INCOMPLETE STREETS

The "Complete Streets" concept and movement in urban planning and policy has been hailed by many as a revolution that aims to challenge the auto-normative paradigm by reversing the broader effects of an urban form shaped by the logic of keeping automobiles moving. By enabling safe access for all users, Complete Streets promise to make cities more walkable and livable and at the same time more sustainable.

Incomplete Streets problematizes the Complete Streets concept by suggesting that streets should not be thought of as merely physical spaces, but as symbolic and social spaces. When important social and symbolic narratives are missing from the discourse and practice of Complete Streets, what actually results are incomplete streets. This volume questions whether the ways in which Complete Streets narratives, policies, plans, and efforts are envisioned and implemented might be systematically reproducing many of the urban spatial and social inequalities and injustices that have characterized cities for the last century or more. From critiques of a "mobility bias" rooted in the neoliberal foundations of the Complete Streets concept, to concerns about resulting environmental gentrification, the chapters in *Incomplete Streets* variously call for planning processes that give voice to the historically marginalized and, more broadly, approach streets as dynamic, fluid, and public social places.

This interdisciplinary book is aimed at students, researchers, and professionals in the fields of urban geography, environmental studies, urban planning and policy, transportation planning, and urban sociology.

Stephen Zavestoski is Sustainability Director at the College of Arts and Sciences and Co-Chair of the Environmental Studies Program at the University of San Francisco, USA.

Julian Agyeman is a Professor in the Department of Urban and Environmental Policy and Planning, Tufts University, USA. He is Founding Editor of *Local Environment: The International Journal of Justice and Sustainability*, published by Taylor & Francis.

Routledge, Equity, Justice, and the Sustainable City series
Series editors: Julian Agyeman, Zarina Patel, AbdouMaliq Simone, and Stephen Zavestoski

This series positions equity and justice as central elements of the transition toward sustainable cities. The series introduces critical perspectives and new approaches to the practice and theory of urban planning and policy that ask how the world's cities can become "greener" while becoming more fair, equitable, and just.

Routledge Equity, Justice and the Sustainable City series addresses sustainable city trends in the global North and South and investigates them for their potential to ensure a transition to urban sustainability that is equitable and just for all. These trends include municipal climate action plans; resource scarcity as tipping points into a vortex of urban dysfunction; inclusive urbanization; "Complete Streets" as a tool for realizing more "livable cities"; the use of information and analytics toward the creation of "smart cities".

The series welcomes submissions for high-level cutting edge research books that push thinking about sustainability, cities, justice and equity in new directions by challenging current conceptualizations and developing new ones. The series offers theoretical, methodological, and empirical advances that can be used by professionals and as supplementary reading in courses in urban geography, urban sociology, urban policy, environment and sustainability, development studies, planning, and a wide range of academic disciplines.

INCOMPLETE STREETS

Processes, practices, and possibilities

*Edited by Stephen Zavestoski
and Julian Agyeman*

Routledge
Taylor & Francis Group

LONDON AND NEW YORK

from Routledge

First published 2015
by Routledge
2 Park Square, Milton Park, Abingdon, Oxon OX14 4RN

and by Routledge
711 Third Avenue, New York, NY 10017

Routledge is an imprint of the Taylor & Francis Group, an informa business

© 2015 Stephen Zavestoski and Julian Agyeman

British Library Cataloguing-in-Publication Data
A catalogue record for this book is available from the British Library

Library of Congress Cataloging-in-Publication Data
Incomplete streets : processes, practices and possibilities / edited by Stephen Zavestoski and Julian Agyeman.
     pages cm—(Routledge equity, justice and the sustainable city series)
     Includes bibliographical references and index.
     1. City planning—Social aspects.   2. Streets—Planning.   3. Bicycle lanes—Planning.   4. Urban transportation—Planning—Social aspects.
     I. Zavestoski, Stephen.   II. Agyeman, Julian.
     HT166.I537 2015
     307.1'216—dc23
                                                                    2014006861

ISBN: 978-0-415-72586-6 (hbk)
ISBN: 978-0-415-72587-3 (pbk)
ISBN: 978-1-315-85653-7 (ebk)

Typeset in Bembo
by Keystroke, Station Road, Codsall, Wolverhampton

CONTENTS

ILLUSTRATIONS

Figures

Tables

CONTRIBUTORS

Julian Agyeman is Professor in the Department of Urban and Environmental Policy and Planning (UEP) at Tufts University, USA. Agyeman's expertise and research interests critically explore aspects of the complex and embedded relations between humans and the environment, and the effects of this on public policy and planning processes and outcomes, particularly in relation to notions of justice and equity. He co-founded and is Editor-in-Chief of *Local Environment: The International Journal of Justice and Sustainability,* and has authored more than 150 publications. Agyeman's most recent book is *Introducing Just Sustainabilities: Policy, Planning and Practice* (Zed, 2013).

Alison Hope Alkon is Assistant Professor of Sociology at University of the Pacific, USA. Her research explores the ways that inequalities affect the production, distribution, and consumption of food and the ways that community based organizations, policy-makers and planners work to create a more just and sustainable food system. She is author of *Black White and Green: Farmers Markets, Race and the Green Economy* and co-editor of *Cultivating Food Justice: Race, Class and Sustainability.*

Anna Livia Brand is an Assistant Professor in the Department of Planning and Urban Studies, University of New Orleans, USA. Her research focuses on the intersection of race and space, specifically looking at black spaces within the context of historical urban changes, gentrification, and issues of power and dominance. Dr. Brand's previous research considers the racial meanings of urban landscapes in New Orleans' Treme and 7th Ward neighborhoods. Currently she is examining the condition and meaning of black meccas in the twenty-first century. Dr. Brand's background is in urban design and planning and she received her PhD from MIT's Department of Urban Studies and Planning.

Josh Cadji, a graduate student in the Community Development Graduate Group at UC Davis, USA, is working on a Master of Science degree in Community Development. His research interests include anti-racism education, social justice pedagogy with youth, gender binary deconstruction, movement building through community leadership development, food justice, and police accountability.

Karen Chapple is Professor of City and Regional Planning at the University of California, Berkeley, USA, where she specializes in community economic development and regional sustainability planning. Her forthcoming book is entitled *Planning Sustainable Cities and Regions: Towards More Equitable Development* (Routledge).

Themis Chronopoulos is a Lecturer in American Studies and History at the University of East Anglia in Norwich, UK. His fields of specialization include urban history, race and ethnicity, immigration, popular culture, public policy, world cities, and human geography. Chronopoulos is the author of *Spatial Regulation in New York City: From Urban Renewal to Zero Tolerance* (Routledge, 2011). He is currently researching and writing a number of articles and book chapters that explore the dynamics of race and class in increasingly multiethnic and multiracial urban neighborhoods both from a historical and a contemporary perspective.

Aaron Golub is an Associate Professor in the School of Geographical Sciences and Urban Planning and the School of Sustainability at Arizona State University, USA. His teaching and research interests include the social and environmental impacts of transportation, planning for alternative transportation modes, and the history of urban transportation in the United States. Dr. Golub received his doctorate in Civil Engineering from the University of California at Berkeley, USA, in 2003.

Erin Goodling is an Urban Studies PhD student at Portland State University, USA. Her research interests include urban political economy/ecology, gentrification/displacement, and popular education related to food and housing justice movements.

Cameron Herrington is an Urban Studies Master's student at Portland State University, USA. He studies community development, housing, and gentrification/displacement in the context of urban sustainability governance.

Melody Hoffmann is a visiting Professor in Communication Studies with a concentration in civic engagement at Gustavus Adolphus College, USA. She received her PhD in Communication Studies from the University of Minnesota, USA, in 2013. Her research interests are focused on analyzing urban planning rhetoric from a critical-cultural perspective. More specifically, her work examines social equity within urban bicycle infrastructure planning. She is a member of Minneapolis Bicycle Coalition's Diversity Task Force.

Sig Langegger is an Assistant Professor in the Faculty of Liberal Arts at Akita International University, Japan. A critical geographer, his research foci are the gentrification of space, homelessness, and social justice, all research contexts that allow him to explore complex intersections between spatial theory and planning practice. He studied sociology at the Universität Wien, Austria, and earned both a Master of Urban Planning and a PhD in Design and Planning from University of Colorado Denver, USA.

Do J. Lee is an Environmental Psychology PhD student at the Graduate Center, City University of New York (CUNY), USA. His research focuses upon the critical exploration of the processes, contexts, and social justice implications of "sustainable" behaviors such as bicycle commuting. Do's professional career has involved work on grassroots sustainability issues for US environmental nonprofits along with service as a US Peace Corps Volunteer in Kazakhstan. His previous degrees include a MPA in Earth Systems Science, Policy and Management from Columbia University, USA, and a BA in Molecular Cell Biology from the University of California at Berkeley, USA.

Amy Lubitow is an Assistant Professor in the Department of Sociology at Portland State University, USA. Her research explores issues of environmental policy and activism, environmental justice, and social sustainability. She is currently conducting research on cycling infrastructures and bike share programs in urban areas. She teaches courses on topics related to her research and hopes to enhance transit justice and equity in Portland through research and activism.

Vikas Mehta, PhD, is an Associate Professor and the Fruth/Gemini Chair and Ohio Eminent Scholar of Urban/Environmental Design at the College of Design, Architecture, Art and Planning at the University of Cincinnati, USA. He is interested in the various dimensions of urbanity through the exploration of place as a social and ecological setting and as a sensorial art. Dr. Mehta's work focuses on the role of design and planning in creating a more responsive, equitable, stimulating and supportive environment. He is the author of *The Street: A Quintessential Social Public Space* (Routledge, 2013).

Thaddeus R. Miller is an Assistant Professor of Urban Civic Ecology and Sustainable Communities in the Nohad A. Toulan School of Urban Studies and Planning at Portland State University, USA. His research explores the social, ethical and political dimensions of science and technology and urban sustainability. He is currently working on research examining the techno-politics of sustainable infrastructure, including smart cities and information and communication technology. Prior to joining Portland State, Thad received his doctorate in Sustainability at Arizona State University's School of Sustainability.

Lusi Morhayim is an Architectural Researcher focusing on social and cultural processes in architecture and urban design. Her research interests include urban social movements, right to the city, sustainability, health and built environment, and post-occupancy evaluations. She has taught architectural research and theory classes at the University of California, Berkeley, USA, and Academy of Art University in San Francisco, USA. Currently, she is co-editing an edited volume on social research in the built environment. She holds a PhD in Architecture from the University of California Berkeley, USA.

Peter Norton is Associate Professor in the Department of Engineering and Society at the University of Virginia, USA, and the author of *Fighting Traffic: The Dawn of the Motor Age in the American City*. He is a historian of technology with particular interests in traffic, streets, and people. His article "Street Rivals: Jaywalking and the Invention of the Motor Age Street" won the Usher Prize of the Society for the History of Technology.

Mark Vallianatos is Policy Director of the Urban and Environmental Policy Institute and an Adjunct Instructor at Occidental College in Los Angeles, USA. Mark serves on the steering committees for Los Angeles Walks, a citywide pedestrian advocacy organization; the Los Angeles Street Vendors Campaign, a coalition seeking to legalize sidewalk vending; and Take Back the Boulevard, a local street-changing initiative. He is co-author of *The Next Los Angeles: The Struggle for a Livable City* and is a regular contributor to Streetsblog Los Angeles. Mark received his BA from the University of Virginia, USA, and JD from the University of Virginia School of Law, USA.

Stephen Zavestoski is Associate Professor of Sociology and Environmental Studies at the University of San Francisco, USA. He is the co-editor, with Phil Brown, of *Social Movements in Health* (Blackwell, 2005), and with Phil Brown and Rachel Morello-Frosch, of *Contested Illnesses: Citizens, Science, and Health Social Movements* (UC Press, 2012). His research areas include environmental sociology, social movements, sociology of health and illness, and urban sustainability. Dr. Zavestoski is also co-editor of the Routledge series Equity, Justice and the Sustainable City.

PREFACE

Incomplete Streets is the first book in the Routledge Equity, Justice and the Sustainable City series. The series is intended to address both the challenges and opportunities confronting the world's cities—whether old or emerging or part of the global South or North—in the face of the growing sustainability imperative. These challenges and opportunities are being met with great urgency and optimism by municipal leaders, urban planners, designers, architects, engineers, social movement organizations, and others. We hope that the series will give those engaged in delivering sustainable cities the critical perspectives needed to achieve simultaneously the goals of ecological sustainability, economic opportunity, and social justice and equity. We call this "just sustainability".

The series as a whole foregrounds equity and justice as being central to the transition toward sustainable cities. We anticipate that future books in the series will emphasize the imperative of a "just sustainability" approach. Meeting this imperative will require a different set of understandings and practices in urban planning, policy, and associated social movements than the more technological and scientifically-focused approaches typically associated with "greening" and "environmental" planning, policy, and practice.

Incomplete Streets nicely introduces the series with its aim of problematizing the Complete Streets concept. In contrast to streets as designed and engineered during the century of the automobile's dominance, Complete Streets are streets that enable safe access for all users—pedestrians, bicyclists, motorists, and transit riders. Complete Streets policies are typically justified in a number of ways, including their ability to meet a city's sustainability goals by making alternatives to the automobile viable. *Incomplete Streets* critically examines whether, or how, Complete Streets policies might undermine sustainability goals by exacerbating various forms of inequality. This is precisely the kind of critical approach to urban sustainability and social justice that we envision for the series: one that moves beyond techno-centric exercises where contestations over rights, access to basic resources and services, and ideas about what the city should be and for whom are ignored. Readers can look forward to future books in the series that, like *Incomplete Streets*, investigate emerging trends in the global North and South for their potential to ensure an equitable and just transition to sustainable cities.

ACKNOWLEDGEMENTS

This book was inspired by, and is dedicated to, those who are invisibilized and silenced in the face of the waves of Complete Streets "improvements" leading to greater "livability" and "walkability" in our cities. We hope, in undertaking this project that we make you more visible and less silent to those politicians, policy-makers, planners, and activists who see such projects as a major part of the answer to achieving sustainable cities.

We would also like to thank the contributors whose promptness in submitting their work and responding to editorial requests allowed us to move this project along smoothly, and who like us feel the time is right to join in the growing contestation and debate over our most used public space: the street.

We would very much like to acknowledge our partners Marion and Janet for putting up with our long nights poring over the manuscript, and to Janet for her generous commitment of time and energy in the final stages of preparing the manuscript. Last, but not least, thanks to Khanam Virjee and Helen Bell at Routledge who have provided invaluable support at all stages in this project.

"The 'Complete Streets' approach seems to be a feasible way to improve access, health, and economic activity. But are we really challenging inequality and inequity by designing and building 'Complete Streets'? This edited volume is thought provoking, and a good way to start the conversation about this urgent question."
–Lois M. Takahashi, University of California, Los Angeles, USA

"*Incomplete Streets* asks important questions about how equitable Complete Streets really are. While seemingly benign, authors in this well-edited collection argue that this vision of street design ignores key street users from sidewalk venders to low-wage auto commuters. This is a timely critique that deserves attention."
–Ann Forsyth, Harvard University, USA

"Over the last 30 years our urban spaces have become increasingly neo-liberalised commodities and *privatised* public places. This timely collection reveals the contested space tensions and the successes that can be achieved in local streets. The Complete Streets movement will challenge attitudes of highways and engineering professionals, and those of urban planners too. We should refocus our attention to 'people and places' rather than 'land users' to become truly equitable and sustainable; after all it is people that make places."
–Mark Tewdwr-Jones, Newcastle University, UK

"This important book takes a hard look at the emerging movement for livability and asks the essential question: For whom? The authors' unflinching, good humoured perspectives are essential reading for anyone who cares about the shape of our cities."
–Elly Blue, Bikenomics Industrial Complex, USA

1

COMPLETE STREETS

What's missing?

Stephen Zavestoski and Julian Agyeman

Cities in the United States have suffered from 80 years of development shaped by an undying commitment to the automobile as the primary mode of transit. This commitment has left a physical legacy of air pollution and associated health risks and impacts, poor public transit options and unsafe conditions for pedestrians and bicyclists in both old metropolitan areas (e.g., New York, Chicago, Atlanta, and Detroit) and newer urban centers (e.g., Denver, Los Angeles, Phoenix, and Las Vegas). In each of these cities, and in many other smaller cities, low income and minority communities have borne the worst effects of auto-centric development. Not only have these communities been disproportionately utilized as the locus of industrial and other unwanted development, they have also been used as transportation corridors facilitating the speedy movement of people and goods through (or often over) their neighborhoods. This benefitted the suburban dweller and downtown employer, but not the highway-dissected community.

Recent trends in urban planning and policy aim to challenge this auto-normative paradigm by reversing the broader effects of an urban form shaped by the logics of keeping automobiles moving. The aim of creating "Complete Streets" in "walkable" and "livable cities" is an example of such an effort. *Transportation Alternatives Magazine* (2007) boldly asserts: "The Complete Streets revolution has begun." Everyone, it seems, from planners to public health professionals to politicians wants them. According to *Mobility Magazine*: "North America is on the verge of a new paradigm . . . At the forefront of the 'street revolution' is the concept of Complete Streets" (Whitney 2010).

The New York Chapter of the American Association of Family Physicians has proclaimed the health benefits of Complete Streets:

> The pedestrian plazas, car-free spaces, neighborhood bike networks and world-class bicycle lanes . . . [of New York City] are vital to the public health

of our city. These changes help pave the way for a city that breathes cleaner air and is in better physical condition.

(Murphy 2011)

Elsewhere, Complete Streets are seen as a strategy to fight childhood obesity. "The road was very clear," a report of the Michigan Department of Community Health tells us, discussing an initiative sponsored by the Division of Nutrition, Physical Activity, and Obesity of the Centers for Disease Control and Prevention's National Center for Chronic Disease Prevention and Health Promotion. The report continues:

> In 2009. as the state with the 9th highest rate of obesity, Michigan had much work to do . . . [T]he Michigan Department of Community Health created a five-year strategic plan to reduce childhood obesity in Michigan. One of its first initiatives? A statewide effort to address Complete Streets.
>
> *(Centers for Disease Control and Prevention 2011)*

Complete Streets policies are even seen as a tool for diversity, as Annise Parker, Mayor of Houston, Texas, explains about the city's new policy:

> Houston is a city that embraces its diversity. This Complete Streets policy applies the same approach to our mobility system by meeting the diverse needs of all Houstonians while also creating more accessible and attractive connections to residential areas, parks, businesses, restaurants, schools and employment centers.
>
> *(City of Houston, Mayor's Office 2013)*

Perhaps the greatest evidence of the "revolution," at least in the US context, is the proliferation of policies and laws institutionalizing and codifying Complete Streets as a guiding principle in urban planning. "Communities of all sizes are transforming their streets into more than just a way to move people in cars from one place to another," reports the National Complete Streets Coalition. "These communities are part of a growing national movement for Complete Streets." In fact, the National Complete Streets Coalition's 2013 report on best Complete Streets policies of 2012 claims that there are now 488 Complete Streets policies across the US. These exist at all levels of government, including 27 statewide policies. More than 25 percent of the existing policies were passed in 2012 alone (National Complete Streets Coalition 2013).

If there is indeed a Complete Streets revolution, then the objective must be to challenge the paradigm that produces *in*-Complete Streets. So, what exactly do we mean in calling this book *Incomplete Streets*?

Complete Streets

First introduced to the lexicon in 2003 by Barbara McCann, a staff member of the advocacy organization America Bikes, Complete Streets was proposed as an alternative to the term "routine accommodation," which was being used to convey the need to include bicycles in transportation planning. As McCann recounts, "Right away, we knew that we had a concept that was bigger than bicycles" (McCann 2010). The coalition model that McCann developed between America Bikes and the League of American Bicyclists quickly expanded to include AARP, the American Planning Association, the American Public Transportation Association, the American Society of Landscape Architects, and the American Heart Association. Advocates and transportation planners were brought together and eventually developed the following definition of a Complete Streets policy:

> A Complete Streets policy ensures that the entire right of way is routinely designed and operated to enable safe access for all users. Pedestrians, bicyclists, motorists and transit riders of all ages and abilities must be able to safely move along and across a complete street.
>
> *(McCann and Rynne 2010, p. 3)*

The concept began garnering national and international media attention from outlets such as *The New York Times* (Kral 2008), *USA Today* (Ritter 2007) and *Time Magazine* (Padgett 2009), and from organizations like Streetsblog, Transportation Alternatives, 8-80 Cities, and the National Complete Streets Coalition in North America, as well as organizations such as Living Streets in the UK, the Bicycling Empowerment Network in South Africa, and international organizations like Walk21 and Embarq.

While Complete Streets is the zeitgeist in the US, it is rhetorically linked to concepts commonly used outside the US such as "Livable Cities" and "Cities for People." These concepts and their associated discourses have exploded in urban planning, transportation planning, environmental policy and sustainable communities circles. Developing as part of and related to the urban planning über-narrative of "place-making," the movement has transformed the frames of livable, walkable streets into a mobilizing frame that has led to coalition building and activism, influenced legislation and policy, and provided the average citizen with a compelling and tangible vision of the potential of their streets beyond that of mere automobile conduit. Indeed, the American Association of State Highway and Transportation Officials (AASHTO) notes that the purpose of street design is to ensure "operational efficiency, comfort, safety, and convenience for the motorist."

For the National Complete Streets Coalition in the US, the movement is about changing the AASHTO transportation paradigm from "moving cars quickly" to "providing safe access for all modes," including pedestrians, bicyclists, motorists and transit riders of all ages and abilities. The Coalition adds that the Complete Streets movement "encourages and provides for safe access to destinations for everyone, regardless of age, ability, income, ethnicity, or mode of travel." The extent to which the Complete Streets discourse has been adopted by professional planning and transportation associations, the way it gives shape to the efforts of walking and bicycling advocacy organizations, and the inspiration it provides for ordinary citizens aiming to make their communities more livable, is remarkable.

Implicit in the Complete Streets concept is the notion that streets are not currently designed to meet the needs of all users. It conveys the message that streets are ultimately public spaces, and that everyone in the community—from pedestrians to bicyclists to public transit users—should have equal rights to space within them, irrespective of whether they are driving a car or not. As Agyeman (2013) notes: "[This] street-level spatial justice, this 'democratization of the street' through the redistribution of rights to (and in) public space, may make the street look physically different, but I think it also fundamentally rewires our brains, affecting the way we think." In this way, adding these "other" street users effectively de-centers the motorist and problematizes the auto-normative paradigm while potentially bringing together previously disconnected interest groups—people with disabilities, bicyclists, senior citizens, public transit advocates and others—into a powerful coalition. Streets, the movement implies, are incomplete when they are designed, constructed and maintained with the primary objective of moving automobiles efficiently.

Incomplete streets

While we certainly agree with its challenge to auto-normativity, the aim of this book is to problematize the Complete Streets concept in ways that might provoke its more critical use and application by urban planners, policy-makers, and academics. We have asked the authors in this volume to investigate the question: "Complete for whom?" If the movement claims that Complete Streets policies, when implemented, "complete" previously incomplete streets, then we ought to ask whether all street users are, in fact, gaining safe access to streets "regardless of age, ability, income, ethnicity, or mode of travel" (National Complete Streets Coalition). The accepted definition of Complete Streets, while recognizing "diversity," refers to "users" of streets. This effectively reduces people primarily to their mode of transportation. Yet not everyone's mode of transportation is a choice. Some people choose to cycle while others are forced to. What mistakes might we be making in assuming that redesigning streets with the goal of providing safe access to all users of streets can sufficiently address the broader historical, political, social, and economic forces shaping the socioeconomic and racial inequalities embedded in and reproduced by the spaces we call streets?

Like Massey (1995), we see places (and streets are places) as having no fixed meaning; rather, they are "constantly shifting articulations of social relations through time." Yet much of the current physically-focused Complete Streets rhetoric disconnects streets from their significant social, structural, symbolic, discursive, and historical realities. Economically, ethnically, and racially diverse members of communities are referred to monolithically as "users." Assumptions are made that "users" make rational choices about different "modes" of transportation available to get themselves from point A to point B. This book calls for a (re)conceptualization of Complete Streets that humanizes "users" by acknowledging their difference and diversity and by asking questions about how individuals' experiences as historically marginalized members of society (and users of streets), among other identities, impinge on their ability to participate in dialogues about Complete Streets, and whether their lack of voice in turn gives shape to urban spaces that subtly, and not so subtly, exclude certain individuals.

In the wake of the rapid and largely unproblematized rise of the Complete Streets movement (see for example Schlossberg *et al.* 2013; McCann 2013), the types of questions asked in the chapters of this book are vital if the movement is to fully deliver on its promises. We draw our critical, theoretical and intellectual inspiration from the works of, among others, Henri Lefebvre (1974) and Ed Soja (2010) on the trialectics of space, and on spatial justice; from Henri Lefebvre (1974), David Harvey (2008) and Don Mitchell (2003) on the right to the city; from Julian Agyeman (2013) on "just sustainabilities"; and from Doreen Massey (1995) and Talja Blokland (2009) on social relations and historical narratives regarding place. Yet few urban planners are asking the types of questions we explore here. Academics, especially in fields such as urban geography, planning and sociology, where we might expect to see an interest, have given the Complete Streets phenomenon scant attention. Although they do not engage the Complete Streets concept directly, Cutts *et al.* (2009) are nevertheless concerned with how the combination of walkability and access to parks—two features common in the Complete Streets discourse—promote physical activity and reduce obesity. Other studies come at Complete Streets, or their correlates, from public health (Bassett *et al.* 2008; Geraghty *et al.* 2009; Moreland-Russell *et al.* 2013) or transportation engineering perspectives (Burden and Litman 2011; Dock *et al.* 2012; Laplante and McCann 2008).

Much of this existing research is limited. The public health focus on the influence of the built environment on physical activity and health typically leaves out an analysis of other important social processes shaping how people interact with space and place, whether symbolic or material. Transportation engineers focus almost exclusively on the technical aspects of the design of Complete Streets, with occasional interest in political processes that open and close doors for Complete Streets projects. Long champions of Complete Streets, progressive urban planners have yet to engage in a specifically socially just framing within their discourse. A possible exception is Day's (2006) argument that planning for active living—defined as urban planning and design to promote physical activity—needs to address low-income, Black and Latino communities due to higher rates of obesity in these communities and fewer resources for dealing with the problem. Another application of a social justice frame, in this case from a public health perspective, occurs in Taylor *et al.*'s (2006) meta-analysis of published research that discusses disparities in physical activity, dietary habits, and obesity among different populations. As expected, their analysis reveals modest support for the conclusion that there is disproportionate lack of access to health-promoting urban features such as sidewalks, parks and calm traffic in low income and racial/ethnic minority communities, in turn contributing to higher rates of obesity.

Beyond peer-reviewed publications, there are a handful of reports and other analyses or recommendations for addressing the issue of equity with respect to Complete Streets policies and practices. Clifton, Bronstein and Morrissey's undated report, "The Path to Complete Streets in Underserved Communities: Lessons from U.S. Case Studies," makes a number of recommendations for building equity concerns into Complete Streets policies. But their approach focuses solely on the issue of transportation equity without consideration of the broader structural, historical, political, and economic factors that are the focus of this book and that shape people's places within urban systems. Litman's report (2013) for the Victoria Transport Policy Institute, "Evaluating Complete Streets: The Value of Designing Roads for Diverse Modes, Users and Activities," also tackles the issue of equity with respect to Complete Streets from a transportation equity perspective:

> Planning practices that favor mobility over accessibility and automobiles over other modes tend to be unfair and regressive, since they reduce the transport options available to non-drivers. In a typical community, 20–40% of residents cannot or should not drive due to physical impairment, poverty or age. In automobile dependent communities non-drivers tend to have significantly less accessibility, and therefore reduced economic and social opportunity, than motorists. Complete Streets help achieve equity objectives by giving non-drivers a fair share of road space, by reducing risks motor vehicles impose on pedestrians and cyclists, and by improving mobility and accessibility options for non-drivers.
>
> *(Litman 2013, p. 14)*

Whether Litman's claim that Complete Streets can achieve equity objectives remains to be seen, as too few Complete Streets policies have resulted in implementation of the types of projects that would allow such an analysis. More troubling is the way in which Complete Streets are abstracted and treated as theoretical ideals. Inarguably, if the non-driving population is overrepresented by the poor, people of color, seniors, and people with disabilities, then designing streets that give non-drivers a fair share of road space, in theory, will make streets more equitable. But streets do not exist in the abstract. They are (usually) paved surfaces that exist in physical spaces within a city. The spaces in between the streets, and sometimes the streets themselves, provide places for city dwellers to reside, work, recreate, worship, and engage in countless other activities that constitute city life. Streets connect these spaces in ways that advantage certain parts of the city, or certain residents within the city, over other parts of the city and its residents. A Complete Streets project, when implemented, might cover a mere three or four city blocks. Ambitious projects in larger cities might cover more. Regardless, when implemented incrementally, Complete Streets will inevitably benefit certain people in certain urban spaces and not others.

Complete Streets' design and mobility principles and preferences include the introduction of bicycle lanes, street accessibility improvements, mass transit expansions and upgrades, and pedestrian zone placements. However, as the chapters in this volume show, these physical changes can make certain street users and the dwellers in some neighborhoods, invisible, further diminishing their rights and roles in the community. In these predominantly low-income communities and neighborhoods of color, people worry that such changes will foster gentrification.

Historical narrative and the right to the city

This book, then, is concerned both with streets that are incomplete from the urban planner's perspective (i.e., streets that exclude non-drivers), as well as with the incompleteness of ostensibly "complete" streets. In employing the concept of Incomplete Streets, we intend to draw attention to important missing narratives in the Complete Streets discourse and practice. Blokland (2009), through her study of New Haven, Connecticut, shows how place-making (and by extrapolation Complete Street-making) can be seen as a struggle between residents' different historical narratives (which thereby define "the community"). If any of the historical narratives are absent from the dominant picture of who the community is, that picture will therefore be distorted. In short, we contend that there are important missing people—namely people of color, immigrants, the poor and other historically disenfranchised individuals—in popular narratives of Complete Streets. Similarly, the notion of Incomplete Streets evokes an understanding of streets as lived and ultimately contested spaces and asks us to consider the types of spaces, for example, recreational, religious, commercial, and, most importantly, public, that may or may not be missing from hypothetically Complete Streets. Finally, Harvey reminds us of the broader context for participation in Complete Streets at the discursive, narrative, and physical levels, namely, that they are a part of our Right to the City: "The freedom to make and remake our cities and ourselves is . . . one of the most precious yet most neglected of our human rights" (2008, p. 23).

The range of disciplines and practices represented by our authors, together with the styles of analysis and criticism they employ, present different approaches to the question of whether the ways Complete Streets narratives, policies, plans, and efforts are envisioned and implemented might be systematically reproducing and even amplifying many of the urban spatial and social inequalities and injustices that have characterized cities for the last century or more. The conclusions drawn ought to push planners and policy-makers, academics, activists, and laypeople to think more critically about streets, not just as physical and material amenities that function to move people and goods, but as significant social and symbolic spaces where users are linked to intersecting economic, transportation, food, cultural, and governance systems, as well as personal, group, and community histories and experiences.

The following chapters will reveal how streets and the communities they connect are physical and symbolic spaces with great potential. They can reflect and reproduce the social structures, inequalities, and injustices that continue to shape and define many urban lives. But they can also empower and engage, build civic and social capital, and create opportunities, if seen in the wider contexts that we suggest in this book.

Processes, practices, and possibilities

The book is divided into three Parts: Processes, Practices and Possibilities. Part I, "Processes," addresses both the historical processes through which streets came to be designed almost exclusively to accommodate automobiles, as well as the contemporary processes through which the *in*completeness of streets becomes contested, opening the door for the rapid growth of Complete Streets rhetoric, planning and policy development. In Chapter 2, Peter Norton argues that this process is rooted in discursive campaigns aimed at winning the debate over whether we build streets for people or for cars. Norton argues that "Motordom" won the debate by offering a persuasive narrative linking automobiles to progress and ultimately to American values such as independence and freedom. This narrative was carefully crafted in the 1920s by representatives of an emerging public relations industry. The Complete Streets movement, he concludes, would benefit by learning from the automotive industry's success in gaining control of the narrative and thereby control of streets, to develop a compelling counter-narrative (re)defining streets as spaces for all users, as they once were. Aaron Golub extends Norton's historical analysis in Chapter 3 while adding a political economy perspective on urban development. In addition to discourses, Golub maintains that the rise of Fordist social structures facilitated automobility for many. Complete Streets discourse, he argues, emerges out of a post-Fordist neoliberal context, which raises questions regarding how, or whether, the use of transportation innovations like rail to attract investment will threaten minority communities with displacement. In Chapter 4, Themis Chronopoulos' analysis of congestion pricing schemes in London, Stockholm, and New York City continues the interrogation of neoliberalism. He demonstrates how neoliberalism provides the political rationality to justify congestion pricing, which is essentially a form of spatial exclusion that makes driving in certain parts of a city a costly endeavor that only the affluent can afford. Chronopoulos asks whether congestion pricing, to the extent that it fits into the Complete Streets objective of balancing the needs of various modes of transportation, introduces new problems of access and inclusion that might result in the same types of injustices produced by auto-centric transportation planning. The theme of neoliberalism's deep influence on the character of streetscapes continues in Chapter 5. Do Lee explains our acceptance of the automobile's role in extraordinary rates of death and damage by examining how a streetscape of "cumulative irresponsibility" arises when the absence of collective responsibility turns the harm caused by cars into a naturalized burden of everyday life. Chapter 6, which concludes Part I, "Processes," proposes that streets be understood and appreciated from an ecological perspective. Vikas Mehta's concern is that the Complete Streets approach fails to see streets in a holistic way, instead flattening the rich ecology of streets by focusing on mobility and a particular quality of urban life that Complete Streets promise to provide. Together, the chapters in Part I explain how dynamic processes ranging from ideological discourses to hegemonic economic policies have created the current context from which Complete Streets strategies—with their promises of producing more socially desirable, vibrant, active, fit, healthy, and green cities—have emerged with high levels of public and political support.

Part II, "Practices," focuses on the formal and informal practices of urban planners, policy-makers, civic organizations, and others to make streets safer, more pedestrian friendly, and more livable (i.e., "complete"). Sig Langegger's analysis in Chapter 7 foregrounds the largely Latino cultural practice of "lowriding" and "cruising," and attempts in north Denver, Colorado, by city officials and the police to curb the practice. It points to two notions of the street: (1) Complete Streets as efficient and orderly thoroughfares for the movement of people; and (2) streets as spaces of *la vida pública*, sites where cultural practices and traditions are enacted and performed. As Langegger shows us, the practice of tight regulation toward "safe and predictable streets" provides a platform for gentrification. Chapter 8 extends this line of thinking by implicitly placing much of the bicycle advocacy and planning happening in cities like Minneapolis into the "streets as efficient and orderly thoroughfares for the movement of people" category. Of course, the movement for better infrastructure and accommodations for bicyclists seeks orderly and efficient streets that include bicyclists. Melody Hoffmann's argument is that advocates must be acutely aware of how their visions of bicycle friendly cities might clash with the race, class, and other identity markers that define local understandings and narratives of the functions that streets ought to serve. Otherwise, in Minneapolis and elsewhere, as in Langegger's anti-lowriding north Denver, planning for bicycle infrastructure in certain parts of a city will be seen by some as yet another driver of gentrification. In Chapter 9, Josh Cadji and Alison Hope Alkon examine an attempt in Oakland, California, to respect a neighborhood's history and diversity while introducing a feature that is often seen as central to Complete Streets and livable cities more broadly: access to fresh local produce through farmers' markets. Yet even while attempting to tackle the gentrification that often follows or is part and parcel of neighborhood street enhancements like farmers' markets, Phat Beets Produce, a food justice organization dedicated to creating a healthier, more equitable food system in North Oakland, itself becomes a victim of gentrification. Whereas previous chapters in Part II point to the practices of planning and implementing Complete Streets or practices of resistance when Complete Streets are seen as harbingers of gentrification, in Chapter 10, Erin Goodling and Cameron Herrington detail how equity and social justice objectives can be explicitly integrated into sustainability strategies (and Complete Streets planning) by operationalizing equity as an objective in planning. Their analysis of a watershed planning program in Portland, Oregon, documents the extensive steps taken by one public agency to ensure public resources were being spent equitably, and shows how emphases on Complete Streets and livability in city planning and municipal governance will not necessarily result in equitable outcomes without advocates in public agencies being willing to reinvent the ways we think about equity in planning processes and practices.

Part III, "Possibilities," explores possible outcomes of Complete Streets policies, practices and projects. More broadly, do truly Complete Streets in the way we have described them have the potential to undo decades of structural inequalities that are so deeply inscribed in the landscape of our cities? Or, if not, can Complete Streets planning and implementation happen in ways that recognize and endeavor to avoid perpetuating past inequities? In Chapter 11, Mark Vallianatos describes the rich history that Los Angeles' primarily Latino street food vendors have had in producing the types of layered and diverse street ecologies that Mehta describes in Chapter 6 and Langegger describes in Chapter 7. Yet new permitting requirements and other city policies have made it more and more difficult for vendors to conduct business. Vallianatos offers a set of policy prescriptions that have the potential not only to ensure the ongoing practice of the Latino street food vendor tradition, but also to continue the tradition in a way that could bring healthier foods into parts of Los Angeles that are otherwise considered food deserts.

Further north in California, Lusi Morhayim examines, in Chapter 12, emerging practices of "Do-It-Yourself" (DIY) Urbanism in San Francisco as responses to the same neoliberalization of cities critiqued in earlier chapters by Golub, Chronopoulos and others. In San Francisco, for example, the city-sanctioned closure of streets during monthly "Sunday Streets" events has its roots in grassroots mobilizations like Critical Mass and Park(ing) Day. Morhayim asks what the equity and justice implications are when a city's approach to Complete Streets depends, in part, on institutionalizing the practices of DIY urbanists. In Chapter 13, Anna Livia Brand points to the possibilities that arise from the co-optation of Complete Streets discourse. The neighborhoods of New Orleans' North Claiborne Avenue were first devastated in the 1960s when a new Interstate highway bisected them and then again by Hurricane Katrina in 2005. Brand documents the public participation process surrounding a plan to take down the urban portion of the highway and attract redevelopment by promoting the neighborhood's historical roles in celebrated African–American cultural traditions such as jazz and brass bands. The redevelopment strategy is rooted in a vision that the planners say would develop "the most complete street in the world." Whether Claiborne Avenue will become the "most complete street in the world" is uncertain. Brand concludes that we must be reminded of the importance of recognizing how redevelopment strategies, especially those in New Orleans, couched as they are in the benevolent and unassailable historic and nostalgic rhetoric of Complete Streets, gloss over the "brutalities of racial discrimination and segregation." She also reminds us of the roles people play in evolving local culture and traditions, and how neighborhoods and their traditions, in many cases, have been impacted by past planning decisions that may have benefitted urban economic development, but not the lives of those immediately affected. Her analysis points to the possibility for Complete Streets discourse to be used in a way that co-opts a community's own historical narratives and contributions to local culture and its own vision for its re-development.

Where Brand highlights the dark underbelly of Complete Streets-style planning, Thaddeus Miller and Amy Lubitow showcase the possibilities for Complete Streets planning that gives voice to the victims of historical injustices in a community. Chapter 14 begins with Miller and Lubitow asking how a bikeway enhancement project became so contested in "America's Bicycle Capital." A "Traffic Safety and Operations Project" on Portland's North Williams Avenue triggered a public debate that brought "to the surface legacies of racist policies and planning projects, frustrations over the city's priorities, concerns about continuing gentrification and equitable public participation in city decision-making." Yet whereas North Claiborne's future in New Orleans is yet to be determined, planners in Portland, Oregon, put a halt to their original plan so that the public participation process could be restarted in a manner that not only engaged the neighborhood's long-time African–American residents, but made listening to the personal accounts of historical injustice a central part of the process. What planners heard, in essence, is that bikes and by extension Complete Streets-style projects represented to the neighborhood's historical residents forms of yet another wave of gentrification. As a result, the project was scaled back from its original bicycle-centric plan. Miller and Lubitow explain the process in terms of the potential for dominant frames, such as the "safety and access" frame common in Complete Streets rhetoric, to focus on technical changes to streets in ways that obscure how streets are "inextricably tied to race and the historical social and physical development" of cities.

Finally, in Chapter 15, Karen Chapple broadens the Complete Streets debate in two ways. First, she frames her analysis not at the level of the street but of the region. Second, she offers an analysis of regional transportation patterns that highlights the unique needs for street space among low-income families, and, in particular, low-wage workers. Both groups tend to be heavily dependent, when they can afford them, on automobiles as a primary mode of transportation. To the extent that Complete Streets policies might make automobile transportation more costly, whether in terms of money or time, such policies are likely to inequitably impact poor families and low-wage workers. Chapple also asks the provocative question "What is diversity?" and "In the specific case of urban design, given the impossibility of envisioning all potential users, how can designers keep diversity in mind when planning a public space?" These questions, as well as an attempt to synthesize the analyses and assertions of the volume's authors, are taken up in Zavestoski and Agyeman's concluding Chapter 16.

Combined, the chapters in this volume offer a critical analysis of both the concept of and movement for Complete Streets. We ask readers to embrace a fluid conceptual space in which a diversity of lenses, perspectives, and methods, not just among but also within chapters, can help us to understand streets as more than physical spaces. Ultimately, our intent is to demonstrate the power of seeing streets not as fixed, but as constantly adapting and evolving physical, social, and symbolic spaces of creativity and contestation, and that social equity is essential in facilitating the constant adaptation and evolution that streets must undergo in response to the changing communities around them. Inequality creates powerful vested interests committed to maintaining the status quo, which sees streets as spaces whose primary functions are to move privileged people using privileged modes of transportation in order to get them to places of work, consumption, and recreation. Yet for various reasons, streets may need to adapt to facilitate multiple functions such as mobility, economic activity, and cultural practice. Can such adaptation occur when streets are shaped primarily, or even exclusively by market forces? Or will more democratic and equitable streets be better suited to the challenge? We hope that this volume initiates the kind of dialogue and future research that can help answer these questions.

References

Agyeman, J., 2013. *Introducing just sustainabilities: Policy, planning and practice*. London: Zed Books.

Bassett, J. R., Pucher, J., Buehler, R., Thompson, D.L., and Crouter, S.E., 2008. Walking, cycling, and obesity rates in Europe, North America, and Australia. *Journal of Physical Activity & Health*, 5 (6), 795–814.

Blokland, T., 2009. Celebrating local histories and defining neighbourhood communities: place-making in a gentrified neighbourhood. *Urban Studies*, 46 (8), 1593–1610.

Burden, D., and Litman, T., 2011. America needs Complete Streets. *Institute of Transportation Engineers, ITE Journal*, 81 (4), 36–43.

Centers for Disease Control and Prevention, 2011. Taking it to the (complete) streets: Michigan's road to fight obesity. *CDC/DNPAO Stories from the Field: Michigan*. Available from: www.cdc.gov/obesity/downloads/field/Stories-from-the-Field_Michigan-Web_3-7-12.pdf [Accessed 12 January 2014].

City of Houston, Mayor's Office, 2013. Mayor Annise Parker announces visionary Complete Streets policy for Houston. Press release, October 10. Available from: www.houstontx.gov/mayor/press/20131010.html [Accessed 12 January 2014].

Clifton, K.J., Bronstein, S., and Morrissey, S, Undated. The path to Complete Streets in underserved communities: Lessons from U.S. case studies. Portland State University. Available from: www.smartgrowthamerica.org/documents/cs/resources/complete-streets-in-underserved-communities.pdf [Accessed 12 January 2014].

Cutts, B.B., Darby, K.J., Boone, C.G., and Brewis, A., 2009. City structure, obesity, and environmental justice: An integrated analysis of physical and social barriers to walkable streets and park access. *Social Science & Medicine*, 69 (9):1314–1322.

Day, K., 2006. Active living and social justice: Planning for physical activity in low-income, Black, and Hispanic communities. *Journal of the American Planning Association*, 72 (1), 88–99.

Dock, F.C., Greenberg, E., and Yamarone, M., 2012. Multimodal and Complete Streets performance measures in Pasadena, California. *Institute of Transportation Engineers, ITE Journal*, 82 (1), 33–37.

Geraghty, A., *et al.*, 2009. Partnership moves community toward Complete Streets. *American Journal of Preventive Medicine*, 37 (6 Suppl. 2), S420–S427.

Harvey, D., 2008. The right to the city. *New Left Review*, 53 (Sept–Oct), 23–40.

Kral, G., 2008. In wake of two deaths, making streets safer. *The New York Times*, October 3, Available from: www.nytimes.com/2008/10/05/nyregion/connecticut/05streetsct.html?_r=2& [Accessed 12 January 2014].

Laplante, J., and McCann, B., 2008. Complete Streets: We can get there from here. *Institute of Transportation Engineers, ITE Journal*, 78 (5), 24–28.

Lefebvre, H., 1974. *The production of space*. Oxford: Blackwell.

Litman, T., 2013. Evaluating Complete Streets: The value of designing roads for diverse modes, users and activities. Victoria Transport Policy Institute, June 6. Available from: www.vtpi.org/compstr.pdf [Accessed 12 January 2014].

Massey, D., 1995. Places and their pasts. *History Workshop Journal*, 39 (1), 182–192.

McCann, B., 2010. Happy anniversary, Complete Streets! Smartgrowth America/National Complete Streets Coalition. Available from: www.smartgrowthamerica.org/2010/12/03/happy-anniversary-complete-streets/ [Accessed 12 January 2014].

McCann, B., 2013. *Completing our streets: The transition to safe and inclusive transportation networks*. Washington, DC: Island Press.

McCann, B., and Rynne, S., 2010. *Complete Streets: Best policy and implementation practices*. Planning Advisory Service Report Number 559. New York, NY: American Planning Association.

Mitchell, D., 2003. *The right to the city: Social justice and the fight for public space*. New York, NY: Guilford Press.

Moreland-Russell, S., *et al.*, 2013. Diffusion of Complete Streets policies across U.S. communities. *Journal of Public Health Management Practice*, 19 (3) E-Supp, S89–S96.

Murphy, M., 2011. 140 medical professionals prescribe "Complete Streets" for a healthier New York City: Letter to city hall lauds bike lanes and other street safety improvements. Transalt, September 22, Available from: www.transalt.org/news/releases/5460 [Accessed 12 January 2014].

National Complete Streets Coalition (with Smartgrowth America), 2013. The best Complete Streets policies of 2012. Available from: www.smartgrowthamerica.org/documents/cs-2012-policy-analysis.pdf [Accessed 12 January 2014].

Padgett, T., 2009. Florida's deadly hit-and-run car culture. *Time Magazine*. November 29. Available from: http://content.time.com/time/nation/article/0,8599,1942986,00.html [Accessed 12 January 2014].

Ritter, J., 2007. "Complete Streets" program gives more room for pedestrians, cyclists. *USA Today*, July 31. Available from: http://usatoday30.usatoday.com/news/nation/2007-07-29-complete-streets_N.htm [Accessed 12 January 2014].

Schlossberg, M., Rowell, J., Amos, D., and Sanford, K., 2013. Rethinking streets: An evidence based guide to 25 Complete Street transformations. Sustainable Cities Initiative. University of Oregon. Available from: http://www.rethinkingstreets.com/download.html [Accessed 3 June 2014].

Soja, E., 2010. *Seeking spatial justice*. Minneapolis, MN: University of Minnesota Press.

Taylor, W.C., *et al.*, 2006. Environmental justice: Obesity, physical activity, and healthy eating, *Journal of Physical Activity & Health*, 3 (Suppl. 1), S30–S54.

Transportation Alternatives Magazine, 2007. A lot can happen between the lines: Completing NYC streets. Fall issue. Available from: http://transalt.org/files/news/magazine/2007/fall/10-13.pdf [Accessed 12 January 2014].

Whitney, R.A., 2010. Why Complete Streets are the answer. *Mobility*, 10 (Oct/Dec): 48–51. Available from: http://rideyourcity.files.wordpress.com/2011/07/complete-streets1.pdf [Accessed 12 January 2014].

PART I

Processes

PART 1

Processes

2

OF LOVE AFFAIRS
AND OTHER STORIES

Peter Norton

Introduction

Jane Jacobs never wrote of "Complete Streets," but in other terms she championed them as the "life" of cities. "How can you know what to try with traffic," she asked, "until you know how the city itself works, and what else it needs to do with its streets?" (Jacobs 1961, p. 7). Less well known today, however, is an indirect reply to her appeal that many millions more Americans heard. Just two weeks after Random House released *The Death and Life of Great American Cities*, NBC Television presented an hour-long defense of all things automotive.[1] Though their visions could not have been more different, both works exemplified the use of stories—characters, settings, and plots—to influence discussions of streets.

On October 22, 1961, hosting an episode of NBC's Sunday evening program, *DuPont Show of the Week*, Groucho Marx explained to millions of television viewers that the history of the automobile in America was the history of a "burning love affair"—a "romance" between American men and "the new girl in town" (NBC Television 1961). DuPont, which owned a 23 percent share in General Motors, to which it sold varnishes and fabrics (Freeland 2001, p. 4), promoted this "affectionate report" as "the story of America's love affair with the automobile."[2] "Merrily We Roll Along" thereby introduced what would become the most overworked metaphor in discussions of the car in the United States: Americans' love affair with the automobile. It was not chosen at random; instead, Marx used it to make an explicit point. Love will find a way. Automobiles and the drivers who loved them overcame extraordinary obstacles—poor roads, the disapproval of the older generation, intrusive regulation. And love is blind. Americans would accommodate their beloved cars at any cost—at the dealership, at the gas station, and in traffic jams. If cars wouldn't fit into Americans' cities, Americans would not accommodate the car to the city—they'd rebuild the city for the car. On an ample freeway, from the wheel of a Chevrolet, Marx explained the lesson of the history he'd just told. "Our romance with the automobile—it's still going on. Our honeymoon ended . . . but we're still very much married to Lizzie." Marx—who was then on his third marriage—concluded: "We don't always know how to get along with her, but you certainly can't get along without her. And if that isn't marriage, I don't know what is."

The history of streets—including the Complete Streets movement—is ultimately inseparable from the stories about them. Stories about streets—stories we grew up with, stories we know so well and so deeply that we no longer think about them, stories with lessons that seem as true as natural laws—secure the status quo in streets, make them hard to change, and constrain our imaginations. Yet within the past century, well-told new stories have attracted listeners to new possibilities, despite older mental models. In so doing they have also fostered a kind of collective forgetting of the conditions that came before. The past, seen by the lights of the present, shows "how far we've come," serving the present as a flattering mirror of progress. Seen by its own lights—or in terms of its own stories— the past offers the present forgotten possibilities. As critics of the status quo, advocates of Complete Streets have much to learn from reexamining streets as they were before the motor age. To examine them either with uncritical nostalgic admiration, or as lower steps on the stairway of progress, would be to commit varieties of the same error—to project a present story onto the past. It remains to see streets as they were seen, in what has become another age. This will require not just reexamining the factual historical record but also the stories by which street users understood streets, and with which they promoted their values, defended the status quo, or advocated change.

Stories

"Merrily We Roll Along" was a brilliant but strangely forgotten rebuttal to the car's critics. Jane Jacobs (1956, 1958, 1961), William H. Whyte (1957), John Keats (1958), Lewis Mumford (1958, 1961), Daniel Patrick Moynihan (1960), and others had attacked not automobiles themselves but the excesses to which Americans— city planners, highway engineers, and motorists—went to accommodate them. By comparing Americans' relationship to cars to a "love affair," "Merrily We Roll Along" sidestepped the attack, dispensing with any pretense of a rational defense of a world rebuilt for cars. Such excesses were expressions of mass preference, subject to criticism from an aloof elite but finally to be accepted as the free preference of a free people. And the message was extraordinarily successful. Before 1961, the love affair metaphor scarcely existed, even as a passing figure of speech.[3] The program elevated it to a thesis. Its origins in a narration by Groucho Marx were soon forgotten, as were details of the metaphor (the driver as man, the car as "girl"; the honeymoon; the marriage), but the thesis itself survived. Ever since the 1960s, even intellectuals who attacked the lavish accommodation of automobiles generally accepted the validity of the love affair thesis—and frequently invoked it themselves. They thereby also implicitly accepted their own relegation to a class of elitist social critics.

The legacy continues. Advocates of Complete Streets are, as Keats, Mumford, and Jacobs were, frequent and easy targets for accusations of elitism; today, in response to the charge, the defendants frequently confess: "Let's face it, Americans love cars" (Preservation 2012). To their accusers, automobiles' critics are "anti-car elitists" ignorant of "what cars mean to real people" (DiCarlo 2006). As of this writing, Google will autocomplete a search for "American love affair with—" to "American love affair with cars," seven times the number of the only auto-completed alternative ("American love affair with guns"). Fifty years after "Merrily We Roll Along," the "love affair" thesis still prevails.

That Americans love cars—or that most people (in any country) have tended to welcome cars when they could get them—is typically treated as axiomatic in discussions of mobility and of streets. The thesis proposes an absolute preference to explain a choice made in distinct circumstances. While the thesis has been questioned (White 1994, p. 152; Wells 2012), such dissents are rare. The love affair thesis seems true because it surely is, indeed, half-true: people (Americans and others) tend to like cars. But it seems true also because, as George Orwell (1944) observed, "history is written by the winners." In this case, the winners told the history of the automobile in America as the history of heroic invention and eager acceptance. To agree with Orwell on this point does not entail subscribing to a rigid conception of hegemony. Agreement may be (as it is here) merely an admission that power relationships are typically imbalanced, that the historical record is subject to influence, and that more powerful groups, correctly recognizing the legitimating power of stories (including histories), exercise their power to foster and advance the historical accounts they prefer. The winners must write history to justify the status quo. And in writing history to justify the status quo, they must prefer the plausible half-truth to the far-fetched "big lie," or risk inviting doubt. The half-truth more effectively conceals the lie.

To call the love affair story a lie would be to compound one half-truth with another. It is best understood not as a lie but as a strategy in a much older struggle over streets. What are streets for? Street users have disagreed as long as there have been streets. To prevail over their opponents, participants in these struggles have resorted to diverse exercises of raw power. For a century, examples have included the motorist whose menacing driving clears the street of pedestrians—and the pedestrian who brazenly compels a driver to concede the right of way. They include the residents who finally succeed in getting the curb parking on their block limited to residents only, and the coalitions that manage to get zoning ordinances amended to require retailers to provide off-street parking. They include the stopped delivery truck that blocks traffic and the traffic code that empowers police to order the driver to move on.

But exercises of raw power invite resistance. At small scales, drivers subvert low speed limits through spontaneous collective civil disobedience; residents respond to fast driving with traffic calming measures; pedestrians use superior agility to match motorists' superior horsepower. At larger scales, such subversion takes the form of alternative conventional wisdoms manifested in editorial pages, in popular fiction, or in popular nonfiction, such as *The Death and Life of Great American Cities*. The effective exercise of power requires more than power alone; "only legitimacy can transform brutal power into recognized authority" (Dogan 1992, p. 116). By fostering compliance and dampening resistance, legitimized power is far less expensive to those who exercise it.

Storytelling and streets

The struggles for the American city street—including the substantial initial resistance to automobiles a century ago, the motor age redefinition of streets as places for motor vehicles alone, the challenges of Jane Jacobs and other social critics, and the rise of movements such as Livable Streets and Complete Streets—are best understood in these terms. Complete Streets advocates did not invent or join in a new struggle to reconceive streets; they entered a stage as players in a new act of an old drama. Their predecessors and the predecessors of their opponents have fought for power and for legitimacy at least since the arrival of the automobile in substantial numbers in American city streets a century ago. In 1920, Bessie Buckley, a Milwaukee schoolteacher objected to motor vehicles' growing prevalence in streets and the cost imparted on the children and the pedestrians of her city. "Are streets for commercial and pleasure traffic alone?" she asked rhetorically. Her voice was one in a massive movement of resistance to the automobile's domination of streets—a movement which stood for practically the same causes as the Complete Streets movement many decades later.

The preferred technique on both sides has been storytelling. Plausible stories work better than lies, and when the events are complex and the historical record is a stew of facts, omissions, public relations, propaganda and fabrication, plausible stories are wonderful in their variety. As in the film *Rashomon* (1950), the story-tellers' biases and limited perspectives constraint their accounts. Among the many genres, favorites include history (or historical fiction, depending on the reader's point of view), melodrama, visionary futurism, dystopian fantasies, political thrillers—and love stories.[4] Among the stories told by participants in the struggle for the street, "Merrily We Roll Along" is unusual in representing itself explicitly as a story about a love affair. But just as a love interest is rarely absent from works in any genre of popular fiction, love interests populate many other stories about streets and who belongs in them. Indeed *The Death and Life of Great American Cities* is a kind of love story, explicitly dedicated to a city.[5] Like "Merrily We Roll Along," *The Death and Life of Great American Cities* defends the irrational as human. Planners' oppressive quest for cold order neglects the bonds of warm affection that sustain successful neighborhoods. The love affair, in Jacobs' telling, is not between Americans and their cars, but between urban people and their streets and neighborhoods. Both in "Merrily We Roll Along" and in *The Death and Life of Great American Cities*, love justifies what rationality cannot.

The history of stories about streets—and stories about histories of streets—have much to offer advocates of Complete Streets and their critics. In the very name for their movement, proponents of Complete Streets set themselves in opposition to a dominant legitimating story—though one of which they are generally little aware. This story's success is apparent in a powerful governing assumption: streets are for cars. The assumption is seldom stated because its apparent truth is as obvious as gravity. Like gravity, people learn to live with it. They don't question it and they don't have a lot to say about it. Drivers accept that streets are for cars and don't have much to say about it—until another street user behaves as if streets are for anything else. More significantly, pedestrians, cyclists, and other street users typically also accept that streets are for cars. But unlike gravity, streets-are-for-cars is of course not a natural fact. It is a social invention secured to some extent by mass preference and by raw power (it can be physically and legally dangerous to challenge it) but legitimized and perpetuated by successful storytelling.

When streets were not for cars[6]

There was nothing self-evident in the proposition that streets are for cars. The stories that account for the proposition's ultimate success are not well known. They were devised in the 1920s as people who wanted a future for cars in cities collided with the limits that the then prevailing stories imposed upon them. These status quo stories and story fragments were diverse, but they were consistent with the conclusion that streets were *not* for cars. Against this constraint, motorists often found themselves perceived as unwanted, space-hungry and dangerous intruders.

This perception reflected and perpetuated a status quo that pre-dated automobiles, and that therefore had not been influenced by people who wanted a place for cars in cities. The city street of 1900 was unmarked. There were no signals and, except in unusual circumstances, no traffic police. While commercial signage was abundant, almost no official signs governed traffic, and indeed there were no distinct official traffic codes to regulate it. While pedestrians preferred sidewalks, neither laws nor social norms prevented them from roaming streets at will and crossing them wherever they wished. Mud and manure often deterred pedestrians, but on the paved streets of larger towns and cities such nuisances were usually well managed by busy street cleaning departments. There were no marked crosswalks. Indeed, because streetcars loaded and unloaded passengers along the centerlines of streets, pedestrians of all kinds crossed them wherever they could. Young children played in quieter streets and crossed the busy ones at will and unescorted; their right to them was defended by parents and judges. Anything faster than a streetcar was "speeding." In the absence of traffic codes, common law principles prevailed; these gave pedestrians rights of access to streets that were at least equal to those of any other street users. Social norms mattered much more than laws, and these too granted pedestrians generous access. Busy streets were, in brief, much like crowded city parks today—places welcoming diverse uses, provided users did not obstruct or menace others.

As they proliferated in cities, automobiles exposed the incompatibility between motor traffic and this social construction of streets. The distinct advantage of cars over the alternatives lay in their speed—drivers who exploited this advantage even to just 20 miles per hour could be condemned as dangerous speeders. Pedestrians forced to concede the street to menacing motorists expressed their anger in letters to their newspapers. Far more explosive, however, were the many casualties. In 1925 alone, motor vehicles killed about 21,000 Americans. In cities of more than 25,000, pedestrians—most of whom were not drivers—accounted for more than two-thirds of the dead. Many were young; children accounted for 7,000 of the 1925 fatalities.

Defenders of cars often eagerly joined in the consequent safety efforts. Auto clubs, auto dealers, and well-meaning drivers joined other safety advocates to call for greater caution from everyone, especially motorists. They joined and transformed a larger "Safety First" movement, which had originated a decade earlier in the railroads and heavy industries. The expanded movement extended the Safety First movement's publicity techniques, summarized by Edward Bernays, the founder of public relations, as the "use of every form of appeal, from poster to circular, from lecture to law enforcement, from motion picture to 'safety weeks,'" to change "the attitude of a safety-deserving public towards the taking of unnecessary risks" (Bernays 1923, p. 91). To the widespread condemnation of dangerous cars and drivers, they added stories—often comic in tone—blaming foolish "jay walkers." But they soon found themselves ensnared in a more sensational melodramatic narrative that damned them. Cars were "modern Molochs" to which drivers sacrificed children in crowds. Motorized Grim Reapers mowed early harvests of immature victims. The casualties, in the usual tellings, were always innocent and were even memorialized officially as public losses, like war dead.

In these and other ubiquitous fragmentary stories—in the form of sensational news items, editorial cartoons, and safety posters—cars and drivers were villains. Such depictions were the staples of the many public safety campaigns of the period. In the popular fiction of the 1910s and 1920s, traffic victims were typically innocents on foot; the killers were often privileged aristocrats of dubious character (Tarkington 1918; Miller 1921; Manslaughter 1922; Fitzgerald 1925; The Crowd 1928). Such stories and story fragments were conspicuously absent from later histories of streets and cars.[7] History would be written by true winners, and the melodramas of villainous automobiles and innocent pedestrian victims were products of a losing side in the struggle for the street.

But first the defenders of the car found themselves players in another kind of drama, in which they, again, were scripted as the villains. As cars clogged city streets in the 1920s, coalitions of city businesses hired engineers to study the problem and propose remedies. Chambers of commerce and other business groups feared that traffic jams threatened the value of major investments, and constrained retail business. Large department stores, automobile dealers and clubs, and electric railways were generally well represented. The engineers, many of them experienced in "municipal engineering" (the provision of city services such as water and gas) conducted traffic surveys to spot inefficiencies. Their findings were diverse, but they tended to agree that spatially demanding automobiles were the culprits, and to advise against expensive reconstruction to accommodate them. Cincinnati's city manager (a trained engineer) expressed a typical position: congestion created a "necessity of giving precedence to vehicles in the streets in the order of their capacity for moving the greatest number of riders in the least possible time and using the least possible space in doing so." To him, this procedure put "private motorcars" in last place (Sherrill 1926, p. 648). While their recommendations were many, traffic engineers particularly favored curb parking bans and coordinated timing of traffic signals. As a way to relieve traffic jams and ease traffic flow, such recommendations could gain support from automotive interest groups as temporary remedies.

Motordom's crisis

Until the mid-1920s, people who wanted a future for cars in cities—auto clubs, auto dealers, taxicab companies and other motor fleet operators—tended to accept the stories others wrote for them. In the early to mid-1920s, however, automotive interest groups began to see stories of homicidal, spatially profligate cars as a threat. Industry leaders, in step with the rise of the idea and practice of public relations, concluded they needed to devise and propagate stories of their own.

Among the several reasons, two are salient. First, an unexpected sales slump in 1923 alarmed car dealers and manufacturers. The economy was in recovery following the recession of 1921, but somehow car sales fell, especially in large cities. Auto industry insiders warned of coming saturation of demand for automobiles. Americans would soon have all the cars they wanted; many—especially people in cities—would never want them. Demand would be sustained only by replacement sales, some of which would be lost to the growing used car market. Like an evangelist's warning of Judgment Day, it was a frightening story for people whose fortunes depended on reliable auto sales.

Meanwhile, city people, disturbed by high pedestrian casualties, began demanding restrictions of cars. Since cars were the villains in the prevailing story, the solution (many agreed) lay not in pedestrian regulation. Rather, automobiles had to be restricted until they conformed with the street as it had been before their introduction. Such sentiment was common in large cities; it manifested itself most strikingly in Cincinnati in 1923. There, 42,000 residents signed petitions for an initiative that would require all cars operating in the city to be equipped with mechanical governors limiting their speed to 25 miles per hour.

Together, saturation of demand and blame for high traffic casualties were threats to the automobile's urban future. In the face of these threats, people in the automobile business abandoned the stories that characterized cars as inherently dangerous congesters of traffic. They needed new stories—fables, so to speak, with different morals to teach. Automotive interest groups needed a better image, and the new field of public relations promised to deliver it. The National Automobile Chamber of Commerce (NACC)—an automobile manufacturers' trade association representing major automakers except for Ford—and the American Automobile Association (AAA) became the leaders in this effort. Both organizations could trace their origins back to 1903, but neither had a major, coordinated, national public relations effort until the threats of the early to mid-1920s mobilized them. Automotive interest groups joined in common cause, cooperating with each other and sometimes even referring to themselves as "motordom." While most of the consequent public relations effort was planned and led by automotive industry executives, NACC had on its staff a professional public relations man. John C. Long saw his job as "building collective good will" for the industry (cited in Long tells 1922, p. 1353). In 1923, the effort began in earnest.

For the automobile saturation threat, some in NACC advanced a different explanation. There was no saturation of *demand*. "Every single man and woman [and] every family that possibly can dig, scrap, borrow, beg or steal enough money is going to have an automobile," one manufacturer told his colleagues in the industry. "The problem," he explained, "is not one of temporarily policing, arrangements of streets, and traffic signals and everything of that sort, but the fundamental problem is one of floor space" (Jordan 1923). From this perspective, traffic jams indicated saturation of *street capacity*. Far from offering a way out, engineers' cure-all of efficiency would only limit the urban future of the car by precluding more ambitious efforts to accommodate it. In this story, only greater road capacity would save the automobile. Accommodating cars would take ambitious projects. To justify them, motordom needed an alternative to engineers' sober efficiency message.

On the safety front, both NACC and AAA were leaders, each in its own theater of operations. In response to the speed governor threat from Cincinnati, NACC formed a new Traffic Planning and Safety Committee. It ignored existing safety efforts associated with the old stories: that speed is inherently dangerous and that pedestrians struck by cars are the innocent victims of motorists. Its members contended instead that speed can be safe provided roads are well designed and that a reckless minority of motorists is kept off the road. They backed efforts to target reckless drivers for harsh punishment. They redirected responsibility to the pedestrian, redoubling older efforts by local automotive interest groups to stigmatize free-roaming pedestrians as "jaywalkers" (now more often a single word).

In its effort to redirect much of the responsibility for safety from motorists to pedestrians, NACC applied state-of-the-art public relations techniques. According to Edward Bernays, the leading pioneer of public relations, such efforts work best when the information comes through existing, trusted sources. "People accept the facts which come to them through existing channels. . . . They have neither the time nor the inclination to search for facts that are not readily available to them" (Bernays 1923, pp. 137–138). To NACC's public relations man John C. Long, the most effective channel was clear: "the leading medium of expression for the Trade Association is the newspaper" (Long 1924b, p. 201). Newspapers routinely reported pedestrian accident victims; indeed, it was in newspapers that the prevailing story of traffic safety was told. Through newspapers, NACC proposed to redirect responsibility for most of the accidents to the pedestrians themselves.

To do so, NACC offered a service to newspapers. NACC gave editors blank forms on which to fill in details about each traffic accident. Newspapers sent the completed forms to NACC, which drew its own conclusions from them. NACC sent its reports back to the newspapers, which presented them as authoritative. NACC's plan was to "make the newspaper a clearing house" for its "safety suggestions," and newspapers would "be influenced . . . to give greater publicity to the *real* causes of traffic accidents." NACC was confident it could use the "clearing house" to show that "In a majority of automobile accidents the fault is with the pedestrian rather than with the automobile driver" (Graham 1924a, 1924b; Trying 1924).

Within a year newspapers in about 300 cities and towns were participating, gathering data for NACC to assemble and interpret. In the resulting reports for 1924, NACC blamed 591 fatalities on recklessness by drivers—specifically "excessive speed" (371 deaths) and "violat[ing] the rules of the road" (220); these were far outnumbered, however, by deaths blamed on pedestrians (1,010)—specifically adults who were jaywalking (654) and children who were at play (356) (Jenkins 1925; see also More Playgrounds, 1925). By the fall of 1924, the character of newspaper coverage of accidents had changed enough to catch the notice of people unaware of NACC's service. With some exaggeration, the magistrate of New York City's traffic court commented: "It is now the fashion to ascribe from 70 to 90 percent of all accidents to jaywalking" (cited in Nation Roused 1924). Newspapers' use of the term rose sharply; indeed in 1924 *jaywalker* entered a standard dictionary for the first time (*Practical Standard*, 1924). Under the new logic of traffic safety that NACC promoted, pedestrian casualties were to be solved by spreading the word: Streets are for cars. Free-range pedestrians are jaywalkers.

AAA and its member auto clubs joined in the effort. To promote pedestrian responsibility, local auto clubs and dealers had been propagating the term *jay walker* since 1913. In Los Angeles, the Auto Club of Southern California and a local association of business groups calling itself the Los Angeles Traffic Commission conducted traffic surveys and wrote a traffic control ordinance for the city, paying for implementation themselves. Modified and backed by motordom as the Model Municipal Traffic Ordinance in 1927, it became a template for cities across the nation. It encoded cars' supremacy in streets, relegating pedestrians to crossings. At least as important, however, were the auto clubs' safety education efforts. In the early to mid-1920s, some local clubs, notably the Chicago Motor Club and the Auto Club of Southern California, went into the public schools to teach children that streets are for cars and to sponsor existing school safety patrols or start new ones. In the late 1920s, the national AAA coordinated a major, national, and permanent safety education campaign. Children pledged not to play in streets and to look both ways before crossing, and learned that streets are for autos.

These efforts were not a total success. Pedestrians took advantage of their agility to retain access to streets, children continued to play in streets where they could, and motorists continued to share in the blame for pedestrian casualties. Yet motordom's success was sufficient and substantial. By 1930, pedestrians using streets in ways considered perfectly normal just a decade earlier were now jaywalkers, engaged in at least somewhat disreputable conduct. Witnesses to the injury of a child at play in the street might still blame the motorist, but by 1930 at least some of the blame went to parents as well. Above all, a generation of children was growing up to believe that streets are for cars—and to believe it almost like they believed in gravity, as an immutable natural law, not subject to question. Through this achievement, motordom had gone far toward securing the automobile's future in the American city.

The reckless driver, the foolish jaywalker, and the careless child were new characters in an evolving new drama—but the story was incomplete. Although the "floor space" metaphor achieved some currency within motordom, for wider audiences it was a narrative dead-end, a showroom analogy only an auto dealer could admire. Something greater was needed—something less defensive and more positive that would free automobiles and their drivers from precedents and engineering models that saddled them with responsibility for traffic congestion and traffic casualties. By the mid-1920s, some in motordom had found what they were looking for: new, inspiring stories, sufficient in their appeal to justify new mental models and new courses of action.

New stories

One new narrative made the automobile a character in a new chapter of a story of progress, international in scope. The automobile and the airplane were not merely two impressive new inventions, but symbols of an essential departure from steam-age past. The "motor age" promised faster and more individualized mobility, more personal and more democratic. Fulfillment of its promise would require escape from outmoded precedents left over from another age. "We are living in a motor age," explained John Hertz, president of Chicago's Yellow Cab Company, in 1926. The problem, to Hertz, was not to make automobiles conform to ways of the preceding age, but to reeducate people for life in the new age: "we must have not only motor age education, but a motor age sense of responsibility" (cited in Agree on Code 1926).

A second, related story was more distinctly American. In it, the automobile was an expression of American ideals, in particular of personal freedom against official restraint, of economic freedom against regulation, of political freedom against regimentation, and of individualism against collectivism. While isolated and fragmentary examples of such appeals had not been unusual before, beginning in the fall of 1923 NACC developed a more consistent, extensive and durable version. Only thereafter did its themes become persistent mainstays in and out of motordom.

NACC rolled out its new story in the eye of the speed governor storm in Cincinnati. A few weeks before the November referendum, NACC's general manager, Alfred Reeves, traveled to Cincinnati to address the city's automobile dealers' association. Reeves explained that "America is converted to rubber-tire transportation" because "the flexible independent transportation afforded by the motor vehicle appeals inherently to an independent people" (cited in Accidents 1923). Heartened by motordom's victory in the referendum, Reeves took the message to the wider public, applying it to the proposition that greater street and road capacity was the solution to congestion. In a 1924 article promoting the "floor space" analogy, Reeves found more inspiring words. He appealed to the patriotism of those alarmed at what it would take to rebuild American cities for the motor age: "No physical feat need seem staggering to a nation that can build the Panama Canal, can blast Hell Gate and can construct the Croton Reservoir" (Reeves 1924, p. 31).

For expert audiences, others in NACC presented the new story in journals that had featured work by the efficiency experts NACC opposed. In November 1924, NACC's Roy Chapin, President of the Hudson Motor Car Company, published a version of it in the *Annals of the American Academy of Political and Social Science* (Chapin 1924). To explain the popularity of the automobile in the United States, Chapin invoked not mass production, America's prosperity, or the practical advantages of cars to a country of great distances. Instead he appealed to more exalted ideals, the kind associated with American exceptionalism. To him, "American instincts" were at stake. "Americans are a race of independent people," Chapin explained. "Their ancestors came to this country for the sake of freedom and adventure. The automobile satisfies these instincts." Americans "seized upon motor travel so rapidly and with such intensity" because of their "craving for freedom of the individual" and because "the automobile supplies a feeling of escape from this suppression of the individual" (1924, pp. 4–5).

Working closely with Chapin was NACC's professional public relations man, John C. Long (1924a). Making no mention of his affiliation with NACC, Long adapted Frederick Jackson Turner's famous frontier thesis, which emphasized America's distinct character to its frontier history. Long argued that the automobile had revived the frontier. It induces a "pride of ownership" with the "sense of freedom that accompanies ownership," which together form "the chief reason for the wide-spread acceptance of the motor car by the American public" (ibid., 112). "We come of independent pioneering stock," Long argued, echoing Chapin. "Our forefathers were impatient of restraint and adventurous in spirit." From industrialization's regimentation, "the automobile furnishes a release. It makes the individual the overlord of his own transport system; he can go where he wants, at such time as he desires" (ibid., p. 112). "The hunger for new scenes is inherent in the American people. The automobile makes this new territory available, it satisfies a pioneering desire, which is a large part of the popular appeal of the motor car" (ibid., p. 118).

By its own terms, NACC's new story and its descendants were not stories of stability but of progress, not of efficiency but of abundance, not of rational control but of personal expression. In its diverse versions, the story united these themes through appeal not to universal principles but to a self-conscious Americanism. Appeals to popular versions of the American past—to the struggle for inde-pendence, to pioneering and the settlement of the West, and to technological inventiveness—legitimized appeals to fundamental change. To evoke pioneering and to celebrate change over stasis, General Motors promoted the metaphor of "new horizons" in its 1952 film Key to Our Horizons:

> Our horizons have been expanded by the motor car. And the greatness of America has been that we are never content to stop at the horizon we can see. We know that there is another, and another, horizon beyond . . . The motor car has been the key to open new horizons.

By delivering "individual freedom of movement . . . the motor car will be the key to our ever-widening horizons of tomorrow" (Chevrolet 1952). By representing history as constant improvement—progress—motordom challenged the status quo's self-legitimizing character, freeing the transportation problem from standards of assessment that automobiles could not win.

Motordom's new story was soon retold and extended in countless variations. Miller McClintock, the leading traffic expert of the 1920s, had begun his career as a critic of automobiles in cities, on grounds of their spatial inefficiency. Recruited in 1925 by Studebaker to direct a new, Studebaker-funded, national traffic planning group, McClintock gradually joined the cause. By 1927 he was a champion of it. He adopted motordom's new story. Cities, McClintock said, must "adjust their physical layout . . . to the requirements of an automobile age" (McClintock 1927). The automobile was an expression of American ideals. "This Country was founded on the principle of freedom," he told the Society of Automotive Engineers; "the automobile has brought something which is an integral part of the American spirit—freedom of movement" (McClintock 1928).

At the 1939–40 New York World's Fair, the story was presented as a futuristic motor age epic, told through twentieth-century technology for an audience of millions. At General Motors' vast pavilion, entirely modern in its design, fairgoers waited for hours to see Futurama—the "World of Tomorrow," a "magic city of progress" depicted as an enormous model (GM 1940, p. 21). While Futurama has already been frequently referenced in scholarship on automobility in American history, it is worth commenting here specifically on the story it told.[8] In the first summer of the fair, five million tourists took it in; millions more saw it in the second summer or as a color film: To New Horizons (1940). Both in terms of the numbers of visitors and visitors' expressed preferences, it was also by far the most popular exhibit at the fair (Marchand 1992).

After they entered the pavilion but before they reached the model, fairgoers already heard Futurama's soothing, recorded "Voice." It explained that "The history of American roads is the history of our civilization as it marched westward from the Atlantic to the Pacific—roadways forging ever onward through mountain, desert and forest barriers, leaving in their wake great thriving cities, industrial centers and prosperous farms" (GM 1940, p. 4). History, as GM presented it, was dynamic—"highway progress of the future" demanded constant change, through "modern pioneering" (ibid., p. 4; *To New Horizons*). But in 1939, the Voice warned, "in many sections today's traffic is moving on roadways designed for yesterday." At this point, fairgoers saw a graphic warning of the crushing congestion "that might occur, if for the next twenty years our highways were not improved." But there was hope. "Express Motorways—particularly through and between our larger cities," would avert disaster, and deliver "highway progress" (ibid., pp. 4–5).

Fairgoers were then invited to take a seat in the exhibit's 552-seat "Carry-Go-Round," a moving trolley of comfortable chairs facing the Futurama model (ibid.). As if from an airplane window, visitors observed the city of 1960—depicted in three dimensions in a model four-fifths of an acre in size. The Voice continued its story, this time from speakers discretely mounted in the seats themselves. Passengers saw and heard about the "wonder world of 1960." It was a narrative of "progress and achievement," a "drama of highway and transportation progress" a visual fantasy—but the Voice was at pains to explain that it could be reality: "Strange? Fantastic? Unbelievable? Remember, this is the world of 1960!" On a highway bearing seven lanes of traffic in a single direction, drivers could safely maintain 100 miles per hour; they could take exit ramps at 50 mph. The power to deliver this motor-age utopia lay in the visitors' hands. "Is this Motorway actually the roadway of 1960? Perhaps. We only know that the world moves on and on, and that the highways of a nation are what set the pace for advancing civilization." The moral of the story, in case any fatigued tourists had missed it, was that the status quo must be left behind. As fairgoers ended their journey, the Voice intoned "ALL EYES TO THE FUTURE" (ibid.). A year later, GM's public relations director called Futurama "an object lesson in PROGRESS" (cited in Marchand 1992, p. 35).

Versions of this story, invoking American exceptionalism and the pioneer past, celebrating progress and individual freedom, remained staples of the more modest public relations efforts after World War II. Counter-narratives existed: for example, in 1948 General Electric, manufacturer of electric streetcars and trolley buses, released a color film called *Going Places*. Arguing in rational terms that cities should not be reconstructed for the sake of a motoring minority, the film advocated spatial and economic efficiency through mass transportation instead. The moral of GE's story: "We've been trying to move traffic when the basic intent is to move people." Yet such stories were overwhelmed by the heirs of Futurama.

In the 1950s, to mobilize support for a massive new interstate highway program, motordom's public relations experts went into high gear. In a 1954 color film called *Give Yourself the Green Light*, General Motors again evoked horizons new and old. "Freedom of the road is as old as the first man and as new as this moment." In soothing (almost plodding) tones, reminiscent of Futurama's Voice, the narrator offered a frontier history of road freedom: "Once we fought for it through forest and river, wild animals and Indians, across desert and mountain range—and we won our right of way." Switching to views of a freeway with fast traffic, he explained: "This is the American dream of freedom on wheels—an automotive age traveling on time-saving super highways." In 1956, the Ford Motor Company joined in, releasing a book and a film both called *Freedom of the American Road*. Henry Ford II introduced both with an American exceptionalist case: "We Americans always have liked plenty of elbow room—freedom to come and go as we please in this big country of ours" (Ford 1956; *Freedom of the American Road*).[9]

The love affair

Motordom's very success induced new and stronger counter-narratives. Major projects—of which the new National System of Interstate and Defense Highways was but one—could be cast as villains in new dramas. According to these stories, Americans were irrational idolaters, sacrificing themselves financially and bodily to an insatiable demonic deity: the automobile. At least one writer (Evans 1954, p. 197) even attributed the madness to a "love affair." Lewis Mumford and John Keats best represent the new narrative; William H. Whyte and Jane Jacobs offered variants that engaged in less demonization of the car and more celebration of a model of streets—small in scale, diverse in character and use—long since rejected by highway engineers.

It is in this context that "Merrily We Roll Along" is best appreciated. Love requires no rational defense. Critics of true love look foolish. The program characterizes the first three decades of the automobile in America as a disapproved courtship between the American (man) and the automobile ("the new girl in town"). The lovers were bedeviled by Victorian busybodies. Prudish chaperones—officious lawmakers, close-minded curmudgeons, and unimaginative skeptics—hemmed the young couple in at every turn. That the lovers succeeded despite such obstacles is the proof of their love. They were made for each other.

In the light of this program, 1960s critics of the car could seem elitist, antidemocratic, and out of touch. "Merrily We Roll Along" was too plebeian in style, too elementary in its content, to attract intellectual discussion. Intellectuals—critics of the automobile and others—ignored it. Strangely, however, its mantra gradually became the most widely accepted and the single most common explanatory metaphor for the automobile in American life. By this standard, the program must rank as motordom's greatest public relations success since Futurama. Both among intellectuals and in the popular press, "Americans' love affair with the automobile" and close variants became a ubiquitous presence in discussions of the automobile, and have remained so.[10] The automobile's critics accepted the notion at least as much as its defenders, unwittingly accepting the role in which the program cast the car's critics: as backward looking enemies of fun. Indeed, the thesis was so successful with the car's critics that the car's defenders have even mistakenly attributed it to them. As Joel Schwartz of the American Enterprise Institute sees it, "From the perspective of the automobile's critics, Americans have an irrational love affair with the automobile" (Schwartz 2005, p. 37). Schwartz contends that preference for cars is universal and economically rational—and in so doing, he inadvertently undermines the dual moral of GM's fable—that the love affair is distinctly American and, as the free choice of a free people, requires no rational defense.

The legacy persists. Criticisms of autocentric urban design have proliferated; alternative concepts and schools—Livable Streets, New Urbanism, Walkability, bicycle-friendly design, Complete Streets—have become ubiquitous. None of them, however, has yet told a story to compete with Futurama or "Merrily We Roll Along," and all have been frequent and easy targets for the accusations of elitism that "Merrily We Roll Along" invited. Before the advocates of such alternatives can challenge these stories, they must first recognize them for what they are. "Americans' love affair with the automobile" is neither self-evident truism, nor organic folk wisdom, nor socio-anthropological theory, though it has been presented as all three. It is a masterstroke of public relations, an invention intended to serve a distinct purpose: to make autocentric design normal design. It contains validity. Americans, like most people, embrace cars when they can—all the more in an environment that has been rebuilt for them and which offers meager alternatives. But this partial validity does not diminish its public relations power. To the contrary, it magnifies it, by concealing its more misleading aspect. Americans resisted cars fiercely, especially in cars' first three decades, and certainly not only for foolish reasons. The depth and extent of this resistance are best indicated by the panic it induced in motordom in the 1920s and by the energy of its consequent effort to change the story.

Motordom did not believe Americans loved cars enough to bring about the motor age unaided. Rather, it so feared the hostility to automobiles, especially in cities, that it organized perhaps the greatest private-sector public relations effort ever undertaken. It could not have succeeded if the car had not held powerful attractions, which it certainly did. But motordom knew that it would take more than that to convince Americans to recommit their streets to the almost exclusive use of motor traffic, and to rebuild their cities around cars. Advocates of alternatives have much to learn from their success.

Notes

1 Random House released *The Death and Life of Great American Cities* on October 9, 1961; the NBC broadcast ("Merrily We Roll Along") came 13 days later, on October 22. "Merrily We Roll Along" was in production well before *The Death and Life of Great American Cities* was released; it was a "reply" only in the sense that both works were part of a larger continuing debate—a debate in which Jacobs had been prominent since a speech she delivered at Harvard in 1956, published as Jacobs (1956) and adapted as Jacobs (1958).

2 *New York Times*, October 23, 1961, p. 53.

3 Before 1961, expressions of the metaphor were extremely scarce and little developed; all were critical of the relationship (Evans 1954, p. 197; Canaday, 1961). Lippincott marketed Keats (1958) as a book that was "all about America's love affair with the automobile" (*New York Times*, November 30, 1958). Five and a half months before "Merrily We Roll Along" aired, advance marketing billed it as the story of "the nation's love affair with the automobile" (*Chicago Tribune*, May 13, 1961). Weeks before NBC aired "Merrily

We Roll Along," IBM's *Think* magazine published an article titled, "Our Love Affair with the Automobile," celebrating the relationship (Purdy 1961).

4   Important examples include "Merrily We Roll Along" (history); Alice Duer Miller's 1921 novel *Manslaughter*, esp. pp. 119–123, adapted as the film *Manslaughter* (melodrama); General Motors' Futurama exhibit (1940) at its Highways and Horizons pavilion at the New York World's Fair of 1939–1940 (visionary futurism); Ray Bradbury's 1951 story "The pedestrian" (dystopian fantasy); Bradford Snell's 1974 testimony to the U.S. Senate Subcommittee on Antitrust and Monopoly, "American Ground Transport" (political thriller). In the designation of genres no assessment of the validity of these narratives is intended.

5   "To New York City, where I came to seek my fortune . . ."

6   Most of the material in this section ("When Streets Were Not for Cars") and in the following one ("Motordom's Crisis") is documented in the author's book *Fighting Traffic* (Norton, 2008), and adapted here in support of a different thesis.

7   Clearly both *The Magnificent Ambersons* and (especially) *The Great Gatsby* survived the era as major works of fiction (indeed *Gatsby* became a success only decades after its publication). Yet the period-specific significance of the characteristic auto accidents in them—in both works, pedestrians were struck by motorists—was generally lost to later generations of readers, who read these books when the trope was no longer recognizable.

8   Probably the most thorough scholarly account is Marchand (1992).

9   Similar promotional films, telling variations of the same story, were common. Examples include *Key to Our Horizons* (Chevrolet 1952), *Highway Hearing* (Dow 1956), *Freedom Highways* (Greyhound 1956), and *We'll Take the High Road* (ARBA 1958).

10 Perhaps the best indication of the acceptance of the "love affair" metaphor by critics of the automobile is a 1976 film *The American Love Affair*, by Lee Rhoads. In nonfiction books, the metaphor gained currency in the 1970s. Important early examples of such books include Leon Mandel, *Driven: The American Four-Wheeled Love Affair* (New York: Stein and Day, 1977); John B. Rae, *The American Automobile Industry* (New York: Twayne, 1984). More recent examples of nonfiction books (popular and scholarly) in which the love affair thesis is accepted uncritically include Karal Ann Marling, *As Seen on TV: The Visual Culture of Everyday Life in the 1950s* (Cambridge, MA: Harvard University Press, 1994); Lynn Dumenil, *The Modern Temper: American Culture and Society in the 1920s* (New York: Hill and Wang, 1995); Frank Coffey and Joseph Layden, *America on Wheels: The First 100 Years, 1896–1996* (Los Angeles: General Publishing Group, 1996); Katie Alvord, *Divorce Your Car! Ending the Love Affair with the Automobile* (Gabriola Island, BC: New Society, 2000); Richard Merrill Dalton, Jr., *Car People: America's Love Affair with Cars* (Bloomington, IN: Xlibris Corp., 2001); Maury Klein, *Rainbow's End: The Crash of 1929* (New York: Oxford University Press, 2003); David Blanke, *Hell on Wheels: The Promise and Peril of America's Car Culture, 1900–1940* (Lawrence: University Press of Kansas, 2007); Douglas Farr, *Sustainable Urbanism: Urban Design with Nature* (New York: Wiley, 2007); Tom McCarthy, *Auto Mania: Cars, Consumers, and the Environment* (New Haven, CT: Yale University Press, 2007); Randy Salzman, *Fatal Attraction: Curbing Our Love Affair with the Automobile Before It Kills Us* (CreateSpace, 2012). In 1982 Alan Drengson cited the "love affair with the automobile" (in this case, not a distinctly American affair) in support of a more general phenomenon he called technophilia; see Drengson (1982).

References

Accidents, 1923. Accidents can be prevented, *Cincinnati Enquirer* (Automobile Section), October 21.

Agree on Code, 1926. Agree on code of sane speed for speedy U.S. *Chicago Tribune*, March 25.

Bernays, Edward, 1923. *Crystallizing pubic opinion*. New York, NY: Liveright, 1961.

Bradbury, Ray, 1951. The pedestrian, *The Reporter* 5 (August 7), pp. 39–40.

Buckley, Bessie, 1920. Letter to editor, in "Where can the kiddies play? Send views to *Journal*," *Milwaukee Journal*, September 29.

Canaday, John, 1961. Art critic finds hint of sanity in styling. *New York Times*, April 2.

Chapin, 1924. The motor's part in transportation, *Annals of the American Academy of Political and Social Science* 116 (November), 1–8.

DiCarlo, Rachel, 2006. Hit the road: The fallacy of anti-car environmentalism (blog post), *Weekly Standard* (January 24). Available from: www.weeklystandard.com.

Dogan, Mattei, 1992. Conceptions of legitimacy. In: Mary Hawkesworth and Maurice Kogan eds. *Encyclopedia of government and politics*, vol. 1. London: Routledge, 116–126.

Drengson, Alan, 1982. Four philosophies of technology. *Philosophy Today*, summer: 103–117.

Evans, B., 1954. *The spoor of spooks and other nonsense*. New York, NY: Knopf.

Ford Motor Company, 1956. *Freedom of the American road*. Dearborn, Michigan.

Fitzgerald, F. Scott, 1925. *The Great Gatsby*. New York, NY: Scribner's.

Freeland, Robert F., 2001. *The struggle for control of the modern corporation: Organizational change at general motors, 1924–1970*. Cambridge: Cambridge University Press.

GM (1940). General Motors Corporation, *Futurama*. Includes a transcript of the recorded narration visitors heard. A scan of the book is available courtesy of Bob Catania at: www.1939nyworldsfair.com.

Graham, George, 1924a. Education, punishment and traffic safety (address, February 14), in bound collection marked "Pamphlets." New York: National Automobile Chamber of Commerce, Library, Washington, DC: U.S. Department of Transportation.

Graham, George, 1924b. Stern action is urged to banish death from highways. *Automotive Industries* 50 (February 28), 495–98, 511.

Jacobs, Jane, 1956. The missing link in city redevelopment. *Architectural Forum* 104 (June), 132–133.

Jacobs, Jane, 1958. Downtown is for people. *Fortune* 57 (1958), 133–40; 236, 238, 240–242.

Jacobs, Jane, 1961. *The death and life of great American cities*. New York, NY: Random House.

Jenkins, J.L., 1925. Motor speed and jaywalking roll up death totals. *Chicago Tribune*, February 15.

Jordan, Edward S., 1923. The future of the automobile. In: National Motorists Association, *Report on the National Convention of automobile club officials, Cleveland, September 20–22* (mimeographed typescript). Headquarters Library, American Automobile Association, Heathrow, Florida.

Keats, John, 1958. *The Insolent Chariots*. Philadelphia, PA: Lippincott.

Long, John C., 1924a. Motor transport and our radial frontier, *Journal of Land and Public Utility Economics*, 2 (January), 109–118.

Long, John C., 1924b. *Public relations: A handbook of publicity*. New York, NY: McGraw-Hill.

Long tells ad men of trade body aims, 1922. *Automotive Industries* 46 (June 15), 1353.

Marchand, Roland, 1992. Designers go to the fair II: Norman Bel Geddes, the General Motors "Futurama," and the Visit to the Factory Transformed. *Design Issues*, 8 (spring), 22–40.

McClintock, Miller, 1927. How the city traffic problem will be solved. *The Automobilist*, May, 5–7.

McClintock, Miller, 1928. Remedies for traffic congestion. *S.A.E. Journal*, 23 (November), 443–446.

Miller, Alice Duer, 1921. *Manslaughter*. New York, NY: Dodd, Mead.

More Playgrounds, 1925. More playgrounds needed by motorists of America. *Washington Post*, July 26.

Moynihan, Daniel Patrick, 1960. New roads and urban chaos. *The Reporter*, 22 (April 14), 13–20.

Mumford, Lewis, 1958. The highway and the city. *Architectural Record*, 123 (April), 179–186.

Mumford, Lewis, 1961. *The city in history: Its origins, its transformations, and its prospects*. New York, NY: Harcourt, Brace and World, esp. pp. 508–510.

Nation Roused, 1924. Nation roused against motor killings. *New York Times*, November 23.

Norton, Peter D., 2008. *Fighting traffic: The dawn of the motor age in the American city*. Cambridge, MA: MIT Press.

Orwell, George, 1944. As I please, *Tribune*, February 4.

Practical Standard (1924, 1936). Jaywalking. In: *Practical standard dictionary of the English language*. Springfield, MA: Merriam, 1331.

Preservation, 2012. Preservation or "progress" (anonymous post). *Environmental Geography*, May 6. Geography 360, Ohio Wesleyan University (blog). Available from: www.environmentalgeography.wordpress.com.

Purdy, 1961. Our love affair with the automobile. *Think* (IBM) 27(9), 14–18.

Reeves, Alfred, 1924. Have we enough highway floor space? *Nation's Business*, 12 (December), 30–31.

Schwartz, Joel, 2005. The social benefits and costs of the automobile. In: Wendell Cox, Alan Pisarski, and Ronald D. Utt, eds. *21st Century highways: Innovative solutions to America's transportation needs*. Washington, DC: Heritage Foundation, 37–66.

Sherrill, Clarence O., 1926. Congested streets are costly. *Electric Railway Journal*, 68 (October 9), 648–650, 648.

Snell, Bradford C., 1974. American ground transport: A proposal for restructuring the automobile, truck, bus and rail industries. U.S. Senate, Committee on the Judiciary, Subcommittee on Antitrust and Monopoly, February 26, 1974. Washington, DC: U.S. Government Printing Office.

Tarkington, Booth, 1918. *The magnificent Ambersons*. New York, NY: Doubleday.

Trying, 1924. Trying to get newspapers to tell accident causes. *Automotive Industries*, 50 (January 17), 125.

Wells, Christopher W., 2012. *Car country: An environmental history*. Seattle, WA: University of Washington Press.

White, Michelle J., 1994. Housing and the journey to work in U.S. cities (1991). In National Bureau of Economic Research, *Housing markets in the United States and Japan*, edited by Yukio Noguchi and James M. Poterba. Chicago: University of Chicago Press, 130–160.

Whyte, William H., 1957. Are cities un-American? *Fortune* 55 (September), 123–125, 213–214, 218.

Films and television

The American Love Affair, 1976, Film. Lee Rhoads.

Freedom Highways, 1956. Film. Greyhound Lines.

Freedom of the American Road, 1956. Film. Ford Motor Company. MPO Productions.

Give Yourself the Green Light, 1954. Film. General Motors Corporation.

Going Places, 1948. Film. General Motors.

Highway Hearing, 1956. Film. Dow Chemical Company.

Key to Our Horizons, 1952. Film. Chevrolet Motor Division, General Motors.

Manslaughter, 1922. Film. Cecil B. Demille. Paramount Pictures.

Merrily We Roll Along, 1961. NBC Television. Produced and directed by Robert L. Bendick, *Du Pont Show of the Week*, first aired October 22, 1961.

Rashomon, 1950. Film. Akira Kurosawa, Shinobu Hashimoto, and Kazuo Miyagawa, Daiei Film Co. Produced by Minoru Jingo and Masaichi Nagata; from the story, "In a Grove" (1922), by Ryonosuke Akutagawa.

The Crowd, 1928. Film. King Vidor and John V. A. Weaver. Metro-Goldwyn-Mayer.

To New Horizons, 1940. Film. General Motors Corporation.

We'll Take the High Road, 1958. Film. American Road Builders Association (ARBA).

3

MOVING BEYOND FORDISM

"Complete Streets" and the changing political economy of urban transportation

Aaron Golub

[T]o bring the pedestrians back into the picture, one must treat him [sic] with the respect and honor we now accord only to the automobile: we should provide him with pleasant walks, insulated from traffic, to take him to his destination.

(Lewis Mumford 1963)[1]

A right delayed is a right denied.

(Dr. Martin Luther King, Jr. undated)[2]

Introduction

"Complete Streets" have emerged as a new paradigm for roadway design which would "enable safe access for all users, regardless of age, ability, or mode of transportation" (SGA 2013, see also Clifton *et al.* 2012). Such designs would vary depending on rural or urban context, right of way dimensions, adjacent land uses, community preferences, etc. and might include: "sidewalks, bike lanes (or wide paved shoulders), special bus lanes, comfortable and accessible public transportation stops, frequent and safe crossing opportunities, median islands, accessible pedestrian signals, curb extensions, narrower travel lanes, roundabouts, and more" (SGA 2013). Complete Street standards are important ideas now long overdue. Shouldn't streets accommodate all users safely? Aren't public safety and equal accommodation (not to mention basic human dignity) a core goal of the civil engineering and urban planning professions?

Sadly, that Complete Streets is even lauded as an innovation illustrates the level of ignorance displayed by generations of transportation planners and engineers for the daily risks facing an actually highly diverse set of road users. But, planners and engineers don't act in a vacuum—they are situated within city and county governments, directed by elected officials and pressured by wider groups of citizens and stakeholders, all of which reflect and reproduce broader social norms and expectations. Similarly, Complete Streets concepts didn't fall to Earth from outer space—they also arise in a particular social context, and similarly, didn't arise in other contexts. This chapter situates innovations in urban transportation planning such as Complete Streets into those social contexts. Lewis Mumford's (1963) quote above reminds us that these ideas are now decades old, and so I ask in this chapter: "Why now?" In doing so, I offer some tough challenges to planners and engineers hoping to use Complete Streets to achieve transportation equity goals.

In this chapter, I explore those contexts in which Complete Streets did and did not arise, and connect them to larger processes of social change. I synthesize analyses from the fields of political economics, critical geography, and public history focused on issues of economic and social change. Then I focus further on the history of transportation and planning and policy for automobile transportation, as well as the process of racial and class segregation and discrimination within the process of urban development and transportation planning in the United States during the timeframe in question.

First, I trace the rise and fall of the Fordist social structure of consumption, beginning in the early part of the twentieth century, which produced a century-long, nearly secular, increase in automobile travel and ownership in the United States. I highlight, however, the mechanisms which marginalized large segments of society, and specifically the role that transportation planning played in that process. As white Americans fled to the suburbs in their cars, urban minorities were left to rely on the shrinking mobility of the sidewalk, the bus, and the train. Yet little was done to improve conditions for these non-drivers.

I then turn to the contemporary reconfiguring of the American social and urban landscape. The dismantling of Fordist social structures has reduced support for public welfare and services, stagnated wages, and now challenges the assumed patterns of suburban growth and automobile consumption. I describe the rapid reinvestment in urban development as cities respond to the competitive pressure for investment dollars in the increasingly volatile world of international finance and the widespread embracing of alternatives to the automobile, for reasons both good (growing interests in active travel) and bad (rising costs of mobility). At the same time, however, mounting forces of gentrification and displacement are at play in many urban areas. This only adds to the century-long story of urban marginalization—from early century segregation, to white suburbanization and urban containment, to present-day white "re-urbanization."

I close with an interpretation and discussion. We will ponder how transportation planning rarely, if ever, challenged the dominant processes of urban exclusion and marginalization. We consider how many communities harmed by that process may wonder why this time will be any different. What promises do innovations like Complete Streets or modern streetcars offer for transportation equity? In the words of Dr. King as in the opening quote to the chapter (see Bell 2013), will the denied right finally be honored? Or will Complete Streets merely pave the way for a reconfigured process of suburbanization of central cities? What can planners do differently this time?

Fordism

The seeds of "Fordism" were sown as industrial production turned its focus increasingly from luxury to consumer goods and grew increasingly dependent on workers' consumption for returns (de Janvry 1981; Aglietta 2000; Fairfield 2010). Low wages and weak articulation between workers' productivity and wages limited consumption capacity and challenged the broadening of industrial production. The introduction of scientific labor management (Taylorism) and its "assembly line" in the 1910s only exacerbated these imbalances and by the 1920s the system flirted with stagnation (Baran and Sweezy 1968; Gordon 1984; Aglietta 2000). The resulting Great Depression revealed the underlying fragility of concentrated industrial capitalism: the mismatch between consumption (wages) and productivity could lead to underconsumption and overproduction, leading to general divestment and stagnation.

The Depression inspired new ways of thinking about the interaction between the economy and society and between production and consumption. Influenced by British economist John Maynard Keynes and shaped by negotiations between capital, organized labor, and the government through the New Deal legislations, a pattern of private and public policies, often labeled "Fordist" grew to manage and stabilize the economy (Fraser and Gerstle 1989; Cohen 1990; Aglietta 2000). This pattern, still largely in place today, emphasized government intervention in the economy (through monetary and fiscal policy) to manage consumption, inspire investment, and stabilize growth. The government, most powerfully at the federal level, would play a significant role in funding and building infrastructure, regulating business and finance, moderating competition, subsidizing and insuring credit, funding a social safety net, and becoming a more significant economic actor more broadly. Workers trade higher wages and job stability for more intense exploitation in the workplace and management of their consumption behaviors at home (Harvey 1985; Cohen 1990; Fairfield 2010). While the immediate results of the arrangement were overshadowed by substantial wartime spending during World War II, the general structure led to relatively stable and sustained growth for the 30 years following the end of the war.[3]

Mass automobility

Fordism had a particular spatial and industrial character as most of the policies and investments synergized with the fastest growing sectors of the day—namely the automobile, the freeway, and the suburban tract home filled with mass produced durable goods. This was also a time of growing disdain for the often overregulated, underfunded, and under-maintained urban transit systems (Whitt and Yago 1985). Infrastructure investment programs through the New Deal spent many times more on roads, highways, and bridges than on public transit systems.[4] The automobile industry, subordinate downstream and upstream industries (oil, steel, rubber, car dealers, credit finance, service stations, etc.), other consumer goods industries (household appliances, etc.), and the dozens of large banks, insurance companies, and other financial institutions became functionally and managerially inter-dependent during this period (Snell 1974; Ullmann 1977; Gordon 1984; Whitt and Yago 1985; Gartman 2004; Urry 2004). This "automobile-suburban complex" dominated the mid-century economy and was reinforced by public policy (which it often managed[5]), public investments (e.g. the 1956 Interstate Highway Act, federal mortgage guarantees, etc.), and inter-firm coordination (interlocking directorates and ownership, industry associations, etc.). Dominance was further fortified by efforts to shape consumers' identity around suburbanization and automobile ownership (Flink 1975; Gartman 2004; Paterson 2007; Seiler 2008). The profound effect of these processes on the social and physical landscape of the country cannot be overstated.

The widespread acceptance of automobility bolstered by the increased federal and state presence in local transportation policy and planning combined to reconceive the use of street spaces in urban areas around the country (Foster 1981; Bottles 1987; McShane 1995; Norton 2008). These public spaces were transformed from loosely managed thoroughfares carrying a mixture of pedestrians, horses, buggies, and streetcars to spaces to be managed and optimized (Foster 1981; Rose 1990; Urry 2004). The process of optimization, however, became the purview of complex bureaucracies staffed by experts, effectively removing it from public debate and oversight (Rose 1990). Optimization was achieved through roadway invest-ments (widening) or operations improvements (traffic signaling, removing on-street parking, consolidating driveway entries, etc.) (Henderson 2011). Often, needed crosswalks are removed or not implemented, traffic speeds are raised, and signal timings are adjusted to favor through movement, placing cyclists, pedestrians, and transit users at great disadvantage while potential cyclists, pedestrians, and transit users are discouraged. Regionally, transportation planning was reconfigured to link already exploding suburbs to central cities, facilitating further outward expansion through new freeway links or suburban mass transit systems. The construction of such systems was fueled by a series of federal highway legislations and a dedicated funding stream through the Highway Trust Fund and gasoline taxes, again insulating the programs from regular debate.

Fordism, suburbanization, and exclusion

Significant segments of the population were excluded from the general process of Fordist development. While the "New Deal Liberalism" from which Fordism grew was perhaps less overtly racist than the Jim Crow South (Fraser and Gerstle 1989), blacks and other minorities were faced with various forms of discrimination in most of the country's metropolises. The rise of Fordism preceded the modern civil rights movement during a time when most minorities were subjected to discrimination in nearly all aspects of their lives—in employment, wages, housing, access to credit, education, etc. Minorities were limited in where they could rent or buy a home while the neighborhoods in which they lived were systematically underinvested by municipalities, "redlined" by public and private lenders, and often targeted for infrastructure (freeways, warehousing, etc.) or "urban renewal," which destroyed more housing than it created (Hirsch 1993). These forces severely retarded the integration of many minorities into the mainstream of the Fordist economy.[6]

Though most of these openly racist practices ended with the end of legalized discrimination following the Civil Rights Act and related legislation, most of the segregation and inequality persisted through the Fordist period (Massey and Denton 1993). Earnings for blacks as a share of white earnings in the U.S. were 54 percent in 1947 and remained basically unchanged (56 percent) in 1982; the record for Hispanics is roughly the same (Baran and Sweezy 1968; Wolff 2010, pp. 52–53). Fordist suburbanization exacerbated these existing processes of exclusion and segregated regions and abandoned working-class and minority communities in central cities. Transportation planning largely aided and abetted these broader processes in three ways: (1) unequal access to participation in the planning process; (2) unequal exposure to localized environmental burdens; and (3) unequal distribution of mobility benefits from transportation investments (Golub et al. 2013a).

Numerous barriers existed to prevent minority and low-income communities from participating in the regional transportation planning processes (Pucher 1982; Denmark 1998; Sanchez et al. 2003; Bullard et al. 2004). While early on, transportation planning agencies were not required to consult with the public about their plans in a meaningful way, urban minorities were still further ignored in the larger narrative of urban development (Pulido 2000; Golub et al. 2013). Even to this day, regional transportation decision-making has been shown to be biased to favor the needs of whiter and more suburban jurisdictions (Sanchez 2006; Golub et al. 2013).

With the growing suburbanization of residents, tax bases, and industry, regional mobility was increasingly important, yet challenging, for urban minorities facing rising transportation costs and divested urban public transit systems (Kain 1968; Ihlanfeldt and Sjoquist 1998). This mismatch between workers and geographies of opportunity is further perpetuated by the standard transportation planning methods which focus resources at particularly congested links in the regional transportation networks; central city populations who are less mobile and pose fewer demands on the road network will benefit less from transportation investments than the most mobile, who become even more mobile after the investments are made (Martens et al. 2012). Today, staggering differences in performance between the road network and public transit services result from decades of uneven investments (Kawabata and Shen 2007; Grengs and Levine 2010; Golub et al. 2013a).[7] Furthermore, a substantial body of research finds that many transportation investments have been used to purposely isolate minority communities (Pucher 1982; White 1982; Bayor 1988; Mohl 1993; Bullard et al. 2004; Henderson 2004; Golub et al. 2013).[8]

Differences in wealth and income have obvious implications for minorities' access to transportation. Figure 3.1 shows the share of households with no vehicles, clearly illustrating the significant difference in access to vehicles especially among black households. Data from 1995 showed that black households traveled only about 75 percent as much as the average household (in terms of vehicle miles traveled) (Battelle 2000, p. 42).

Transportation systems produce significant localized environmental burdens such as air pollution, dust, noise, blight, and create barriers within and between neighborhoods (Bullard et al. 2004; Schweitzer and Valenzuela 2004). Because of the history of segregation and confinement of minorities to central cities, and the common placement of freeway facilities proximate to or directly through those communities, urban minorities are often disproportionately exposed to resulting environmental burdens (Bullard et al. 2004).[9] There are impacts on safety as well; the combination of urban confinement, higher rates of walking, lack of recreational space, and high exposure to traffic cause urban minorities to face greater risk of injury and death due to motor vehicle traffic, especially as pedestrians, than the white population (Daniels et al. 2002; Campos-Outcalt et al. 2003; Hilton 2006).[10]

One final point should be made regarding the relationship between minority communities and transportation during this period. Paul Gilroy powerfully illuminates in his essay "Driving While Black" the roles that slavery, confinement, and restricted mobility (from "Sundown Laws" to today's Trayvon Martins) have

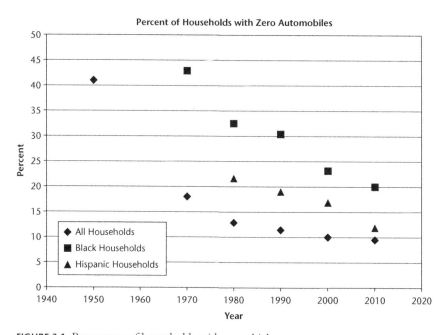

FIGURE 3.1 Percentage of households with no vehicles

Sources: Flink (1975) and Murakami and Long (2013). Note: 2010 data is actually from the 2007 to 2011 (5-year) American Community Survey.

played in the lives of minority communities in the United States, and thus the special significance mobility plays in response (2001, p. 94):

> For African-American populations seeking ways out of the lingering shadows of slavery, owning and using automobiles supplied one significant means to measure the distance travelled toward political freedoms and public respect. Employed in this spirit, cars seem to have conferred or rather suggested dimensions of citizenship and status that were blocked by formal politics and violently inhibited by informal codes. Later, the same freedom-seeking people would be confined to the disabling options represented by rural poverty on one side and inner city immiseration on the other. Here again, the car provided handy solutions to the eco-political problems it had occasioned and multiplied.

This creates a tension between the degrading influences automobility has had on urban livability, and its liberating potential for status and physical mobility. This highlights the differences with which certain communities may view mobility, consumption, and changes in transportation planning, with clear implications for post-automobile planning.

Fordist social structures had numerous internal contradictions and limits, and by the late 1960s, were showing signs of stress and decline. Next, we explore the reconfiguration of the economic planning process and the transition to deregulation as Fordism was replaced by new paradigms of governance. The effects of this transition on urban development and transportation planning are significant as growth in automobility stagnates, interests in alternatives to the automobile grow, and urban areas find themselves now the focus of redevelopment.

Post-Fordism[11]

High wages and concomitant declining and volatile levels of profits, and increasing international competition, placed U.S.-based capital, constrained by Fordist bargains, under increasing pressure.[12] By the middle of the 1970s, economic stagnation, unemployment, and high rates of inflation were causing serious and extended slowdowns to the U.S. economy. Responding to this crisis, capital cultivated a broad cultural and political support for a pattern of deregulatory policies often called neoliberalism (named for its emphasis on classical "Smithian" free-market liberalism). These policies would effectively liberate capital from costly Fordist bargains and compromises (Jessop 1994; Brenner and Theodore 2002; Harvey 2005).

Support for general social welfare—education, health care, infrastructure, and housing—was privatized, downscaled, or terminated. Responsibilities devolved from national levels (Fordism's primary structures of governance) to city and state governments or even special districts or private contractors. Neoliberal policies created new means of extracting, commodifying, and securitizing value, credit, and risk to satisfy increasingly mobile investment capital (Weber 2002).

The breakdown of Fordism also meant that wages no longer tracked with changes in productivity, worsening the already skewed wealth distributions inherited from the Fordist period (Fleck *et al.* 2011).[13] The end of *de jure* discrimination notwithstanding, income ratios between minorities and whites have remained basically unchanged to 2010.[14] Reliance on debt, however, doubled between 1983 and 2010, as households attempted to retain Fordist consumption patterns amidst stagnating real earnings.[15]

Neoliberalism and gentrification

These processes have had particular effects on urban development and planning. Without the support and structure from national-scale planning and financing for housing, urban renewal, infrastructure, and other urban services, metro areas have been forced to become "entrepreneurial" to attract investment to support growth, employment, and vibrancy (Weber 2002). The suburban growth model, of which the automobile is integral, remains a central fixture of the U.S. economy, though significant investment has shifted to more prized sites scattered throughout the metropolis, often including urban infill redevelopment projects (often buoyed by public subsidies and transfers) (Smith 2002; Weber 2002). To critical geographer Neil Smith (2002), urban infill and resulting gentrification are the defining and dominant mode of urban spatial development in the post-Fordist era. Though waves of gentrification have occurred for decades (Hackworth 2007), the past decade has witnessed both a broadening and deepening of its effects, described here by Smith (2002, p. 443):

> [G]entrification as urban strategy weaves global financial markets together with large and medium-sized real-estate developers, local merchants and property agents with brand-name retailers, all lubricated by city and local governments for whom beneficent social outcomes are now assumed to derive from the market rather than from its regulation. Most crucially, real-estate development becomes a centerpiece of the city's productive economy, an end in itself, justified by appeals to jobs, taxes and tourism. In ways that could hardly have been envisaged in the 1960s, the construction of new gentrification complexes in central cities across the world has become an increasing unassailable capital accumulation strategy for competing urban economies.

Stagnating household incomes and increasing dependence on debt now threaten dominant consumption patterns such as automobile ownership (Golub 2013). Significant volatility in world energy markets no longer guarantees the low and stable gasoline prices upon which Fordism depended. Indeed, the rising costs of automobility may be a significant factor motivating the reurbanization of white and middle-class households and the significant decline in licensure rates among millenials (Dutzik and Baxandhall 2013).[16]

Other factors compound cost increases to further challenge the dominant pattern of automobility. There is a growing recognition of the health impacts of sedentary lifestyles associated with suburbanization and automobiles, and an explosion in interest in active travel, especially cycling (Pucher *et al.* 2011). Furthermore, as suburbs themselves diversify, there is a declining need for regional travel to meet most needs (Newman and Kenworthy 2011). Though not currently a factor, significant demographic shifts including increasing rates of retired workers, households without children, and households of unrelated adults, will likely further alter the dominant process of automobility and suburbanization (Nelson 2009). Indeed, based on vehicle travel data, since 2006, we have entered an extended, perhaps permanent, period of stagnating growth in automobility (Dutzik and Baxandhall 2013), something transportation scholars have called "peak car" (Millard-Ball and Schipper 2011; Goodwin 2012; Golub 2013; Metz 2013).

Figure 3.2 presents various indicators relevant to transportation activity and costs since the end of the Fordist period. As incomes stagnate in real terms, costs of gasoline and automobiles have increased significantly. Meanwhile, automobile purchases have declined and registrations per household and vehicle miles traveled have stagnated. Figure 3.3 shows, however, that while walking and transit use are

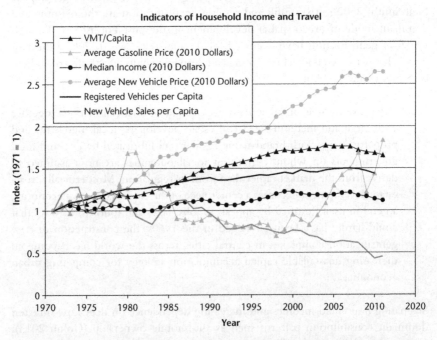

FIGURE 3.2 Various indicators of transportation consumption, household income, and fuel costs

Sources: Energy Information Agency, Real Prices Viewer; BEA Table 7.2.5S, Auto and Truck Unit Sales, Production, Inventories, Expenditures, and Price; Federal Highway Administration, Table VMT-421C; U.S. Census Bureau, Historical Income Tables, Table H-5.

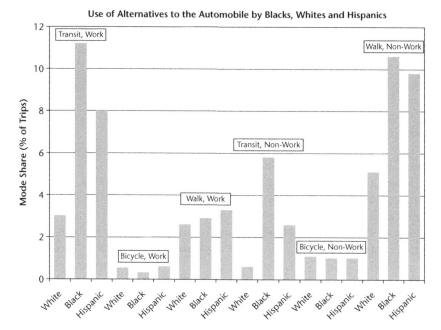

FIGURE 3.3 Walk, bicycle, and transit mode share for work and non-work trips by ethnicity

Source: Data for non-work travel is for 1995 (Battelle, 2000), and work travel is for 2010 (Murakami and Long 2013; League of American Bicyclists and the Sierra Club 2013).

being rediscovered by the middle classes, minorities never forgot them; they've been walking and using transit at high rates all along.

Unfortunately, while these data show there are real existing and growing needs for alternatives to the automobile, the processes of urban entrepreneurialism have recast transportation investments as tools to attract investment rather than to create viable system-wide solutions (Grengs 2004). For example, public transportation investment programs have been reconfigured to match the increasingly finer scales of urban interventions; the Federal Transit Administration now offers grant programs for transit projects as small as a single streetcar line of only a few miles in length.[17] This allows investments to be tailored for specific economic development activities, turning them into simple upgrades for areas needing a re-branding or the right mix of amenities to attract the attention of the so-called "creative class." Furthermore, it enables regions previously too small or too suburban to receive grants without making a large commitment to a comprehensive public transit program (though possibly threatening existing bus services as these new boutique services often consume disproportionate amounts of operating budgets). Meanwhile, the needs of existing transit users can be ignored, since they may only marginally overlap with the investment, or may eventually be priced out of areas nearby the transit investments (Pollack *et al.* 2010). For example, Stephens *et al.*

(2013) document significant demographic changes near rail stations in Los Angeles; in many station areas, rent burdens, the share of households with more than two vehicles, and the share of workers who drive alone to work increase, while the number of car-free households and the share of workers who take the transit to work decline. Residents and advocates in the San Francisco Bay Area forced the metropolitan planning organization to calculate and monitor the "potential for displacement" as part of its environmental justice analysis of its regional transportation plan (MTC 2013).

These issues can also extend to bicycle facilities in some places. Later chapters in this volume explore the cases of Portland, Oregon (Miller and Lubitow, Chapter 14), Minneapolis, Minnesota (Hoffmann, Chapter 8) and Brooklyn, New York (Chronopoulos, Chapter 4, see also Stein 2011) where ongoing processes of gentrification are accompanied by bicycle infrastructure investments and proposals. These cases illustrate how such interventions are often tied to wider forces of land development and branding while being disconnected from existing community concerns and desires.

Though we see a change in the character, scale, and location of transportation planning, there still exists tremendous momentum behind the Fordist paradigm. Most workers in the United States still drive to work, live in automobile-oriented areas and engage in an economy of mass production and consumption. Indeed, at the national level, we witnessed a resurgence of Fordist policies in the wake of the 2008 economic crisis as large banks and automobile manufacturers were propped up with federal funds. What's more, the 2009 American Recovery and Reinvestment Act spent very little to support alternatives to the automobile—very much in step with the same patterns of federal spending over the past 50 years.[18]

Discussion

Complete Streets standards represent a significant improvement over the status quo approaches to urban traffic engineering, reflecting a clearer concern for health and safety, fairness, sustainability, and even basic human dignity. This potential notwithstanding, their implementation in practice, and their resulting impacts on social equity will be modified by a host of social and political forces which shape the impacts of any innovation. The century-long record of urban development and transportation innovation reviewed here shows how strongly they have been intertwined with broader issues of social reproduction. It is difficult to understand the implications of innovations like Complete Streets for social outcomes without appreciating this context.

The essential task of Fordism was to stabilize and insure growth by coordinating the institutions and investments necessary for consumption. The growth in automobility was integrated into a larger process of Fordist economic development, as well as the process of regional racial segregation through suburbanization—both fundamental components of social reproduction during the post-war years (Jackson 1985). With Fordism's unraveling, social reproduction has become dependent on competition for increasingly mobile capital, where the roles of Fordist automobility and suburbanization are less clear. What's more, their costs are both better understood and have clearly escalated relative to stagnant earnings, so it is unlikely that we will see growth in automobility and suburbanization at the same pace as during the Fordist period. Awakened interests in health and active travel and significant demographic shifts have recast denser urban living and the more active lifestyles they generally provide as something to be desired rather than avoided.

But those hoping to ride this new wave of urban living into existing downtowns are forced into a rude awakening. Harsh traffic conditions and inhumane roadway designs mean that the active consumption patterns to which they aspire are unsafe and unpleasant. It is from this context that Complete Streets innovations were conceived—streets and their operations were technically out of sync with "emerging" uses and users, and need to be retrofitted. And as Lewis Mumford reminded us earlier, these ideas are already decades old. As always, the technical issues are the most simple: these street upgrades are something any municipal engineering staff with a street works crew can perform. As this volume will illustrate, however, these are not the only challenges for such innovations, as others have noted before (e.g. Clifton et al. 2012; League of American Bicyclists and the Sierra Club 2013).

Those challenges arise when the "new" urbanists arrive to find there are communities existing in situ, many for decades, whose long-term marginalization recasts these questions of urban innovations in a completely different light. Indeed, even the very idea of mobility and the historical struggle for the right to mobility may differ among communities (Gilroy 2001; Bullard et al. 2004; Cresswell 2006). Urban redevelopment and its highly competitive and commodifying nature pose significant challenges to existing central city minority neighborhoods. As before with the freeway and optimized urban street, transportation innovations and investments can be a threat to urban communities. The processes through which investments are planned and the effects of those investments on neighborhoods have been problematic in the past, and there is little reason communities should believe this time will be different (see the frank discussion on race and planning by Harris 2013). This is separate from the fact that urban communities can benefit tremendously from Complete Street investments. As Figure 3.3 shows, urban minorities have been walking and taking transit for decades in these environments with long unmet calls for improved safety (Daniels et al. 2002).

Thus, the key questions for Complete Streets and their impacts on social equity must surround their planning process, and not technical issues. Are Complete Streets being implemented because it is something a planning or streets department prioritizes? Are Complete Streets used to attract investments? Or, are Complete Streets a piece of a wider planning process addressing a variety of pressing issues (which may not even immediately prioritize street upgrades)? Are Complete Streets used in neighborhoods with no particular potential for attracting investments, and can instead benefit current residents immediately and for the long term? How does this wider planning process work? Who is involved and how?

The cases in this volume focus extensively on these questions. Brand's chapter (Chapter 13) on New Orleans highlights the problematic role the post-Katrina recovery process has played in recasting urban redevelopment in long-standing minority communities. There, proposals for street upgrades, freeway off-ramp removals, and expanded parks have elevated the typical issues of land development and re-branding, with unclear reflection of existing community desires. Communities, who have been asking for these improvements for nearly 40 years, must be wondering—why now? Brand's chapter leaves us with only uneasy answers. In a more hopeful case, Miller and Lubitow in Chapter 14 chronicle how history and storytelling played a key role in a street planning process involving a marginalized community in Portland, Oregon. There, the technical questions were secondary to those of process—who was involved, and what range of concerns were addressed. What began as a simple process to plan a bike lane became a much richer discussion about the history and future of the neighborhood and its residents' needs—in effect, a process of reconciliation, perhaps long overdue, was begun.

To close, there are two dimensions at play here—urbanization or suburbanization, and racial integration or segregation. Transportation innovations in the past—the automobile and the freeway—facilitated suburbanization with segregating outcomes. New evidence shows that contemporary urban redevelopment relying on transportation innovations like light rail, heavy rail, and the modern streetcar may produce similarly problematic racialized outcomes—a new wave of "suburbanization" in the city. Whether Complete Streets will contribute to this pattern will depend on how they are planned and implemented.

Acknowledgments

Jenna Nash provided assistance with some of the research appearing in this chapter.

Notes

1 L. Mumford (1963), from the essay "The Highway and the City," in Mumford (1963, p. 244).
2 Quote is loosely attributed to Dr. King, see Bell (2013).
3 Other macro-economic factors were also important, such as the post-war re-positioning of the U.S. economy and currency at the apex of the world economy, protection from international competition, underpriced or unpriced external costs (such as resource consumption, soil degradation, or water pollution), and a political economy of international petroleum highly favorable to the United States' exploding energy needs.
4 The ratio of spending from the Public Works Administration and the Works Progress Administration was more than 12 to 1 and 80 to 1, respectively (Foster 1981, pp. 166, 231).
5 The Clay Committee, in charge of developing a proposal for the Interstate Highway System which was eventually modified by Congress, contained representatives of some of the major actors in the automobile-centered economy (Rose 1990). Its namesake, General Lucius D. Clay, was also on the board of General Motors, and the committee contained Francis du Pont of the DuPont family, a supplier to the automobile industry (Weingroff 1996), Steve Bechtel of the Bechtel Corporation (Civil Engineering), Bill

Roberts of Allis-Chalmers Manufacturing Company (Civil Engineering) (Weingroff 2005). For other work concerning these policy processes, see Snell (1974), Rose (1990) and Whitt and Yago (1985).

6   There are numerous works on this process of exclusion, for a general overview, see Chapter 1 of Massey and Denton (1993).

7   For instance, in the Bay Area, within 45 minutes of travel time, the average driver can reach about 150,000 manufacturing jobs, compared to just 23,000 for the average transit user (Golub et al. 2013a, p. 24).

8   In a confidential 1968 memo, former HUD Secretary George Romney described America's housing patterns as a "high-income white noose" around the black inner city (Hannah-Jones 2012).

9   For example, in a recent analysis of its long-range transportation plan, the Southern California Association of Governments found that minorities and low-income populations were disproportionately concentrated within 500 feet of heavily traveled corridors where pollution and noise impacts are most concentrated and therefore face higher respiratory hazard and cancer risk (SCAG 2012, pp. 108–116).

10   African Americans account for more than 40 percent of traffic-related injuries nationally, compared to their 13 percent share of the overall population (Daniels et al. 2002). Black children who are killed by motor vehicles are 50 percent more likely to be killed as pedestrians, compared to children overall (Hilton 2006). A study in Arizona covering the years 1990 to 1996 showed that Hispanic and African-American males were 1.33 and 1.75 times as likely, respectively, to be killed as a pedestrian as Non-Hispanic Whites (Campos-Outcalt et al. 2003).

11   This section borrows heavily from an article by the author published in the journal, Planners Network (Golub 2011). The author wishes to thank the Planners Network editors Ann Forsyth and Tom Angotti for the permission to use the material and acknowledges Ann for her role in the detailed editing of the piece.

12   Social scientists point to various conditions in the domestic and world economy at the end of the 1960s that reduced the viability of the Fordist model. While there is much debate as to the relative significance of these conditions, here are some of note: (1) high wages from effective worker bargaining power and historically low unemployment; (2) inflation from low unemployment and high and prolonged domestic and military spending; and (3) the declining role of U.S. manufacturing and increased competition from abroad coinciding with the resuscitation of the European and Japanese economies. The OPEC oil embargo of the U.S. at the close of 1973 put the system into further stress.

13   Between 1983 and 2007 (before the recession), the top 20 percent of households experienced a doubling of real (median) wealth, while the bottom 40 percent experienced a 63 percent decline. Income records are similar—increases for the top 20 percent of households were over 60 percent (and over 120 percent for the top 1 percent), while incomes increased only 7 percent in real terms for the bottom 40 percent of households (Wolff 2010, p. 46).

14   From 1982 to 2009, the median income ratios between blacks and whites and Hispanics and whites remained roughly unchanged from 56 percent to 59 percent, and from 66 percent to 67 percent, respectively. The household median wealth ratio between blacks and whites declined from 7 percent to 5 percent, and for Hispanics and whites it declined from 4 percent to 1 percent (Wolff 2012, pp. 73–76).

15   From 1983 to 2010, the overall debt to income and debt to equity ratios for all households grew from 68 percent to 127 percent and from 15 percent to 21 percent, respectively (Wolff 2012, p. 61). For the middle 60 percent of households by wealth, their ratios grew from 67 percent to 134 percent and 37 percent to 71 percent (ibid., p. 65). Meanwhile, these debt ratios for the top 1 percent wealthiest households fell.

16   Drivers licensing rates among 16–24-year-olds has dropped from around 80 percent in the 1970s and 1980s, to around 67 percent currently (Dutzik and Baxandhall 2013, p. 21). The overall licensure rate for the U.S. population has dropped from 90 percent to 86 percent since 1992 (ibid., p. 12).

17 The Federal Transit Administration offers competitive capital grants for small projects, called "Small Starts" (up to $250 million in total costs) (FTA 2006). "Evidence of economic development" is an important element of project ranking for funding; applicants are asked to show how local market conditions support growth and how land development will be positively impacted by the project (ibid.). These grant programs, however, are not without controversy, see, for example, Vock (2013).
18 A very small share of total transportation funding has been spent on bikes and pedestrians: 1 percent of total Highway Trust Fund funding since 1956, and only 2 percent of 2009 American Recovery and Reinvestment Act (FHWA Table FE-210, see www.fhwa.dot.gov/policyinformation/statistics/2010/fe210.cfm).

References

Aglietta, M., 2000. *A theory of capitalist regulation: The US experience.* New York: Verso.
Baran, P.A., and Sweezy, P.M., 1968. *Monopoly capital: An essay on the American economic and social order.* New York: Monthly Review Press.
Battelle, I., 2000. *Travel patterns of people of color* [online]. Available from: www.fhwa.dot.gov/ohim/trvpatns.pdf [Accessed 4 November 2013].
Bayor, R.H., 1988. Roads to racial segregation: Atlanta in the twentieth century. *Journal of Urban History*, 15 (1), 3–21.
Bell, J.L., 2013. *Martin Luther King and "A right delayed"* [online]. Available from: http://ozandends.blogspot.com/2013/01/martin-luther-king-and-right-delayed.html [Accessed 20 December 2013].
Bottles, S.L., 1987. *Los Angeles and the automobile: The making of the modern city.* Berkeley: University of California Press.
Brenner, N., and Theodore, N., 2002. *Spaces of neoliberalism: Urban restructuring in North America and Western Europe.* Oxford: Blackwell.
Bullard, R., Johnson, G., and Torres, A. eds., 2004. *Highway robbery: Transportation racism and new routes to equity.* Cambridge, MA: South End Press.
Campos-Outcalt, D., Bay, C., Dellapena, A., and Cota, M.K., 2003. Motor vehicle crash fatalities by race/ethnicity in Arizona, 1990–96. *Injury Prevention*, 9 (3), 251–256.
Clifton, K., Bronstein, S., and Morrissey, S., 2012. *The path to Complete Streets in underserved communities: Lessons from U.S. case studies.* Portland, OR: Portland State University.
Cohen, L., 1990. *Making a new deal: Industrial workers in Chicago, 1919–1939.* Cambridge: Cambridge University Press.
Cresswell, T., 2006. The right to mobility: the production of mobility in the courtroom. *Antipode*, 38 (4), 735–754.
Daniels, F., *et al.*, 2002. The role of the African-American physician in reducing traffic-related injury and death among African Americans: consensus report of the National Medical Association. *Journal of the National Medical Association*, 94 (2), 108.
de Janvry, A., 1981. *The agrarian question and reformism in Latin America.* Baltimore, MD: Johns Hopkins University Press.
Denmark, D., 1998. The outsiders: planning and transport disadvantage. *Journal of Planning Education and Research*, 17 (3), 231–245.
Dutzik, T., and Baxandhall, P., 2013. *A new direction: Our changing relationship with driving and the implications for America's future.* Santa Barbara, CA: U.S. PIRG Education Fund and Frontier Group.
Fairfield, J.D., 2010. *The public and its possibilities: Triumphs and tragedies in the American city.* Philadelphia, PA: Temple University Press.
Fleck, S., Glaser, J., and Sprague, S., 2011. The compensation-productivity gap: a visual essay. *Monthly Labor Review*, 134, 57–69.

Flink, J.J., 1975. *The car culture*. Cambridge, MA: MIT Press.

Foster, M., 1981. *From streetcar to superhighway: American city planners and urban transportation, 1900–1940*. Philadelphia, PA: Temple University Press.

Fraser, S., and Gerstle, G., 1989. *The rise and fall of the New Deal order: 1930–1980*. Princeton, NJ: Princeton University Press.

FTA (Federal Transit Administration), 2006. *Small starts: Program overview* [online]. Available from: www.fta.dot.gov/12304_222.html [Accessed November 15, 2013].

Gartman, D., 2004. Three ages of the automobile: the cultural logics of the car. *Theory, Culture & Society*, 21 (4–5), 169–195.

Gilroy, P., 2001. Driving while black. In: D. Miller, ed. *Car cultures*. New York: Berg.

Golub, A., 2011. Liberalism, neoliberalism and urban transportation. *Progressive Planning: The Magazine of Planners Network*, Fall, 23–25.

Golub, A., 2013. *Peak auto or peak Fordism?* Working Paper, School of Geographical Sciences and Urban Planning, Arizona State University.

Golub, A., Marcantonio, R.A., and Sanchez, T.W., 2013. Race, space, and struggles for mobility: Transportation impacts on African Americans in Oakland and the East Bay. *Urban Geography*, 34 (5), 1–30.

Golub, A., Robinson, G., and Nee, B., 2013a. Making accessibility analyses accessible: A tool to facilitate the public review of the effects of regional transportation plans on accessibility. *Journal of Transportation and Land Use*, 6 (3), 17–28.

Goodwin, P., 2012. *Peak travel, peak car and the future of mobility: Evidence, unresolved issues, policy implications, and a research agenda*. International Transport Forum Discussion Paper 2012-13. Paris: OECD.

Gordon, D., 1984. Capitalist development and the history of American cities. In: W.K. Tabb, and L. Sawers, eds., *Marxism and the metropolis: New perspectives in urban political economy*, 2nd edn. New York: Oxford University Press, 21–53.

Grengs, J., 2004. The abandoned social goals of public transit in the neoliberal city of the USA. *City*, 9 (1), 51–66.

Grengs, J., and Levine, J., 2010. Intermetropolitan comparison of transportation accessibility: sorting out mobility and proximity in San Francisco and Washington, D.C. *Journal of Planning Education and Research*, 29 (4), 427–443.

Hackworth, J., 2007. *The neoliberal city: Governance, ideology, and development in American urbanism*. Ithaca, NY: Cornell University Press.

Hannah-Jones, N., 2012. Living apart: How the government betrayed a landmark civil rights law. *Pro-Publica* [online]. Available from: www.propublica.org/article/living-apart-how-the-government-betrayed-a-landmark-civil-rights-law [Accessed November 19, 2013].

Harris, W.M., 2013. The South: the race culture sustained. *Progressive Planning: The Magazine of Planners Network*, Spring, 2–5.

Harvey, D., 1985. *The urbanization of capital*. Oxford: Blackwell.

Harvey, D., 2005. *A brief history of neoliberalism*. New York: Oxford University Press.

Henderson, J., 2004. The politics of mobility and business elites in Atlanta, Georgia. *Urban Geography*, 25 (3), 193–216.

Henderson, J., 2011. Level of service: the politics of reconfiguring urban streets in San Francisco, CA. *Journal of Transport Geography*, 19 (6), 1138–1144.

Hilton, J., 2006. *Race and ethnicity in fatal motor vehicle traffic crashes 1999–2004*. Washington, DC: US Department of Transportation, National Highway Traffic Safety Administration.

Hirsch, A., 1993. With or without Jim Crow: Black residential segregation in the United States. In: A. Hirsch and R. Mohl, eds. *Urban policy in twentieth-century America*. New Brunswick, NJ: Rutgers University Press, 65–99.

Ihlanfeldt, K.R., and Sjoquist, D.L., 1998. The spatial mismatch hypothesis: A review of recent studies and their implications for welfare reform. *Housing Policy Debate*, 9 (4), 849–892.

Jackson, K.T., 1985. *Crabgrass frontier: The suburbanization of the United States*. New York: Oxford University Press.

Jessop, B., 1994. Post-Fordism and the state. In: A. Amin, ed. *Post-Fordism: A reader*. Oxford: Blackwell.

Kain, J., 1968. Housing segregation, negro employment, and metropolitan decentralization. *Quarterly Journal of Economics*, 82 (2), 175–197.

Kawabata, M., and Shen, Q., 2007. Commuting inequality between cars and public transit: The case of the San Francisco Bay Area, 1990–2000. *Urban Studies*, 44 (9), 1759–1780.

League of American Bicyclists and the Sierra Club, 2013. *The new majority: Pedaling towards equity*. League of American Bicyclists and the Sierra Club.

Martens, K., Golub, A., and Robinson, G., 2012. A justice-theoretic approach to the distribution of transportation benefits: implications for transportation planning practice in the United States. *Transportation Research Part A: Policy and Practice*, 46 (4), 684–695.

Massey, D.S., and Denton, N.A., 1993. *American apartheid: Segregation and the making of the underclass*. Cambridge, MA: Harvard University Press.

McShane, C., 1995. *Down the asphalt path: The automobile and the American city*. New York: Columbia University Press.

Metz, D., 2013. Peak car and beyond: the fourth era of travel. *Transport Reviews*, 33 (3), 255–270.

Millard-Ball, A., and Schipper, L., 2011. Are we reaching peak travel? Trends in passenger transport in eight industrialized countries. *Transport Reviews*, 31 (3), 357–378.

Mohl, R.A., 1993. Race and space in the modern city: Interstate-95 and the black community in Miami. In: A. Hirsch and R. Mohl, eds. *Urban Policy in Twentieth-Century America*. New Brunswick, NJ: Rutgers University Press, 100–158.

MTC (Metropolitan Transportation Commission), 2013. *Plan Bay Area: Equity analysis report*. Oakland, CA: MTC.

Mumford, L., 1963. *The highway and the city*. New York: Harcourt, Brace and World.

Murakami, E., and Long, L., 2013. Vehicle availability and mode to work by race and Hispanic origin, 2011 [online]. Available from: www.fhwa.dot.gov/planning/census_issues/ctpp/articles/vamtw.cfm [Accessed 20 September 2013].

Nelson, A.C., 2009. The new urbanity: the rise of a new America. *Annals of the American Academy of Political and Social Science*, 626 (1), 192–208.

Newman, P., and Kenworthy, J., 2011. Peak car use: understanding the demise of automobile dependence. *World Transport Policy and Practice*, 17 (2), 31–42.

Norton, P.D., 2008. *Fighting traffic*. Cambridge, MA: MIT Press.

Paterson, M., 2007. *Automobile politics*. Cambridge: Cambridge University Press.

Pollack, S., Bluestone, B., and Billingham, C., 2010. *Maintaining diversity in America's transit-rich neighborhoods: Tools for equitable neighborhood change*. Boston, MA: Dukakis Center for Urban and Regional Policy at Northeastern University.

Pucher, J., 1982. Discrimination in mass transit. *Journal of the American Planning Association*, 48 (3), 315–326.

Pucher, J., Buehler, R., and Seinen, M., 2011. Bicycling renaissance in North America? An update and re-appraisal of cycling trends and policies. *Transportation Research Part A: Policy and Practice*, 45 (6), 451–475.

Pulido, L., 2000. Rethinking environmental racism: White privilege and urban development in southern California. *Annals of the Association of American Geographers*, 90 (1), 12–40.

Rose, M.H., 1990. *Interstate: Express highway politics, 1939–1989.* Knoxville, TN: University of Tennessee Press.

Sanchez, T.W., 2006. *An inherent bias? Geographic and racial-ethnic patterns of metropolitan planning organization.* Boston, MA: The Brookings Institution.

Sanchez, T., Stolz, R., and Ma, J.S., 2003. *Moving to equity: Addressing inequitable effects of transportation policies on minorities.* Boston, MA: Civil Rights Project at Harvard University.

SCAG (Southern California Association of Governments), 2012. *Regional transportation plan: Environmental justice appendix.* Los Angeles: SCAG.

Schweitzer, L., and Valenzuela, A., 2004. Environmental injustice and transportation: the claims and the evidence. *Journal of Planning Literature*, 18 (4), 383–398.

Seiler, C., 2008. *Republic of drivers*, Chicago: University of Chicago Press.

SGA (Smart Growth America National Complete Streets Coalition), 2013. *What are Complete Streets?* (online). Available from: www.smartgrowthamerica.org/complete-streets/complete-streets-fundamentals/complete-streets-faq [Accessed 1 November 2013].

Smith, N., 2002. New globalism, new urbanism: gentrification as global urban strategy. *Antipode*, 34 (3), 427–450.

Snell, B., 1974. *American ground transport: A proposal for restructuring the automobile, truck, bus, and rail industries.* Washington, DC: U.S. Government Printing Office.

Stein, S., 2011. Bike lanes and gentrification: New York City's shades of green. *Progressive Planning: The Magazine of Planners Network,* Summer, 2011.

Stephens, P., Coleman, E., Liu, C., and Shah, P., 2013. *Rail impact: Mapping gentrification in Los Angeles* [online]. Available from: www.its.ucla.edu/RAILimpact/index.html [Accessed November 20, 2013].

Ullmann, J.E., 1977. *The suburban economic network: Economic activity, resource use, and the great sprawl.* New York: Praeger Publishers.

Urry, J., 2004. The "system" of automobility. *Theory, Culture & Society*, 21 (4–5), 25–39.

Vock, D.C., 2013. Cities turn to streetcars to spur economic development. *Pew State and Consumer Initiatives* [online]. Available from: www.pewstates.org/projects/stateline/headlines/cities-turn-to-streetcars-to-spur-economic-development-85899518491 [Accessed 2 October 2013].

Weber, R., 2002. Extracting value from the city: neoliberalism and urban redevelopment. *Antipode*, 34 (3), 519–540.

Weingroff, J., 1996. Federal-Aid Highway Act of 1956: creating the interstate system. *Public Roads*, 60 (1).

Weingroff, J., 2005. *General Lucius D. Clay: The president's man* (online). Available from: www.fhwa.dot.gov/infrastructure/clay.htm [Accessed 23 October 2013].

White, D., 1982. The black sides of Atlanta: a geography of expansion and containment, 1870–1970. *Atlanta Historical Journal*, 26, 208–213.

Whitt, J.A., and Yago, G., 1985. Corporate strategies and the decline of transit in US cities. *Urban Affairs Review*, 21 (1), 37–65.

Wolff, E.N., 2010. *Recent trends in household wealth in the United States: Rising debt and the middle-class squeeze. An update to 2007.* Working Paper No. 589, Levy Economics Institute.

Wolff, E.N., 2012. *The asset price meltdown and the wealth of the middle class* (online). Available from https://appam.confex.com/appam/2012/webprogram/ExtendedAbstract/Paper2134/Wealth Trends 1962 to 2010 Sept 2012 Version WOLFF.pdf [Accessed 10 November 2013].

4

URBAN SPATIAL MOBILITY IN THE AGE OF SUSTAINABILITY

Themis Chronopoulos

The fall 2007 issue of the *Transportation Alternatives Magazine* highlighted "The Complete Streets Revolution." Various articles provided overviews of how the streets of New York City were surrendered to the needs of the automobile during the twentieth century and contended that this trend was undermining the quality of urban life. The articles also underscored the determination of the contemporary city government in reversing this trend through the creation of green streets, and emphasized the important role of Transportation Alternatives (TA) in advocating Complete Streets.[1] The writers of the magazine viewed Complete Streets as one of three important complementary policies that sought to reduce the dominance of the automobile in urban infrastructure; the other two were congestion pricing and parking reform. Congestion pricing sought to charge drivers to enter a large portion of Manhattan while parking reform called for the elimination of free curbside parking on residential streets. According to TA, the proceeds from congestion pricing would fund mass transit (In Focus 2007).

TA magazine's issue on Complete Streets was published a few months after Mayor Michael R. Bloomberg (2002–2013) announced a plan to make New York the most livable and sustainable city in the world, and the simultaneous release of a blueprint entitled *PlaNYC: A Greener, Greater New York* (City of New York 2007). The proposals of PlaNYC were more far-reaching than those of TA and included six general categories: Land, Water, Transportation, Energy, Air, and Climate Change. PlaNYC included no plan to charge for street parking in non-commercial areas. Moreover, there was no emphasis on Complete Streets, though proposals spread in different parts of the report resembled some elements of the scheme. However, a plan for congestion pricing was featured prominently, and in the months that followed the Bloomberg Administration promoted it with unusual fervor.

Although a year later, New York City's Department of Transportation (DOT) announced a program called "Sustainable Streets" that gradually made Complete Streets a prominent public policy feature in New York City (DOT 2008), the initial emphasis on congestion pricing is not surprising. The Bloomberg Administration accelerated the process of neoliberal urbanization in New York City under which most spheres of urban governance and urban living were increasingly permeated by the forces of commodification. Despite the encouraging signals of PlaNYC regarding environmental responsibility, the city government's main priority remained the enhancement of New York's global city status, so that it could attract more multinational corporations and affluent individuals (Brash 2011, 2012; Chronopoulos 2013). Congestion pricing was a measure originally proposed and championed by the Partnership for New York City, an organization comprised of the city's two hundred most important corporate CEOs that seeks to promote big business interests. After some lobbying, the Bloomberg Administration designed its own congestion pricing plan and tried to sell it as an environmentally shrewd smart-growth proposal that would reduce pollution, minimize automobile traffic, improve the provision of public transportation, and benefit New Yorkers of all backgrounds living in all locations of the city (Chronopoulos 2012).

This chapter examines urban spatial mobility in the age of sustainability with an emphasis on congestion pricing in London, Stockholm, and New York City. These three cities are the largest and most important urban centers in their respective countries with significance and outlook that are truly global when it comes to business and finance (Sassen 2001; Scott 2001). With the exception of Singapore, which introduced congestion pricing in 1975 (Phang and Toh 2004), London, Stockholm, and New York were the first global cities to propose such a system. Congestion pricing is a neoliberal proposal that, if implemented correctly, seeks to transform driving in certain parts of the city into an expensive undertaking that only the affluent can afford.[2] Given that most low-income people in large dense cities have no automobiles (Eliasson and Mattson 2006), congestion pricing generates a conflict between the middle classes and the upper classes (Chronopoulos 2012). This conflict is becoming a salient feature of neoliberal urbanization. As Jimmy Carter recently stated, many of today's middle-class people resemble Americans who lived in poverty when he was president in the late 1970s (Leff 2013). This trend goes beyond the United States and especially applies to residents of global cities in which the cost of living is becoming prohibitive for middle-class households. And while this conflict about congestion pricing itself does not involve as many low-income individuals, in such unequal societies and urban areas as the ones that have developed since the late 1970s, complementary spatial mobility proposals such as Complete Streets pose serious questions about access, inclusion, and social justice. As Aaron Golub (Chapter 3, this volume) observes, transportation planning has seldom taken into consideration excluded and marginalized populations, and the danger is that Complete Streets initiatives may be following the same path of urban exclusion.

Neoliberalism as a political rationality

Neoliberalism goes beyond the realm of ideology and functions as a political rationality. According to Michel Foucault (2008), a political rationality operates as a normative political reason and has the capacity to organize state and society. Using this concept, Wendy Brown (2006, p. 693) argues:

> While neoliberal political rationality is based on a certain conception of the market, its organization of governance and the social is not merely the result of leakage from the economic to other spheres but rather of the explicit imposition of a particular form of market rationality on these spheres.

In the realm of spatial mobility, this has profound implications. Mobility depends on prevailing power relations and restrictions in mobility can interfere with citizenship and individual rights (Cresswell 2006). However, under neoliberal urban governance, citizenship has been transformed from a possession of rights to a capacity to act (Rose 2000; Murray 2008). Powerholders guided by their period's ideological predispositions configure and organize space in ways that serve their interests (Chronopoulos 2011) and this includes the facilitation of certain types of movement and the restriction of others (Henderson 2009, 2013; Cresswell 2010).

Congestion pricing is a prime example of neoliberal political rationality. Despite the existence of other non-market mechanisms to reduce vehicular congestion in central urban areas, under a neoliberal political–economic system, the commodification of road use is presented as the only sensible and possible alternative. As Colin Leys (2001, pp. 211–212) argues:

> Market-based provision of services is not just another way—allegedly more efficient—of providing public services. To be marketed they must be commodified, and commodification first transforms them into "products," and then further transforms them into different products, serving different ends.

In that sense, urban spatial mobility with an automobile is rendered as environmentally and socially unsustainable, transformed into a transaction, and marketed as a product that in theory is governed by the forces of the free market. In practice, this type of spatial mobility becomes a privilege for affluent individuals who can afford to pay the fee and drive without experiencing interference from lower-income drivers (Chronopoulos 2012).

David Harvey (2005, p. 31) argues that above all "neoliberalization has been a vehicle for the restoration of class power." Schemes like congestion pricing go beyond the realm of class power and enter that of class privilege, which is an expectation that the affluent develop once class power has been accomplished. Although class power achieved through the accumulation of spectacular levels of wealth is important, it is not fully realized unless its beneficiaries enjoy the privileges that most ordinary people cannot. Under existing neoliberalism, social relations are defined through an expectation of deference under which ordinary people are obligated to defer to the elites. In most cases, the elites are able to buy such deference or at least the pretense of it. However, deference of any degree is not achieved whenever the elites drive in public roadways. Traffic rules apply to everyone and it is possible for affluent people to be delayed and inconvenienced by wage workers. Schemes like congestion pricing seek to restore class privilege to the elites in a realm that their affluence has been unable to penetrate (Chronopoulos 2012).

What has happened so far is that governments have not increased the congestion fee to levels that would exclude most middle-income drivers. This has occurred because elected officials are reluctant to relinquish the existing revenues from congestion charging and because they are fearful of potential political costs. This does not mean that congestion pricing is not a regressive tax or that it is not based on neoliberal reasoning. It means that the promises of significantly reduced congestion and cleaner air are not true. Middle-income drivers continue to pay fees while upper-income drivers still have to share the roads with them.

Congestion charging proponents argue that the scheme is successful because of a reduced number of vehicles in the congestion zones. However, this requires some qualification. In recent years most people's incomes have stagnated while the costs of owning and maintaining automobiles have increased considerably (Chapter 3, this volume). This has led to a stagnation in miles traveled that goes beyond congestion zones. This decline is not substantial enough yet to decongest city centers, despite the institution of fees. But the trend is there.

The implementation of congestion charging in London

Officials designing their congestion charging plans in London were aware that opposition to the scheme threatened the electoral fortunes of local politicians, but also that this opposition declined if proceeds from congestion charging benefitted mass transit. Indeed, three MORI surveys in England (Commission for Integrated Transport 2000, 2001, 2002) found that public support for congestion charging at peak hours was only 27 percent, 37 percent, and 30 percent, respectively. However, public support increased to 39 percent, 54 percent, and 58 percent when the revenue raised from congestion charging was earmarked for mass transit. Similarly, the ROCOL Working Group (2000) survey found that 67 percent of the public felt positive about congestion charging, if net revenues were used for transport improvements. The European Union's TransPrice (2000) project discovered a similar increase in support (to as much as 64 percent) when respondents were told that proceeds from congestion charging would be redistributed to improve transportation infrastructures. To be sure, drivers favored the improvement of roadways as opposed to non-drivers who preferred improvements in public transportation. Still, without public transportation improvements, popular support for road pricing schemes declined significantly.

The London congestion charge scheme began in February 2003 and covered a 22 square kilometer area in central London. The congestion charge area represented London's center of finance, entertainment, business, government, and law. Vehicles were charged a daily fee of £5 to drive or park on public roads inside the congestion charging zone between 7 a.m. and 6:30 p.m., Monday to Friday. Alternative fuel vehicles, motorcycles, vehicles for disabled people, emergency vehicles, London taxis, military vehicles, and roadside assistance vehicles were exempted from the charge. Car owners from inside the zone received a 90 percent discount. Weekends and holidays were excluded from the scheme. The main goals of the program were to reduce motor vehicle congestion, increase journey time reliability for car users, make the distribution of goods and services more efficient, and use net revenues to improve mass transit in London (TfL 2003a). These goals were achieved almost immediately. Vehicular congestion inside the zone decreased by 15 percent, mass transit was able to accommodate higher demand, car travel time improved, and mass transit also improved (ibid.).[3] When it came to the affordability of congestion charges, almost a quarter of drivers surveyed claimed that they were experiencing difficulty in paying it. In terms of geography, residents of Greater London experienced more difficulties in paying the charge than residents of Inner London, whereas borough residents were more likely to experience affordability difficulties than people living in the West End (TfL 2004b).

In London, congestion charging was implemented by Ken Livingstone, a leftist politician who was elected mayor in 2000 as an independent, because the Labour Party opposed his candidacy and expelled him. Livingstone's congestion charging was part of a comprehensive London plan (Mayor of London 2002). The plan for London argued that the local government should promote growth that is environmentally sustainable while protecting its existing residents from the underside of this growth. Livingstone's plan for London included many proposals that could be characterized as progressive, in effect, trying to combine corporate economic development with equitability and social justice. Livingstone was also aware of the neoliberal credentials of congestion charging and the dangers that such an imposition could cause to his political future. In an interview, he admitted that it was a policy that members of the Tories had been proliferating: "I was initially sceptical about the congestion tax. I was aware of the origins of the tax. It comes from the Thatcherite right. Milton Friedman and others have argued for it . . . It is a flat-rate tax, like the poll tax. It would not be the tax of first choice" (Beckett 2003). Besides its regressive nature, a congestion charging initiative was politically risky for Livingstone who would have to stand for reelection in 2004. Although members of Livingstone's administration were optimistic that once implemented, congestion charging would become popular with Londoners, the actual beginning of the program would be dangerously close to the election. Bob Kiley, Livingstone's Commissioner of Transport for London (TfL), advised him in the end of 2001 to delay the congestion charge scheme until he was reelected (Harper 2001). But Livingstone ignored that advice, tying his political career to the success and acceptability of congestion charging. He was confident that his mass transit initiatives and his assurance that proceeds from congestion charging would be diverted to public transportation would assuage public opposition.

Toward that end, TfL implemented a number of bus improvements before and during congestion charging. In particular, TfL introduced new bus routes and larger buses; initiated faster direct service and frequency improvements of existing routes; and increased service in the evenings, nights, and weekends. In a few months, passenger capacity improvements had been introduced in 114 bus routes while there was also an emphasis on bus service reliability so that buses arrived on time and required less time to reach their destination. To improve the speed of buses, TfL enhanced driver training programs, introduced mechanisms for faster boardings, increased the number of bus lanes, intensified traffic enforcement in bus lanes, and improved infrastructure in bus stops. TfL also reduced the overall ticket cost for bus passengers (TfL 2002; 2003a; 2004a; Santos 2008). Other mass transit improvements included regular service increases in the London Underground after the central government handed it over to TfL in July 2003 and more departures in the National Rail and the Docklands Light Rail. Overall, mass transit in London improved to unprecedented degrees (TfL 2002, 2003b). Livingstone planned to continue improvements in mass transit by using the proceeds from congestion charging as well as other funds. In 2006, TfL announced a four-year plan that included the further improvement of bus service and mass transit accessibility, the development of segregated bus lanes and trams, and the enhancement of transport mode interchanges (Santos 2008). These improvements were embraced by Londoners. Passenger satisfaction reached the highest levels in the Underground's history and this with a higher ridership and more train kilometers traveled than before. Something similar happened with the other modes of transportation with London buses improving the most in terms of frequency, ridership, punctuality, and distances traveled. In 2004–2005, bus ridership grew to its highest level since 1965 (TfL 2005). An Ipsos-MORI poll in the lead-up to the 2005 general election showed that 40 percent of Londoners identified public transport as one of their defining voting issues. Nationwide polls in 2007 showed similar trends with support for congestion charging rising to 61 percent (from 49 percent) and opposition dropping to 21 percent (from 29 percent), if the revenue was invested in improving public transportation. In London, the percentages were probably higher given that its population utilized public transportation more and had consistently supported congestion charging in higher numbers than the people from the rest of the country (Klahr and Marshall 2007).

During his second term, Livingstone increased the congestion charge fee and almost doubled the congestion charging area. In July 2005, the charge was increased to £8 (TfL 2006). In February 2007, the charging zone was extended west to include Westminster and portions of Kensington and Chelsea while the charging hours were shortened by half an hour in the evening (Santos 2008). Bus and other mass transit services were improved in and around the extended zone before the new charge took place. The Western Extension did not make as much of a difference as the original congestion zone, mostly because the number of employees in the original zone was more than one million as opposed to 170,000 in the area of expansion (TfL 2008; Santos 2008). In 2008, while running for a third term, Livingstone unveiled plans to charge 4x4 cars £25 a day and to exclude them from the 90 percent discount if they belonged to a driver from the charge zone.

In the election of 2008, Conservative candidate Boris Johnson defeated Livingstone. Congestion charging did not play a major role in this election despite Livingstone's efforts to present the scheme as a great and successful achievement and Johnson's promises to reconsider the Western Extension. Johnson did not increase the charge for drivers of 4x4 cars or for drivers from inside the cordon zone. After public consultation, Johnson removed the Western Extension of congestion charging in 2010. In 2013, he raised the congestion charge fee to £10. Although he originally appeared lukewarm to congestion charging, in 2013 Johnson announced a number of measures that would favor less polluting cars (TfL 2013).

Ten years after the introduction of congestion charging in London, the results are mixed. From a neoliberal perspective, it has been a failure. The corporate sector and the city's elites hoped for a serious reduction of middle-income drivers and higher traffic speeds. Instead, they got a small reduction in traffic and almost no congestion improvements. Transit riders believed that the proceeds from congestion charging would improve mass transit and freeze fares. As it turned out, fares increased significantly. Mass transit also improved, but mainly because of other funding sources. The environmental benefits from congestion charging were also questionable, possibly because the cordon area is small and the reduction in gridlock not as dramatic (Kelly *et al.* 2011). Indeed, the congestion of vehicles inside the cordon area declined by 15 percent in 2003 and an additional 6 percent in 2004. In the years that followed congestion stabilized and even worsened because of public works and the removal of road space for buses, bicycles, and pedestrians (TfL 2008).[4]

Congestion charging has not been successful in London because of its contradictions. If the scheme is to remain profitable, serious increases of the congestion fee have to be avoided. However, unless the fee rises considerably, congestion in the cordon zone will not decline in any significant way. In the beginning, the scheme's operational costs proved so high that it took three years to show a profit. Dissatisfied with the level of net revenues, Livingstone tried to increase them by adding the Western Extension despite fierce opposition. This worked, though after 2007–2008, the gross revenue begun to decline because of the economic downturn.[5] In 2010, Johnson eliminated the Western Extension and this made for even less revenues (Table 4.1). Meanwhile, mass transit expenditures rose sharply and so did fares. Between 2004 and 2014, when paying for a single trip in cash, bus fares increased by 140 percent and underground fares by 90 percent. When paying for a single trip with an Oyster travel card, bus fares increased by 107 percent and underground fares by 36 percent.

While congestion charging is not one of Livingstone's most meaningful accomplishments, the improvement of pedestrian, bicycle, and mass transit infrastructures

TABLE 4.1 Annual revenue from congestion charging in London in thousands of British pounds

Year	Revenue	Net revenue
2002–2003	18.5	−58.3
2003–2004	186.7	45.3
2004–2005	218.1	96.4
2005–2006	254.1	106.3
2006–2007	252.4	89.1
2007–2008	328.2	137
2008–2009	325.7	148.5
2009–2010	312.6	158.1
2010–2011	286.5	173.5
2011–2012	226.7	136.8
2012–2013	222	132.1

Sources: TfL Annual Reports 2002–2013.

is. Many of these improvements are elements of what has become known as Complete Streets. While causal explanations are not easy to make, and the correlation between non-automobile use and improvements is not as straightforward, they chronologically developed together. If we take into consideration central London, an area larger than the congestion zone, the following trends are identified in the mode of transport that people use to enter it during the weekday morning peak between 2000 and 2010: a 57 percent increase in bus use; a 134 percent increase in cycling; a 4.4 percent increase for all combinations of rail modes; and a 51 percent decline in the number of people using the car (TfL 2011). These trends preceded the introduction of congestion charging and similar trends can be seen in the rest of London.

Implementation of congestion charging in Stockholm

In Stockholm, the leading politician of the Social Democratic Party, Annika Billström, promised to consider environmental charges if she was elected mayor in 2002. Almost immediately, conservative parties expressed their opposition to "Social Democratic tolls." Weeks before the election, in a televised debate Billström backed away and promised not to introduce road pricing. The election outcome was a slender majority both locally and nationally for the coalition of the Social Democratic Party, the Green Party, and the Left Party. In order to participate in the coalition, the Green Party demanded the implementation of congestion charging in Stockholm. Eager to form a national government, the leader of the Social Democratic Party Göran Persson accepted the demands of the Green Party and became the prime minister. Billström reversed her election promise, formed a local coalition with the Green and Left Parties as well, and accepted the institution of a trial of congestion charging with the possibility of making it permanent. In response, the alliance of opposition parties along with motorist organizations demanded a voter referendum on the issue, arguing that the Social Democrats had lied to the voters during the election campaign. At the time, polls showed that an overwhelming majority of voters opposed congestion charging. In June 2003, the national government defined congestion pricing as a tax and took over the implementation of the scheme, as according to Swedish law only the national parliament can introduce taxes (Vägverket 2006). The national parliament delayed the implementation of congestion charging because of disagreements over the length of the trial. The Green and Left Parties wanted the trial to last longer. However, the Social Democrats argued that the trial should be shorter and that the referendum should be held in conjunction with the general election of 2006. In the end, the coalition parties decided to end the congestion charging trial by 31 July 2006; what they did not expect was that court challenges would delay the beginning of the trial to January 3, 2006 (Isaksson and Richardson 2009).

During the Stockholm trial, charges were imposed on vehicles passing a cordon around the inner city of Stockholm between 6:30 a.m. and 6:30 p.m. weekdays. Evenings, nights, weekends, holidays, and the day before public holidays were excluded from the charge. Vehicles were charged either entering or leaving the city center and the fee was 10 SEK, 15 SEK, or 20 SEK depending on the time of day. Vehicles that crossed the cordon boundaries multiple times paid a maximum fee of 60 SEK. Buses, taxis, eco-cars, motorcycles, diplomatic vehicles, military vehicles, emergency vehicles, vehicles with disability parking plates, and bypass traffic from the island of Lidingö were exempted, meaning that about 30 percent of vehicles did not pay the fee (Vägverket 2006). The toll zone, which covered about 30 square kilometers, had about 300,000 residents and 23,000 workplaces employing 318,000 people. About two-thirds of these employees commuted to work from outside the zone. Moreover, about 30,000 people who lived inside the zone commuted to workplaces located outside the zone (Eliasson *et al.* 2009; Schuitema *et al.* 2010). As expected, the congestion tax trial succeeded in reducing the number of vehicles crossing the cordon area and managed to dissuade less affluent drivers from entering or exiting the center of Stockholm frequently. During the congestion tax trial, the number of vehicles crossing the cordon decreased by about 22 percent. The decrease was largest in the afternoon peak (-23 percent) and smaller in the morning peak (-18 percent). Traffic inside the cordon area decreased to a lesser extent, as vehicles moving there were not charged (Eliasson *et al.* 2009). Households with high discretionary income paid nearly three times as much congestion tax as households with low discretionary income. Affluent men living in the inner city paid the most. The people who paid the most congestion tax were not necessarily the commuters driving to work from outside the cordon area, but the people with the highest incomes. This happened because affluent people drove more frequently, lived closer to the inner city, and could afford to pay the tax (Transek 2006).

As in London, the Swedish national government promoted congestion charging as one of many urban life proposals and emphasized public transportation services and more park and ride facilities near city access roads and train stations. In fact, the public transport expansion began in the fall of 2005 and went on for 16 months. Although limited track capacity made it difficult to increase rail services during peak hours, there were some additional peak hour departures as well as lengthened trains. More than this, the transportation agency increased the frequency of non-peak train traffic. In addition, 20 of the existing bus lines were strengthened with extra departures and 14 new express bus routes were instituted. The new bus lines were direct and fast and sought to alleviate heightened public transit demand in busy areas and to make for a more comfortable commute. As it turned out, trains and the metro did not experience increased crowdedness because of the additional bus service. Finally, garages near train stations and other mass transit centers were retrofitted and extra parking spaces were created. The number of parked vehicles in park and ride garages was increased by 23 percent (Stockholmsförsöket 2006). The improvements helped to accommodate the 58 million additional mass transit journeys during the congestion tax trial. Most people who gave up their cars to take public transportation were from the municipalities around Stockholm. The average resident of Stockholm County made 350 trips in mass transit during 2006 (*The Local* 2007).

In Stockholm, the congestion charging trial would become permanent only if a majority of voters approved it. The referendum, which coincided with the general election of 2006, revealed how the congestion charge tax in Stockholm was still a controversial and unpredictable issue. The Social Democrats tried to dissociate themselves from the tax, claiming that the voters had a chance to reject the tolls and still vote for them. The Liberals and Moderates tried to equate the Social Democratic Party with road tolls and hoped that voter discontent would help them to prevail in both the local and the national elections. Yet, as public opinion in Stockholm became more positive toward congestion charges during the mass transit and vehicular trials, the Social Democrats attempted to take up the issue while opposition parties stopped talking about it. Originally, only the Stockholm municipality was planning a referendum with its leaders arguing that the cordon was located inside the city and that it was up to the city residents to decide about the charges. Several surrounding municipalities objected to this, contending that congestion taxes affected their residents as much as those who lived inside the city of Stockholm. In the end, 14 of the 25 municipalities of the county of Stockholm arranged their own referendums. The municipalities that held referendums were governed by the Alliance, and the municipalities that did not were governed by the Social Democrats. In the city of Stockholm, a majority of 53 percent voted to keep congestion charges, with 47 percent voting against. In the neighboring municipalities, a 60 percent majority voted against, and a 40 percent minority supported congestion charges. The Alliance of the Moderate Party, the Liberal Party, the Center Party, and the Christian Democratic Party prevailed in both the national and the Stockholm elections. After taking time to figure out how to interpret the outcome of the referendums, the Alliance decided to permanently reintroduce the congestion tax, but to earmark the revenues for road improvements, so that the residents of municipalities around Stockholm would be appeased (Agius 2007; Eliasson *et al.* 2009). The Social Democrats had used the income from the congestion charge tax to fund mass transit.

Congestion charging was reintroduced in the summer of 2007. Under the permanent system the congestion fees did not increase, meaning that over time they declined in real terms because of inflation. The congestion fee became deductible from the income tax and this amounted to a 60 percent reduction of the charges. Taxis were no longer exempted from the fee after 2007 and the same applied to alternative fuel vehicles bought after 2008. The reduction of vehicles crossing the cordon remained steady. However, the real congestion measure is that of traffic volumes. Inside the cordon area they have declined by about 8–9 percent and this is not as significant (Börjesson *et al.* 2012).[6] For a significant decline the fee would have to increase markedly, but the government appears unwilling to take the political risk and to lose a portion of the net income.

Congestion charging has become part of the local government's branding of Stockholm as one of the greenest cities in the world. However, Karin Bradley, Anna Hult, and Göran Cars (2013) problematize this claim. For example, the city government argues that Stockholm has reduced its greenhouse gas emissions per capita, though the opposite is true. The city promotes cycling, but when compared with Copenhagen or Amsterdam, the cycle routes are irregular and dangerous. Investments in public transport focus on the central city instead of the region, making suburban residents cynical of the city's green profile, which they view as a marketing tool. Meanwhile, affordable housing is becoming more challenging to obtain, commuter trains from the suburbs are becoming more crowded, and social inclusion appears increasingly difficult to achieve.

Congestion pricing in New York City

New York City's congestion pricing scheme remained a proposal, as it was not implemented. The proposal was devised by the Bloomberg Administration and recommended that passenger vehicles entering (or exiting) Manhattan below 86th Street be charged a fee of $8 between 6 a.m. and 6 p.m. on weekdays. Trucks would be charged $21 and large trucks $42. Passenger vehicles traveling only inside the congestion pricing zone would be charged $4. Vehicles crossing tolled bridges and tunnels would be able to deduct that toll from the congestion fee. The plan would exempt the two highways running north–south in the western and eastern parts of Manhattan as well as the approaches of all bridges and tunnels so that vehicular travel from neighborhoods outside the congestion area to other neighborhoods outside the congestion area would be possible without paying the fee. Moreover, the plan would exempt taxis, emergency vehicles, livery cars, and automobiles with disabled license plates from the fee (City of New York 2007). As this congestion pricing scheme was never implemented, there have been no concrete distributional impacts and redistributive effects. However, studies by the city administration and the state assembly indicated that the majority of the people affected by the charge would be middle-income drivers from the boroughs outside Manhattan (Brodsky 2007).

The Bloomberg Administration's credibility over the scheme began to suffer once it became clear that the mayor had no specific plan for improving mass transit as part of congestion pricing, despite promises to the contrary. Unlike the mayor of London, the mayor of New York has absolutely no control of mass transit. Public transportation in New York City is operated by the New York City Transit Authority (NYCTA). The NYCTA is a subsidiary of the Metropolitan Transportation Authority (MTA). Chartered by the New York State Legislature, the MTA is a quasi-autonomous public authority whose 17-member board is nominated by the governor of New York and confirmed by the state senate. Only four members of the board are recommended by the mayor of New York City (Chronopoulos 2012). Despite its quasi-independence, the MTA answers to the state legislature and the governor who provide direct funding, appoint or remove board members and directors, and allow the authority to embark on capital campaigns with state-backed bonds. For various reasons that include an unfriendly local media, many residents of New York City distrust the MTA and blame it for fare increases and inadequate services. They also understand that the mayor of the city has little to do with the MTA, and when Bloomberg promised improved mass transit during congestion pricing, they did not believe him. Moreover, Bloomberg's promises to provide services in southeast Queens and other parts of the city that are not serviced by buses or trains were also considered to be exaggerations. Such promises have been proliferating since 1929 (City of New York 2007).

Nonetheless, the Bloomberg Administration continued to argue that congestion pricing was not regressive because most of its proceeds would benefit mass transit riders who tend on the average to have a lower-income than drivers. However, there was no plan for a mechanism that would channel the revenues from congestion pricing to mass transit. Moreover, in June 2007, the Republican state senators proposed the elimination of hundreds of millions of dollars of new state money earmarked for the city's mass transit, arguing that the city would have its own slush fund of congestion pricing proceeds (Hakim and Rivera 2007). Given the budget constraints that the state had been facing and the anti-city sentiment by many upstate and suburban legislators, it was possible that the funding formula from Albany would change if the city was able to spend other funds for mass transit. To make things worse, many subway lines, especially the 4, 5, and 6 trains in the east side of Manhattan, had been operating beyond capacity during rush hour. The problem was too many riders with no room in the tracks to run additional trains, meaning that many subway improvement promises would be difficult to enact (Neuman 2007). Finally, once the city administration began to face difficulties in the state assembly over its congestion pricing proposal, its members claimed the quality of mass transit provision in New York City would suffer, without the federal money earmarked for the establishment of congestion pricing. Many politicians considered this claim to be disingenuous.

Committees of the state assembly held hearings on the issue in June 2007 with many assembly members questioning the regressive nature of the proposal. The Bloomberg Administration was unable to counter the charge that congestion pricing was regressive. According to data provided by the Bloomberg Administration as well as by other government agencies, congestion pricing in Manhattan would disproportionately affect middle-income drivers from the city's outer boroughs: Queens, the Bronx, Brooklyn, and Staten Island. If set at $8, congestion pricing would cost these drivers about $2000 annually (Brodsky 2007). While low-income drivers would be penalized by congestion pricing even more, their numbers appeared to be not as substantial and the expectation was that they would stop driving into the congestion pricing zone. Manhattan real estate agents supported the idea and ran an advertising campaign, expecting congestion pricing to make Manhattan's high-rent districts even more exclusive and desirable (Barbanel 2007).

In the hearings, Bloomberg admitted that New York's elites would benefit from congestion pricing and argued that this is the way things work in a capitalist society. In his words, "Assemblyman Gantt talked about whether this is regressive, in the end, it is true if you charge something, those who are wealthier find it less onerous" (Brodsky 2007, p. 11). In the hearings, Bloomberg offered frequent glimpses of his view on the socioeconomic structure by saying:

> I think one of the answers is we live in a capitalistic society. We use economics to encourage lots of things and there's nothing necessarily wrong with that. Those that want it more will pay more. And it is true, some people have more so that is in their benefit. But we've always done that.
>
> *(ibid., p. 11)*

With these statements, the mayor offered an unapologetic acceptance of the class inequality inherent to congestion pricing. Despite efforts to emphasize the environmental benefits of the proposal, the distributive impact of congestion pricing dominated the hearings. Bloomberg and administration officials were also adamant in exempting taxis from the fee. According to state assembly members, this added to the regressive nature of congestion pricing. The average annual income of a taxi rider was calculated to be $127,510, a figure that placed it above the middle class. More than this, taxis were considered to be one of the main causes of traffic gridlock in Manhattan (ibid.).

The state assembly also speculated that the city administration would substantially increase the congestion fee once the charging system was in place, making it even more difficult for middle-class drivers to enter the zone. This was because the mayor's report estimated that with its proposed fee scale, traffic within the congestion zone would decrease by 6.3 percent and that speeds would increase by 7.2 percent (City of New York 2007). This meant that less than one in ten automobiles driving in the Manhattan central business district would be eliminated under the plan and that speeds would increase by a mere 0.6 mph. These figures defeated the economic rationale of congestion pricing and made Bloomberg's proposal appear like a commuter tax without any environmental or traffic benefits. In the hearing by the State Assembly, John Folcocchio, Director of the Urban ITS Center at Polytechnic University, and a supporter of congestion pricing, noted that in order to increase vehicular velocity in the congestion area by 30–40 percent, the fee would have to be set in the neighborhood of $15–20 (Brodsky 2007).

In the end, the members of the state assembly decided to represent themselves as champions of the middle class and refused to even consider congestion pricing. This occurred after the state legislature agreed with the governor to create a 17-member commission to study Bloomberg's plan. The majority of the commission's members were appointed by the mayor and the governor; both of them had supported congestion pricing. In the beginning of 2008, the commission recommended the imposition of congestion pricing, but shortened the cordoned area. However, the state assembly, citing opposition among its members, refused to put the issue for a vote and effectively killed it (Confessore 2008).

The sustainable city and its discontents

In April of 2010, while conducting field research on gentrification in Williamsburg-Greenpoint—an area of Brooklyn that has been gentrifying at least since the 1980s (Curran 2007; Marwell 2007; Chronopoulos 2013; Campo 2013)—an elderly resident who had lived there for decades, pointed to Kent Avenue (Figure 4.1) and asked: "Do you really believe that these streets are for us?" I was surprised by this question, because at the time I had not given enough consideration to the creation of Complete Streets. This resident was criticizing the Bloomberg Administration's handling of the re-zoning of the area, which went against the wishes of more than 40 neighborhood groups, as well as the majority of its residents, and Brooklyn Community District One, which is the local political subdivision. The re-zoning transformed industrial areas into residential ones and gave the green light to developers to build luxury condominiums. The opponents to the re-zoning made comprehensive counter-proposals with an important one being the requirement that developers set aside 40 percent of the new housing units for moderate-income families and reserve 50 percent of these units for existing residents of Community District One. In exchange for the inclusion of moderate-income units, developers would be able to build denser and taller structures, meaning that the number of market-rate apartments would be close to the original (Brooklyn Community Board One 2004). City agencies refused to require developers to build moderate-income apartments in their buildings and instead provided only incentives (Marwell 2007). Because of this, thousands of condominiums were built in the area, but almost none of them were moderate-income units (Hoffmann 2013). As this redevelopment unfolded, many existing residents of Williamsburg-Greenpoint feared that they would be displaced from their neighborhood because of gentrification pressures and government policies. Like this particular resident who was skeptical of the redesign of Kent Avenue, these individuals viewed Complete Streets as nothing more than government overtones toward gentrifiers. Indeed, these neighborhood residents were experiencing what Melissa Checker (2011, p. 212) defines as environmental gentrification:

> Environmental gentrification describes the convergence of urban redevelopment, ecologically-minded initiatives and environmental justice activism in an era of advanced capitalism. Operating under the seemingly a-political rubric of sustainability, environmental gentrification builds on the material and discursive successes of the urban environmental justice movement and appropriates them to serve high-end redevelopment that displaces low income residents.

Environmental gentrification has been taking place in gentrified or gentrifying neighborhoods in New York City, contributing to a series of displacements that make local residents skeptical of the language and practice of urban sustainability.

The conversation in Kent Avenue reminded me of ones that I had three years before in Bushwick, a Brooklyn neighborhood east of Williamsburg. At the time, I was researching intensified gentrification pressures in Bushwick, which were similar to what had been happening in Williamsburg-Greenpoint since the 1990s. Other than being able to rent a decent place, many of the families there considered the ability to own and maintain an automobile as one of the greatest achievements of their lifetime (Figures 4.2 and 4.3). At the time, the Bloomberg Administration was working toward the institution of congestion pricing in Manhattan. Although most of the people I encountered seldom drove in the parts of Manhattan slated

FIGURE 4.1 A redesigned Kent Avenue in Williamsburg, Brooklyn

Source: Photograph by Themis Chronopoulos, 2010.

for congestion pricing, they felt that the city government was "out to get them" and that the mayor was "hypocritical" in his quest to brand himself as an environmentalist. Their sentiment was that the mayor was against the private automobile, unless it was used by himself or his corporate friends. Many of them mentioned news reports which criticized the multibillionaire mayor's riding of the subway—a gesture meant to humanize a mayor considered to be as out of touch with the problems of ordinary people. They were referring to the fact that whenever the mayor decided to ride the subway to city hall, a couple of sizable Chevrolet Suburbans picked him up from his house in the Upper East Side of Manhattan and drove him 22 blocks to an express stop of the subway where he and his security detail continued their commute by train. Then the SUVs went to city hall and drove the mayor to places that he needed to go throughout the day and back home in the evening. Bloomberg, who at the time was condemning subway riders complaining of overcrowded conditions as unrealistic and bragged that he took the subway almost every day and that his commute was comfortable, could have walked to his local subway stop, which was not express and avoided the use of two king-size SUVs (Grynbaum 2007). However, this did not happen. The use of the subway was a public relations affair. With the exception of these highly publicized events during some mornings, Bloomberg seldom used public transportation, and this contributed to the cynicism that many people developed toward urban sustainability.

FIGURE 4.2 A series of off-street garages in Bushwick, Brooklyn. With real estate values being low for many years, space was reorganized to accommodate the automobile.

Source: Photograph by Themis Chronopoulos, 2007.

FIGURE 4.3 There are numerous apartment buildings in Bushwick like the ones that appear in this photograph without off-street parking. Indeed, the majority of automobile owners park in the street and constantly move their cars because of street cleaning. Parking late in the evening and at night becomes a difficult undertaking because there is not enough street parking. Reflecting the demographics of the area, the great majority of these car owners are Latinos and African Americans.

Source: Photograph by Themis Chronopoulos, 2007.

Like congestion pricing, Complete Streets are about spatial mobility. They should not be, because streets are more than just corridors facilitating the movement of purpose-oriented individuals, but this is how they are defined. Complete Streets are designed in a way that enables the safe movement of a diversity of users, irrespective of age and ability, along and across the street. Comprehensively designed Complete Streets include well-built sidewalks, protected bike lanes, meaningful areas for vehicular parking, accessible bus, light-rail, and metro stops, exclusive bus lanes, crosswalks, automobile lanes, and designated loading areas (McCann and Rynne 2010). To be sure, not all of these elements may be possible or needed in every street, but the idea is to include as many of them as possible. For example, the redesign of Kent Avenue—one of the busiest truck arterials of waterfront Williamsburg—meant the following: the rebuilding of the sidewalks that had been crumbling on both sides of the street; a two-way bike path along the west curb; a "floating" parking lane on the west side that was separated from the bike path; a one-way northbound vehicular lane right next to the "floating" parking lane; and a loading lane on the east curb (DOT 2009; Figure 4.2).

Unlike congestion pricing, Complete Streets initiatives are not explicitly seeking to charge their users. However, there is something unsettling about the redesign of Kent Avenue in late 2009. During this period, luxury condominiums had either been completed or were being completed on Williamsburg's waterfront (Figures 4.4, 4.5, and 4.6). The cheapest and smallest of these units cost more than half a million dollars. It does not take much to conclude that the city government became suddenly interested in the area because of the development of these condominiums and that having a busy truck thoroughfare right outside of them was viewed as unacceptable. In this case, despite the rhetoric of user inclusiveness, Complete Streets represented an effort to provide the new affluent residents with more exclusivity and a luxury infrastructure.

Ironically, when the re-zoning of the area was challenged in 2005, the city government agreed to set aside more land for parks and to make the waterfront accessible. Nicole P. Marwell (2007, p. 91) argues that this reflected the power of an environmentally conscious middle class:

> The efforts of the North Brooklyn Alliance to reshape the designs of capital on Williamsburg and Greenpoint through political engagement yielded certain concessions in the rezoning plan. It is notable that the comparatively middle-class, professional interests in Greenpoint and the Northside of Williamsburg achieved greater success in their efforts to preserve open space and waterfront access than did the low-income Latinos in the Southside who sought to secure their number-one priority: affordable housing.

FIGURE 4.4 The waterfront development of luxury condominiums in Williamsburg, Brooklyn. More buildings are supposed to be erected, but the Great Recession slowed the process down.

Source: Photograph by Themis Chronopoulos, 2010.

FIGURE 4.5 Luxury condominium on Kent Avenue. It is virtually located across the street from the waterfront development.

Source: Photograph by Themis Chronopoulos, 2013.

FIGURE 4.6 Another luxury condominium on Kent Avenue

Source: Photograph by Themis Chronopoulos, 2010.

Once again, the development of sizable parkland adjacent to the new luxury developments may be inclusive, but can also be seen as an amenity for the new residents.

Conclusion

This chapter discussed congestion pricing as a neoliberal spatial mobility proposal and its relationship to Complete Streets. Proponents of congestion pricing are also proponents of Complete Streets, because the two are viewed as ways to reverse a historical planning commitment to the automobile and to build new livable and sustainable cities. In the process, the proponents of these schemes—many of whom are progressive—ally with powerholders, whose priority is to financially benefit from the production of space. These alliances reproduce existing social injustices in the name of sustainability and environmentalism, which are transformed into market-based initiatives that favor affluent individuals in their pursuit of comfort and profit.

From the experience of London, Stockholm, and New York City, it appears that congestion pricing becomes politically viable when it includes a redistributive measure that benefits mass transit. However, long-term improvements and the affordability of mass transit because of congestion pricing appear to be as questionable as the promise of less congestion and cleaner air. In recent years, bus fares in London have increased substantially and well above the rate of inflation. In this sense, even if London designs the most comprehensive Complete Street system in the world, what does this mean in terms of bus access? The bus stops may be located in ideal locations and equipped with the latest accessibility infrastructure, but individuals with the inability to pay will still have no access to public transportation.

In the end, congestion pricing is a strategy rooted in conceptions of streets as conduits for the efficient movement of automobiles. However, livable streets should go beyond this and Complete Streets policies represent a good beginning. There is a need for a conception of streets as public spaces with far more diverse functions than the movement of automobiles or movement in general.

Julian Agyeman, Robert D. Bullard, and Bob Evans (2003) argue that environmental justice is based on the myth that environmental measures benefit everyone equally and harm no one excessively. This is a myth that needs to be deconstructed and rejected. Sustainabilities based on social justice are possible, but not when they are based on the requirements of a neoliberal political–economic system and its urban growth narratives. This possibility of social justice should begin with the community organizations that advocate measures like Complete Streets. Unless these organizations take into consideration the needs of ordinary people and understand that not everyone benefits from the neoliberal vision of sustainability, initiatives like Complete Streets will remain incomplete.

Notes

1   "Complete Streets" is mostly a U.S. term that has been used almost interchangeably with "green streets," and "sustainable streets."
2   There are disagreements over what it means to implement the fee correctly. As I show, governments become addicted to the income of congestion charging and are reluctant to increase the fee to levels that will actually amount to significant vehicular congestion reductions. Neoclassical economists call for differential congestion fees, so that peak-time traffic gets diverted to other times. However, the London scheme has no differential fee and the New York proposal did not include one either.
3   When I use the term vehicles in this chapter, I mean motor vehicles with four wheels or more.
4   Average congestion in the original charging zone during 2006 was 8 percent lower than before congestion charging implementation. After that it worsened.
5   The net income did not necessarily decline because of a more efficient operation of the scheme.
6   Many observers including the authors of the article cited consider this reduction to be significant enough.

References

Agius, C., 2007. Sweden's 2006 parliamentary election and after: Contesting or consolidating the Swedish model? *Parliamentary Affairs*, 60 (4), 585–600.

Agyeman, J., Bullard, R.D., and Evans, B., 2003. *Just sustainabilities: Development in an unequal world*. Cambridge, MA: MIT Press.

Barbanel, J., 2007. Crossing the golden line. *The New York Times*, 24 June.

Beckett, A., 2003. Ready, Ken? *The Guardian*, 10 February.

Börjesson, M., Eliasson, J., Hugosson, M. B., and Brundell-Freij, K., 2012. The Stockholm congestion charges—5 years on: Effects, acceptability and lessons learnt. *Transport Policy*, 20, 1–12.

Bradley, K., Hult, A., and Cars, G., 2013. From eco-modernizing to political ecologizing: Future challenges for the green capital. In: J. Metzger and A.R. Olsson, eds. *Sustainable Stockholm: Exploring urban sustainability in Europe's greenest city*. New York: Routledge, 169–194.

Brash, J., 2011. *Bloomberg's New York: Class and governance in the luxury city*. Athens: University of Georgia Press.

Brash, J., 2012. The ghost in the machine: the neoliberal urban visions of Michael Bloomberg. *Journal of Cultural Geography*, 29 (2), 135–153.

Brodsky, R., 2007. *Interim report: An inquiry into congestion pricing as proposed in PlaNYC 2030 and S.6068*. Albany, NY: Committee on Corporations, Authorities and Commissions.

Brooklyn Community Board One, 2004. *Greenpoint-Williamsburg rezoning. ULURP applications: 050111ZMK, N050110ZRK, 040415MMK, 040416MMK, 040417MMK, 040418MMK. Position and recommendations*. Brooklyn: Community Board One.

Brown, W., 2006. American nightmare: neoliberalism, neoconservatism, and de-democratization. *Political Theory*, 24 (6), 690–714.

Campo, D., 2013. *The accidental playground: Brooklyn waterfront narratives of the undesigned and unplanned*. New York: Fordham University Press.

Checker, M., 2011. Wiped out by the "Greenwave": Environmental gentrification and the paradoxical politics of urban sustainability. *City & Society*, 23 (2), 210–229.

Chronopoulos, T., 2011. *Spatial regulation in New York City: From urban renewal to zero tolerance*. New York: Routledge.

Chronopoulos, T., 2012. Congestion pricing: The political viability of a neoliberal spatial mobility proposal in Stockholm, London, and New York City. *Urban Research and Practice*, 5 (2), 187–208.

Chronopoulos, T., 2013. The politics of race and class and the changing spatial fortunes of the McCarren Pool in Brooklyn, New York, 1936–2010. *Space and Culture*, 16 (1), 104–122.

City of New York, 2007. *PlaNYC: A greener, greater New York*. New York: The City.

Commission for Integrated Transport, 2000. *The CfIT report 2000: Public attitudes to transport in England (MORI)*. London: The Commission.

Commission for Integrated Transport, 2001. *The CfIT report 2001: Public attitudes to transport in England (MORI)*. London: The Commission.

Commission for Integrated Transport, 2002. *The CfIT report 2002: Public attitudes to transport in England (MORI)*. London: The Commission.

Confessore, N., 2008. $8 traffic fee for Manhattan gets nowhere. *The New York Times*, 8 April.

Cresswell, T., 2006. *On the move: Mobility in the modern western world*. New York: Routledge.

Cresswell, T., 2010. Towards a politics of mobility. *Environment and Planning D: Society and Space*, 28 (1), 17–31.

Curran, W., 2007. "From the frying pan to the oven": gentrification and the experience of industrial displacement in Williamsburg, Brooklyn. *Urban Studies*, 44 (8), 1427–1440.

DOT, 2008. *Sustainable streets: Strategic plan for the New York City Department of Transportation 2008 and beyond*. New York: The City.

DOT, 2009. *Kent Avenue improvement plan: Implementation update*. New York: The City.

Eliasson, J., Hultkrantz, L., Nerhagen, L., and Smidfelt Rosqvist, L., 2009. The Stockholm congestion-charging trial 2006: overview of effects. *Transportation Research Part A*, 43 (3), 240–250.

Eliasson, J., and Mattson, L., 2006. Equity effects of congestion pricing: Quantitative methodology and a case study for Stockholm. *Transportation and Research Part A*, 40 (7), 602–620.

Foucault, M., 2008. *The birth of biopolitics: Lectures at the Collège de France, 1978–1979*. Ed. M. Senellart. Trans. G. Burchell. Basingstoke: Palgrave Macmillan.

Grynbaum, M.M., 2007. Mayor takes the subway—by way of S.U.V. *The New York Times*, 1 August.

Hakim, D., and Rivera, R., 2007. City traffic pricing wins US and Spitzer's favor. *The New York Times*, 8 June.

Harper, K., 2001. Kiley tells mayor to delay road charges. *The Guardian*, 13 December.

Harvey, D., 2005. *A brief history of neoliberalism*. New York: Oxford University Press.

Henderson, J., 2009. The spaces of parking: Mapping the politics of mobility in San Francisco. *Antipode*, 41 (1), 70–91.

Henderson, J., 2013. *Street fight: The politics of mobility in San Francisco*. Amherst: University of Massachusetts Press.

Hoffmann, M., 2013. City built less than 2 percent of affordable units promised to Williamsburg. *DNAinfo New York*, 20 May.

In Focus, 2007. A lot can happen between the lines: Completing NYC streets. *Transportation Alternatives Magazine*, 13 (4), 10–13.

Isaksson, K., and Richardson, T., 2009. Building legitimacy for risky policies: The cost of avoiding conflict in Stockholm. *Transportation Research Part A*, 43 (3), 251–257.

Kelly, F., Anderson, H.R., Armstrong, B., Atkinson, R., Barratt, B., Beevers, S., Derwent, D., Green D., Mudway, I., and Wilkinson, P., 2011. The impact of the congestion charging scheme on air quality in London. *Health Effects Institute Research Report*, No. 155.

Klahr, R., and Marshall, B., 2007. *Road pricing at the crossroads: A paper reviewing new and existing public opinion research on road pricing schemes*. London: Ipsos MORI.

Leff, L., 2013. Carter: Middle class today resembles past's poor. *The Associated Press*, 7 October.

Leys, C., 2001. *Market-driven politics: Neoliberal democracy and the public interest*. London: Verso.

Marwell, N.P., 2007. *Bargaining for Brooklyn: Community organizations in the entrepreneurial city*. Chicago: University of Chicago Press.

Mayor of London, 2002. *The draft London plan: Draft spatial development strategy for London*. London: Greater London Authority.

McCann, B., and Rynne, S., eds., 2010. *Complete Streets: Best policy and implementation practices*. Washington, DC: The American Planning Association.

Murray, M.J., 2008. *Taming the disorderly city: The spatial landscape of Johannesburg after apartheid*. Ithaca, NY: Cornell University Press.

Neuman, W., 2007. Some subways found packed past capacity. *The New York Times*, 26 June.

Phang, S.Y. and Toh, R.S., 2004. Road congestion pricing in Singapore: 1975 to 2003. *Transportation*, 43 (2): 16–25.

ROCOL Working Group, 2000. *Road charging options for London: A technical assessment*. London: The Stationery Office.

Rose, N., 2000. Governing cities, governing citizenship. In: E. Isin, ed. *Democracy, citizenship, and the global city*. New York: Routledge, 95–109.

Santos, G., 2008. *London congestion charging: Brookings-Wharton papers on urban affairs*. Washington, DC: Brookings Institution Press, 177–234.

Sassen, S., 2001. *The global city: New York, London, Tokyo*. Princeton, NJ: Princeton University Press.

Schuitema, G., Steg, L., and Forward, S., 2010. Explaining differences in acceptability before and acceptance after the implementation of a congestion charge in Stockholm. *Transportation Research Part A*, 44 (2), 99–109.

Scott, A.J., ed. (2001). *Global city-regions: Trends, theory, policy*. New York: Oxford University Press.

Stockholmsförsöket, 2006. *Facts and results from the Stockholm trials: Final version—December 2006*. Stockholm: City of Stockholm.

TfL, 2002. *TfL report to the mayor on the readiness of public transport for central London congestion charging*. London: Mayor of London.

TfL, 2003a. *Congestion charging 6 months on*. London: Mayor of London.

TfL, 2003b. *Central London congestion charging impacts monitoring: Annual report*. London: Mayor of London.

TfL, 2004a. *Central London congestion charging: Impacts monitoring. Second annual report, April 2004*. London: Mayor of London.

TfL, 2004b. *MORI: Central London congestion charge social impacts surveys 2002, 2003*. London: Mayor of London.

TfL, 2005. *Annual report*. London: Mayor of London.

TfL, 2006. *Central London congestion charging impacts monitoring: Fourth annual report, June 2006*. London: Mayor of London.

TfL, 2008. *Central London congestion charging impacts monitoring: Sixth annual report, July 2008*. London: Mayor of London.

TfL, 2011. *Travel in London*. Report 4. London: Mayor of London.

TfL, 2013. *Mayor's transit strategy*. Available from: www.tfl.gov.uk/corporate/11610.aspx [Accessed 27 November 2013].

The Local, 2007. Congestion charge increased public transport use. *The Local*, 31 July.

Transek, 2006. *Equity effects of the Stockholm Trial*. Stockholm: Transek.

TransPrice, 2000. *Trans modal integrated urban transport pricing for optimum modal split*. Brussels: The European Union.

Vägverket, 2006. *Trial implementation of a congestion tax in Stockholm, 3 January–31 July 2006*. Borlänge: Swedish Road Administration.

5

THE UNBEARABLE WEIGHT OF IRRESPONSIBILITY AND THE LIGHTNESS OF TUMBLEWEEDS

Cumulative irresponsibility in neoliberal streetscapes

Do J. Lee

Introduction

"First, Kill All the Cyclists" are the words that Will Leitch, a *Deadspin* movie reviewer, blares out in the title of his review of *Premium Rush*, a 2012 movie about bike messengers in New York City. Leitch (2012) begins his review with a diatribe concerning New York bicyclists:

> It's difficult to overstate how much I dislike bicycle riders in New York City ... Bike riders have taken over this city, and they are, almost entirely across the board, rude, dismissive ... Cyclists in New York always complain about how dangerous the cars are ... bikes are far more a menace than cars. I've never seen a car drive down the wrong side of the street, brazenly run every red light, or just pop up on the sidewalk whenever the driver feels like it. I see a bicyclist do this every 10 seconds. And cars haven't ruined the Brooklyn Bridge either.

Remarkably, Leitch's comments reflect the public sentiment that understands car culture and its impacts as deeply normal while finding bicyclists as harmfully deviant and dangerous through their lack of conformity to the rules of the road. Within this streetscape, drivers enjoy privileges where the police frequently define the fatality of a bicyclist in a collision with a motor vehicle as blameless and as an "accident" (e.g. Bowen 2011). However, by widening our perspective, the aggregation of isolated motor vehicle "accidents" reveals an environment of irresponsibility that results in a staggering human toll in which motor vehicles killed 268 and injured 69,995 car occupants, pedestrians and bicyclists in car accidents in New York City in 2011 (NY Department of Motor Vehicles 2011). In addition, the high intensity of car use around the world has resulted in "killing fields" (Urry

2007, p. 124) with millions of deaths and injuries per year (World Health Organization 2013) while contributing substantially to climate change and influencing social factors that negatively affect human population health (Woodcock and Aldred 2008).

Our car-based society is maintained by absolving all but egregious violations of individual driving behavior while inhibiting oppositional collectivity for alternatives. This describes *cumulative irresponsibility*, where no single person or institution can be solely blamed for the harm of car culture, yet we are unable to enact collective responsibility for the mass damage. On the surface, the "Complete Streets" model of street design appears to address this problem through upending car dominance by equalizing access and safety for all transportation users in the street (Smart Growth America 2013). However, without examining and addressing fundamental issues of how responsibility for car damage is constructed, erased, and misdirected, Complete Streets may instead perpetuate unjust inequalities that privilege some and exclude others in the streetscape. As such, this chapter explores the production of cumulative irresponsibility in neoliberal streetscapes and speculates about an approach for reconstructing shared collective responsibility for more Complete Streets.

Cumulative Irresponsibility

In public discourse, injustices such as poverty are often understood through the frameworks of personal responsibility and structural causation (Young 2011). The stance of individual or personal responsibility contends that injustices are caused by poor personal behavior and the result of a few bad apples. Therefore, the blame for a driver who maims or kills a pedestrian or bicyclist remains at the individual level of analysis and results in responsibility being charged to the person most at fault. In contrast, structural causation argues that many injustices are rooted in systems and structures so that the responsibility to address injustices belongs at the collective group level (e.g. government). A collective responsibility perspective might then approach motor vehicular violence by intervening in societal structures and systems, such as building safer pedestrian and bicycling facilities, improving the design of streets and traffic signal, and decreasing the speed limit for motor vehicles in areas of high pedestrian and bicyclist usage.

Iris Marion Young (2011, p. 3) notes a momentous change in the political and academic discourse in the United States in the 1980s whereby the dominant explanation of the injustice of poverty shifted from structural processes to personal responsibility. Underlying this debate is the false assumption that an injustice must be exclusively located in either personal responsibility or structure but not both (ibid.). In contrast, Young elaborates a deeply intertwined relationship between individual responsibility and socio-structural processes in the production and maintenance of structural injustice. Social structures result from the accumulation and combination of the actions and relations of many individuals and institutions who pursue their own projects with varying coordination with others (ibid.). This means that past actions and decisions are not only embedded within the current shape of physical structures and social relations in places, but the past also frames the potential for future action (ibid., p. 55). Mobility must then be understood within contexts as each individual is embedded within a "charged" environment that requires a "negotiation of interests within an already existing social and time/space arrangement that supports some activities, discourages others, and makes some impossible" (Saegert 1993, p. 81). For example, the physical transportation infrastructure of roads and public transit represents a multitude of past decisions that would require enormous amounts of energy and money for any substantial alterations. Accordingly, injustices in social structures enable some to unfairly gain substantial benefits while constraining others in ways that cause deficits. As such, Young differentiates structural injustice as distinct from an injustice that results from a deficit of personal responsibility. To address the critique of structural explanations as being overly deterministic for the individual actor, Young (2011) maintains the connection to the individual by defining structural injustice as emerging from socio-structural processes resulting from the accrued actions of many individuals and institutions. Young proposes the social connection model of responsibility in which the responsibility for a structural injustice is shared by those whose actions constitute the processes that produce the injustice; shared responsibility means that structural injustices can only be resolved through collective action.

Within this responsibility framework, cumulative irresponsibility materializes when social structures shatter shared collective responsibility into minutely fine shards of individual responsibility that in turn collectively aggregate into cumulative irresponsibility. Under neoliberal regimes, social structures are particularly prone to fragmenting shared collective responsibility due to an emphasis on personal responsibility. In the process of shattering collective responsibility and producing cumulative irresponsibility, the shards of individual responsibility become deeply embedded within the many layers of social and material fabric of daily life. In this situation, no single individual can be blamed for the mass injustice. For example, one particular driver cannot be held to account for the totality of harm resulting from all car collisions even if the driver causes a devastating accident. Nor can the automotive industry, oil companies or others who profit from an auto-centric society bear the entire blame for mass injury and death. By subdividing collective responsibility, the resulting individual responsibilities are each inadequate to take the blame for mass harm and therefore, responsibility altogether disappears. Thus, cumulative irresponsibility manifests as the erasure of responsibility for mass injustice when blame or responsibility is difficult or even impossible to assign at the individual level, but mass harm and injustice materialize when minute or imperceptible damages aggregate exponentially. Speculatively, cumulative irresponsibility could also characterize other structural injustices such as climate change, persistent racial segregation in the U.S., and a global economic system that exploits workers and externalizes costs onto the public.

An environment of cumulative irresponsibility is produced and reproduced through a complex dialectic of remembering and forgetting (Billig 1995). Billig argues that the remembrance of national identity is constructed and embedded in everyday life so that there is continuous remembering that results in the "movement from symbolic mindfulness to mindlessness" (ibid., p. 41). For example, streets are littered with constant reminders of its dangers with signs such as one that warns drivers to slow down because children are at play or are often crossing because of the school located nearby. Because these signs are prevalent, we do not experience the signage and their warnings in active, conscious thought but rather, these signs are experienced as forgotten. Yet these safety signs remind us unconsciously that streets are unsafe for children. Therefore, we experience these safety signs as a forgotten reminder. Likewise, many have noted similarities in the forgotten naturalization of car culture so that "transport, and primarily the private car, [are] fundamental to people's everyday lives and hence their identities, although this often goes unrecognized thanks to the motor-car's very ubiquity" (Urry 2007, cited in Aldred 2010, p. 35). In addition, the private car has been so deeply embedded within a complex system of social relations and physical infrastructure so that undoing this structure would require "disembedding each of these different elements from the overall *ensemble* – an extremely difficult task" (Rosen 2002, p. 156). Often people have little control over their transportation choices as many are coerced into "intense flexibility" (Urry 2007, p. 120), which describes how people must rely on car mobility because our required destinations for daily life (e.g. home, work, errands) are spatially distant from each other with precious little time allotted for travel between places. Thus, the automobile generates a locked-in social life that reinforces car-centric lifestyles while laying the foundations for the expansion of automobility (Urry 2004).

Within this naturalized car-based landscape, the aggregated mass injury and death toll from car collisions becomes an unnoticed part of everyday life so that harm from "accidents" is erased into individual blamelessness. Assigning individual responsibility in car collisions is often very difficult because drivers often do not actively intend to harm others. Collisions often occur under conditions that obscure individual responsibility—such as slippery roads, high speeds, and human error, limitation, and distraction. Criminalizing fatalities of car collisions from unintentional mistakes could criminalize any driver. Furthermore, since the system of transporting commonplace products, food, and waste is dependent on automotive transportation, everyone is guilty by association because of how each of us directly and indirectly benefits. This situation creates a dilemma for a society that uses a system of personal liability to assign blame because, "Where all are guilty, nobody is. Guilt, unlike responsibility, always singles out; it is strictly personal" (Arendt 1987, cited in Young 2011, p. 71). Illustrating the inability of liability to handle cumulative irresponsibility, New York City police cited less than 100 drivers per year for careless driving despite over 13,000 pedestrians and bicyclists injured per year from 2008 through 2010 (Aaron 2012). Thus, Jörg Beckmann (2004) contends, "automobility 'works', *because its accidents are denied*. Collective denial enables individual mobility" (p. 94). In order to maintain daily life in a car world, the individual responsibility of the impacts of driving moves into the realm of forgotten remembering because individual responsibility cannot adequately address cumulative harm. Furthermore, while technologists tout the future of driverless cars as the remedy for human driver error and thus reducing car accidents, increasing the capacity of roads and increasing mileage efficiency (Markoff 2010), a driverless car may further distance the individual from personal responsibility for the harmful outcomes of automobility. This technological solution disguises and diverts attention from the root problems and inequalities of an incomplete street. Thus, collective or structural actions that alter social and material conditions would be the most direct way to address injustices of cumulative irresponsibility.

Irresponsibility and neoliberal streetscapes

The automobile, the iconic manufactured product of twentieth-century capitalism (Urry 2007), transformed the space-time of urban and rural areas and led to explosive suburban growth (Knox and McCarthy 2005). Before the automobile, the urban street served as a mixed use public space not only for travel, but also as informal marketplaces and vital social purposes for the neighborhood (McShane 1994). In the 1920s, though exponentially growing numbers of people came to enjoy the freedom of mobility afforded by the low cost private automobiles from Henry Ford's mass production process, urban driving was commonly perceived as a danger to public safety and a disruption to normal urban mobility (Furness 2010, p. 48).

At the inception of the automobile, both urban and rural communities reacted with fierce contestation over the use of public street space and the escalating number of deaths from car collisions (McShane 1994). For example, children in particular waged a war against the automobile, which had invaded the play area of children on public streets, causing spatial conflicts and many deaths. To deal with anti-car biases, automobile interests and mass media with the support of financial and political elites steered and changed public discourses to socially reconstruct urban streets for motor vehicle traffic (Furness 2010, p. 49). To deal with opposition from children, automobile interests funded efforts with the support of media, schools, and the police that transformed the meaning of the street as hazardous for children and led to the construction of playgrounds in schools and parks that shifted the space of children's play away from the street (McShane 1994, p. 224). Furthermore, the development of suburban homes with yards not only offers substitute spaces for children's play (ibid., p. 202), but also privatizes play spaces. These changing discourses accompanied alterations to rules and social norms that controlled pedestrian mobility in order to fundamentally change the streetscape from mixed used environments of pedestrians and vehicles into simple and efficient thoroughfares for motor vehicles (Furness 2010). The rapid growth of automobility aligned well with the goals of industrial capitalism as the car is the "essential technology to access consumer society" (Cahill 2001, p. 634). To this end, the corporate controlled media has fabricated and institutionalized the idea that consumerism is the primary basis for gaining citizenship and the right to the street

(Furness 2010, p. 136). Since the 1970s, capitalism in Western countries has shifted into a neoliberal form that not only emphasizes free markets, deregulation, and privatization (Knox and McCarthy 2005), but also reifies and expands the system of private automobility. Cumulative irresponsibility gains particular strength within neoliberal systems by privileging privatization, competition, and personal responsibility, which makes collective actions less likely to occur and thus solidifying structural injustices.

Privatization involves the takeover of public space and systems through increasing demarcations of private territories. Public streets are the "largest and most important piece of public open space in the city. They account for up to 30% of the total surface area of the city, yet we consider them only as afterthoughts. Streets are everyone's open space" (Switzky 2002, p. 189, cited in Furness 2007). Despite being public spaces, streetscapes are essentially privatized by personal spaces of motor vehicles that impede the entry of other potential users of public streets (Furness 2007). Streetscape privatization manifests through the subdivision of street spaces with segregating indicators (e.g. painted lines) that demarcate the type of person who has a right to space. While bike lanes create a small rupture in the dominant space-time of the automobiles, designated bike lanes simultaneously fortify the privatization of public spaces. Likewise, traffic rules and systems that inform and control traffic and pedestrians are designed to facilitate automobile traffic flow. For example, automobile interests with the assistance of print media familiarized Americans with the term *jaywalker* in order to constrain pedestrians from entering the street in ways that impede traffic flow (Furness 2010, p. 49). Thus, both the subdivision of public streets and the performance of traffic rules serve as forgotten reminders (Billig 1995) indicating that cars are privileged above all other users on the street.

Neoliberalism can also influence the distribution of injustice through rules, implementation, and procedure (Deutsch 1975). Other sections of this chapter imply injustices of rules (e.g. traffic rules) and implementation (e.g. failure to enforce traffic violations by drivers). Procedural injustice can occur when a legal system is designed to only accept certain forms of evidence. With the permeation and embedding of neoliberalism in the justice system, personal responsibility and direct damage become the lens in which evidence is valued. As documented, courts do not accept systematic evidence to prove damage in cases of racial discrimination (Weich and Angulo, 2000) because the court is solely concerned with proving individual causation of damage. Since individual responsibility is both difficult to prove and marginally consequential in an environment of cumulative irresponsibility, the failure to accept systematic evidence is an example of procedural injustice that maintains the status quo of car privilege in neoliberal streetscapes.

Cumulative damage moves into the body

Car privilege increases "the risk of accidents by absolving drivers from having to use their intelligence and engage with their surroundings" (Hamilton-Baillie and

Jones 2005, p. 44). In essence, not only are the users segregated from each other within privatized public streets, drivers are severed from context within their privatized "carcoons" (Wickham, 2006) whereby they "create an increasingly pleasant environment for those inside of them, they themselves produce an unpleasant environment around them, through noise, pollution and risk of injury" (Jones 2012, p. 655). Therefore, cars create spaces of sensory privacy for the occupants (Bijsterveld 2010, p. 190) that reflect class divisions and structure as the interior of the car environment becomes increasingly more pleasant as the car becomes more expensive. This segregation of driver from environment creates a situation where the "western middle-class sensescape is, however, increasingly managed, deodorized and commodified" (Edensor 2007, cited in Jones 2012, p. 656) through the strict disciplining of sensory stimulation because it is perceived as interfering with consumption or that sensory stimulation should be controlled and commodified (Jones, 2012). By providing for the sensory privacy of carcoons, the car's negative sensory impacts are externalized upon the car exterior that leads to the erosion of the quality of the public commons on the streets whereby people learn that "public services are inherently inferior to private ones" (Fine and Ruglis 2009, p. 23).

Fine and Ruglis (ibid.) describe the movement of institutional damage into the physical bodies of alienated students. Likewise, the cumulative damage from car spaces inscribes into and onto bodies with not only death and injury but also with a fear of public streets. This fear is not only produced from physical danger and damage from cars, but ironically, it is also reproduced through informational campaigns and media that appear to attempt to make cycling safer, but instead they implicate cycling as hazardous (Horton 2007). Movement of damage into the body can occur when fear of the violent streets becomes "embodied through obesity, diabetes, and cardiovascular disease" (Woodcock and Aldred 2008, p. 6). The movement of damage to the body can also be understood through the production and maintenance of habits. Based upon the frameworks of philosophers such as Ravaisson and Dewey, Schwanen *et al.* (2012) conceptualize a habit as:

> An emergent property of a body-mind-world assemblage – something that is fabricated out and ties together the fluid and continuously changing ensembles of limbs, muscles, sensory organs, the brain, neurochemical processes within the corporeal body, artefacts (including transport technologies), infrastructures, bodies of other human beings, rules, procedures, ideas, norms and other agents encountered as part of the flows and rhythms of everyday life.
>
> *(p. 526)*

As such, habitual behavior is the embodiment of the sensory experience of the individual in the environment. Through this pathway, the sensory experience of harm from cumulative irresponsibility in neoliberal streetscapes manifests as everyday habits and behavior. For example, "responsible" parenting involves socializing children in street safety rules such as looking both ways before crossing the street, not playing in the street, waiting on the sidewalk for the traffic signal to turn green, and wearing a helmet while bicycling. Damage occurs even when pedestrians obey the prescribed rules of vehicular traffic as Dultz *et al.* (2013) found that of the injuries incurred by pedestrians in car collisions in New York City, 44 percent occurred when the pedestrian was in the crosswalk with the traffic signal indicating their right of way and 6 percent occurred when the pedestrian was on the sidewalk. The resulting fear and harm have strongly influenced the withdrawal of children and other vulnerable citizens from street life, which further affects the well-being of those alienated from an important source of public life (Aldred 2010, p. 38). The sensory privacy afforded by cars proves to be a false illusion of sensory security as drivers themselves experience the movement of damage into their bodies through their own personal experiences in crashes and from the stories told by other drivers about car collisions. Since drivers are often bicyclists and pedestrians too, cumulative damage moves into drivers through these identities. Thus, the neoliberalization of space facilitates alienation from public life and the movement of the damage of cumulative irresponsibility into and onto the body.

The movement of the damage of cumulative irresponsibility to the body is also characterized by forgotten remembering. The cumulative damage of neoliberal streetscapes acts as an oppressive weight upon all who bear it; people become so accustomed to the cumulative weight that the added burden becomes forgotten but ever present. When cumulative irresponsibility becomes deeply embedded into daily life, the burden of cumulative damage becomes erased from memory. In addition, the numerous everyday practices and the ghosts of the historical material production of space also become forgotten remembering, which in turn amplifies the burden of cumulative damage. A few examples of historical material space production and everyday practices include public transcripts like that of Will Leitch's movie review that cast bicyclists as deviant, the failure to enforce traffic rules for motor vehicles (Aaron 2009), the risk of bike theft, the defiance of building owners to let cyclists bring their bikes into buildings despite city ordinances to the contrary (Ortiz 2010), the construction of the daily practices of home and work that places unspoken requirements for driving, and the public discourse that casts bicycling as unsafe (Horton 2007). These ghosts of historical materialism and everyday practices accumulate and move into and onto the body in the same way as the damage of cumulative irresponsibility and, altogether, they form a forgotten cumulative pressure upon the public and disciplines the public in conformity to an unjust streetscape. Only when bicyclists venture away into the shelter of car-less and separated bike paths does the cumulative weight become apparent because the weight is suddenly and temporarily lifted from the body. With the momentary removal of burden, these sheltering spaces for bicyclists are "Open and free yet sheltering as a nest . . . We all want this: an expanse of sky, possibility without barrier and also protection, shelter, and enduring love . . . When sheltered, our essence can unfold" (Robinson 2011, p. 11). Sheltering bicycle spaces can allow the bicyclist to gather experience, strength, and skill with far less fear, damage, and burden than the streetscape choked with cars. However, sheltering spaces reinforce privatization of public space and they are the physical manifestation of our reaction to the movement of car damage to our bodies. This damage informs our embodied habitual preferences for bicycling in sheltering spaces away from car traffic because the cumulative burden of damage returns upon the unavoidable reentry into oppressive car spaces.

Construction of the good–bad bicyclist binary

Neoliberalism's strong inclination for personal responsibility facilitates the subdivision of collective responsibility into many microscopic pieces of individual responsibilities that are reassembled into cumulative irresponsibility. As part of this process, cumulative irresponsibility helps reallocate individual responsibility onto the non-automobile users of street space. In this environment, each pedestrian and bicyclist is individually responsible for their own health and well-being instead of the responsibility of damage belonging to those (i.e. drivers) who have by far a disproportionate amount of power to inflict harm. This is not to suggest that bicyclists should not bear personal responsibility when they harm others, but bicyclists are often held to account for the harm incurred by their actions to an extent not experienced by drivers (Furness 2010). In a system of individual responsibility, the only drivers accountable for inflicting harm are those who make poor individual decisions, e.g. drunk driving. This shifting of personal responsibility onto the bicyclist occurs because the bicyclist is socially constructed as the strange and deviant "other" in order for the driver to be cast as "normal" (Horton 2007). In addition, when the bicyclist moves from roads to off-road bike and pedestrian paths, the bicyclist transforms from being the one of many users vulnerable to harm from cars on the road to being the source of danger to pedestrians on off-road paths (ibid.). This not only helps transfer responsibility from the driver upon the bicyclist, but also creates conflict and division that impedes collectivity between bicyclists and pedestrians. Thus, the bicyclist functions as the scapegoat (Gemmill 1989) that allows drivers to redirect the attention away from the damage and failings of automobility.

By carrying the burden of individual responsibility, there is a "persistent binary discourse that constructs the 'good cyclist' against the 'bad cyclist'. This discourse focuses the 'good cyclist' to display credentials (whether by swearing off the 'anti-car' ideology, signing the 'Stop at Red' Pledge, or wearing a helmet)" (Aldred 2010, p. 40). Wearing a helmet reinforces the notion of individual responsibility being placed upon the bicyclist and also creates a visible, public symbol that bicycling is an inherently risky activity (Horton 2007). When bicyclists are killed in car collisions, the question often asked is if the bicyclist was wearing a helmet. Helmets thus produce a stigma of symbolic violence upon bicyclists, while giving the appearance of societal concern (Brotherton 2013, p. 6) for the well-being of bicyclists. An article in *The New York Times* recounts how European cities such as Amsterdam and Copenhagen are among the safest cities to bike despite extremely low rates of bike helmet usage (Rosenthal 2012). In the article, Piet de Jong, a professor of Applied Finance and Actuarial Studies at Macquarie University in Sydney, makes the following observation about cycling in Amsterdam, "Nobody wears helmets, and bicycling is regarded as a completely normal, safe activity. You never hear that 'helmet saved my life' thing" (in ibid.).

The good–bad bicyclist binary also materializes through the constructed hierarchy of bicycling "otherness" as seen in the public discourse about food delivery bicyclists and bike messengers. New York City food delivery bicyclists are described as "kamikaze commercial cyclists who are notorious for mowing down pedestrians, blowing red lights and riding the wrong way down busy city streets" (Durkin 2012). Constructed as deviant "bad" cyclists, food delivery cyclists have attracted societal discipline through New York City Council measures such as the mandatory wearing of reflector vests and attendance of traffic safety classes (ibid.). Food delivery bicyclists in New York City are often Asian, Latino and other immigrants who lack much public support and are often denigrated with descriptions such as being "like dishwashers on wheels" (Goodman 2012). In contrast, while the bike messenger is also considered to be a deviant outsider who flouts road conventions and takes unconscionable risks, the bike messenger is also seen positively as the "'maverick', an individualistic, unorthodox, independently minded person working in a hostile environment and adapting to situations as they arise" (Fincham 2007, p. 190). Despite their "otherness", New York City bike messengers are glamorous enough to be the subject of the movie *Premium Rush*. Since bike messengers have become associated as typically highly educated, starving artists, and hip, rebellious counterculture (ibid., p. 180), bike messengers are constructed as a better "other" than the immigrant food delivery bicyclist. In this way, the construction of the good–bad cyclist within cumulative irresponsibility contributes to the current state of road conditions that promotes unjust hierarchies, class relations, and institutionalized racism (Furness 2007, p. 303).

The construction of the good–bad cyclist within an ethos of cumulative irresponsibility resonates with the way that moral exclusion influences environmental conflicts (Opotow and Weiss 2000). Using the lens of moral exclusion, bicyclists are often perceived to be outside and trespassing upon the boundaries of justice as epitomized by the common absolution of drivers in crashes that result in bicyclist injury or death. However, moral inclusion and exclusion extend further into a nuanced subdivision of cyclists themselves into good and bad cyclists. For instance, the *New York City Bicycle Master Plan* was an important rupture in the assumed car-dominated landscape that created a blueprint for 900 miles of bike routes. However, this plan bases its distribution of bicycle routes on the assumption that "commuters using bicycles wish to travel to the same places as those using automobiles and public transportation. The major destinations include the central business districts, universities, hospitals and educational and cultural institutions" (NYC Department of City Planning 1997, p. 8). By focusing on the central business districts and primary city institutions as route destinations, this plan has dealt a fixed hand that will by default prioritize bicycle lanes in and toward Manhattan. In other words, the benefits of bike facilities have been coopted by the neoliberal agenda to benefit commerce and gentrification. Accordingly, "good" cyclists are morally included by their contribution to this agenda so as long as they comply with the neoliberal rules that define the subdivision of space and responsibility. Furthermore, an examination of the Citi Bike Share program (NYC Department of Transportation 2013) reveals that "good" cyclists receive program benefits as the Bike Share stations are located in and near lower and mid-Manhattan. While bike shares can help normalize bicycling on city streets, Citi Bike Share is also an example of the neoliberal commodification of bicycling where "good" bicycling improves economic productivity and a corporation can own the name of bike sharing. In another example, bicycling advocacy groups like People for Bikes often buttress their advocacy by citing studies that find bikes improve economic productivity, e.g. "Homes located on a bike boulevard are worth $5,757 more than homes not on one" (Rice 2008, cited in People for Bikes 2013). The good–bad bicyclist binary creates constructed hierarchies and divisions among bicyclists that subtly reinforce neoliberal agendas while preventing conditions of collectivity that might disrupt cumulative irresponsibility.

Neoliberal competition in streets

To understand the distribution of bicycling benefits within cumulative irresponsibility, Deutsch's (1975, p. 143) concept of distributive justice, which concerns the distribution of benefits that affect individual well-being, provides a useful lens of analysis. Deutsch (ibid., p. 143) contends that a competition for distributive benefits emerges when given a scarcity of benefits that does not permit all desired outcomes to occur. This description of distributive justice maps well onto New York City where economic productivity is highly privileged and available street space is extremely limited in proportion to a dense population. As Deutsch (ibid., p. 145) predicts, this fosters an atmosphere of contention and competition for scarce street space where the individuals become alienated from each other in this competition, reducing the possibilities for collectivity. In addition, competition can lead to the dehumanization of people, as illustrated when drivers refer to bikes as "road hazards" (e.g. Davis 2003). This competition promotes the neoliberal privatization and subdivision of street space as it helps pick winners and losers in mobility.

However, the very nature of competition for scarce road space results in drivers being in competition with each other to reach their destinations first (Aldred 2010). Hegemonic powers can give a false appearance of working in harmonious concert toward the same set of goals, but within neoliberal competition, hegemonic powers compete with each other too. Thus neoliberal competition leads to an arms race of the streetscape as the numbers of cars proliferate, which results in drivers buying bigger and bigger cars (Anderson and Auffhammer 2011) to take more room on the road and to protect themselves. As cars multiply and swell, the more the cars conflict with each other in the space-time of streetscapes and create gridlock for each other. Thus, because of how large motor vehicles create spatial congestion, the bicyclist actually becomes more mobile than cars (Aldred 2010) and is able to travel through the leftover creases and gaps. These creases are similar to the lines of flight proposed by Deleuze and Guattari (1987) in which "Power centers are defined much more by what escapes them or by their impotence than by their zone of power" (p. 217). Bicyclists moving through these gaps rupture the dominant space-time of cars, but, however, these constantly shifting ruptures are ephemeral, risky, and collapsible at any given moment.

Ruptures in the space-time of automobility

The fragile and fleeting ruptures in the space-time of cars point to some possible forms of disruption of complex of cumulative irresponsibility and neoliberalism so that alternative motilities can be explored. For example, Bogotá, the capital of Columbia, has transformed their auto-centric streetscape to allow for the growth of alternative mobilities through the expansive development of the Bus Rapid Transit and about 300 km of dedicated bike paths (Cervero et al. 2009). In addition, Bogotá transforms mobility in social and physical space through the Cicloviá in which cars are prohibited on 121 km of major streets for seven daylight hours on Sundays and holidays (ibid.). Similarly, one form of resistance has been the Critical Mass bike rides in which a large group of bicyclists reclaim streetscape to offer a temporary alternative space that challenges the ideology and dominance of the car and exposes the injustices of the streetscape (Furness 2007). In addition, Critical Mass is organized as a decentralized framework allowing for the flexible space of participatory discourse, a kind of Occupy movement on wheels before Occupy Wall Street, so that bicycling could be positioned in contrast to the "centralized, corporate institutions of automobility" (ibid., p. 301). Through collective mobility, Critical Mass facilitates a temporary, new, and fun social space where dissent with the dominant mode of automobility is visible and tangible (ibid.).

Another possible disruption is Avery Gordon's (2008) idea of writing ghost stories that "not only repair representational mistakes but also strive to understand the conditions under which memory was produced in the first place, toward a countermemory, for the future" (p. 22). In remarkable resonance to the idea of ghost stories, bicyclists all over the world have begun installing "ghost bikes":

> Ghost Bikes are small and somber memorials for bicyclists who are killed or hit on the street. A bicycle is painted all white and locked to a street sign near the crash site, accompanied by a small plaque. They serve as reminders of the tragedy that took place on an otherwise anonymous street corner, and as quiet statements in support of cyclists' right to safe travel.
>
> (Ghostbikes.org, 2013)

Ghost bikes help bring to light and situate in context the ghosts of the hidden injury and death toll of the automobile paradigm and challenge the viewer to re-imagine justice in streetscapes.

However, Robin Kelley (1993) cautions, "The creation of an alternative culture can simultaneously challenge and reinforce existing power relations" (p. 88). Thus, while ruptures like Bogotá, Critical Mass, and ghost bikes contest the dominance of the car, Bogotá's urban investment in transportation infrastructure could be exacerbating socio-economic divisions (Cervero 2005, p. 28), Critical Mass inadvertently reinforces the stereotype of bicyclists as deviant and aggressive, and the ghost bike underscores the discourse of bicycling risk. In addition, Bogotá and Critical Mass may also strengthen the social construction of neoliberal competition and contention over ownership of public streets. Similarly, while Complete Streets represents a shift toward a model that seemingly does not privilege the car over other modes of transportation (Smart Growth America 2013), the emphasis remains centered upon mobility, which may subtly strengthen the conceit that the right to the street belongs to those who contribute to economic productivity through their movement. As such, critical self-reflexive examination of ghosts reveals how the development of the bicycle resulted in economic, technological, and legal developments that paved the way for automobiles (McShane 1994; Furness 2010). This self-reflexivity can provide the bicycling and Complete Streets movement with an awareness of how bicycling contributed to the production of the cumulative irresponsibility of unjust streetscapes and how to create ruptures that avoid the reproduction of cumulative irresponsibility.

Another radical rupture that changes the social and material conditions that privilege driving is the *woonerf* principles developed in the Netherlands in the late 1960s and early 1970s (Hamilton-Baillie and Jones 2005). *Woonerf* principles experiment with ways to break down the socially constructed segregation of the interiority of private cars and the exteriority of public spaces (ibid.). In a vision for radical redesign of space, all indications (e.g. road markings, curbs, signage) of the neoliberal subdivision of space disappear, which flies in the face of conventional traffic engineering that demarcates space to indicate hierarchies of road users. As a result, the streetscape becomes a much more complex environment for the driver. In order to negotiate complexity where there are no conventional cues to who belongs in space, the driver slows down and reengages in the social world of the street where the "driver becomes a citizen. Eye contact and human interaction replace signs and rules" (ibid., p. 43). In several such small-scale experiments, the numbers of crashes, injury and death have dramatically decreased (ibid.). The *woonerf* approach represents an approach that increases the sensory stimulation for all users of the road, including drivers, while breaking down the notions of neoliberal subdivisions of public street space and responsibility. However, this kind of radical rupture of the dominant space-time of cars is at risk of becoming a miniaturized socio-technical experiment that successfully ruptures the dominant paradigm in isolated spaces, but the rupture is unseen by the wider public (Lezaun 2011). These radical ruptures are often difficult to expand and replicate in scaling up processes because the oppressive aggregate weight from the complex of cumulative irresponsibility and neoliberalism bears down upon and collapses the vertical scaling of such ruptures.

Within an atmosphere of oppressive cumulative weight, perhaps a novel form of horizontal mobility of ruptures might be appropriate. Horizontal scaling allows for spreading rupture through space and time in a way so that the ruptures are not simply copied as replicas as per vertical scaling, but rather, ruptures are molded and formed within local conditions and needs. Metaphorically, the Rose of Jericho might provide a useful strategy for horizontal scaling. The Rose of Jericho is a tumbleweed found in areas of harsh arid conditions in North Africa and the Middle East. This plant grows into a bush with a height of six inches when there are the correct conditions (i.e. water). When the water dries up, the plant curls up into a dry ball with seeds laden in the sheltered interior and lets go of the earth (Hawksworth and Charles Scribner's Sons 1921). At this point, the tumbleweed appears for all intents and purposes to be dead; this tumbleweed gets blown by the desert winds in random directions and travels without a predetermined destination until the tumbleweed comes upon life-supporting conditions (i.e. water). Upon discovery of water, the Rose of Jericho suddenly springs back into life and "promptly unfolds his arms and scatters his handful of seeds on the water; which is precisely the thing he took that journey to do!" (ibid., p. 177). These unfurled seeds blossom into new Roses of Jericho that then get blown into haphazard directions. In this way, perhaps ruptures can better spread horizontally where the vertical growth of rupture is crushed under the oppressive weight of cumulative irresponsibility. Thus, the seeds of rupture can be carried in the seemingly dead tumbleweeds in random directions where the seeds of rupture can blossom into new Roses of Jericho under welcoming social and material conditions and, subsequently, each reiteration of tumbleweed can spread horizontally again. In an interesting example, the first bike lane in New York City was constructed in 1896, but then harsh conditions ensued for bicycling with the rise of the car culture. Yet the seeds of bicycling persisted over time so that despite a lengthy journey without nourishment, the next bike lane blossomed in 1980, a gap of over 80 years (*New York Times* 2010). Thus, not only can a Rose of Jericho persist and spread under harsh conditions, it can also survive long durations of time. Just as cumulative damage moves into the body and becomes embodied in habits, ruptures also move into the body and manifest as habits. Upon the creation of habits, they can "endure below the surface of visibility as latent forces; habits once contracted by a body-mind-world assemblage persist when they are not overt and can be re-activated at a later point in time" (Schwanen *et al.* 2012, p. 526). In this way, ruptures that seemed to have died can resurrect in the most unexpected spaces and times. The randomness of the flight of the rupture is vital to dismantling cumulative irresponsibility because of how deeply cumulative irresponsibility is embedded in the social and material conditions of life. The random spread of ruptures through the unpredictable journey of the tumbleweed can allow for ruptures to blossom into even the most unknowable layers of embedded cumulative irresponsibility. If the widespread and far-reaching proliferation of a diverse set of innumerable seeds of rupture borne by the windblown tumbleweeds can then sprout and grow into the social and materials conditions of everyday life and thus transform it, just maybe, cumulative irresponsibility might then be resurrected as shared collective responsibility along with more Complete Streets.

References

Aaron, B., 2009. TA report: Reckless driving casualties rising as NYPD enforcement lags. *Streetsblog*, 14 July. Available from: www.streetsblog.org/2009/07/14/ta-report-reckless-driving-casualties-rising-as-nypd-enforcement-lags/ [Accessed 10 May 2013].

Aaron, B., 2012. NYPD: 7,371 Pedestrians and cyclists injured, 79 killed, through June 2012. *Streetsblog*, 3 August. Available from: www.streetsblog.org/2012/08/03/nypd-7371-pedestrians-and-cyclists-injured-79-killed-through-june-2012/ [Accessed 8 May 2013].

Aldred, R., 2010. "On the outside": Constructing cycling citizenship. *Social and Cultural Geography*, 11 (1), 36–52.

Anderson, M., and Auffhammer, M., 2011. *Pounds that kill the external costs of vehicle weight.* Cambridge, MA: National Bureau of Economic Research. Available from: http://papers.nber.org/papers/w17170 [Accessed 2 October 2013].

Beckmann, J., 2004. Mobility and safety. *Theory, Culture & Society*, 21 (4/5), 81–100.

Bijsterveld, K., 2010. Acoustic cocooning: How the car became a place to unwind. *Senses and Society*, 5 (2), 189–211.

Billig, M., 1995. *Banal nationalism.* London: Sage Publications.

Bowen, A., 2011. Some say NYPD turns blind eye to bike deaths. *Metro, US*, 26 October. Available from: www.metro.us/newyork/news/local/2011/10/26/some-say-nypd-turns-blind-eye-to-bike-deaths/ [Accessed 10 May 2013].

Brotherton, D., 2013. Artaud, cruelty and everyday exile in the USA. Paper presented at Performance and Justice Symposium, 13–15 March 2013, New York City.

Cahill, M., 2001. The implications of consumerism for the transition to a sustainable society. *Social Policy & Administration*, 35 (5), 627–639.

Cervero, R., 2005. Progressive transport and the poor: Bogota's bold steps forward. *Access: Research at the University of California Transportation Center*, (27), 4–30.

Cervero, R., *et al.*, 2009. Influences of built environments on walking and cycling: Lessons from Bogotá. *International Journal of Sustainable Transportation*, 3(4), 203–226.

Davis, C.W., 2003. Tug of war on the roads: Bikes against cars. *The New York Times*, 10 August. Available from: www.nytimes.com/2003/08/10/nyregion/tug-of-war-on-the-roads-bikes-against-cars.html?pagewanted=all&src=pm [Accessed 10 May 2013].

Deleuze, G., and Guattari, F., 1987. *A thousand plateaus: Capitalism and schizophrenia.* Minneapolis, MN: University of Minnesota Press.

Deutsch, M., 1975. Equity, equality, and need: What determines which value will be used as the basis of distributive justice? *Journal of Social Issues*, 31 (3), 137–149.

Dultz, L.A., *et al.*, 2013. Vulnerable roadway users struck by motor vehicles at the center of the safest, large U.S. city. *The Journal of Trauma and Acute Care Surgery*, 74 (4), 1138–1145.

Durkin, E., 2012. City Council approves mandatory safety classes for commercial cyclists. *New York Daily News*, 11 October. Available from: www.nydailynews.com/new-york/driver-ed-bike-delivery-guys-article-1.1181448 [Accessed 7 May 2013].

Fincham, B., 2007. Bicycle messengers: image, identity and community. In: P. Rosen, P. Cox and D. Horton, eds. *Cycling and Society*, Aldershot: Ashgate, 179–195.

Fine, M., and Ruglis, J., 2009. Circuits and consequences of dispossession: The racialized realignment of the public sphere for U.S. youth. *Transforming Anthropology*, 17 (1), 20–33.

Furness, Z., 2007. Critical Mass, urban space and velomobility. *Mobilities*, 2 (2), 299–319.

Furness, Z., 2010. *One less car: Bicycling and the politics of automobility.* Philadelphia, PA: Temple University Press.

Gemmill, G., 1989. The dynamics of scapegoating in small groups. *Small Group Behavior*, 20 (4), 406–418.

Ghost Bikes, 2013. Ghostbikes.org. Available from: http://ghostbikes.org/ [Accessed 18 May 2013].

Goodman, J., 2012. For deliverymen, speed, tips and fear on wheels. *The New York Times*, 2 March. Available from: www.nytimes.com/2012/03/04/nyregion/for-food-delivery-workers-speed-tips-and-fear-on-wheels.html?pagewanted=all&_r=0 [Accessed 14 March 2013].

Gordon, A., 2008. *Ghostly matters: Haunting and the sociological imagination*. Minneapolis, MN: University of Minnesota Press.

Hamilton-Baillie, B., and Jones, P., 2005. Improving traffic behaviour and safety through urban design. *Proceedings of the Institution of Civil Engineers*, 158 (5), 39–47.

Hawksworth, H., and Charles Scribner's Sons, 1921. *The strange adventures of a pebble*. New York: Charles Scribner's Sons.

Horton, D., 2007. Fear of cycling. In: P. Rosen, P. Cox and D. Horton, eds. *Cycling and society*, Aldershot: Ashgate, 133–152.

Jones, P., 2012. Sensory indiscipline and affect: a study of commuter cycling. *Social & Cultural Geography*, 13 (6), 645–658.

Kelley, R.D.G., 1993. "We are not what we seem": Rethinking black working-class opposition in the Jim Crow South. *The Journal of American History*, 80 (1), 75–112.

Knox, P.L., and McCarthy, L., 2005. *Urbanization: An introduction to urban geography*. Englewood Cliffs, NJ: Pearson Education.

Leitch, W., 2012. First kill all the cyclists: *Premium Rush* Reviewed. *Deadspin*. 23 August. Available from: http://deadspin.com/5937209/first-kill-all-the-cyclists-premium-rush-reviewed [Accessed 9 May 2013].

Lezaun, J., 2011. Offshore democracy: Launch and landfall of a socio-technical experiment. *Economy and Society*, 40 (4), 553–581.

Markoff, J., 2010. Smarter than you think: Google cars drive themselves, in traffic. *The New York Times*, 9 October. Available from: www.nytimes.com/2010/10/10/science/10google.html?pagewanted=all&_r=0 [Accessed 5 October 2013].

McShane, C., 1994. *Down the asphalt path: The automobile and the American city*. New York, Columbia University Press.

New York City Department of City Planning, 1997. *The New York City bicycle master plan*. Available from: www.nyc.gov/html/dcp/pdf/bike/masterpl.pdf [Accessed 21 March 2013].

New York City Department of Transportation, 2013. *Citi bike stations map*. Available from: http://a841-tfpweb.nyc.gov/bikeshare/station-map/ [Accessed 18 May 2013].

New York Department of Motor Vehicles, 2011. *Summary of New York City motor vehicle crashes in 2011*. Available from: www.dmv.ny.gov/Statistics/2011NYCCrashSummary.pdf [Accessed 10 March 2013].

New York Times, 2010. Bike lanes, 1894 to now. *The New York Times*, 22 November. Available from: www.nytimes.com/interactive/2010/11/22/nyregion/20101122-bike-timeline.html?ref=nyregion [Accessed 18 May 2013].

Opotow, S., and Weiss, L., 2000. New ways of thinking about environmentalism: Denial and the process of moral exclusion in environmental conflict. *Journal of Social Issues*, 56 (3), 475–490.

Ortiz, E., 2010. "Bikes in buildings" law takes some on frustrating ride. *AM New York*, 10 October. Available from: www.amny.com/urbanite-1.812039/bikes-in-buildings-law-takes-some-on-frustrating-ride-1.2340555 [Accessed 10 May 2013].

People for Bikes, 2013. Economic statistics. *People for Bikes*. Available from: www.peoplefor bikes.org/statistics/category/economic-statistics [Accessed 24 October 2013].

Robinson, S., 2011. *Nesting: Body, dwelling, mind*. Richmond, CA: William Stout Publishers.

Rosen, P., 2002. *Framing production: Technology, culture, and change in the British bicycle industry*. Cambridge, MA: MIT Press.

Rosenthal, E., 2012. To encourage biking, cities lose the helmets. *The New York Times*, 29 September. Available from: www.nytimes.com/2012/09/30/sunday-review/to-encourage-biking-cities-forget-about-helmets.html?pagewanted=all&_r=1& [Accessed 9 March 2013].

Saegert, S., 1993. Charged contexts: Difference, emotion and power in environmental design research. *Architecture and Behavior*, 9 (1): 69–84.

Schwanen, T., Banister, D., and Anable, J., 2012. Rethinking habits and their role in behaviour change: The case of low-carbon mobility. *Journal of Transport Geography*, 24 (1), 522–532.

Smart Growth America, 2013. *National Complete Streets Coalition*. Available from: www.smartgrowthamerica.org/complete-streets/complete-streets-fundamentals/complete-streets-faq [Accessed 16 May 2013].

Urry, J., 2004. The "system" of automobility. *Theory, Culture & Society*, 21 (4/5), 25–39.

Urry, J., 2007. *Mobilities*. Cambridge: Polity.

Weich, R.H., and Angulo, C.T., 2000. *Justice on trial: Racial disparities in the American criminal justice system*. Collingdale, PA: Diane Pub.

Wickham, J., 2006. Public transport systems: The sinews of European urban citizenship? *European Societies*, 8 (1), 3–26.

Woodcock, J., and Aldred, R., 2008. Cars, corporations, and commodities: Consequences for the social determinants of health. *Emerging Themes in Epidemiology*, 5.

World Health Organization, 2013. *Global status report on road safety*. Geneva: World Health Organization. Available from: www.who.int/violence_injury_prevention/road_safety_status/2013/report/en/index.html [Accessed 7 October 2013].

Young, I. M., 2011. *Responsibility for justice*. Oxford: Oxford University Press.

6

THE STREET AS ECOLOGY

Vikas Mehta

The only legitimacy of the street is as public space. Without it, there is no city.

(Spiro Kostof, 1992)

Introduction

Streets reflect the identity and image of a city: by closely examining its streets, we can decipher the social, cultural, and political life of a city. Streets are arenas for individual and group expression, sites for exchange of information and ideas, forums for dialogue, debate and contestation, spaces for conviviality, leisure, performance and display, places for economic survival and refuge, a system of access and connectivity, and settings for nature in the city. Fulfilling these roles, the street works with its own logic and has its own ecology.

In this chapter, I argue that the holistic way to fathom the street is to understand and appreciate it as ecology. I contrast this with the recent Complete Streets concept and argue that such an approach is inadequate and even deceptive as it flattens this rich ecology to a set of limited mobility-related "quality of life" goals. The street's ecology entails relationships that result from complex webs of interconnected activities and phenomena. Through a micro-analysis of behavior and interactions on neighborhood commercial streets in India and the US, I detail the workings of the street's ecology as a negotiated space of access, travel, commerce, sociability, leisure, learning, and survival. The analysis, using observations and mappings, presents the everyday life on the street as both a place and path. Finally, I suggest a way to think about the street, as a quintessential public space of the city, but not as a finished or complete product of limited predetermined identities and meanings (Massey 1994). Instead, I propose considering the street as an easily accessible place of negotiation between its numerous roles—as a place and path—that is constantly changing through an inclusive process (Madanipour 2010).

As a ubiquitous space, streets are present in all parts of cities, serving a multitude of functions: there are streets in residential, commercial, and industrial areas, in large parks and in sparsely populated suburbs. However, in this chapter, I will focus on neighborhood commercial streets, main streets, high streets, and the like. These local or neighborhood commercial streets are typically a transition between the parochial and public, the neighborly and the civic, and a part of the network of public space of the city. In this chapter, when I use the term street, I am referring to such a public street and not a parochial or a private one.

The street as a quintessential public space

Most urbanites have childhood memories of streets—urban streets, suburban streets, public streets, private streets, street to be on, and streets to stay away from. "[T]he 'street' is often shorthand for the urban world" (Jukes 1990, p. xv). Streets are primary determinants of urban form that constitute a basic unit of space in our experience of the city. Streets hold a special place in the domain of public space and are both literally and metaphorically the most fitting symbol of the public realm. The street "has occupied a cherished place in the lexicon of urbanism" (Keith 1995, p. 297). It is no surprise then that the discussion of the street finds numerous mediums and audiences throughout history. The street has concerned philosophers, political thinkers, social scientists, legal scholars, planners, and architects and also intrigued writers, painters, musicians, and filmmakers among others. Over the centuries cities have changed dramatically and this urban transformation is visible in the streets of cities.

But the history of the street is older than the history of the city. The notion of a linear space for movement and as an extended public space is deeply rooted in human nature. Rykwert (1978) suggests that this conception existed as a pattern even before humans settled down in villages, towns and cities. He writes:

> The very word street, as its etymology suggests, denotes a delimited surface — part of an urban texture, characterized by an extended area lined with buildings on either side. But the manner in which the notion of road or street is embedded in human experience suggests that it has reference to ideas and patterns of behavior more archaic than city building. Light is thrown on this by the way in which some preliterate societies, especially those with very elementary forms of shelter, use the street and also by the way in which children treat the space of play, suggesting a metamorphic notion of the street.
> *(Rykwert 1978, p. 16)*

In the history of the city, streets have accomplished several roles for cities—spiritual, religious, political, social, economic, health, and aesthetic. Streets defined the settlement patterns of cities and towns of Mesopotamia, Egypt, the Indus Valley and China—the four earliest civilizations. Universally, streets have been spaces for defining and directing movement, and to facilitate the exchange of goods. But most importantly, streets have been places *par excellence* for communication and as society's social and symbolic spaces.

The history of the street chronicles its changing culture and use. Used as an essential lifeline for cities of the West until the early twentieth century, the street was reduced to a conduit of rapid movement for most of the post-war decades. Numerous ideas and efforts to reclaim the street from the vehicle have emerged since. These have ranged from completely taking the vehicle away from the street to taming vehicle speeds such that pedestrians and bicyclists feel comfortable and claim the street. Especially in Europe, one of these popular ideas emphasized car-free streets, not only on shopping streets in the commercial and business district (CBD), such as the famous pedestrian-only Stroget in Copenhagen, but also on residential streets. The Dutch *woonerf* (living yard) and the German *wohnstrasse* (livable street) were new ways of modifying existing streets to transform them back to places of interaction and play by making them safe from traffic. In North America, the efforts were primarily aimed at reviving CBDs and downtowns by providing pedestrian-only shopping streets to counter the indoor shopping malls of the suburbs that had sucked most of the retail and shopping from downtowns and main streets of neighborhoods. More recently, following Donald Appleyard's and several other studies documenting the negative effects of traffic on the communal life of neighborhoods, there has been an emphasis on slowing down streets using traffic calming measures. In the twenty-first century, of the many efforts in remaking and claiming the street, the Complete Streets movement has captured the attention of planners, designers, communities, and policy-makers striving to improve the livability of cities.

Complete Streets: not so complete

According to the National Complete Streets Coalition, Complete Streets policies "direct decision-makers to consistently fund, plan, design and construct community streets to accommodate all anticipated users, including pedestrians, bicyclists, public transit users, motorists and freight vehicles."[1] Thus, a more equitable distribution of street space to provide "safe, comfortable, and convenient" travel is the main task of the Complete Streets planner. This approach has several shortcomings but I will focus on two. First, by mainly emphasizing the claiming of space from motorized vehicles and regimenting specific spaces for bicycling and walking (in addition to the already demarcated space for vehicles), the Complete Streets concept reinforces hierarchies and further compartmentalizes an already fragmented space, thus augmenting the path-place dichotomy of the street. This only bolsters the overly regulated nature of the street where institutionalized rules and regulations, instead of the street users, must determine behavior. While attempting to solve mobility-related problems, this approach creates new ones. For example, there are concerns about the addition of bike lanes on a street leading to an increase in the number of pedestrians seriously injured by bicyclists (Tuckel and Milczarskishow 2011). This issue receives much less attention because the focus is on the safety of bicyclists and pedestrians from motorized vehicles while largely ignoring the conflicts between pedestrian-oriented activities and bicyclists. Second, and more importantly, the Complete Streets approach continues to reinforce the myopic reading and understanding of the street as a conduit for movement where mobility is still the sacred objective, making travelers the main beneficiaries. As a Complete Street, regulated for movement, albeit more equitably across various modes, the street continues to be read and understood only as a path. Predominantly addressing mobility conflicts is insufficient as it disregards other social, political, and economic territorial patterns and negotiations possible on the street. The narrow-minded mobility-related focus of the Complete Streets approach ignores much of this and reduces a complex system to a single premise: it does not fully appropriate the street as a public space. History shows that the street has the structure and capacity to be a complex ecology—an interchange for access, travel, commerce, leisure, sociability, and survival. In the process, the street becomes a repository of personal, group, and community histories, experiences, meanings, and identities. In order to understand and appreciate the street, and to counter narrowly defined approaches and current trends such as Complete Streets, I suggest the "street as ecology" approach. Such a view of the street is expansive and it opens up possibilities for streets as places that thrive on diversity and difference.

The street as ecology

Since its origin in the mid-nineteenth century, the definition of "ecology" has included several advances in ecological thinking and has been used in numerous disciplines. However, its primary definition—the relationship between organisms and the environment — remains at the core of its meaning. The fundamental tenet in ecological thinking is that the health of systems is derived not from competition and survival of the fittest but from coexistence. Here survival of metapopulations and metacommunities, through coexistence, works by the processes of distribution and diffusion. Additionally, ecologists (Holling 1996), economists (Buchanan and Vanberg 1994), geographers (Massey 1999), among others in various disciplines recognize that this coexistence in complex systems does not exist in a single state of stable equilibrium. Rather, there are multiple interconnected systems, both stable as well as unstable, that coexist (Thornes 1983). This understanding of systems and ecology is pertinent and useful to fathom and interpret the street. Appreciating the street as ecology means understanding it as a space of dynamic relationships that results from complex webs of interconnected activities and phenomena. This translates into accepting the street as a place that thrives on the coexistence of diverse people, activities, forms, and objects, and modes of control and negotiation, as it operates as a social, cultural, economic, and political space. As a corollary, this also means not thinking of the street as complete and in a stable state of equilibrium, but recognizing the street as a place in flux with some level of conflict.

But the street as ecology is not a novel concept. Historically, the street developed and matured into a space that harbored much of society's workings—a space where the drama of life was enacted, an ecology. This street ecology is legible in several non-Western societies of today, as I will demonstrate later in the chapter. In the West, however, after the decline of the Roman Empire, the narrow labyrinthine medieval street began to emerge during the Dark Ages, as cities, in the wake of invasions, began to consolidate within small walled areas on high ground or in some other way defensible space (Kostof 1995). By the Middle Ages, this consolidation of cities and towns led to the production and use of public open spaces—streets, squares, and plazas—for religious, commercial, political, and communal functions. The street of the Middle Ages was "the place of work, the place of buying and selling, the place of meeting and negotiating, and the scene of the important religious and civic ceremonies and processions" (Jackson 1987, p. 289). But most importantly, in contrast to the town of the preceding time made up of predominantly residential precincts in the countryside with a loose structure of open spaces, the street now existed as an ecology—a place where private, parochial, and public uses overlapped. And this was new and unique. The street ecology supported so many functions that it is impossible to separate the image of a street from that of the medieval city.

> The narrow, overcrowded buildings bordering it spilled out into the street and transformed it into a place of workshops, kitchens, and merchandising, into a place of leisure and sociability, and confrontation of every kind. It was this confusion of functions, the confusion of two different realms of law and custom that made the medieval street a kind of city within a city, the scene of innovations in policing, maintenance, and social reform.
>
> *(Jackson 1987, pp. 289–90)*

Many of these roles and characteristics of the street ecology decreased over the centuries as streets were used to find solutions for problems of defense, transportation, formal social functions, and eventually as vehicles for the display of status and the employment of power. Yet, presently, in many cities, the street exists in numerous forms and multiple images are visible. In some cases, the street ecology has survived and adapted to the social and technological changes, particularly in the cities and towns of several non-Western societies such as India. These streets display the wide-ranging possibilities of the street as a fundamental unit of existence in cities and towns and the street as ecology is easily visible.

A legible ecology: the street in India

In towns and cities in India, the ubiquitous neighborhood commercial street has existed in a centuries-long continuum. Although the Western trend of shopping malls has penetrated the development pattern of cities and regions, there is continued demand for local shopping. Given the limited mobility of a substantial population— women, children, elderly, and the poor—the neighborhood commercial street exists not only as a place of local commerce but also as one of the most vibrant public spaces in the city. An extensive diversity of uses and meanings are visible here: the street as ecology makes itself legible on the neighborhood commercial street in India. Revealing this ecology highlights the qualities of diversity and difference that make the Indian street an equitable, just and sustainable public space.

Image

The familiar image of the oriental street is characterized by a hyper-intense and over-stimulated experience delivered by a space produced by a richly patterned and textured enclosure with a juxtaposition of a panoply of forms. In this image, the street is crowded and chaotic and the visual overload is further pronounced by the aural, olfactory, and tactile quality of the space. Human sounds are intermingled with sounds of traffic; of music playing; of vendors calling out their goods and services; of sounds associated with manufacturing and repairing objects; and of birds and animals. The smells have an immense range too: the soothing scents of flowers and incense, the aroma of spices and oils, and the smell of foods are sometimes intermingled with the stench of garbage and rain water collected in ditches. The street is characterized by a multiplicity of use and meaning and this scene reinforces the image of a seemingly chaotic setting that in fact has a localized and negotiated order and control (Figure 6.1).

FIGURE 6.1 Characterized by a multiplicity of use and meaning, the street in India operates with a localized and negotiated order and control

Source: Photograph by Shilpa Mehta.

Activities on the street

The neighborhood commercial street in India offers shopping as well as opportunities for recreation and other amenities. But more importantly, the street acts as
a complex and wide-ranging public space that is at the core of the workings of
the neighborhood. Because merchants use the street space as an extension of
their shops, several activities associated with shopping spill over onto the street
(Figure 6.2). In many cases goods are sold on the street outside the shop. Wooing
customers, bargaining, and other forms of communication are common on the
street space. Other activities and behaviors related to commerce include making
and mending goods, including activities as diverse as locksmiths making keys,
cobblers repairing and making footwear, mechanics repairing vehicles, and potters
throwing pots. The diverse land use that supports a rich mix of activities, exchanges,
and interactions is further augmented by other fleeting "mobile land uses" in the
form of entertainers, soothsayers, and vendors selling food, small household goods,
and other services. Vendors play a significant role in creating nodes to anchor
stationary activities that seem to randomly appear on the street. They provide places
to sit for a cup of tea or snack, or to gather for a smoke, or listen to a commentary
on a game of cricket, or to get a haircut. Besides providing goods and services these
mobile land uses bring short-term change, stimuli, and novelty to the street. But
more importantly, they widen the range of goods and services and make the street
a suitable, useful, and meaningful place for many more, increasing the diversity and
difference on the street (Figure 6.3).

Non-commercial activities of day-to-day living are juxtaposed with the
commerce-related activities. The street space is a place for walking, sitting,
standing, lying down, sleeping, pan-handling, cooking, eating, smoking, washing
and cleaning, grooming, preaching, praying, playing music, playing games and
sports, and so on. The localized regulatory structure permits more diversity and
difference in the use, forms, and aesthetics of the street (Figure 6.4). The range of
activities visible on the street is a full display of the workings of the neighborhood:
the street as ecology is legible.

Adaptability: space, time, and order

On the Indian street, the use of space considerably changes over time. Often due
to a lack of space, there is extensive use of time to differentiate the use and purpose
of space. Studying the street over the passage of the day reveals how numerous
activities occur on any one space on the street. For example, the space in front of
a shop used as an overflow area for displaying goods during the daytime is used to
sell fresh milk in the morning. The same space transforms into a space of private
occupancy by laying cots for employees to sleep at night. In this sense, the street
is much more flexible and adaptable. A variety of activities occur in various parts
of the street at any given time, and numerous activities occur in the same place
over the hours of the day. The street is distinctive of an environment of complexity and contradictions, a diversity of use and a place of over-stimulated sensory

FIGURE 6.2 Several activities associated with shopping spill over on the street in India as the street space is used as an extension of shops

Source: Photographs by Prem Mehta.

FIGURE 6.3 Vendors widen the range of goods and services making the street in India a suitable, useful, and meaningful place for rich and poor alike

Source: Photographs by Shilpa Mehta.

FIGURE 6.4 A localized regulatory structure on the street in India permits more diversity and difference in the use, forms, and aesthetics of the street

Source: Photographs by Shilpa Mehta.

experience. The location of activities and use of space on the street is always negotiable, morphing to fit the needs of the users. Here order is determined more by the limits of adaptability of the space and the negotiation between individuals and local institutions than by predetermined laws executed by public authorities. Although there are formal rules set in place by jurisdictions, corrupt practices by those in power—politicians, police, landlords, and local gang members—often break and make new rules to their advantage. But the most important rules and regulations are enacted by the negotiations among the users of the street.

Path and place

On the neighborhood commercial street in India, path and place compete for the space on the street; gathering and lingering behavior occurs simultaneously with the act of movement, often negotiating and compromising for space. Multiple speeds and rhythms coexist on the street and movement seldom has hegemony on the street space. Movement on the neighborhood commercial street in India is cumbersome, whether it is in a vehicle or on foot; and it often translates into a negotiated labyrinthine path that pushes, nudges, and squeezes through the myriad territories and ongoing activities. Merchants typically encroach and appropriate substantial space immediately outside their businesses, creating zones for use of the street space but also ones that hinder movement. Vendors and pan-handlers further punctuate the linear space of the street. Whether by choice or not, the slow-moving body on the Indian street acts like a sponge, taking in stimuli and inter-actions as it moves through the street. Interactions are a must even for shopping, as prices are negotiable, and communicating and bargaining are the norm. The street is a place of "social immersion" (Edensor 1998, p. 209) and the body, actively or passively, participates in the ecology of the street. Through such social practices of communication and negotiation the body becomes both a consumer and a producer of stimuli, interactions and meanings.

For all these myriad activities to work, negotiation is paramount. The street, which may have a similar morphology including the dimensions of enclosure to the street in the West, is articulated and used in ways that question its geometry (Figure 6.5). The linearity and unidirectionality of the street are constantly challenged, whether it is by crossing the street at any location or drying *saris* and other large pieces of laundry or playing cricket and other games across the width of the street. In its rich ecology, the Indian street is characterized by difference and diversity and the street is both a path and a place.

A street as ecology in Cambridge, MA, USA

In trying to enliven it and to infuse it with vitality, the street in the West seeks multiplicity, informality, ambiguity in form and use, and a heightened sensory experience. Perhaps the street in the West can never be an unregulated place of unconstrained diversity. But there are streets that counter the prevalent culture of efficiency and consumption and one can find genuine signs of spontaneity and

FIGURE 6.5 The street in India is occupied, articulated and used in ways that defy its linearity

Source: Photograph by Shilpa Mehta.

diversity of people and activities. In this section, I discuss a short stretch of Massachusetts Avenue in Central Square, one of the streets in Cambridge, MA, in the US. Even with its institutional rules and regulations, and limitations, this street, somewhat like the street in New Delhi, is characteristic of diversity and difference.

The Central Square area is a diverse, vibrant, and lively mixed-use area in Cambridge. A myriad of uses, including a wide range of housing from single- to multi-family, various types and scales of retail, offices, and public institutional uses can be found in and around Central Square. Within close proximity are university campuses. Massachusetts Avenue is the main north–south connection and the primary public street and major retail and commercial uses are located here on two blocks north and four blocks south of Prospect Street. On this stretch of approximately six blocks on either side of Massachusetts Avenue, there is a variety of commercial establishments, some small independently owned or local chains, and some regional and national chain stores. These include a variety of restaurants, coffee shops, bars, fast food restaurants, grocery stores, convenience stores, hardware stores, pharmacies, electronics stores, cleaners, apparel stores, barbershops, hair and beauty salons, bookshops, video rental stores, teaching institutes, banks, offices, apartments, and so on. The intersection of Massachusetts Avenue and Prospect Street is also a major transit node for this part of Cambridge, with numerous bus stops and subway ("T") entrances and exits located around the square on Massachusetts Avenue.

Examining such a street is appropriate because it is ordinary. There is a certain authenticity to this street that is visible in the heterogeneity manifest in the types of businesses, the appearance and age of the buildings, and most importantly, the people who use the street. Unlike "invented" or "re-invented" streets (Banerjee *et al.* 1996), this street is not used just for shopping, dining, and promenading. Although it has transformed over time and many people long for the street of the past, it still maintains an everyday feel and grittiness. Neighborhood residents, visitors, workers, and people who call the street their home use the street for myriad purposes of socializing, leisure, everyday and special shopping, dining, lingering, promenading, celebration, protest, and survival.

To provide a sampling of the character of the street I will highlight one short stretch of Massachusetts Avenue that reveals the street ecology. To make it more pedestrian-friendly, the street was modified in the late 1990s, including sidewalk widening, curb extensions, reconfiguration of traffic lanes, addition of bicycle lanes, traffic calming, tree planting, new street lighting on sidewalks, and the provision of benches and other street furniture.

On this stretch of the street, one can find many diverse groups of people and activities. There are at least two community-gathering places where different groups of people linger, socialize and claim the street on this short stretch. People of several age groups and class coexist here and the street serves the many roles of public space discussed in this chapter and in the literature on public space (Figure 6.6). Figure 6.7 shows the locations where certain groups repeatedly claim the street space. In some cases, there are considerable overlaps and a diverse set of people simultaneously claim and territorialize the same street space maintaining a civil distance expected in public space. In other cases, there are spatial distinctions between the groups who establish their claim on the street. In yet other locations, diverse groups claim the same spaces on the street but they do so at different times of the day and week. Table 6.1 lists the range of activities observed on the street during weekdays and weekends. No doubt, this street can shed many of its present rules and regulations and become an even more diverse place but observing the street clearly shows signs of a street ecology.

The street as public space is a space of participation. It is an arena for the collective voice and shared interests but is also the space where the differences and conflicts of various groups play out. The ability to simultaneously be a space for diverse groups is an important role of the street as public space. In discussing the publicness of public space, Mitchell (2003) suggests that the appropriation and use of space by a group to fulfill its needs makes the space public. In many ways, we may think of the street, as public space, as "flexible and ambiguous" (Loukaitou-Sideris and Ehrenfeucht, 2009)—ever changing to accommodate the activities and behaviors of its users. Studying the street, it was evident that Massachusetts Avenue possesses a certain ambiguity and tolerance that allow for more interpretation and freedom of what is possible on the street, who can claim it, and for which activity.

Children's activities – magazine boxes and furniture as play objects

Discussing and learning about art in shop windows

Children interact with people of different background and class – learning of empathy and compassion

Interacting with poor and handicapped – empathy, social capital and support

Place to hang out for homeless – social capital and support

Children's activities – benches for play, not sitting!

Pan-handling – means of survival

Sharing space with people of different class, color, background, etc.

Promoting a cause – public awareness

Interacting with newspaper seller – more than economic transaction

Play a musical instrument – means of survival but also adding sensory stimulus to street

Place to hang out for homeless – social capital and support

People share significant events with friends on the street space

Alone together – place to sit, relax and people watch

Children's activities – cars as objects for play

Alone together – place to sit, relax and people watch

Prospect Street

Massachusetts Avenue

TYPES OF ACTIVITIES

○ Social
△ Economic
◇ Leisure/Play
⬠ Political

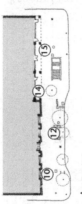

FIGURE 6.7
The plan and photographs show that people of several age groups and class repeatedly occupy, territorialize, and claim the street space on this short stretch of Massachusetts Avenue in Cambridge, MA

Prospect Street

Massachusetts Avenue

LEGEND

1 Families with children
2 Mothers with infants/toddlers
3 Children
4 Middle-age couples
5 Older women

6 Young couples
7 Young women
8 Young men
9 Young women and men
10 Pan-handlers

11 Newspaper vendors
12 Homeless
13 Street musicians
14 Store workers
15 Petition seekers

TABLE 6.1 Postures, behaviors, and activities observed on a short stretch of Massachusetts Avenue in Cambridge, MA

Postures	Adults' behaviors and activities	Children's behaviors and activities
• Walking • Ambling • Standing • Sitting • Lying • Sleeping • Jogging/running • Skateboarding • Bicycling	• Talking • Eating and drinking • Working (typically on a laptop) • Reading • Sharing time with family or friends (eating, drinking, socializing) • Kissing and other intimate physical contact • Cleaning and maintaining shop front and sidewalk • Decorating – putting planters out, hanging planters, putting out advertizing boards, changing signs, etc. • Smoking • Talking on a mobile phone • Playing a musical instrument • Playing board games • Pan-handling • Vending • Greeting others on the street • Walking pets • Observing other people and activities • Window-shopping • Protesting • Soliciting signatures for a petition • Distributing flyers	• Sharing time with family and other children (eating, drinking, socializing) • Greeting adults and children • Assisting grandparents • Walking pets • Observing adults, older children, pets, objects and activities • Inquiring about people, objects and activities • Climbing on and going under objects (furniture, telephone/electrical boxes, bicycle racks, etc.) for play and exploration • Walking in and out of building nooks, entrances, alcoves, etc. • Looking inside shop windows and entrances • Playing hide and seek – using street furniture, trees, parked cars, etc. • Playing chasing games – using street furniture and trees, etc. • Driving toys on building walls and in nooks, entrances, alcoves, etc. • Playing with newspaper dispensing boxes – opening, shutting, hiding things, etc. • Playing with parked cars – leaning, looking in, looking at reflections, etc.

The value of "the street as ecology"

These examples of the street as ecology teach us several important lessons about the potential of creating a just and equitable contemporary city. Foremost, these streets show us that various seemingly incongruent groups and activities have the ability to coexist on the street. This becomes possible when the design and management of the space and the uses on the street represent numerous groups and constituencies of the neighborhood and beyond, and are meaningful to them; when the street is perceived as a neutral ground by many, if not all; when the street is not excessively monitored or overly regulated to favor selected groups and activities; and when the street is designed and managed to support a sociably rich environment that is able to negotiate differences by taking into account (and anticipating) conflicting uses and users.

The street with a rich ecology is one of the ubiquitous transitions between the parochial and the public. This is where the neighborhood meets the city and the resident of the neighborhood becomes the citizen of the city. It is the space where the resident encounters urbanity. As opposed to the limited groups within the neighborhood, such a street is capable of supporting the many publics of the city. When the street performs as a rich ecology, a multitude of small and large businesses, vendors and other uses, spaces, and objects offer opportunities to attract a varied population and people of the neighborhood are able to cross paths with others unlike themselves.

Historically, as a complex ecology, the street has been the place to congregate, to meet, and to enjoy being a part of community, and also a space for expression. A rich street ecology provides a platform for a range of social behaviors and experiences. Although not all are intimate or intense or exceptional, most are meaningful associations for us as social beings. The street even offers the opportunity of being on one's own in the presence of others to be alone, to relax, and to reflect. This variety of behaviors and activities among diverse social groups and classes generates social encounters and experiences that are unique to urbanity. But a rich street ecology is also important because this is where everyday routines overlap with active or passive contact with strangers and "others," people unlike ourselves who may have a different view of the world, who may be more or less fortunate, even some who are down on their luck. Sharing the space with strangers is important. This is how we become tolerant; how we learn about new viewpoints and new ways of perceiving the world around us; how we expand our perspective and become innovative. This is how society in general becomes more complex but richer and advances culture. Thus, a street with a rich ecology creates a context for tolerance where active and passive social contact provides the setting for the "learning of cosmopolitanism."

> [Citizens] in the normal course of their everyday lives, rub shoulders with – accomplish uneventful interactions with – persons of whom they disapprove, with whom they disagree, toward whom they feel at least mild antipathy, or who evoke in them at least mild fear. That means that any city that is capable of teaching urbanity and tolerance must have a hard edge. Cleaned-up, tidy, purified, Disneyland cities (or sections of cities) where nothing shocks, nothing disgusts, nothing is even slightly feared may be pleasant sites for family outings or corporate gatherings, but their public places will not help to create cosmopolitans.
>
> *(Lofland 1998, p. 243)*

Such a street also serves as a public space that fulfills many other crucial social functions including learning, the development of social competence, the exchange of information, the facilitation of social dialogue, the fostering of social awareness, the enhancement of social integrative functions, and the encouragement of ethical conduct (Crowhurst-Lennard and Lennard 1987, 1995).

Decades ago, Jane Jacobs recognized what makes urban neighborhoods livable. She argued for complexity, diversity, and human scale over top-down rationality, homogeneity, and segregation of uses and people. Arguing for the importance of streets as places of contact, her observations, many of which are undisputed as good planning principles, point to the value of coexistence of diverse populations and associated activities, adding not only a certain complexity to the daily rhythms and patterns of use in the neighborhood but also trust and social capital. In essence, Jacobs' accounts of the streets of her neighborhood in Greenwich Village were showcasing the street as ecology.

The street is accessible to many and means different things to different people. For most residents, the neighborhood commercial street is the everyday link to the city and a space that is essential to meeting their day-to-day shopping, leisure, and social needs, and to be in the presence of others and experience urbanity. At times the street is a place to come out and celebrate or to gather and protest and let your voice be heard. For many regular visitors and many who work in the businesses on the street, it is a destination to customarily stop by for eating, drinking, or shopping. But there are people on the street for which it is a place to spend most of their day. Many such users live in very modest accommodations, have meager jobs and some are unemployed and homeless. For them, the street, particularly in mild weather, is as good a place to be as any other. For vendors, the street is a good place to find a constant stream of buyers, as it is for some others who use the street to pan-handle. There are persons who regularly visit the street to look for opportunities, a place where they have some social capital, and where they can get support from friends.

The street with a rich ecology resulting in the coexistence of diverse people, activities, businesses, and other uses within easy reach from home has a direct link to and effect on neighborhood livability. The proximity provides a convenience that promotes walking over driving or taking other modes of travel, thus saving time and resources in addition to the health benefits associated with walking. The clustering of diverse activities and other non-residential uses provides a certain centeredness that often helps in creating a sense of place and giving an identity to the neighborhood. This centeredness enables the use of space over the day, providing the much needed surveillance and resultant sense of safety via the eyes on the street. Another competitive advantage of such a street, due to its location within or near residential neighborhoods, is its ability to make it possible for people of the neighborhood to see and meet one another as a part of the daily round. Where the street provides small businesses, vendors and other uses, it offers economic benefits for many in the community. The neighborhood commercial street thus has a role of being a space that is neighborly and cordial but also civic. With this multiplicity of purpose the street becomes a lived space where myriad economic, transportation, cultural, and governance systems intersect.

Supporting streets as ecologies

The physical improvements to make the street a better place for the pedestrian, often by claiming space from the vehicular domain, are welcome gestures. These days, many design, planning and management decisions that make this possible are visible on the street. But improvements made to the street also make it more suitable and attractive to some users more than others. In the context of movement, multiple speeds and rhythms must exist on the street. To benefit from all that occurs on the street, we must not strive to think about movement as an efficient path but rather as a negotiated journey with multiple encounters filled with experiences and learning. The change in the streetscape is symbolic and it sends messages to welcome some and to deter other users and uses. Even if this does not discourage certain users, at the least, space or time often segregates the use of the street. At the same time, the street, as public space, can have a true identity only if varied groups can use and identify with it. The street must be a place for the display of the genuine constituency of the neighborhood—of all the publics—including the less fortunate and the idiosyncratic. Instead of trying to discourage or conceal them, the street should be designed and managed as a public commons—a space that all have an equal right to claim. This is one of the biggest challenges for policy-makers, designers, planners, and managers of the street who must acknowledge that varied groups have different needs and preferences. They must design and manage the street to be open for various groups to claim it and create their own identities. There is often the urge to resolve conflict by discouraging and curtailing the seemingly uncomfortable uses; by removing uncertainties; by driving out certain groups; and ultimately resorting to accepting a street with homogenized uses and behaviors. But such uncertainties and ambiguities must be seen as opportunities as this is inherently the nature of public space. We must also remember that public space is self-leveling. In places that are open to all and where public and private authorities exert minimum control, some groups inevitably tend to dominate and limit access to others. At most times though, overlaps of occupancy and control of the street are sorted out by using different parts of the street or using it at different times. This is where management and civic authorities must carefully assess and balance the regulations and control of the street such that it continues to retain its publicness and diversity. The management of the street must be open-minded so that the uses remain somewhat open-ended to retain a level of "looseness" (Franck and Stevens 2007) and "slack" (Worpole and Knox 2007). The street as a "stage of a constant struggle between private and public interests" (Kostof 1992, p. 191) has been much discussed in the history of the city. What is crucial on the street is the balancing of the interests of the various publics by the civic authorities and other agencies that have been charged to do so.

Conclusion: let us not Complete Streets

J.B. Jackson, the eminent cultural geographer and landscape theorist, predicted that we will return to the concept of the medieval street and it will be the "true public space of the future" and "they will be playing a social role we have long associated with the traditional public square: The place where we exhibit our permanent identity as members of the community." He argues that for a wide range of social, economic, and aesthetic needs:

> [W]e will be reverting, unconsciously of course, to a medieval urban concept which long preceded the Renaissance concept of the public square. In the Middle Ages it was the street—tortuous, dirty, crowded—and not the public space identified with the church or castle or market, that was the center of economic and social life. The street was the place of work, the place of buying and selling, the place of meeting and negotiating, and the scene of the important religious and civic ceremonies and processions.
>
> *(Jackson 1987, p. 289)*

Jackson's predictions are slowly coming true, perhaps in a more circuitous way. No doubt, observing the contemporary city shows us that with the commodification and privatization of public space, many traditional main streets have been replaced by shopping malls, lifestyle centers, and so on. But the same consumer culture and the need for active and passive engagement and interaction, relaxation, and leisure are also increasingly supporting the concept of publicness and at least some of this public and social life now occurs on streets with coffee shops, restaurants, bars, bookstores, theaters, health clubs, and other public amenities. With the renewed interest in urban living, many people, looking for a lifestyle that offers amenities within easy reach, are opting for neighborhoods with mixed-use streets that accommodate shopping, entertainment, some workspace, and other community-oriented uses. The revitalization of the Main Street across North America is testimony to this. This is an opportunity that policy-makers, planners, and designers cannot miss. The attention toward the street must not be limited: if we settle for the street as a place of mobility, even equitable mobility for all modes, we are settling for too little. Streets can serve many more functions and we should expect no less. We must aim for streets to perform as a rich and sustainable ecology where the social, economic, environmental, and political dimensions must all be considered. These forces that structure society must be able to communicate, interact, and be legible on the street. But this does not translate to completeness. Public space is a contested territory and space is made public through negotiations. As a contested space, the street presents a transient and conflictual ecology. And the presence of conflicts shows the need for and the ability of the street to serve multiple publics. The street ecology is multidimensional: the quality or success of the street must be examined in ways that address issues of politics and democracy, sociability, leisure, and recreation, economic exchange, and symbolic value. Hence, instead of measuring the quality or success of the street in terms of completeness, I suggest evaluating the street in terms of looseness and tightness (Franck and Stevens 2007), or on a continuum of open to closed (Sibley 1995), or gauging the street in terms of its ability to accept diversity and difference (Malone 2002). In this metric, space that is loose or open is diverse, easily adaptable, and often spontaneous whereas tight or closed space is characterized by control, restrictions, and limiting design, and is overly prescriptive.

Diversity is fundamental to ecology. To be a part of society, people have to participate in several social processes. As a ubiquitous space the street must support the diverse processes of working, education, socialization, recreation, production, commerce, and so on. The "street as ecology" approach expands on the possibilities and meanings of the street and counters the narrowly defined approaches such as Complete Streets. In doing so, it opens up possibilities for streets as places to serve many of society's processes and as spaces that thrive on diversity and difference. An increasingly urbanizing world translates into a large number of people who encounter streets. As a vital public and neighborhood space, the street has, and can serve many roles: a pedestrian sanctuary, a place of social capital, support and community, a neighborly territory, a place for play and learning, a place for survival, and a place of rich and diverse experiences, cultural memory, and history. The streets that support these roles will become more important in creating sustainable, just and equitable neighborhoods and cities.

Note

1   "The Best Complete Street Policies of 2012," National Complete Streets Coalition, April 2013. Available from: www.smartgrowthamerica.org/documents/cs-2012-policy-analysis.pdf.

References

Banerjee, T., Giuliano, G., Hise, G., and Sloane, D., 1996. Invented and reinvented streets: Designing the new shopping experience. *Lusk Review*, 2 (1), 18–30.

Buchanan, J.M., and Vanberg, V.J., 1994. The market as a creative process. In: D. M. Hausman, ed. *The philosophy of economics: An anthology*. New York, NY: Cambridge University Press, pp. 315–335.

Crowhurst-Lennard, S., and Lennard, H., 1987. *Livable cities – people and places: Social and design principles for the future of the city*. New York, NY: Center for Urban Well-being.

Crowhurst-Lennard, S., and Lennard, H., 1995. *Livable cities observed*. IMCL Council. Carmel, CA: Gondolier Press.

Edensor, T., 1998. The culture of the Indian street. In: N. Fyfe, ed. *Images of the street*. London: Routledge, 205–221.

Franck, K., and Stevens, Q., 2007. *Loose space: Possibility and diversity in urban life*. London: Routledge.

Holling, C.S., 1996. Surprise for science, resilience for ecosystems, and incentives for people. *Ecological Applications*, 6 (3), 733–735.

Jackson, J.B., 1987. The American public space. In: N. Glazer and M. Lilla, eds. *The public face of architecture: Civic culture and public spaces*. New York, NY: The Free Press, 276–291.

Jukes, P., 1990. *A shout in the street*. New York, NY: Farrar Straus Giroux.

Keith, M., 1995. Shouts of the street: identity and the spaces of authenticity. *Social Identities*, 1 (2), 297–315.

Kostof, S., 1992. *The city assembled: The elements of urban form through history*. Boston, MA: Little, Brown and Co.

Kostof, S., 1995. *A history of architecture: Settings and rituals*. Oxford: Oxford University Press.

Lofland, L., 1998. *The public realm: Exploring the city's quintessential social territory*. New York, NY: Aldine de Gruyter.

Loukaitou-Sideris, A., and Ehrenfeucht, R., 2009. *Sidewalks: Conflict and negotiation over public space*. Cambridge, MA: MIT Press.

Madanipour, A., 2010. Introduction. In: A. Madanipour, ed. *Whose public space? International case studies in urban design and development*. London: Routledge, 1–15.

Malone, K., 2002. Street life: youth, culture and competing uses of public space. *Environment and Urbanization*, 14 (2), 157–168.

Massey, D., 1994. *Space, place and gender*. Oxford: Blackwell.

Massey, D., 1999. Space-time, 'science' and the relationship between physical geography and human geography. *Transactions of the Institute of British Geographers*, 24, 261–276.

Mitchell, D., 2003. *The right to the city: Social justice and the fight for public space*. New York, NY: Guilford Press.

Rykwert, J., 1978. The street: The use of its history. In: S. Anderson, ed. *On Streets*. Cambridge, MA: MIT Press, 14–27.

Sibley, D., 1995. *Geographies of exclusion*. London: Routledge.

Thornes, J.B., 1983. Evolutionary geomorphology. *Geography*, 68, 225–235.

Tuckel, P., and Milczarskishow, W., 2011. Pedestrian-cyclist accidents in New York State: 2007–2010. Unpublished study. Hunter College, New York.

Worpole, K., and Knox, K., 2007. *The social value of public spaces*. York: Joseph Rowntree Foundation.

PART II
Practices

7

CURBING CRUISING

Lowriding and the domestication of Denver's Northside

Sig Langegger

Introduction

The phrase "city streets" evokes thousands of images. Imagine one, a spring afternoon in North Denver in 1990. It's a little warmer than yesterday and the sun is a touch higher in the sky. Brown lawns turn green and neighborly socializing warms once quiet, wintery streets. Just last week playground swings and jungle gyms sat idle, but today they are alive with enthusiastic play and peals of laughter. Teens have shed bulky parkas to reveal summer fashions. A flash catches your eye. Reflecting intense afternoon sun from its buffed chrome bumpers and vivid paint job, a lowrider rolls leisurely down West 38th Avenue. Blaring Tejano hip-hop the car slips into a strip mall parking lot; the Latino at the wheel jokes with a group of youths gathered there. Back on the street, he nods knowingly toward a growing crowd at the entrance to the Elich's Amusement Park. At stop lights, he bounces the front of his car to the rhythm of its booming subwoofers. Taking knowing notice of the lowrider's showboating, a Denver Public Works crew is hard at work distributing traffic barriers at each intersection along West 38th. Each weekend, police erected these barriers as part of a concerted effort to order and rationalize North Denver streets, by straitjacketing cruising circuits. Constantly visible, the barriers serve as a reminder of municipal power. Despite, or perhaps *in* spite of the barriers, each weekend night *Northsiders*, their friends, rivals, and families converge along West 38th to partake in the slow, rhythmic, and loud appropriation of public space known as lowrider cruising.

Framing this scene we find two notions of the street, one eliciting an efficient transportation conduit, the other calling to mind a rich cultural landscape. The terms street cred, streetwise, and even the use of the word street as a vernacular adjective—evoking the urban underground, hip-hop, and a certain edginess—illustrate how the street comes to define the experience of the city. Lefebvre (2003) reminds us that the city is where differences come to know one another. Whereas Complete Streets implies stasis, Lefebvre helps us recognize the city as a contentious and manifold process. As Mehta (Chapter 6 in this volume) argues, use of the term Complete Streets flattens a rich ecology, one replete with calls and responses between performers and audiences, with circular, erratic, and aimless movement, with discovery and growth, into the "origin-destination" logic preferred by transportation planners. Fast forward our imagined scene to present-day Denver: not only has lowriding been all but eliminated from the *Northside* (local vernacular for North Denver), but the four neighborhoods, Sunnyside, Berkeley, Highland, and West Highland bisected by West 38th Avenue are gentrifying. As this chapter deconstructs, eliminating streets as spaces where differences can know one another, the City of Denver established a cultural hegemony by turning surprising places into predictable paths.

In 2006, the completion of a pedestrian bridge across Interstate 25 connected Highland, a heretofore isolated Northside barrio, to Lower Downtown. In a sense, this award-winning span completed North Denver's now pedestrian/bicycle-friendly streets. As I argue below, well before they were completed, these streets played a critical role in neighborhood change. Trendy restaurants, funky boutiques, and bike kiosks currently encourage a decidedly hipster/middle-class publicness along streets that were once public in quite different ways. By deconstructing the complexities of the production of space, this chapter exposes historical conflicts between diverse public practices and shows how Northside streets were dispossessed before they were completed. Diversity in public space is presupposed and often lauded in scholarly discourse; I show that rich potential for diversity can be deliberately regulated, and policed from city streets. Bracing Henri Lefebvre's (1991) theory of the production of space with Stanley Cohen's (2002) notion of the folk devil, I deconstruct formal and informal regulations of lowrider cruising and link them to gentrification processes.

Though it serves as a cornerstone of my argument, gentrification is not an unchallenged concept. It is lauded as an effective urban revitalization mechanism (Freeman, 2005) and it is widely criticized as a covert means of removing "undesirable" people from "desirable" parts of the city. Urban scholars explain how rough and edgy inner-city neighborhoods are slowly domesticated by hip coffee shops (Atkinson, 2003), popularized by trendy restaurants (Zukin 2010), and *re*-authenticated by chic boutiques (Zukin 2011). Approaching this contested terrain, I frame spatial justice (Soja 2000) in terms of the formal regulation of public space and consider the right to the city (Lefebvre 1996) in terms of rights to informally regulate public cultural practices. In the pages that follow, I discuss the significance of lowrider cruising to Latino culture, analyze media constructions of lowrider folk devils, and explore how municipal codes and urban design worked to delegitimize Latino public presence while legitimizing mainstream middle-class public practices along Denver streets (see similarities in Chapter 11 by Vallianatos on food trucks in Los Angeles). Finally, I map these potent discourses onto a discussion of the early gentrification of the Northside.

What is a lowrider? A term packed with vernacular meaning, it is not just a car, it is a person, a symbol, and a practice. Lowriding is a public performance, deriving from and informing the complexities of the Latino experience in the American Southwest. Appropriating public space, lowriders re-enact the *paseo* traditionally practiced in Meso-American church plazas (Richardson 1982) and they rail against modern cultural and racial injustices. Because lowriding reinforces familial and communal bonds, it legitimizes Latino public presence in the city. On the other hand, it directly contradicts many white middle-class expectations of trendy and functional city streets. Well before the Northside began to gentrify, urban pioneers (Smith 1996) implored the city to outlaw the practice of lowrider cruising. Their efforts failed. Cruising, in fact, could not legally be construed a moving violation. Taking it "low and slow" may have annoyed impatient commuters, and bold, artistic paint jobs and machismo-infused public braggadocio may have offended certain neighborhood residents; nonetheless, cruising remains a legal practice. Not able to render the act of operating modified automobiles or hanging out in large groups in publicly accessible space illegal, anti-cruising groups sought to establish demonstrable connections between lowriding and illegal acts. Since both lowrider cruising and street gangs were commonly perceived as part and parcel of dangerous urban youth subcultures, Denver news media and political discourses conflated them into a singular threat to society. These public discourses reframed lowriders as folk devils (Cohen 2002). As such, a component of Latino public presence in the Northside was portrayed as a singular deviant threat to the moral order of the city, which thereby legitimated a decade of extraordinary police policies and protocols that worked to virtually eliminate lowrider cruising from North Denver. Currently, real estate agents and real estate brochures highlight the area's quaint Victorian and Craftsman streetscape, its bikeable proximity to downtown Denver, the foodie scene—dotted with an occasional "authentic" taqueria—in lower Highland, and its walkability. These representations overlay the Latino braggadocio that once animated its streets.

Public space and gentrification

A contested term, gentrification can be measured by myriad outcomes of a suite of political, social, economic, and cultural processes. Gentrification research tends to consider private spaces, focusing on either rented or owned places of residence. In tracking neighborhood change, researchers use a variety of demographic variables including income, education, wealth, and occupation. Picking up a related thread, I focus on another means of measuring neighborhood change, changes in an area's *ethno-racial* composition (Betancur 2011). This type of change occurs in two directions: the settlement of certain ethnic groups into neighborhoods, which often contributes to the displacement of other ethnic groups from their places of residence. Shifting the focus from private places of residence to public space, I explore both cultural and racial components of gentrification, deconstructing how changes to the formal and informal regulation of behavior along city streets affect two distinct ethno-racial groups: the mainstream middle-class and working-class Latino. Well into the late twentieth century, Latino publicness characterized North

Denver. Talking to long-time residents about Northside, I learned that main and side streets used to be congested with cultural activity, noisy with socializing, and punctuated by unexpected encounters. Today, gentrifiers invest in the predictable mobility of North Denver streets and, as one interviewee phrased it, the "trendy livability" of North Denver parks.

The choice of a neighborhood is a central concern of some gentrification scholars (Brown-Saracino 2009). A person's choice of a specific private residence is, of course, a significant factor in her selection of a particular neighborhood. Square footage matters, the number of bedrooms matters, architecture matters. I argue that people also choose homes located in neighborhoods and they choose a neighborhood in large measure because its streetscape, walkability, bikability and the trendy restaurants and hip boutiques that line its streets appeal to them. I argue, for a neighborhood to gentrify, it must appeal to middle-class homebuyers and renters who are drawn to its public spaces as well as its private residences. The fact that a neighborhood's public spaces are comfortable places for newcomers to hang out in and travel through remains underexplored in gentrification scholarship. Unpacking the formal and informal regulation of lowrider cruising, I hope to contribute to a deeper understanding of this complex dynamic.

Researching neighborhood change

Of course, neighborhood change is continual; in fact, its trajectories are ever changing. Families grow; people perish; children grow up and move away; new neighbors move in; old houses are razed or remodeled in what seems like the blink of an eye, many timeworn structures remain, slowly acquiring the subtle patinas of age, while new houses and condominium complexes quickly rise on long-vacant or newly vacated land. In gentrifying neighborhoods change is not only continual, it is rapid. A quick analysis of census data for Highland, the North Denver neighborhood that has experienced the most dramatic neighborhood change in the last decade, goes toward proving this statement. Using the Brown University S4 Longitudinal Track Database, which accounts for shifting census tracts and neighborhood boundaries, I found that between 1970 and 2000 the percentage of Latinos in Highland remained remarkably constant at 65 percent of the neighborhood population. This quickly changed. In the decade spanning 2000–2010, the Latino composition of the neighborhood dropped sharply to 38 percent. White people now make up the majority of Highland. As a resident of West Highland, my conversations with old-timers always revealed a shared sense of awe in how much and how quickly the neighborhoods of North Denver had changed. This change manifests in both physical and social environments. It is noticeable in retail signage and window displays as well as in the people walking down streets, eating in restaurants and drinking at bars.

Such rapid change raised serious methodological problems. Doing fieldwork and conducting interviews in 2011, how was I to explore changes to the formal and informal production of public space during the 1980s and 1990s? Paraphrasing

William Faulkner, the past is never past; it is always present. Yesterday's neighborhood plans shape today's neighborhoods. Present circumstance is always contextualized by personal and collective memories. Relying on narrative interviews—in which neighborhood long-timers told me stories of their individual histories and transportation planners and park planners recounted the histories of their decisions—and archival analysis of news media as well as the evolution of municipal codes, I disentangled the social and political conditions of North Denver before it began to gentrify. Perusing archival evidence uncovered in assessor records, business indexes, neighborhood histories, and other archives, I gained insight into the pre-gentrification physical landscapes of North Denver.

This study is a component of a larger research project that examined the roles various public spaces played in the gentrification of North Denver (Langegger 2013). It draws on 60 narrative interviews with people in critical positions relative to the gentrification of the Berkeley, West Highland, Highland, and Sunnyside neighborhoods, including developers, city officials, middle-class newcomers, Latino long-timers, community activists, and neighborhood parish priests. By means of narrative and casual interviews I gained insight into how a variety of people perceive and sanction an array of public practices. I paid careful attention to uncovering a thematic consistency between interviewee insights, observed behavior, and the empirical evidence uncovered in various archives. Finally, throughout my research selected residents and experts read drafts and verified and/or clarified my preliminary findings and conclusions.

I understand public space to be a place and, like Massey (1994), I see places as ever shifting combinations of social relations. In public spaces, social relations play out within complex webs of physical design, cultural interpretation, and legal regulation. Because public spaces lie in a tangle of municipal regulations and enforcement, considering their legal geographies proves vital. In a word, the publicness of public space is always framed and delimited by interpenetrating and often contradictory layers of legal, municipal, and ethical codes, what Staeheli and Mitchell (2008) define as *tissues of regulation*. Since legal and municipal codes are not observable in the field, I turned to archival research. In addition to researching traffic law, municipal codes, and police protocol, I perused newspaper and magazine articles written at the height of Denver's "cruising crisis" during the late 1990s and early 2000s.

In addition to archival work, I spent considerable time seeking out and talking to individuals who partook in or were impacted by lowrider cruising in North Denver. Speaking with these ex-cruisers and long-time Northsiders, I learned that although lowriding can certainly be understood in terms of the motorized youthful rebellion convincingly portrayed in films such as *The Wild One* or *American Graffiti*, people's memories of cruising centered on the entire community rather than merely on its youth. Since many lowriders are youthful, the practice of cruising can be theorized in terms of teenagers as a separate and new social group (Skelton and Valentine 1998) and in terms of this status on teenager group identity (Cohen 2002). However, my informants insisted that their memories of cruising revolved around families and friends gathering in public space to socialize and partake in the public life of *el barrio*. Although cars offer teens a unique opportunity to frame a uniquely private and mobile space in public (Best 2006), the stories my informants shared centered on cruising as a familial and cultural affair. Their narratives were peppered with rich metaphors of cultural pride and group solidarity, conjuring images of streets as vibrant and diverse public spaces, of which cruising, socializing, and commuting were integral components.

Cruising for a bruising

At once a familial and cultural affair, lowrider cruising is a distinctive public performance with unique mobilities. A subculture within a broader reading of Latino culture, lowriding is a complex, multigenerational, working-class practice that depends upon mutual aid found within car clubs, work relationships, and communal relationships; it strengthens familial bonds across generations; and it emboldens individualistic braggadocio (Chappell 2012). Nevertheless, lowriding remains antithetical to orderly urban governance, traffic management protocols, and, not infrequently, middle-class notions of the urban scene.

Lowriders are highly customized cars featuring airbrushed paint jobs, after-market often gold-plated rims, and significantly modified suspension systems. Popularized by 1980s films like *Boulevard Nights*, *Boyz in the Hood*, and more recently by movies like *Machete*, and *la Mission*, lowrider cruising finds roots deep within the Mexican-American experience, specifically within zoot suit subculture, which arose during the 1930s and 1940s as a response to age and racial discrimination experienced by Latino and Black youth (Alvarez 2008). Inspired by zoot suit grandstanding, a lowrider is a very specific type of customized car, named for their suspension systems that are entirely reconstructed to sit very low to the pavement. Many lowriders have complex hydraulic systems, allowing drivers to raise, tilt, lower, and bounce these distinctive vehicles. Lowrider enthusiasts spend years and many thousands of dollars customizing their cars, which often become family heirlooms. Personalized multi-layered paint jobs, plush upholstery, buffed rims, shiny tires, and thundering stereos are all part of the lowrider package of public display. Occupying space, lowriders assert racial and ethnic symbols, inscribing streets as *barrio places* (Chappel, 2010). Further, lowriding asserts a tenuous cultural control over city streets by practicing a specific type of mobility. Lowrider cruisers call it "taking it low and slow," meaning that the impromptu parades of low-slung cars move down streets well below the posted speed limit. Lowriding thus transgresses both public decorum and personal experiential boundaries. As one informant commented, "Cruising, yeah, the city goes by like a slow dream." An act that is not against the law, lowrider cruising is simply unexpected to anyone traveling near the speed limit. Latinos in low-slung cars slowly cruising, bouncing, and lilting at stop lights, playing rock and hip-hop music, loudly interacting with onlookers, imprinted a mobile *barrio* onto North Denver streets. For many Northsiders this typified a Northside *vida pública* (Valle and Torres 2000).

In Denver, cruising was not always associated with Latinos. By all accounts, between the 1950s and early 1980s, Denver's cruising scene was multicultural, with cars and youths from various inner-city and suburban neighborhoods concentrating in downtown Denver, along 15th and 16th Streets. In 1982, the downtown 16th Street pedestrian mall was inaugurated. Pedestrianizing this traditional cruising strip forced cruisers to find cruisable streets in their own neighborhoods. For North Denver Latinos, this was West 38th Avenue. La Raza Park anchored one end of the cruising strip and Elitch Gardens, an amusement park 2.6 miles west, anchored the other.

This mobile *barrio* raised considerable ire in non-cruising, and specifically non-Latino communities. To many members of the white middle class, impromptu parades of this slowly rolling publicness unsettled urban life in innumerable ways. To some this disruption was welcomed as it represented an essence of the unexpectedness and diverse vibrancy typifying urban life, but to others it was a nuisance, making neighborhoods essentially unlivable. An extended quote from a white man who moved into his house in Highland in 1983 paints this picture:

> The neighborhood has changed a lot, culturally. In the 80s and 90s, weekend stuff was cruising. Cruising on Sundays got to be untenable. It became little Mexico for a day. During the week it was pretty quiet, no big deal. But Sundays *everybody* would leave church and start cruising. It got to where you couldn't drive through the neighborhood. So, yeah, residents were concerned about it. It was noisy. You ended up working your schedule around cruising. You didn't invite guests over on Sunday afternoon. It wasn't going to work. It got tiresome. It's noisy and all that. On the other hand, it was pretty interesting to have this whole other culture rolling *ever so slowly* past your house. Pretty interesting stuff, I found it fascinating. Aside from the souped-up cars, there were a lot of people without particularly fancy rides, just cruising, saying hi to their friends.

While some white residents appreciated this slowly rolling culture, many did not. To illustrate, in the early 1990s, the registered neighborhood organization Highland United Neighbors Inc. (HUNI) initiated a letter writing campaign urging city council to write enforceable laws that would make the legal practice of cruising illegal. Others took matters into their own hands. One Highland resident tells of an Italian-American neighbor who on Sunday afternoons would feign car trouble, park his car perpendicularly in the middle of a popular cruising street and pop the hood. Of course, his DIY roadblock affected *all* traffic along his neighborhood streets. Ignoring protests from his neighbors, he wanted to inconvenience the lowriders to the point that they would simply find somewhere else to cruise. Throughout the 1990s, similar methods of spatial discipline manifested both informally and formally.

As it currently stands in North Denver, cruising is a minor event along Federal Boulevard during Cinco de Mayo; aside from this May weekend, one rarely sees a lowrider on the street. To many North Denver Latinos, lowrider cruising seems a relic of a shared history rather than a part of a splintered present. To some Latino activists the absence of lowriders symbolizes loss in an important battle over cultural legitimacy. Largely ignorant of the cultural history of North Denver, middle-class newcomers appreciate their new neighborhoods' convenient proximity to down-town Denver via *uncongested* and, importantly, *uncontested* streets.

The social practice of cruising

> When I was a kid, me and my friends would cruise with our bikes, cruiser bikes; they're heavy, hard to ride up hill. So one of our friends' dad or an uncle, whoever would drive us up 38th to Tennyson, to Elitch's. We'd hang out there for a while, then ride down to Chubby's to have a coke or a taco. After a while he'd pick us up again, drive us back up. I was little when we were doing that, little. You see, cruising was just a part of the public culture, part of life. Now I'm a grown man, but I've still got lowrider Hot Wheels, you know those little mini-toy cars! I've got a '52 Merc and a '72 Monte Carlo! Cruising is a part of our culture. When I see a lowrider cruising down the street, I like it, bang! Even as an adult. A lot of people don't understand this. A lot of people think that lowriders are gangsters. But it's just part of the Chicano community, you know.

The extended quote above from Cisco Gallardo, program director of Denver's Gang Rescue and Support Project (GRASP), helps us understand the central role cruising played in the reproduction of familial and community relations. Mr Gallardo stresses the significance of cruising as a part of the Chicano experi-ence, and the importance of the geography of the route, from one hang-out—Elitch Gardens—to another—Chubby's, an iconic North Denver taqueria located next to la Raza Park. In a word, he sketches a rich ecology of familial bonds and friendships, commercial land-uses, urban mobility, cultural practice, and personal growth—learning to be cool, how to swagger and pose while fitting in—embedded in the diverse cultural landscape of West 38th Avenue.

Cruising is not only a Chicano public practice. "Mexicans like to show off their pickups and their cowboy boots," says a second generation Mexican American. For many Latinos, cruising the streets of North Denver, either in a lowrider or in "your grandma's jalopy," was an extension of the *paseo*—courtship rites practiced in the plazas of Mexico, in which teenage boys and girls, decked out in their finest, walk in opposite directions around the plaza's fountain, daring a flirtatious glance. While teens courted, families gathered, friends gossiped, and rivals argued. Thus, cruising was a cultural event woven into social fabrics of courtship and community dynamics. Enacted between turnaround points along various Northside streets, it was deeply embedded in a sense of Latino community. Through cruising, many Latinos found comfort in being in public, hanging out on neighborhood streets, and practicing culture (Calhoun and Sennett 2007).

In the late 1980s on summer weekend nights, West 38th Avenue was a Latinized kaleidoscope of sound, color, and motion, with Mexicanos cruising their new Ford 150s, and "old-school" Chicanos in their Fleetliners they call *bombas*. There too were classic lowrider rides like Monte Carlos and Impalas. There were teens flirting and people just sitting on their front porches or hanging out at Elitch's contributing to the public practice of culture. Because gang members were members of the wider Latino community (Venkatesh 2006), they too were there. However, especially if thousands of dollars had been invested in customizing a car, lowriding was most often a family affair. It fostered a means to socialize with other families. As one informant put it, "The gang was there, but cruising's not a gang thing. It's girls talking to guys, guys showing off, it's spending time with the community, looking good. All of it, that's what cruising is all about."

Though not all participated in or even appreciated the cultural diversity of *la vida pública*, it is absolutely normal to Northsiders with whom I spoke. The groups comprising this publicness positively and negatively sanction its constitutive behaviors. Like any diverse community, the Northside comprises many social groups. According to Cisco Gallardo:

> Gang members are members of the Northside community. Are they part of the cruising community? No! That's where the rest of the population makes a mistake. That's where it becomes a cultural difference. We share the cruising, but I think there are three different types of cruisers. There's the actual legitimate cruisers who really take care of their cars—the hydraulics and all that business. And then there's kids who cruise their mom's car, their grandma's car. For them, it's more of a social interaction. And then there's the gang members who use that social interaction to flex, to do their whole "this is my territory" business.

Informal regulation of cruising

No longer children, teenagers are *out of place* (Cresswell 1996) in playgrounds, many spaces are unavailable to them. Usually unwelcome in public space, they are often simply deemed dangerous (Staeheli 2010). As I have shown, cruising allows teens to participate with their community within public space. However, because popular culture and news media correlate cruising with dangerous teenager behavior, the practice of lowriding tends to be directly associated with other disquieting teen activities, such as vandalism, menacing behavior, general mischief, and violence. Consequently, efforts are made to remove them and the unruly practice of lowriding from public space. This linearly spurious logic is all too common. Fulfilling quality of life campaign promises, tough-on-crime mayors and city police use the presence of gang violence to justify all manner of gender-, race- and age-based profiling tactics. In fact, it is not altogether uncommon for municipalities to pass city ordinances that render being in public for Black or Latino juveniles essentially illegal (Geis 2002).

Even though cruising is only tangentially related to the presence of gang members, not gang violence per se, dominant social groups gradually asserted their notions of public decorum along Northside streets. This was sometimes done informally through setting up homemade roadblocks. More often it was accomplished formally, by means of police presence, roadblocks, and towing companies. One longtime North Denver Latino laments this type of spatial discipline, saying, "It's just the way we do things. In our community you see large groups of people hanging out on the sidewalk, cruising, having parties in parks. We just can't do these things anymore, at least without the cops showing up." For him, Northside streets have changed. They have been made *incomplete*, through targeted spatial discipline.

By 1990, cruising had become a problem deemed worthy of considerable increase in police presence. How did dominant groups come to justify the removal of legal activities of marginal groups from ostensibly publicly accessible space? Media coverage played a significant role. Mainstream news media tend to reproduce and reinforce dominant cultural norms, while delegitimizing and even criminalizing the cultural norms of racial minorities. Throughout the twentieth century, news reports linking the behavior of people of Latino descent with crime became a common tool used by police, politicians, and property developers to gain support from otherwise non-racist white individuals for essentially racist policies (Duran 2011). People tend to believe what they see on television. To illustrate, the overuse of racial violence in news media, film, and even video games creates a dissonance between actual crime rates and a generalized fear of becoming a victim of crime (Romer *et al.* 2003). Ironically, most inner-city streets have in fact become safer places, however society harbors a greater fear of these public spaces. This process has a linguistic component. In Denver, the news media's repetitive use of skewed statistics and hyperbolic reporting legitimated words like *cholo gangster* or *gangbanger*—terms used to describe any Latino youth who dresses, acts, speaks, or gesticulates in manners similar to members of gangs, irrespective of actual gang membership—thus conflating cruisers with members of street gangs. In Denver, this media construction of Latino folk devils proved an important component in demonizing cruising.

Denver news reporting and op-eds skewed toward white middle-class notions of public decorum aided and abetted a widespread, implicit tolerance for racial profiling. A close reading of Chuck Green's op-ed column published in the *Denver Post* on May 8, 1996, entitled "Hooligans Don't Know Culture" (Green 1996) shows how blatant racism and overt cultural imperialism (Young 1990) work in tandem to vilify cultural practices of Latinos. Green opens his tirade with the following: "I didn't know that 'cruising' was a Latino cultural thing. I thought it was a 1950s American thing. Now it turns out to be a part of Mexican American/ Hispanic/Chicano/Latino history." To Green, cruising was a part of *his* history, specifically white, middle-class history. He not only denies Latinos their history, but also implies that they stole his. For Green, cruising was:

Lookin' cool, being seen, chasin' girls. Night after night, month after month, we'd be bitchin' our '57 Chevies or '61 Cudas or '65 Mustangs. You'd see all your friends, a few of your rivals. It was a ritual.

In his elegy for white cruising, Green ironically describes cruising precisely as Latinos practiced it. Substitute '45 Fleetliners, '64 Impalas, and '70 Monte Carlos, and he would be aptly describing Latino lowrider cruising. Mid-century, night after night, neighbors had to deal with the nuisance of large groups of white youth cruising Denver streets. Nevertheless, after describing essentially the same behaviors that Latino youth perform in lowriders, he concludes that lowriding "ain't cruisin'; it's hooliganism." Delegitimizing the Latino public practice of cruising while authenticating a similar white public practice works to legitimize racism. It also creates what I call a rights-rift between Latino cultural norms and the practice of cruising by justifying racial profiling and stereotyping as legitimate acts. In a subtle yet powerful turn of phrase, white cruisers remain components of mainstream middle-class nostalgia for simpler times, while Latino cruisers become gangsters and hooligans. Latinos, on the other hand, see cruising as a valid part of their culture, one comprising other public ritualistic practices such as *paseo* and *la vida pública*.

Police response to cruising was legitimated by claims of gridlock, of lowriders denying others predictable mobilities in North Denver. However, according to newspaper articles written during the 1990s and early 2000s as well as stories shared by my informants, gridlock became a problem only after the police showed up and after roadblocks were erected. The North Denver Latino community perceived police actions not as efforts toward guaranteeing public safety or traffic flow, but as attempts to harass and brutalize Latino youth. One Latino informant commented on the persistence of the cruisers in light of the increased police harassment by stating, "I was filled with pride that our Chicano youths so loved who they are that they didn't hesitate to express it to the world in one big spontaneous show of ethnic pride." During the cultural battles for the streets of North Denver, Latino parents distributed fliers that insisted that "cruzin ain't a crime," and ones which quoted Benito Juarez: "Respect for the rights of others *is* peace" (Nicholson 1996). These efforts are clear attempts to justify the validity of Latino ways of being in the world. Put another way, they attempted to legitimize Latino informal regulation of public space. Chicana activist Nita Gonzales puts it succinctly, insisting, "Our culture is communal, and cruising demonstrates the quality inherent in our culture that embraces community" (Gonzales 2001).

Whereas Latino pro-cruising arguments were rooted in statements of cultural pride and the celebration of diversity as well as efforts to censure racist policing, arguments put forward by white middle-class activists were always rooted in folk devil tropes of deviance, public decorum, and traffic congestion. White neighborhood residents drew parallels with Dionysian social deviance, saying lowrider cruising "has more in common with spring break partying than culture" (Keith 2001). Further revealing the cleft between Latino and notions of public decorum, one anti-cruising advocate insisted:

> Residents of the affected neighborhoods often hear the assertion that they
> must show respect for culture. Respect is a two-way street. The desire to
> spend a quiet weekend at home is no less respectable than the desire to show
> off cars, flirt, see friends, have fun, etc.
>
> *(Keith 2001)*

Explicit in this statement is the central component of middle-class public culture I
have been limning. In gentrifying North Denver, middle-class residents regarded
streets as vital components of predictable and unobtrusive mobility, not as sites
of public performance (Sennett 1976). By extending this particularity to the overarching theme of this book, we see how a focus on Complete Streets affords the equitable
mobility of all sorts of transportation modes between all sorts of urban amenities,
while disregarding and even admonishing the use of *completed* streets as public space.

Formal regulation of cruising

Roadblocks and anti-cruising police patrols were intended to move cruising to
other locations, preferably further west to the bordering suburban municipalities.
The police strategy was clear: "eliminat[e] cruising on West 38th Avenue, by
moving it further on" (Miniclier 1991). An important component of this strategy
was a noise ordinance written specifically to target cruisers. Further components
of the strategy included the installation of barriers blocking side streets, which
prevented cruisers from turning off of West 38th Avenue until they reached the
city limits, and the micromanaging of public behavior through strict enforcement
of all moving, parking, loitering, and trespass violations during weekend nights
along this cruising strip. Consequently by the mid-1990s, lowrider cruising shifted
from a five-lane arterial—West 38th Avenue—into the surrounding neighborhood
streets and into neighborhood parks, into places where anti-cruising rhetoric gained
even more traction. Unable to cruise as a part of the everyday practice of culture,
lowriders began to converge en masse during the weeklong Cinco de Mayo
celebrations in May. Eventually, the enormous crowds drawn to this event justified
yet another substantial increase in police discipline.

   Although cruising per se was not illegal, as HUNI's letter-writing campaigns
made clear, disgruntled residents sought to enact codes that would render the act
of cruising illegal. The noise ordinance mentioned above was written specifically
as a component of the general disturbing-the-peace code. Under this code police
are given power to cite drivers whose stereos can be measured at 55 decibels at a
distance of 25 feet (Briggs 1990b). In November 1990, Denver City Council voted
13-0 to amend the disturbing-the-peace ordinance by adding a car-radio noise rider
to the disturbing-the-peace ordinance. Drafted specifically to "curb the cruising
problem" (Briggs 1990a), this rider stipulates that in order to operate a car stereo
at a volume louder than 55 decibels, one needs to obtain a 10 dollar permit or pay
a 50 dollar fine if cited.

   Obvious to most police officers and to the dismay of the anti-cruising lobby,
the noise rider was and remains difficult to enforce. Consequently, mid-decade

efforts to curb cruising were based in outright racial profiling as well as temporary and permanent urban design and traffic calming/control measures. Concerted efforts to render cruising illegal continued. In 1998, Colorado's state legislature debated the merits of two bills intended to eliminate cruising (Young 1998). House Bill 1027 intended to ban the behavior outright by proposing to make driving past the same location more than twice in any two-hour period between 7:00 p.m. and 3:30 a.m. illegal. Senate Bill 34 was designed to ban lowriders from all Colorado streets. Its language rendered illegal any raised or lowered suspension systems that could pose a danger to other vehicles.

Arguments for both bills centered on the rational management of traffic flow, emergency vehicle access, and the inappropriateness of certain public cultural practices. The bills' authors insisted that, "neighborhood residents have the right to peace and quiet and the right of access to their homes." Police representatives argued the new ordinances would be "additional tools to help enforce traffic violations." Those against the bill pointed out its racist overtones, insisting that the bills criminalized a particular type of person engaging in a culturally specific activity. American Civil Liberties Union lawyers argued that both bills "leave too much room for a police officer to define unnecessary driving or legitimate purposes and open too many possibilities for discrimination." Consequently, both House and Senate bills were killed in committee. Despite concerted multi-scaled efforts, the practice of lowrider cruising could not be criminalized.

In the end, a potent combination of extreme traffic code enforcement and racial profiling worked to eliminate lowriding from North Denver streets. Paradoxically, legitimation of racial profiling can be traced to an African American Denver mayor, Wellington Webb. Denver's mayor between 1993 and 2001, Webb was notoriously hard on crime; effects of his stance undulated through the city's African American and Latino neighborhoods. According to some, during Webb's mayoralty, "the Denver Police Department did not fear accountability" (Hermon 2004). Blatant disregard for social justice is evidenced by Webb's gang list, Denver's equivalent of the FBI most wanted list that included two-thirds of all of Denver's black males between the ages of 12 and 20. In all, 97 percent of the individuals on this list were either African-American or Latino (ibid.).

As mentioned above, a primary component of police anti-cruising protocol was the use of barricades to control traffic. In the early 1990s, during weekend nights, once drivers were on West 38th Avenue, they could not get off until they reached the city of Westminster (Jackson 1991). The barriers were but one component of a complex if lopsided strategy of spatial discipline. Latinos were always the focus. For example, during one summer weekend in 1991, Denver police issued 296 tickets for various minor moving violations committed overwhelmingly by Latinos driving lowriders (Gottlieb 1991). Irrespective of claims voiced by the Latino community that the crackdown on Latino youth was not only unfair but also violated their civil rights, police officers insisted that disproportionate traffic control protocols were necessary to reduce the probability of violent crime. Similarly skewed traffic control procedures continued throughout the decade. To illustrate, during weekend nights in 1996, along the 2.6-mile cruising strip of West 38th Avenue, one would find over 80 police cars, various tactical command posts, foot officers donning full riot gear, barricades, helicopter patrols, and motorcycle units (Nicholson 1996). Interestingly, though justifying this remarkable show of paramilitary force with anti-gang tropes, the overwhelming majority of citations were written for moving violations. Importantly, lowriders were not cited for major moving violations such as running red lights or speeding, but for minor infractions including: obstructing an intersection, obstructing traffic, driving without headlights on, cracked wind-shields, illegal turns, sitting on cars in motion, hanging out of cars, hanging objects or body parts out of moving vehicles, failing to signal, hanging objects such as a rosary from rearview mirrors, not coming to a complete stop, stopping in the pedestrian strip, and operating a vehicle with a broken taillight (Callahan 1996).

Lowrider cruising is reproduced in public practice. Rendering this practice difficult if not impossible changed the publicness of North Denver streets. Many Latino long-timers seem to think that cruising faded because kids simply tired of the hassle of constantly dealing with the police, with getting ticketed or arrested, with having their cars impounded. My informants insisted that a decade of racial profiling and police harassment played a significant role in eliminating the public practice of lowrider cruising from the streets of North Denver. Lowriding today is a shadow of its former self.

There is one more element of formal regulation that requires attention: urban design. The use of urban design to regulate behavior is best illustrated through the City of Denver's redesign of an entire Northside park, Sloan's Lake Park, to curb cruising. Ironically, in the 1950s this park was designed to facilitate driving within its boundaries. As such, it featured gently curving internal roads and was dotted with many internal parking lots. For both the white cruisers in the 1950s and the Latino lowriders in the 1980s and 1990s, Sloan's Lake was always a park to drive to and to drive within. As I have shown, who is doing the driving matters a great deal. According to a Denver Parks and Recreation employee, by the late 1980s and early 1990s "lowriding was becoming a real problem, a nightmare in fact." The Parks and Recreation Department initially responded by barricading the entrances to the internal roads during weekend nights. In the early 2000s, the entire park circulation system was redesigned and reconstructed to eliminate cruising; the internal roads were replaced with a system of walking and cycling trails. The language and intent of the Sloan's Lake Master Plan best encapsulate the persistence of Denver's zero-tolerance policy toward cruising. Parking lots were deemed a major problem, contributing to the presence of noise, litter, and in the words of the Master Plan, "unsavory activities associated with certain parking lot users" (DPR 2002). Naming cruising as highly disruptive to other park activities, the plan clearly called for specific design measures to eliminate its practice in the park including: one-way traffic flow, on-street parking used as a traffic-calming device, the installation of a bike lane, and raised crosswalks, which pose a significant road hazard to lowered vehicles. The most significant attempt to remove cruising from the park was the removal of the entire south internal street-loop (Figures 7.1 and 7.2).

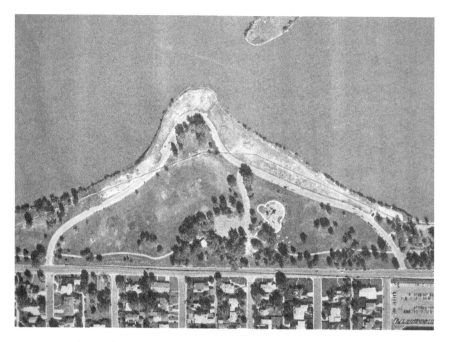

FIGURE 7.1 The south loop of Sloan's Lake Park as a "cruisable" street

Source: Denver Parks and Recreation Archive.

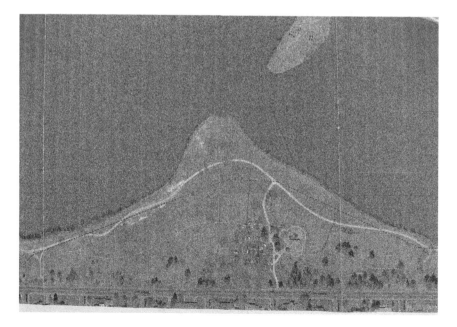

FIGURE 7.2 The redesigned south loop as a walking path

Source: Denver Parks and Recreation Archive.

Reconfiguring the park, urban designers transformed the internal road system's south loop by incorporating it into a lake-encircling walking path. Important to consider here is that the reprogramming of this large North Denver Park facilitated certain activities, namely walking, jogging, and cycling—normalized in mainstream middle-class cultural and spatial practice and constituent parts of Complete Streets discourses—while incontrovertibly frustrating lowrider cruising—an activity authenticated and legitimized in Latino cultural and spatial practice. Put another way, the city drastically altered Sloan's Lake Park, *completing* it for middle-class consumption.

Space and the rights-rift over streets

Henri Lefebvre (1991) theorized that social space is a product of three mutually informing components: (1) spatial practice; (2) conceived space; and (3) lived space. For Lefebvre, spatial practice is empirical human action and inaction in Euclidean space. It is directly sensible and observable, the medium and outcome of human activity and experience. My notion of public practice fits neatly into Lefebvre's concept of spatial practice. In addition to an empirical, observable three-dimensional space, he theorizes two abstract spaces. Lefebvre's model of conceived space is a totalizing abstract view of space assumed by planners, social engineers, architects, and politicians. As such, conceived space is the space of domination, surveillance and the exercise of formal mechanisms of power. Formal regulation can be considered a component of conceived space. Finally, Lefebvre theorized lived space as a poetic moment of human spatial experience. It is what we imagine social space to be, from both aesthetic and ethical standpoints, as we engage with it. Enlivening lived space by focusing on informal regulation, specifically by exploring the production and reproduction of Latino culture and the construction of the lowriding folk devil, I built on this concept by considering how public space is regulated and sanctioned by those who produce it.

In this chapter I have shown how formal and informal regulations have denuded the public practice of a component of Latino culture and in so doing changed North Denver's streets from spaces wherein Latinos publicly practiced their culture into spaces suited for middle-class cultural practices and preferences such as predictable mobilities and Complete Streets. Lefebvre proves helpful here too. In formulating his notion of *the Right to the City*, he insisted that people not only have the right to work and housing but also to public dignity and, importantly, the right to one's culture (Lefebvre 1996). Though guaranteed in the United Nations Charter on Human Rights (UN 2012), the right to practice culture is often not backed with official obligations to satisfy such cultural rights. I argue that the right to practice culture for North Denver Latinos was ignored and eventually stripped by official regulation, media discourse, and urban design.

How this happened becomes clearer when we take a closer look at what exactly constitutes a right. Rights always entail obligations. The philosopher John Searle reminds us of the futility of making claims to rights without recognizing that every claim to a right is a claim against someone or against an institution (Searle 1995). To illustrate, the right to free speech is a claim against the government; its very recognition obligates a State not to intervene in the speech acts of its citizenry. In everyday speech, rights are often demanded. However, they are far more complicated than passionately voiced requests. Rights are relational; they cannot be demanded or granted without legally obligating a person or an institution to satisfy them.

Rights-claims and subsequent obligations do not exist in a static relation; instead they lie along a flexible continuum of formal regulations. The closer a rights-claim is to formal mechanisms to satisfy it, such as the middle-class claim to the right to peace and quiet, the greater chance that it will be satisfied. Conversely, the further a rights-claim lies from formal mechanisms, such as the claim to be able to publicly practice culture through lowriding, the less chance that it will be satisfied. I call this dynamic the *rights-rift*: a disconnect between rights attached to people and the regulation of people's behavior. To illustrate, while Latinos retain the right to their culture, many lost the legal grounds to practice that culture because the behavior of cruising was rendered impossible through urban design and spatial discipline. On the other hand, the rights-rift closed for members of the middle class, who claimed the right to practice the behaviors of enjoying peace and quiet and navigating orderly streets. Consequently, North Denver streets slowly changed from spaces marked by music, cruising, and spontaneous interaction to highly regulated spaces that facilitated predictable mobilities and a middle-class notion of livability.

Positioning the notion of the right cultural practices in the rift between a term I explored at length, *la vida pública*, and the woolly term *livability* require further attention. By foregrounding safe and predictable streets, I elided a fundamental driver of contemporary gentrification. Gentrifiers are not staid creatures that slip unnoticed into swank residences to recharge before quietly commuting back to the office. They too want to party and hang out. It follows that gentrifying neighborhoods tend to be replete with trendy restaurants, bars, boutiques, and coffee shops. Today in North Denver, there is plenty to do and much noise is made doing it. The salient point here is that deconstructing the spatiality of trendy neighborhood amenities *vis-à-vis* performative public spaces broadens our understanding of livability. Whose livability, and where it happens, matter a great deal. Complete Streets policies leave out much of the city. They privilege the mobility of diverse modes of transportation between amenities as the primary function of streets. This aligns perfectly with neighborhood development plans that foster livability—lively commercial centers linked to leafy residential areas by Complete Streets. On the other hand, *la vida pública* brazenly positions a diverse publicness in the middle of the street. Expanding this notion of public life in Complete Streets rhetoric would require policy-makers to include not only varied modes of transportation but also wide-ranging public practices in neighborhood and transportation plans. As it stands, contemporary Complete Streets rhetoric, like the historical curbing cruising efforts, widens the rights-rift for the working class and closes it for the middle class.

Critically, I suggest that the dislocation of Latino practice from streets and the gentrification of North Denver are interrelated. In so doing, I highlight a non-economic driver of gentrification. Near the beginning of this chapter I suggested that an award-winning pedestrian bridge completed North Denver streets. Every so often the phrase "This is Gentrification" is spray-painted on one of this bridge's trusses, structural elements normally kept gleaming white by Denver's anti-graffiti task force. Obviously a bridge cannot be an urban process; however, it can facilitate gentrification. It works to do so by continually privileging the notion of streets as paths for diverse transportation modes between connected places over the idea of streets as public spaces that facilitate the connection of diverse practices.

When focusing on movement and connection, most gentrification scholarship highlights residential displacement. However, neighborhood change is propelled by more than economic mechanisms. Often following a calculus marginally related to property valuation, people simply choose to relocate (Freeman 2005). According to real estate broker informants, some Latinos sold their homes to cash in on rising real estate prices. In other cases, some Latino families left North Denver in order to remove their children from the influence of its street gangs. I learned that several Northsiders relocated because they no longer felt at home in North Denver's public spaces. Some moved simply because, as one former resident phrased it, "*el barrio* became too quiet, too monotonous, too lifeless." I argue that the elimination of lowrider cruising—a markedly loose, capricious, and animated practice—facilitated the replacement of vibrant, *barrio*-inscribed, public spaces with calm, orderly, and predictable conduits. Northside streets, once places for Latino residents, became paths for neighborhood newcomers. Latinos who came to feel uncomfortable publicly practicing their culture moved away, while people who value quiet and predictable streets moved in. Though certainly not the only factor in its gentrification, delegitimizing and disciplining lowriding facilitated changing the ethno-racial composition of the Northside. An historical deconstruction, this chapter makes manifest the need for additional scholarship to tease out and analyze relationships between gentrification and the design, use, and regulation of city streets.

References

Alvarez, L., 2008. *The power of the zoot: Youth culture and resistance during World War II*. Berkeley, CA: University of California Press.

Atkinson, R., 2003. Domestication by cappuccino or a revenge on urban space? Control and empowerment in the management of public spaces. *Urban Studies*, 40, 1829–1843.

Best, A., 2006. *Fast cars, cool rides: The accelerating world of youth and their cars*. New York, NY: New York University Press.

Betancur, J., 2011. Gentrification and community fabric in Chicago. *Urban Studies*, 48, 383–406.

Briggs, B., 1990a. Car-radio noise bill gets loud city yea. *The Denver Post*, Tuesday, November 20.

Briggs, B., 1990b. Proposed law would limit noise level of car stereos: mobile music lovers face a daily, $10 noise permit. *The Denver Post*, Wednesday, November 14.

Brown-Saracino, J., 2009. *A neighborhood that never changes: Gentrification, social preservation, and the search for authenticity*. Chicago, IL: University of Chicago Press.

Calhoun, C., and Sennett, R., 2007. Introduction. In: C. Calhoun and R. Sennett, eds. *Practicing culture*. New York, NY: Routledge.

Callahan, P., 1996. Public meeting set on cops' crowd control: civilian review board responds to complaints. *The Denver Post*, Thursday, May 23.

Chappell, B., 2010. Custom contestations: lowriders and urban space. *City and Society*, 22, 25–47.

Chappell, B., 2012. *Lowrider space: Aesthetics and politics of Mexican American custom cars*. Austin, TX: University of Texas Press.

Cohen, S., 2002. *Folk devils and moral panics: The creation of the mods and rockers*. London: Routledge.

Cresswell, T., 1996. *In place/out of place: Geography, ideology and transgression*. Minneapolis, MN: University of Minnesota Press.

DPR 2002. *Sloan's Lake Park Master Plan*. In Denver, C. A. C. O., ed., Denver, CO.

Duran, R., 2011. Racism, resistance and repression: the creation of Denver gangs, 1924–1950. In: A. Aldama, ed. *Enduring legacies: Ethnic histories and cultures of Colorado*. Boulder, CO: University Press of Colorado.

Freeman, L., 2005. Displacement or succession?: Residential mobility in gentrifying neighborhoods. *Urban Affairs Review*, 40, 463–491.

Geis, G., 2002. Ganging up on gangs: Anti-loitering and public nuisance laws. In: R. Huff, ed. *Gangs in America III*. Thousand Oaks, CA: Sage Publications.

Gonzales, N., 2001. Cruising on Cinco de Mayo: A celebration or a nuisance? PRO Embrace our youth, our fiesta. *The Denver Post*, April 29.

Gottlieb, A., 1991. 296 tickets issued in cruising crackdown: W. 38th businesses, residents complain about traffic, noise. *The Denver Post*, Tuesday, May, 21.

Green, C., 1996. Hooligans don't know "culture". *The Denver Post*. May 21.

Hermon, G.J.R., 2004. Community development and the politics of deracialization: The case of Denver, Colorado, 1991–2003. *Annals of the American Academy of Political and Social Science*, 594, 143–157.

Jackson, R., 1991. Cruising curbs begin Friday on West 38th. *Rocky Mountain News*, (CO), Tuesday, May 14.

Keith, H., 2001. Cruising on Cinco de Mayo: A celebration or a nuisance CON noise, intrusions unjustified. *The Denver Post*, Sunday, April 29.

Langegger, S., 2013. Viva la Raza: A park, a riot, and neighborhood change in North Denver. *Urban Studies*, 50.

Lefebvre, H., 1991. *The production of space*. Malden MA: Blackwell Publishing.

Lefebvre, H., 1996. The right to the city. In: E. Kofman and E. Lebas, eds. *Henri Lefebvre: Writings on cities*. Malden, MA: Blackwell Publishing.

Lefebvre, H., 2003. *The urban revolution*. Minneapolis, MN: University of Minnesota Press.

Massey, D., 1994. *Space, place, and gender*. Minneapolis, MN: University of Minnesota Press.

Miniclier, K., 1991. W. 38th cruising facing a bruising. *The Denver Post*, Tuesday, May 14.

Nicholson, K., 1996. Cops take cruising safeguards: Citizens join efforts to forestall troubles. *The Denver Post*, May 11, 1996.

Richardson, M., 1982. Being-in-the-market versus being-in-the-plaza: Material culture and the construction of social reality in Spanish America. *American Ethnologist*, 9, 421–436.

Romer, D., Jamieson, K., and Aday, S., 2003. Television news and the cultivation of fear of crime. *Journal of Communication*, March, 88–104.

Searle, J., 1995. *The construction of social reality*. New York, NY: The Free Press.

Sennett, R., 1976. *The fall of public man*. New York, NY: W.W. Norton and Company.

Skelton, T., and Valentine, B., 1998. *Cool places: Geographies of youth cultures*. New York, NY: Routledge.

Smith, N., 1996. *The new urban frontier: Gentrification and the revanchist city*. London: Routledge.

Soja, E., 2000. *Postmetropolis: Critical studies of cities and regions*. Malden, MA: Blackwell Publishing.

Staeheli, L., 2010. Political geography: Democracy and the disorderly public. *Progress in Human Geography*, 34, 67–78.

Staeheli, L., and Mitchell, D., 2008. *The people's property?: Power, politics, and the public*. New York, NY: Routledge.

UN, 2012. Universal Declaration of Human Rights [online]. Available from: www.un.org/en/documents/udhr/ [Accessed July 12, 2012].

Valle, V., and Torres, R., 2000. *Latino metropolis*. Minneapolis, MN: University of Minnesota Press.

Venkatesh, S., 2006. *Off the books: The underground economy of the urban poor*. Cambridge, MA: Harvard University Press.

Young, I., 1990. *Justice and the politics of difference*. Princeton, NJ: Princeton University Press.

Young, R., 1998. Curbs on cruising collide with foes. *The Denver Post*.

Zukin, S., 2010. *Naked city: The death and life of authentic urban places*. Oxford: Oxford University Press.

Zukin, S., 2011. Reconstructing the authenticity of place. *Theory and Society*, 40, 161–165.

8

RECRUITING PEOPLE LIKE YOU

Socioeconomic sustainability in Minneapolis's bicycle infrastructure

Melody Hoffmann

Introduction

Research suggests that there is a link between bicycling and the socioeconomic status of a city. Richard Florida (2011, 2012) describes riding a bicycle as a signifier of the "creative class"[1] and suggests that cities where people bike commute have more affluent and highly educated residents, and fewer residents with working-class jobs. The creative class and its members' expendable income have become desirable to cities across the United States. Cities that once built bicycle infrastructure to promote environmentally friendly lifestyles now build it to attract young, educated workers. This chapter provides evidence of this shift and explores its implications for equity and justice in the twenty-first-century city. The City of Minneapolis, its bicycle advocacy organizations, and a bustling bicycle culture serve as a case study in this chapter. Minneapolis has closely followed Portland, Oregon, as a top bicycling city due to its commitment to building off-street bicycle trails and bicycle lanes.

Discussing the power dynamics between Complete Streets rhetoric and bicycling is not a new phenomenon. As noted in Chapter 1, the term "Complete Streets" was originally used in 2003 to "convey the need to include bicycling in transportation planning." Although the City of Minneapolis does not overtly utilize Complete Streets terminology,[2] particular values of having Complete Streets are upheld in the mainstream bicycle advocacy organizations. It is worth noting that in Minneapolis, bicycle advocacy organizations work in tandem with the local government.[3] It is not uncommon for the city's and advocates' bicycle planning agendas to be one and the same. Through local organizations, advocates continually work towards making streets complete for bicyclists. For example, the Minneapolis Bicycle Coalition has an impressive record in filling county-led transportation planning meetings with residents to demand bicycle lanes.[4] As is made clear in this book, the definition of a Complete Street is up for contestation and interpretation.

My findings suggest that both the City of Minneapolis and advocacy organizations operationalize *their* definition of a Complete Street, a definition that does not necessarily resonate with other residents. This result expands upon Zavestoski and Agyeman's definition of inequality in Chapter 1; transportation inequality functions to "move privileged people using privileged modes of transportation." Additionally I have found that it is not always about *what* the privileged mode of transportation is, but *where* that mode of transportation is prioritized. In my observations of bicycle advocacy and planning in Minneapolis, a particular brand of bicyclist now has power in the city to make important decisions regarding how our streets look.

The city's focus on making it attractive in strategic ways reflects a distinguishing marker of young creative workers: they do not move for jobs, they move for the city. This trend benefits cities competing for creative talent, or, as Florida (2005, p. 3) argues, "Today, the terms of competition revolve around a central axis: [the] ability to mobilize, attract, and retain human creative talent."[5] This form of recruitment is a significant characteristic of young creative workers; it is not uncommon for them to decline a job promotion that requires relocation because they would rather continue to live in a "hip" city. To make it cool for the creative workforce to live in Minneapolis, the city has chosen to engage in strategic sustainability projects. They are strategic in that the focus is on livability, not radical environmental solutions that perhaps would be more connected to sustainability (Krueger and Gibbs 2007). One of these livable city sustainability projects is making Minneapolis a top city for bicycling.[6]

Most Minneapolis bicyclists would agree that former Mayor R.T. Rybak was one of the biggest bicycle advocates in the city government.[7] Even among the general population, Rybak is known for being extremely supportive of bicycle transportation. He was responsible for creating a bicycle coordinator position in the city government, a position that Rybak implies was not common in other city governments.[8] He also rallied to bring neon green bicycles to Minneapolis, otherwise known as the Nice Ride bike share program: an amenity popular in Europe but not present in the U.S. until Minneapolis's program.[9] Rybak's support for bicycle infrastructure allows him to build his environmental credentials and simultaneously use these credentials as a sales pitch for why Minneapolis is hip, eco-friendly and thus a great place for the creative class.

Rybak is not shy about how economic competition with other U.S. cities, vis-à-vis recruiting young talent, is connected to sustainable city living. If the goal is to be the most "green" city filled with creative workers, then Minneapolis is certainly trying to win. Rybak explains, "Our very public bike culture has been an enormous asset in attracting talented people here. Not just in the bike fields but in advertising, in financial services, the arts, politics."[10] Rybak sees economic potential for bicycle infrastructure through his claim that Minneapolis is a frontrunner in re-envisioning the city scape:

> It's completely clear to me that we're in a midst of a total revolution in the way we get around. Most public governments haven't quite gotten anywhere

nearly where the public is at on this. We [the city government] have. So, I recognize that congestion is up, global warming, gas prices, all add to the fact that we're reinventing the American city that's going to be much more pedestrian and bike-oriented.

Rybak seamlessly conflates increasing sustainable transportation with competing with other city governments and appears proud that his government is keeping up with public demand for a less car-centric city. This approach to sustainability mirrors the observations made by Jonas and While (2007, p. 129), who argue that "the new urban politics is as much about sustainability as it is about urban competition."

Rybak's sentiments also reflect perhaps the most genius part of utilizing bicycle infrastructure to promote economic growth in specific industries: the ability to hide it behind sustainability messaging. This sustainability messaging is successful in part because climate change poses a serious threat to large cities and addressing these realities allows city governments to adopt an eco-friendly political identity. Moreover, the concept of sustainable development is an "empty signifier" wherein it appears to be addressing environmental concerns but in effect "is largely deployed to maintain the priority of economic growth for achievement of global competitiveness" (Gunder and Hillier 2009, p. 20).

"Greening" cities through sustainability projects is "part of neoliberal competition between global urban centers," but this wave of greening comes at a price because sustainability ensures its benefits are distributed unequally (McDonogh et al. 2011, p. 113). Sustainability practices negatively impact specific social groups and so it is important to consider who benefits and who loses from these practices (ibid.). Thus, there is potential for sustainability marketing through bicycle infrastructure to be a gain for some and a loss for others. In urban planning, the sustainability concept has replaced concepts such as equality and social justice that were once planners' "ideological pivot" (Davidson 2010, p. 391). This rhetorical shift has had a negative impact on people who most need transportation resources (Portney 2003; Bullard et al. 2004).

In this chapter, I argue Minneapolis builds bicycle infrastructure to recruit young, educated workers with little regard to the infrastructure's impact on residents who fall outside of that demographic. My argument is supported by interviews with the mayor, members of a local bicycle advocacy organization, and a realtor in a "bike-friendly" part of town. As a bicycle commuter in Minneapolis for four years, I engaged in participant ethnography of the bicycle infrastructure and numerous bicycle planning meetings, including a public meeting about a new bike path in an area of town with low bicycling rates. This research is contextualized through theories and concepts of the creative class, environmental gentrification, and urban sustainability. The case study will explore the City of Minneapolis's economic-driven approach to bicycle infrastructure planning, the construction of a greenway that changed the demographic landscape of an old railroad corridor, and the current plans to build a new greenway in a neighborhood not typically prioritized for transportation amenities.

Although bicycling as a form of transportation has been historically perceived as a radical political act (Furness 2010), bicycling politics are becoming realigned with neoliberal and economic interests. In Minneapolis, I see this realignment happening in two ways: first, the city tends to place new bicycle amenities in areas that already have a burgeoning bicycle culture; and second, *if* bicycle infrastructure is placed in an area with a low level of bicycling, the *primary* reason is for economic growth, not to support the needs of underserved people. The bicycle then becomes a rolling signifier of environmental friendliness and bourgeois leisure, doing economic work that has little to do with progressive bicycle politics such as increased mobility for *all* people regardless of class position.

Sustainability and social justice: the oil and water of transportation planning

Although there has been much critical scholarship done on urban sustainability, very little has specifically focused on how bicycle infrastructure planning fits into the sustainability narrative. It is important to bring bicycles into this discussion because the skepticism scholars have revealed about sustainability practices, *vis-à-vis* development and motorized transportation planning, is also being echoed by people impacted by bicycle infrastructure planning.

Urban geographers and political scientists tend to come to similar conclusions in their studies on sustainable communities and development, finding that sustainability initiatives are not meant for a diversity of users. This is largely due to the oft-repeated observation that people involved with sustainability projects typically ignore broader social concerns, especially justice and equity. Sustainability initiatives are often crafted for middle- to upper-class populations and the needs of other communities are rarely considered (Krueger and Gibbs 2007). Government intervention that utilizes transportation planning to produce sustainable communities is contingent on particular communities' transportation needs, such as bus routes to local factories or schools. This requires a continual process of crafting strategies to specific communities (Horan *et al.* 1999).

Scholarship that is critical of local sustainability initiatives claims that "sustainability is motivated by an expressed desire for middle-class White residents of cities to systematically undermine efforts at racial, ethnic, or socioeconomic integration" (Portney 2003, p. 167). In regards to whether a city takes socioeconomic equity into consideration with sustainability projects, Portney found that:

> Sustainable cities initiatives in the U.S. do not seem to take [equity issues] very seriously. Perhaps it would be more accurate to say that as practices in most cities, equity issues do not appear to be integral parts of cities' definitions of sustainability.
>
> *(ibid., p. 175)*

If city planners *did* consider how equity and sustainability intersect, they would also have to consider how sustainability projects intersect with gentrification.

Although not always talked about together, gentrification can impact access to transportation, including the "environmentally friendly" options of bus lines and bicycle lanes. Sustainability planning can be understood as a gentrification tool that enables upwardly mobile populations to move into historically underserved, working-class areas. Referred to as *environmental* gentrification, this process works by building upon the successes of the environmental justice movement and appropriating its goals to serve upper-class interests and displace low-income residents (Checker 2011). Environmental gentrification is marketed as a "green lifestyle" which is attractive to affluent and "eco-conscious" residents (ibid., p. 212). This type of neighborhood improvement is typically presented as "positive and politically neutral" and may mask "unequal urban development" (ibid., p. 212).

Inequity in urban development can easily be operationalized through a city's transportation planning. Scholars committed to transportation justice tend to focus on equity issues in mass transportation and vehicle-centric roadways such as freeways. Case studies suggest that transportation funding, including bus systems and light rail, prioritize the needs of the middle- to upper class (Bullard and Johnson, 1997; Bullard, *et al.* 2004; Agyeman 2005). Although counterintuitive, mass transportation systems often privilege those less dependent on public transportation with better resources. Furthermore, government transportation planners often destroy neighborhoods for freeway construction (Gibson 2007); neighborhoods typically populated with people less likely to travel on freeways. Classism and racism are embedded in transportation programs, and unfortunately transportation injustice has also made its way into bicycle infrastructure planning.

Transportation justice scholars suggest that the demographics of transportation users directly impact the funding and attention city governments allocate for the upkeep of the infrastructure. There "appears to be an unwritten rule that the poor and people of color transit riders deserve fewer transit amenities than white suburbanites who own cars" (Bullard *et al.* 2004, p. 5). It is not a coincidence then that, in moments of urban revitalization, urban planners started paying attention and catering to the urban, white, educated bicyclist with little regard to the needs of day workers, food deliverers, and third-shifters who use bicycles to commute to work. "With demographic changes taking place in the American urban core, biking has come to symbolize white re-population" (Zewde 2011). To extend transportation justice to the bike movement means finding ways to support bicycling in diverse communities (Lugo 2012). My research alerts scholars invested in sustainability and transportation justice that a critical lens needs to be turned upon those responsible for advocating for and planning bicycle infrastructure in urban spaces.

Recruiting people like you: the case study of Minneapolis's bicycle infrastructure

Do Minneapolis city planners and bicycle advocates really promote bicycle infrastructure to attract particular demographics or is this merely a theory based on perceived need and placement of such amenities? There is no need to read between the lines of one of the biggest proponents of and powers behind Minneapolis's bicycle infrastructure. The mayor of Minneapolis, R.T. Rybak, clearly sees a link between building bicycle infrastructure and competing with other U.S. cities for creative talent:

> The key to economic growth is attracting talent. Especially in the creative field, talent is very mobile. [Our bicycle infrastructure] has attracted this wide swath of people to get something they can't find in a freeway-oriented place like Houston. Even in a city with a great reputation like Austin, for attracting cutting edge talent, they are not even in the same league as Minneapolis on bike culture. That gives us a huge competitive advantage.

His sentiment echoes Florida's (2002, 2011) theory that "cutting edge talent" has high economic value to businesses and cities. The quality of place is important to the creative class; Florida (2002) refers to this place as a "people's climate." This climate is not necessarily based on creating things for people to do, but rather on establishing an aura of a vibrant street-level culture. A creative class member does not necessarily need to interact or participate with every element of this climate; rather, the climate sets a general tone that is attractive to the creative class.

For example, the people's climate includes bicycle infrastructure, regardless of how often it is utilized by people. A city with ample bicycle lanes and paths is simply a signifier to the creative class that the city is a high quality place for them to live. I asked Minneapolis realtor Michael Gross whether his clients convey a desire to live by the Greenway, an off-street bicycle trail, regardless of their desire to *utilize* it. Gross responded, "Yes, very often. And when you look at how things are advertised, if they are within four or five blocks from the Greenway it usually ends up on the advertisement . . . [the Greenway] has a high property value."[11] This is part of the city's economic strategy of building a bicycle path in Minneapolis. Not only does the city look eco-friendly in its dedication to building bicycle infrastructure but the infrastructure simultaneously attracts desirable residents and development investors.

Through urban development such as the Greenway and conjoining apartment buildings with high property value, Minneapolis appears to be emerging as the blueprint in recruiting the creative class. Rybak's approach to bicycle infrastructure planning echoes many of Florida's sentiments about the creative class lifestyle. For example, Florida (2002) cites Austin, Texas, as an example of a city that has recruited creative talent via its strategic recruitment and Rybak cited Austin as a clear competitor for attracting the creative class. Rybak even alluded to creating a people's climate, in saying that even though he loves riding his bike and benefits from the infrastructure, he admitted that "it's more about what kind of city we want."

One "benefit" of the people's climate, such as off-road bike paths, is that it is "open to a larger population" (Florida 2002, p. 294). Or put more cynically, the creative class generates growth and others may live off their spoils. Even in the

Greenway's construction, undesirable populations were directly impacted by the bicycle path but there was little concern shown for the impending displacement. In the subsequent section, I will explore how the Midtown Greenway morphed from a homeless and youth hangout into a bourgeois leisure space. Harnessing the latter image, the city is constantly finding new areas to develop bicycle infrastructure, as is the case in North Minneapolis, where the economic benefits of a new Greenway appear to outweigh the needs and values of current residents.

Greenways and environmental gentrification

If you are the mayor, a bicyclist, or someone who lives near it, you may view the Greenway as a pride and joy in Minneapolis's alternative transit amenities. Officially known as the Midtown Greenway, it is certainly impressive in quality and efficiency. Not many U.S. cities have bike paths that allow you to travel for miles in high-density areas without having to interact with vehicle traffic. The Greenway, as most people call it, includes two lanes for bicyclists and one lane for pedestrians. It is the site of a former railroad corridor, and runs east–west for 5.5 miles. The Greenway is popular because it connects a large swath of neighborhoods and rarely intersects with city streets. Scholars who study bicycle infrastructure usage argue that off-street paths are the most effective in attracting new people to bicycling because of their segregation from vehicular traffic (Baker 2009). Because of its multiple usage potential, the Greenway is an easy sell for diverse lifestyles and is not an obvious marker of environmental or developmental gentrification. The initial construction of the Greenway was even an easy sell to residents because the city conceptualized it as taking over unused space.

Bicycle paths have the potential to "clean up" blighted areas of a city and this certainly was the case for the Greenway. A longtime Minneapolis resident and avid bicyclist, Spencer Haugh, described the space that existed before the Greenway construction: "Urchins and hooligans. And graffiti writers. And awesomeness. I like the Greenway, but it makes me sad. It was a five mile long art gallery" (personal communication, 11 July 2011). The Midtown Greenway Coalition describes the same "awesome" space as once "a trash-filled trench that was a disgrace to our city" (www.midtowngreenway.org). The intentional rhetoric of a disgraceful space follows the pattern of cities using transportation development to improve depressed areas (Nogrady and King 2004). The hooligans who utilized the corridor knew changes would be coming when their graffiti, that usually never got touched, started to be painted over. To many, the tall brick walls and overgrown bushes created a hideaway and an autonomous space. By no means was this type of space desirable in the eyes of a city government. While the underground inhabitants were largely left alone day-to-day, the Greenway construction that started in the early 2000s would eventually oust them. Through the construction of the Greenway, a communal space was taken from the poor, the marginalized, and the defiant and given to a more "civil" group of citizens. It is clear that there were transitional problems, as people who once used to hang out on the tracks learned they were not allowed to any longer. It was a "disgrace to the city" for some, but a place to sleep and socialize for others.

In Minneapolis, this narrative continues with new plans for expanding the Greenway system. Twin Cities Greenways, a non-profit organization, is run by volunteers who promote the construction of "greenway-quality trails" to better connect the Twin Cities.[12] The proposed Greenway in North Minneapolis is a form of environmental gentrification, as exemplified by residents' reactions to the project, the reasons given for constructing the Greenway, and the benefits assumed to come from the Greenway. My interviews with two Twin Cities Greenways board members, one white man and one woman of color, suggest divergent views on building bicycle infrastructure in a diverse, underemployed neighborhood. The existing Greenway system, and its impact on property values, produces concern about the future of North Minneapolis.

The first of ten public meetings in North Minneapolis about the proposed Greenway path suggested future tensions between bicycle advocates and residents. About 15 people attended this meeting, held in September of 2011. Three white people, including myself, were in attendance; the rest were people of color. The meeting was run by Carrie Christensen, a white woman, from Community Design Group, a consulting group involved in many local bicycle projects. The main purpose of the meeting was to present information about and justification for a Greenway and three different proposed designs;[13] the plan for the rest of the meeting was for a brief question and answer period to be followed by meeting attendees being broken into small groups and asked to write down their opinions on the three designs. The planned structure of the meeting was derailed fairly quickly. When Christensen got to the point in the presentation where she presented the three designs, she was peppered with attendees' questions. Many people did not understand the designs, if only because none of the proposed street designs existed in North Minneapolis.

This break in the planned presentation left room for people to ask questions about the larger project. Robert Woods, a community organizer in North Minneapolis, asked about the consulting group. "Where is this information going? How diverse is your staff?" Christensen admitted that Jose, a Latino man, was the planned presenter but he had to go to Peru. She reported that the group employed three white people and two Latinos—two of these employees lived in North Minneapolis. "That's good," Christensen said about the group's demographic. A Black woman attendee responded, "It is?! For you, maybe." Woods continued, "Listen, I'm trying to be cute about [talking to a white person about race issues]." A Black woman confirmed, "We are looking for ethnic diversity and people who live and work in North Minneapolis." Another attendee tried to calm the conversation by reminding people that this was their "chance to add value to the project." Without much group discussion about the Twin Cities Greenways organization, board member Matthew Hendricks offered up his promise to add more diversity to the board.

Other participants pressed Christensen on the funding for the project, who would be hired to build the Greenway, and the current state of bicycle infrastructure in

North Minneapolis compared to their public works necessities. An attendee argued, "It's an insult to throw [bicycle lanes] down on uneven roads. We can't even get our streets plowed, how will the bike paths be maintained?" Another attendee referenced the new bicycle lane on a busy street reporting that the street is down to one lane with bus traffic. "Who did you ask about that?" she asked Christensen. Overall, it was obvious that Christensen was not prepared for an alternative meeting structure to take place as she tried many times to get back to her presentation. She also appeared unprepared to answer the critical questions posed by attendees.

Per the meeting's schedule, attendees were broken up into small groups to discuss the proposed plans. In my small group I worked with Woods, an older Black woman, and a young white woman. We were given a large sheet of paper with a visual of the three designs and asked to put Post-It notes with comments on each design. The older Black woman immediately began questioning the necessity of this project due to larger issues, saying, "If you take my street, and don't plow my alley like usual, then what?" I talked with Woods in more detail about the criticisms he shared with the large group. He told me he majored in urban studies in college, which he summarized as studying "how to control populations." He also argued that city planners' ideas and "our ideas" do not usually match. Woods said that city planning can be used to drive people out. I offered up my own critique to Woods, saying, "I think that these sorts of bike trails can be used to push people out, to clean up certain areas. I mean that is my cynical answer." Woods, nodding along and looking at me with intense, focused eyes responded, "Yeah, but you are right." Checker, who witnessed similar "drama" at a public meeting about a park's planned improvement, argued that this sort of challenge creates a difficult paradox: "Must [low income] residents reject environmental amenities in their neighborhoods in order to resist the gentrification that tends to follow?" (2011, p. 211). The paradox that Checker presents is unanswerable at this moment, especially in light of sustainable urban development following such a predictable, profit-driven pattern. But it is a question that should be at the forefront of discussions with those who are committed to building a more environmentally conscious, just, and equal city.

Matthew Hendricks of the Twin Cities Greenways board responded to concerns about the proposed North Minneapolis Greenway by suggesting that people think through the ways lower-income people will truly benefit from the new bicycle infrastructure. "I think the questions that were asked [at the public meeting] were certainly valid and they were concerns we had as well," Hendricks said.[14] When asked about whether the North Minneapolis Greenway could spur gentrification, he responded that gentrification was a concern the board had as well:

> Gentrification is such a complicated issue because there are pieces of neigh-borhood improvement that everybody wants. Everybody wants to live in a neighborhood with less crime, with property value that is stable, so if you invest in a home it's actually an investment not a mistake . . . You can still want good things for the neighborhood, you just want to make sure everybody has a part of it, it's not displacing a lot of people who live there.

Hendricks reframed the discussion about gentrification by suggesting that someone who lives in a poor neighborhood is not necessarily averse to improving their surroundings. But, one of the "benefits" of improving and/or gentrifying a neighborhood is the increase in property values.[15] This of course is typically only a benefit for property owners. North Minneapolis has seen a sharp increase in foreclosed homes that are then bought up by investors and turned into rental properties. The number of owner-occupied houses is declining in North Minneapolis and so if property values rise, investors are the ones most likely to benefit (Furst 2012).

Another concern raised by residents is the discordance between Twin Cities Greenways touting the raising of property values as a positive outcome of building more Greenways and the issue of rent then being raised for those who do not own houses. Hendricks responded with two points. One, property values are already so low in North Minneapolis that if the Greenway led to an increase in property values, it would be still affordable to live there. "I mean there are homes that are going for 10, 20, 30 thousand dollars that are under foreclosure, that need work, but that's a very affordable home today. Even double that or triple is very affordable." Two, community members using the Greenway to commute to work and to run errands will be saving money. "If your transportation bill goes down by 300 or 400 bucks a month because you can bike downtown easily then you can afford, when your rent goes up by 100 bucks a month, you are still ahead. And you live in a nicer neighborhood." Gross reflected on the planned North Minneapolis Greenway and its impact on access to employment downtown:

> So maybe it does allow for easier access to downtown and maybe for a certain percentage that really does benefit them in their options for jobs, you know? So the economic status is increased. It's not necessarily the case that a poor person remains a poor person always.

Gross's theory is that the North Minneapolis Greenway could possibly *decrease* the likelihood of people moving out because it eases access to downtown and downtown employment. But some North Minneapolis residents are not convinced that they are the ones being considered when new bicycle infrastructure is constructed in their neighborhood.

Hendricks and Gross are working with the assumption that those in North Minneapolis who have access to downtown would then be able to commute to *work* downtown. Debra Stone, the only person of color on the Twin Cities Greenways board, believes that the access is not necessarily envisioned for current residents. According to Stone, North Minneapolis has the highest unemployment rate in the Twin Cities and:

> Where they want to put the Greenway is the most economically challenged area and I would argue not all those people who live in that community, in that neighborhood, in those blocks, are working downtown. If they are working at all.[16]

At the public meeting about the North Minneapolis Greenway, access to downtown was not presented as an incentive to building the bicycle path.

The proposed Greenway brings potential economic benefits and parallel consequences to North Minneapolis's primary residents: the poor, the working class, and people of color. "Maybe it's true that not only does it increase property values but it also increases socioeconomic health of a community. But I would hypothesize that it more pushes [North Minneapolis residents] out," Gross argued. Stone has observed North Minneapolis residents talking about the threat of gentrification and displacement potential of the Greenway:

> We see the gentrification happening right now. I mean, North Minneapolis is very close, it's an ideal situation for downtown Minneapolis so it definitely is a concern for residents up in the North side and I think rightly so . . . research shows that with bikes and Greenways, neighborhoods become safer. They certainly would become more appealing, especially as being so close to downtown, yeah. But who has the jobs downtowns? Not people of color.[17]

What Stone's comment illustrates is not only a literal link between a North Minneapolis Greenway and jobs downtown, but also a concern that the people who have been living in North Minneapolis would not all benefit from this economically driven plan. Stone alluded to a future vision of more affluent people moving up into North Minneapolis due to its increased access to downtown.

If the planned Greenway has potential to contribute to gentrification, then should people who are against such changes be supporting the vision? Although Stone said gentrification is a concern, she also said: "I don't think it should stop us. What it should do is make us more pro-active in making sure that we get our say about what the Greenways are going to look like." Stone's point reiterates that those in neighborhoods with low rates of bicycling do not stand idly by while bicycle advocates come in and plan bicycle infrastructure. Rather, they need to get involved with the planning and remind advocates that not everyone sees bicycle paths as a priority or a desired urban adjustment. The Greenway does have potential to positively impact the neighborhood, as long as the neighbors are part of the planning process. The initial community meeting I attended represented some of the tension that occurs when outsiders come into a neighborhood and plan *around* the community members. Due to this tension, bicycle organizations came together in 2013 to plan more community engagement in North Minneapolis about the Greenway. Currently, Blue Cross Blue Shield is funding a long-term community engagement strategy in an attempt to re-sell the Greenway to skeptical residents.

Conclusion

In this chapter I have presented Minneapolis government rhetoric about bicycle infrastructure, the changing landscape of the Greenway, and plans for a future one, to argue that the city builds bicycle infrastructure to recruit the creative class with little regard to the infrastructure's impact on residents who fall outside of that demographic. This situation also reflects the inequality in privileged people being granted privileged modes of transportation. For example, because of North Minneapolis's systemic poor financial situation and low rates of bicycling, Nice Ride deemed the residents an improper fit to pilot the bicycle share program. *Zero* stations were installed in North Minneapolis during the first year of operation. North Minneapolis would have been a perfectly fine place to pilot the program *because* of its low bicycling rates. In this instance, for purely economic reasons, bicycles were placed where there were plenty of them already. Once again we see the privilege of the creative class operationalized to isolate the poor and working class from bicycle access (Rose 2013).

This narrative about a bike share program in Minneapolis is just one example of subtle yet materially significant consequences of strategically placing bicycle infrastructure in particular places in the city. North Minneapolis residents not only noticed the absence of the neon green bikes but had to demand them before Nice Ride installed any stations. As the Nice Ride bikes roll through North Minneapolis, residents may not identify with them as much as other residents would. Although I do not see this sort of strategic placement of bicycle amenities ending anytime soon, I do want to suggest some approaches to bicycle infrastructure planning that may alleviate some of this tension and disappointment for city residents who have been overlooked in the bicycle infrastructure planning process.

Bicycle advocates involved at the governmental, non-profit, or individual level need to consider alternative visions of what bicycling could look like. Advocates often get frustrated when their plans are not accepted without critique. But in some communities, trash collection and snow removal are more of a concern than a bicycle path. There is a significant amount of race and class privilege associated with bicycle infrastructure and its place in urban planning. As was obvious at the public meeting in North Minneapolis, bicycle advocates need to be acutely aware of how identity markers affect residents' relationship to bicycle infrastructure. It is problematic that white people are coming into North Minneapolis and suggesting very intensely that people need a Greenway. According to Hendricks, no one asked for a Greenway in North Minneapolis. Gross described this approach to urban development by saying, it's "this kind of paternalistic tendency that we know what's good for you, here it is." Bicycle advocates argue that bicycle infrastructure will help solve problems residents currently have: abandoned buildings, low levels of home ownership, unemployment, and poverty. But before advocates go into communities that lack bicycle infrastructure and present different bicycle paths for residents to vote on, it would be worth talking through the beneficial side effects of bicycle infrastructure with residents. The residents may accept the arguments or they may not. It would also serve city planners and advocates well to approach community meetings aware of resident concerns about bicycle infrastructure. There are numerous examples of community meetings across the U.S. wherein the presenters appeared unprepared for critical questions about representation and gentrification. In general, bicycle advocates have a hard time dealing with opposition and in some ways the advocates' perseverance has produced some excellent bicycle amenities across the country. But if a community does not see bicycle infrastructure as a priority, then advocates and city planners need to slow down the plan and work more directly with residents. We have seen this already happen in North Portland (see Chapter 10) and now in North Minneapolis with grant-funded community engagement.

My case study in Minneapolis suggests environmental justice activism is practically silenced in government-sanctioned planning. When residents insist that bicycle infrastructure is a radical political issue, those in power are made uncomfortable. Unfortunately, the creative class reaps the most benefits from bicycle infrastructure. But those who lack political power, such as the residents in North Minneapolis, are reminding bicycle advocates and the city that everyone has a right to a sustainable urban future. The findings in this chapter should be a concern to bicycle advocates and community organizers because if bicycle planning continues to be used as a tool to recruit young "creative talent," then we do a huge disservice to the rest of the community. Those not hailed by Complete Streets visions are not ignorant of their unacknowledged presence. If the *real* reason for planning a North Minneapolis Greenway and decisions about where to place Nice Ride stations were any indication, North Minneapolis residents may expect to be left out of future visions of bicycle infrastructure. And when these residents are *used to* and *expect* to be left out of these conversations, they may automatically reject the idea of the infrastructure on the grounds of their exclusion. Now how complete is that?

Notes

1 Florida (2012) says the distinguishing characteristic of the creative class is its members "engage in work whose function is to create meaningful new forms" (p. 38). Florida argues he is also able to ascertain things about this class, such as their main values— individuality, meritocracy, diversity, and openness (ibid., pp. 56–57).

2 This term is not used in the city's marketing of bicycle culture but the Minnesota government passed a Complete Streets statute (174.75) in 2013, requiring the Minnesota DOT commissioner to "implement a Complete Streets policy."

3 The partnership is also monetary. For example, the city started the non-profit Transit for Livable Communities with the same federal transportation funds that paid for much of the existing bicycle infrastructure.

4 Perhaps the most successful organizing was demanding that Hennepin County move and reconstruct the bicycle lanes on Park and Portland Aves—two conveniently located but dangerous streets for bicyclists (Fawley 2012).

5 My use of Richard Florida's research does not mean I align myself with such scholarship. In fact, I find his methodology and celebration of the creative class to be quite problematic (for a more thorough critique, see Peck 2005). But Florida's work is important here because the City of Minneapolis has dedicated itself to recruiting people under the "creative class" descriptor and Mayor R.T. Rybak discusses Minneapolis as if he is one of Florida's clients. Therefore, to understand Minneapolis's standpoint I found it necessary to use the same economic and cultural theories that underlie the sustainable development.

6 This goal has been relatively achieved as Minneapolis is constantly ranked as the #2 Bicycling City in America, according to *Bicycling* magazine. In 2011, Minneapolis was ranked #1, beating out longtime placeholder Portland, Oregon (Friedman 2011).

7 After 12 years as Minneapolis's mayor, Rybak did not run for another term in the 2013 election.
8 This job position created controversy in Minneapolis because Rybak had recently laid off ten firefighters, citing budget issues (Roper 2011).
9 Rybak is currently a board member of Nice Ride.
10 All quotes from R.T. Rybak come from personal communication with author on 20 May 2012.
11 All quotes from Gross come from personal communication with author on 31 January 2013.
12 This organization is also closely tied to the City of Minneapolis in collaboration on planning and harnessing funding for future greenway projects. Moreover, board members work for the city government and Department of Transportation.
13 The three designs were a bike boulevard, "half and half" where one lane is a greenway and the other lane allows one-way vehicle traffic, and a linear park where the entire street would be turned into a greenway with no vehicle traffic allowed.
14 All quotes from Hendricks come from personal communication with the author on 29 November 2011.
15 On the Twin Cities Greenways website, "Increasing property values" is a listed reason for how a community would benefit from a greenway (*Why Greenways?*, n.d.).
16 All quotes from Stone come from personal communication with the author on 8 August 2012.
17 To be clear, there are plenty of people of color who *do* work downtown—as janitors, food workers at the stadiums, construction workers, and bus drivers. But interestingly Stone's comment suggests that these workers are not the ones coveted by the supporters of the North Minneapolis Greenway project. Here Stone seems to be referring to the creative class sector of labor that is largely void of people of color.

References

Agyeman, J., 2005. *Sustainable communities and the challenge of environmental justice.* New York, NY: NYU Press.
Baker, L., 2009. How to get more bicyclists on the road (online). *Scientific American.* Available from: www.scientificamerican.com/article.cfm?id=getting-more-bicyclists-on-the-road [Accessed 4 September 2013].
Bullard, R.D., and Johnson, G.S., eds., 1997. *Just transportation: Dismantling race and class barriers to mobility.* Gabriola Island, BC: New Society Publishers.
Bullard, R.D., Johnson, G.S., and Torres, A.O., eds., 2004. *Highway robbery: Transportation racism and new routes to equity.* Cambridge, MA: South End Press.
Checker, M., 2011. Wiped out by the "greenwave": Environmental gentrification and the paradoxical politics of urban sustainability. *City and Society*, 23 (2), 210–229.
Davidson, M., 2010. Sustainability as ideological praxis: The acting out of planning's master-signifier. *City*, 14 (4), 390–405.
Fawley, E., 2012. *Great Park and Portland public meeting* (online). Minneapolis Bicycle Coalition. Available from: www.mplsbike.org/blog/posts/great-park-and-portland-public-meeting/ [Accessed 4 October 2013].
Florida, R., 2002. *The rise of the creative class: And how it's transforming work, leisure, community and everyday life.* New York, NY: Basic Books.
Florida, R., 2005. *The flight of the creative class: The new global competition for talent.* New York, NY: HarperCollins Publishers.
Florida, R., 2011. American's top cities for bike commuting: happier, too [online]. *The Atlantic.* Available from: www.theatlantic.com/national/archive/2011/06/americas-top-cities-for-bike-commuting-happier-too/240265/ [Accessed 13 October 2013].

Florida, R., 2012. *The rise of the creative class, revisited.* New York, NY: Basic Books.

Friedman, S., 2011. #1 bike city: Minneapolis (online). *Bicycling.* Available at: www.bicycling. com/news/featured-stories/1-bike-city-minneapolis [Accessed 4 October 2013].

Furness, Z., 2010. *One less car: Bicycling and the politics of automobility.* Philadelphia, PA: Temple University Press.

Furst, R., 2012. Homesteaders are giving way to renters in Twin Cities [online]. *Star Tribune.* Available from: www.startribune.com/local/minneapolis/157667005.html?refer=y [Accessed 28 July 2013].

Gibson, K.J., 2007. Bleeding Albina: A history of community disinvestment, 1940–2000. *Transforming Anthropology* 15 (1), 3–25.

Gunder, M., and Hillier, J., 2009. *Planning in ten words or less: A Lacanian entanglement with spatial planning.* Farnham: Ashgate.

Horan, T.A., Dittmar, H., and Jordan, D.R., 1999. ISTEA and the new era in transportation policy: sustainable communities from a Federal initiative. In: D.A. Mazmanian and M.E. Kraft, eds. *Toward sustainable communities: Transition and transformation in environmental policy.* Cambridge, MA: The MIT Press, 217–245.

Jonas, A.E.G., and While, A., 2007. Greening the entrepreneurial city? Looking for spaces of sustainability politics in the competitive city. In: R. Krueder and D. Gibbs, eds. *The sustainable development paradox: Urban political economy in the United States.* New York, NY: The Guilford Press, 123–159.

Krueger, R., and Gibbs, D., eds., 2007. *The sustainable development paradox: Urban political economy in the United States.* New York, NY: The Guilford Press.

Lugo, A.E., 2012. Planning for diverse use/rs: Ethnographic research on bicycling in Los Angeles. *Kroeber Anthropological Society Papers,* 101 (1), 49–65.

McDonogh, G., Isenhour, C., and Checker, M., 2011. Sustainability in the city: Ethnographic approaches. *City and Society,* 23 (2), 113–116.

Nogrady, B., and King, A., 2004. Transit activism in Steel Town, USA. In: R.D. Bullard, G.S. Johnson, and A.O. Torres, eds. *Highway robbery: Transportation racism and new routes to equity.* Cambridge, MA: South End Press, 121–144.

Peck, J., 2005. Struggling with the creative class. *International Journal of Urban and Regional Research,* 29 (4), 740–770.

Portney, K.E., 2003. *Taking sustainable cities seriously: Economic development, the environment, and quality of life in American cities.* Cambridge, MA: The MIT Press.

Roper, E., 2011. Despite fiscal woes, Minneapolis aims to hire bike coordinator (online). *Star Tribune.* Available from: www.startribune.com/local/minneapolis/128358623.html ?refer=y [Accessed 25 October 2013].

Rose, J., 2013. Shifting gears to make bike-sharing more accessible [online]. National Public Radio. Available from: www.npr.org/blogs/codeswitch/2013/12/12/243215574/ shifting-gears-to-make-bike-sharing-more-accessible [Accessed 22 December 2013].

Why Greenways? [online] Twin Cities Greenways. Available from: www.tcgreenways.org/ why-greenways/ [Accessed 1 November 2013].

Zewde, S., 2011. Biking advocacy and race: where's the disconnect? [online]. Plurale tantum: A new project on identity and urbanism. Available from: http://pluraletantum. com/2011/02/24/biking-advocacy-and-race-wheres-the-disconnect/ [Accessed 1 October 2013].

9

"ONE DAY, THE WHITE PEOPLE ARE GOING TO WANT THESE HOUSES AGAIN"

Understanding gentrification through the North Oakland farmers market

Josh Cadji and Alison Hope Alkon

Introduction

Stanford Avenue runs nearly all the way across North Oakland, California. It breaks off of the I 80 freeway amidst the skyscrapers and chain stores of Emeryville, which stand upon the native Ohlone burial sites. Stanford then glances back across the bay to San Francisco, before heading east. At the other end of the road is Martin Luther King Junior Way, historically a dividing line between black and white, investment, and the lack thereof. The street dead-ends at a patch of grass under the elevated train tracks, where 8-foot tall sculptures of the words "HERE" and "THERE" stand up against the lawn. "HERE" points toward one of Berkeley's most Complete Streets, which includes the Ashby train station, the brand new transit-oriented Ed Roberts Campus, which houses non-profits working with people with disabilities, and the Berkeley Bowl, a 40,000 square foot independent supermarket specializing in fresh produce. "THERE" points toward Oakland, where the street widens and follows under the train tracks. It passes by homes and apartments, some run-down, interspersed with small strips of struggling stores. A few blocks further, MLK flows into Ghost Town, an Oakland neighborhood so named for the high rates of displacement through eminent domain in the 1960s, as well as the large number of shootings in the 1980s.[1]

Like the Oakland side of MLK, Stanford Avenue is a wide street, difficult to cross. Its few traffic lights and stop signs make it an easy choice for cars driving through, rather than to the neighborhood. Bikers and pedestrians—common sights in this flat, sunny locale—avoid this street whenever possible. It is precisely the kind of street that urban planners criticize through the Complete Streets discourse.

And yet on Saturdays, Stanford Avenue brings you to the North Oakland Farmers Market. It is managed by Phat Beets Produce, a food justice organization dedicated to creating a healthier, more equitable food system in North Oakland.

Phat Beets' other projects include a profitable community supported agriculture (CSA) program, a market garden, and neighborhood farm stands connected to health clinics and elementary schools. The produce for these programs comes from the market garden, as well as from farmers of color within the region. The produce is generally cheaper than at more upscale farmers markets in Berkeley and wealthier parts of Oakland, and the fees to participate as a vendor are significantly lower.

Phat Beets has also worked with neighborhood residents to develop the Crossroads Co-op Café, a small, co-operatively owned restaurant adjacent to the farmers market. Phat Beets and other cooperative members fundraised to retrofit a dilapidated neighborhood landmark as a community and commercial kitchen, as well as a home for the organization's office, workshops, and fundraisers. Local residents seeking to start food businesses rotate shifts in the café, and serve up a wide variety of specialties. On any given day, you might find Southern, Japanese, Thai or Ethiopian food, depending on who's cooking. Phat Beets helps to make the café viable by bringing an established customer base each Saturday and promoting the new venue through its various social media outlets. In turn, Crossroads helps to make the farmers market more of a destination. Neighborhood residents tend to walk or bike to the market, do their shopping, and stay for brunch. In the parlance used by Langegger in Chapter 7 of this volume, Phat Beets helps to create the street as a place, rather than a mere path.

Phat Beets' customers differ significantly from those who have historically inhabited the neighborhood. In the early 1900s, North Oakland was a mixed race, working-class area, but in the 1930s, most white residents took advantage of Federal Housing Authority loans and moved to newly constructed housing in the Oakland hills. World War II brought an influx of additional black residents, who were excluded from other parts of the city through racial covenants. Since that time, the neighborhood has been predominantly black, and is well known as the birthplace of the Black Panther Party (Self 2003).

Only in the past 10–15 years have the neighborhood demographics begun to change again. Leona, an African-American long-term resident and vendor at the farmers market, describes the neighborhood's transition:

> [When] white people were moving up into the hills, this area [was] under-handedly zoned off to blacks. Since [whites] were finding other areas to invest and move into, they didn't care. [But] my father predicted that, one day, the white people are going to want this land and these houses again. When their children get older and can't afford those properties in the hills and they're making their start, they're going to look at these houses and want them again. It was absolutely true.

North Oakland's population is shifting for a number of reasons. San Francisco's tech-boom continues to first push younger artsy types, and then the more affluent, towards the east side of the bay. In addition, Oakland is undergoing something of a national publicity boom, and was recently named by Movoto, a major real-estate blog, as the most exciting city in the country (Cross 2013). This draws in new residents, particularly young people, from across the country. Indeed, Phat Beets' organizers, many of whom live in North Oakland, are a multiracial group of mostly young, formally educated, countercultural types of middle-class backgrounds from many parts of the US. Many of them have had to work to develop relationships with long-term residents. Organizers have hired long-term, working-class residents of color as additional market staff, managers, and vendors, and some of them have joined the collective as well. The market's clientele is mostly new, white residents of the neighborhood, as are subscribers to the organization's profitable community supported agriculture program, which subsidizes many of its other activities.

Nonetheless, Phat Beets prioritizes the needs, interests, and visions of long-term residents. The farmers market remains a chance for long-term residents to purchase healthy food, initiate a food-based business in a low-overhead setting, and connect with community activists in a vibrant public place. Phat Beets creates a complete street that offers more than just multiple modes of transportation. It invites participation from a socially, racially, and economically diverse community, and attempts to contend with the neighborhood's history of institutional racism and economic divestment. Moreover it's a chance to use the street as celebration, as a way to create a healthy, vital, and interconnected neighborhood.

This chapter examines Phat Beets Produce and the North Oakland Farmers Market in order to explore the tensions that arise when progressive and even radical middle-class activists seek to create Complete Streets in areas undergoing rapid gentrification. It asks whether and how food justice activism can create economic opportunities for long-term and low-income residents in these areas, giving them a financial and cultural stake in the changes their neighborhood is undergoing. Simultaneously, we ask how food justice activists such as Phat Beets can be implicated in the gentrification process. We argue that despite Phat Beets' intentions to the contrary, the Complete Streets they help to create implicitly signal to young, white, potential neighborhood residents that this area is a good fit for them, encouraging them to settle in the area. Phat Beets organizers have been remarkably reflexive about these tensions, and have responded by initiating creative strategies to further cement their collaborations with long-term residents. Their goal is to craft a role for food justice in promoting economic development without displacement. In doing so, they offer important lessons for planners and policy-makers looking to create Complete Streets that reflect the desires of diverse urban populations, and for low-income communities looking to create livable public spaces while continuing to live in them.

(In)Complete Streets, gentrification, and food justice

In contrast to decades of automobile dominated urban planning, the Complete Streets movement advocates for the development of places equally accessible to many types of users, including bicyclists, pedestrians, people with disabilities, and riders of public transportation. Advocates claim that Complete Streets democratize this important public space, providing what Agyeman (2013) calls "street-level spatial justice." Moreover, advocates argue that Complete Streets hold benefits for the economy by linking residential to commercial destinations, environmental advantages through reduced automobile emissions, and improved public health by enabling walking and bicycling (Smart Growth America n.d.; see also Cutts *et al.* 2009; Day 2006).

The Complete Streets concept is a relatively new idea that compliments many of the tools already present in the planner's lexicon. These include concepts such as the New Urbanism, Smart Growth and sustainable development. All of these models seek to create vibrant streets and contribute to the broader process of place-making, which, according to the Project for Public Spaces "facilitates creative patterns of activities and connections (cultural, economic, social, ecological) that define a place and support its ongoing evolution. Place-making is how people are more collectively and intentionally shaping our world, and our future on this planet" (Project for Public Spaces, n.d.).

Farmers markets are very much aligned with these notions of Complete Streets, Smart Growth, and the like. Advocates similarly stress their economic, environmental, and public health benefits, as well as their potential to create vibrant public places and a strong sense of community. While farmers markets might seem an odd fit for a book primarily concerned with transportation, they share many guiding social, economic and environmental principles with the Complete Streets approach.

In addition, many of the critiques this book aims at the concept of Complete Streets have been made towards farmers markets as well. Farmers markets and other venues dedicated to the promotion of local and sustainable food have long been accused of failing to ask the "*for whom?*" question that guides this volume. Many scholars have noted that farmers markets tend to be white spaces, even when located in more demographically mixed neighborhoods, and that the narratives supporters espouse about why local and sustainable food is important often implicitly draw on white histories and traditions (Slocum 2007; Guthman 2008). Farmers markets, particularly those highlighting sustainably produced food, also tend to be quite expensive, which can compound critiques of elitism. Moreover, farmers market supporters and popular food writers commend market customers for doing the right thing by "voting with their forks" for more sustainable food systems, without acknowledging the wealth and racial privilege that make such purchases more accessible. This has the unintended consequence of promoting a course of action that is far from equally available to all, and can leave low-income people and people of color out of the struggle for sustainable food systems (Alkon 2012). This is one impetus for the rise of the food justice movement, through which organizations like Phat Beets seek to create local food systems in low-income communities and communities of color as a form of resistance to institutional and environmental racism (Alkon and Agyeman 2011).

This chapter suggests an insidious and unintended consequence of even the most progressively minded food justice projects, including Phat Beets: despite its explicit opposition to gentrification and privileging of the needs and views of long-term and low-income neighborhood residents, Phat Beets nonetheless contributes to it. Given that farmers markets and Complete Streets share unacknowledged racial and class connotations, it seems possible that attempts to create Complete Streets in low-income, urban communities of color might similarly appeal to the tastes and cultural proclivities of gentrifiers.

Gentrification

Gentrification is a complex and "politically charged" term indicating "the process by which higher income households displace lower income residents of a neighborhood, changing the essential character and flavor of that neighborhood" (Kennedy and Leonard 2001). Over 40 years of case studies, surveys, ethnographies, and other forms of research on gentrification have examined the processes by which working-class and urban communities become inhabited by middle-class individuals and families looking for affordable housing; how public agencies and private investors target these neighborhoods and economic markets for development; and the implications this has on historic residents in terms of displacement (which is extremely difficult to measure because of the displacement factor itself) (Slater 2006; Lees *et al.* 2013; Quastel, 2009).

New studies on gentrification also employ not only approaches that include political economy and consumption but also political ecology—"the ways in which material relations and uneven resource consumption, concepts of nature, and the politics of environmental management are worked into gentrification processes"— to articulate how discourses of environment are used by the state and its private partners to serve the interests of gentrification (Quastel 2009, p. 697). Despite the lack of literature on how farmers markets intersect with gentrification, an analysis of "eco-gentrification" comes close to explaining the processes that produce gentrification as it relates to "greening," of which farmers markets are one aspect. Eco-gentrification is the "displacement of vulnerable human inhabitants resulting in the implementation of an environmental agenda driven by an environmental ethic" (Dooling 2008, p. 41). Melissa Checker (2011), for example, writes about how environmental justice activists in the Bronx fought for the clean-up of locally unwanted land uses, only to see an influx of new, wealthier and whiter residents to their newly improved neighborhood. These new residents drove up local prices, displacing the very activists who had worked to make the neighborhood so attractive to them.

Many scholars tend to understand gentrification as a process occurring in various waves, though we question the implied linearity of this model. Generally, early gentrification occurred as a result of the post-World War II urban planning policies and principles of the 1940s and 1950s that have come to be known as "urban renewal," which saw federal subsidies fund slum clearance for new housing developments in low-income communities. The creation of new highways that intersected and isolated urban neighborhoods from one another led to suburbanization and subsequent disinvestment from local governments, not coincidentally once people of color remained as whites fled for the suburbs (Cameron 2003).

What most laypeople, including Phat Beets organizers, commonly think of as gentrification consists of progressive and counter-cultural individuals, and later middle-class, predominantly white families, moving into low-income communities of color, using sweat equity to squat buildings or otherwise renovate older units to reside in (Ocejo 2011). These gentrifiers, whom cultural geographer Neil Smith (1996) refers to as middle-class pioneers invading the downtown area of the urban frontier, tend to be white-collar, politically liberal, environmentally friendly, and interested in ethnic and cultural diversity (Quastel 2009, p. 699). Their movements are supported by local government policies and development plans, and city services tend to be elevated once these newcomers arrive (ibid.).

In large cities like San Francisco and New York, this process gives way to so-called super-gentrification. Here, wealthy bankers and financiers re-gentrify surrounding residential areas that were previously gentrified by earlier groups, thus displacing them (Lees 2000, p. 398). Early gentrifiers, through their sweat equity and willingness to move into impoverished and ethnically diverse neighborhoods, signified the "cleaning up" of the neighborhood, therefore making them "safer" and more appealing for the super-gentrifiers to move in (Shaw 2007, p. 90; Smith 1987). It is this dynamic that *The Onion* mocks by reporting that a "recent influx of exceedingly affluent powder-wigged aristocrats [have moved] into the nation's gentrified urban areas [and] is pushing out young white professionals, some of whom have lived in these neighborhoods for as many as seven years" (*The Onion* 2008). In Oakland, super-gentrification has brought a number of development projects, as well as the large-scale purchase of foreclosed homes by speculators, who charge rents that well exceed their mortgages (Glantz 2012).

In part, because it is so difficult to study the displaced, much of the academic literature on gentrification focuses on the consumptive tastes of gentrifiers, and the kinds of businesses they or others create to cater to them. These culturally constructed tastes prioritize authenticity above all else for its distinctiveness from the mundane and mainstream (Zukin 2008). Authenticity can include a "neighborhood's gritty, ethnic and cultural diversity" (Ocejo 2011, p. 286) as well as its "'authentic', historical buildings, converted lofts, walkable streets, plenty of coffeeshops . . . 'organic and indigenous street culture' as well as consumptive patterns that 'reject suburbia' and the "generica" of chain stores and malls" (Peck 2005, p. 745). Farmers markets, often heralded as an alternative to the monocultural corporate food system, fit neatly into this aesthetic. Indeed, while she does not mention farmers markets per se, urban sociologist Sharon Zukin describes how "[new residents'] desire for alternative foods, both gourmet and organic . . . encourages a dynamic of urban redevelopment that displaces working-class and ethnic minority consumers" (1987, p. 724).

Many Phat Beets organizers are among those young, educated, middle-class individuals who have come to a neighborhood searching for this cultural aesthetic. Like many gentrifiers, they are drawn to North Oakland for its urban gardening, alternative lifestyles, radical politics, and cultural diversity. They also share with many gentrifiers a desire for alternative foods, and the collective works to increase these options in the neighborhood. Organizers' goals here, however, are not only to help themselves, but to increase access to healthy food for long-term residents, and to support them in claiming an economic stake in the neighborhood's transformation through the development of food-based businesses. In this way, they are similar to Brown-Saracino's (2004) "social preservationists" who move into gentrifying neighborhoods and seek to become members of the community, while working to preserve a history of which they were never a part.

Phat Beets organizers recognize that gentrification is counter to the organization's mission because it undermines the ability of long-term residents to afford and access the fresh, organic produce they sell to the neighborhood. In addition, Phat Beets has itself become a victim of gentrification, as it recently lost its lease to a wealthier tenant, an anecdote that will be visited later in this chapter. Simultaneously, though, organizers understand that they are visible symbols to investors, developers, city officials, and first-time home buyers that money and resources are flowing back into North Oakland, making it safe for subsequent waves of gentrifiers. Becoming victims of gentrification has strengthened the organization's will to better understand this process and develop resistance to it through food justice activism.

This study has implications beyond farmers markets and food justice activists, including many projects that comprise the Smart Growth, sustainable development and Complete Streets planning initiatives. Phat Beets' experience suggests that efforts to extend such projects to long-term residents of low-income communities of color that are experiencing gentrification may nonetheless serve to empower gentrifiers to feel safe, comfortable, and catered to in their new homes.

Methodology

This chapter is based on nine months of participant observation as an organizer with Phat Beets Produce in 2012, as well as 21 interviews with other organizers and North Oakland Farmers Market vendors. All primary research was conducted by Cadji, with Alkon serving in an advisory role. As a participant observer, Cadji attended Phat Beets meetings, as well as the farmers market each Saturday. He usually stayed the length of the market (from 10 a.m. to 3 p.m.), splitting time between observing and working. Working included answering questions from customers, setting up and taking down equipment, troubleshooting, and helping to pack the Community Supported Agriculture (CSA) box, which subscribers could pick up at the market. Cadji's constant presence facilitated his observations, which allowed him to witness and analyze interactions that transpired there.

Ethnography is the appropriate social science method for researchers seeking to understand those emic perspectives employed by participants in a particular setting and drawing on them to shape etic concepts and frameworks from social science discourses (Pike 1967; Watson-Gegeo 1988). This is precisely what our study seeks to do as it works outward from the perspectives offered by Phat Beets organizers and North Oakland Farmers Market vendors to address academic and other outsider understandings of gentrification and the role that progressive, neighborhood revitalization projects can play in it. In this way, the call and response between emic and etic perspectives resemble Michael Burawoy's extended case method (2009).

In addition to observations, it is important to understand the ways that participants in a research setting understand their own experiences. For this reason, ethnographers often supplement their participant observation with formal and informal interviews. Before beginning this study, Cadji organized with Phat Beets for two years, working in various roles and capacities within the organization, including as Volunteer Coordinator and Community Supported Agriculture Coordinator. When he began to formally conduct research, Cadji started informally interviewing organizers and vendors, either asking them questions as they worked and recording their dialogues or observing and then later taking down notes. He later developed a more formal interview schedule. His sample included vendors, organizers, as well as new and long-term residents (some of whom are vendors and organizers, while others are customers and neighbors). Interviews were audio-recorded and transcribed and lasted an average of one hour. These interviews helped us develop a fuller picture, context, and timeline for understanding the role the North Oakland Farmers Market plays in gentrification, and how individual organizers and vendors are implicated in the process.

Although this is not a study focused on gender, Cadji sought to deploy feminist ethnographic methods in the manner suggested by Alkon (2011). This choice is important because it approaches the research not as the pursuit of some disembodied, value-free "truth" but rather as a form of socially constituted knowledge that could emerge from vendors and organizers in a holistic and systemic way. This approach avoids the notion that researchers can detach themselves from their social positionalities in order to produce an objective depiction of a social environment. Instead, feminist methodologies require researchers to reflect on our own positionalities and their effects on the research process. This allows researchers to better understand, rather than seek to neutralize, the specific historical, social, and political context that informs our subjectivity and the lens from which we look (Bordo 1990).

Cadji identifies as a mixed-race, heterosexual man of Moroccan and Polish descent, while Alkon is a white, straight woman. We also share the economic and educational privilege that allows us to study others within an institutional academic setting, and to earn income from doing so, though Alkon's faculty position is more secure than Cadji's role as a graduate student. In addition, both of us have long been involved with efforts to create sustainable local food systems, and are troubled by the lack of accessibility for low-income communities and communities of color. In response, Alkon spent years working with a farmers market in West Oakland during her dissertation research, and continues to write and teach about food justice. She has also recently joined Phat Beets' advisory board. As a long time organizer with Phat Beets, Cadji shares an emic perspective with many of his peers, and a much stronger sense of familiarity with the vendors. In short, Cadji has been an essential participant in the narrative we have constructed, while Alkon shares demographic similarities with the Phat Beets organizers but offers a more etic perspective.

On intent and effects: gentrification at Phat Beets and the North Oakland Farmers Market

The North Oakland Farmers Market is the kind of lively, vibrant public space that advocates of Smart Growth, sustainable development and Complete Streets initiatives work to create. It is easily accessible by foot or bicycle from every direction, and indeed the limited parking suggests that most constituents use alternate means of transportation. Fresh produce and healthy prepared foods are readily available and sold by regional farmers and local residents. Like many farmers markets, this is a social space, as customers are encouraged to get to know vendors, Phat Beets organizers, and one another. In this way, what the market provides are economic benefits as well as opportunities for community development and improved health. Moreover, while sustainable development projects like bike lanes and farmers markets tend to take place in affluent and white neighborhoods, Phat Beets attempts to extend the benefits of sustainability to working-class communities of color, and particularly to long-term residents in danger of displacement from gentrification. This makes Phat Beets a prime example of what Agyeman (2003) describes as "just sustainability."

However, as described above, the demographics of farmers market customers reflect newer rather than long-term residents. In Chapter 7 of this volume, Langegger argues that people "choose homes located in neighborhoods and they choose a neighborhood in large measure because of its streetscape, its walkability, its bikeability." Although he mentions restaurants and boutiques specifically, farmers markets are also among those businesses that reflect and shape neighborhood character. At Phat Beets, customers are largely though not exclusively white, young and middle-class. Some are "broke but not poor," meaning they lack steady income but have middle-class families that serve as safety nets, while others have found stable and well-paying jobs. Some older, African-American, long-term residents increasingly make use of the market as well, but their numbers are still small when compared to newcomers.

Catering to the community

Unlike many local food organizations in gentrifying neighborhoods, Phat Beets has worked to build its appeal to local residents, developing relationships with community members, and ensuring that they play leadership roles in the area's budding local food system. Phat Beets is dedicated to making its work relevant to long-term residents, and the name and logo of the organization, for example, draw on a hip-hop aesthetic chosen for its potential to resonate with the African-American community.

Phat Beets also explicitly seeks to employ long-term residents. For example, the market manager Thomas is an African-American man in his late twenties who has spent almost his entire life in the Bay Area. Neighborhood residents are also encouraged to become vendors. For example, William, an African-American man from East Oakland, sells raw, vegan foods, including pizza and cookies, while Leona, an African-American woman born in Berkeley, offers polarity therapy and mudras practice to customers looking for spiritual consultations. By supporting local residents and creating opportunities for them to become leaders in the food justice movement, "[Phat Beets is] trying to change the face of farmers markets," explains Terrance, an African-American vendor for one of the market's farmers and a long-term resident of Oakland.[2]

Another way Phat Beets helps to foster economic opportunities for local residents is through its Kitchen Incubator Program, which provides support for small, healthy food businesses. Long-term residents are given priority to participate in this program. Maurice, a self-identified white male who founded Phat Beets in 2007, explains:

> I think the reason I pushed for the Kitchen Incubator Program is so that we can have a farmers market that was an economic powerhouse in the area. Giving opportunities to people who wouldn't normally be able to start a business [and] can now do so and use the farmers market as a platform.

The Kitchen Incubator Program supports long-term residents in starting their own businesses, while the farmers market and café become venues for sales and distribution. These kinds of economic opportunities do not prevent gentrification, but they foster the ability of long-term residents to benefit from it.

Phat Beets' efforts are not lost on at least some long-term residents. When asked about whether Phat Beets contributes to gentrification, Valerie, an older, African-American woman, a long-term resident of Oakland, and informal advisor to Phat Beets, offers a positive assessment of the organization:

> If you're looking at just a slice, yes, [Phat Beets] is part of the problem, you're new too! But if you look at it, the intentionality, your mission, and how you're moving to fulfill that mission, then I say the answer is no . . . I don't think the farmers market and Phat Beets are implicated in gentrification. Think of gentrification as moving in with more entitlement and ability and taking over something already there, making it impossible for what's there to continue. That's different from moving in to add something to the community . . . I view Phat Beets as more of a community of people who want to do something in the community and move in to work with something that's there. The part where you're displacing – you moved in where there was nothing. You brought something. You added a contribution.

For Valerie, it seems that the value of newcomers' contributions hinges on their intentions and their willingness to work with long-term residents.

North Oakland Farmers Market vendors largely agree that Phat Beets is focused on the community, and appreciate the opportunities Phat Beets brings. Terrance elaborates:

> We don't carry ourselves like a business but more like a community, trying to spread the word and get others involved . . . [It] seems like 70 percent of the people that come to [nearby markets in Berkeley] are white, and [these markets] are expensive. Phat Beets separates itself from other markets based on the way it carries itself.

This is certainly what Phat Beets organizers intend to do, and some organizers and staff agree with this flattering portrayal. Sandy, a Korean immigrant, who has spent much of her adult life in the Bay Area, is Phat Beets' Kitchen Incubator Program Coordinator. She explains, "The great thing is how Phat Beets is trying to create products that are affordable and appropriate for low-income residents in the neighborhood. We are catering to the community, not the gentrifiers."

A completely different look

And yet, the gentrifiers continue to come, not only to the neighborhood but to the farmers market itself. This can be seen clearly in the farmers market's clientele, and more specifically in attendance at the educational workshops held there. Angelica, a 20-something immigrant from Columbia and UC Berkeley graduate who organizes the Food n' Justice workshops, explains:

> The idea [of the workshops] is to bring the knowledge of how to be more resilient in an urban setting [and] make it accessible to the community . . . [but] one big thing I notice in the workshops I organize [is that they are] attended mostly by white folks, young families, often people who have just moved to the neighborhood.

Some of Phat Beets workshops, like mushroom cultivation or fermentation, seem likely to draw this privileged crowd. But the same demographic can be found at the market's political workshops as well. Rico, a mixed-race woman from Illinois who also studied at UC Berkeley, and is the point-person for delivering CSAs for Phat Beets, describes two workshops that organizers believed would appeal to historic residents:

> Last year, Billy X, a former Black Panther, led a walking tour of North Oakland, starting at the North Oakland Farmers Market. It was probably 100 people. From what I remember, I didn't see many historic residents other than Billy on the walking tour. It was mostly people like us that have an interest

in the Panthers, either because of food justice or our own politics trying to learn the history of North Oakland. As a political project, it's great that those types of things happen and that we're trying to do those things . . . [but] I don't think it changes what the role of the farmers market is in the neighborhood. Even our political workshops like on the PIC [prison industrial complex] tend to attract white, alternative new residents.

Other food justice studies have pointed to the Black Panthers and prison abolition movements as political themes that resonate with low-income African-American communities (Alkon 2012). In this case, however, workshops appealed to newer residents instead, in part, we believe, because of greater access to and more comfort in the farmers market environment itself.

For vendors, the drawing in of young, predominantly white supporters is a mixed blessing. Terrance, for example, is quite critical of gentrification. When asked about the process in general, he replied, "It's a completely different look when white people come into our area. They [the city government] care about the potential of new people moving in. [They're] trying to make Oakland a crime-free city. I get that. But their way to do it is to flush everybody out, get clean streets, re-do streets." But when asked about gentrification's relationship to the farmers market, he takes a more measured approach:

> Gentrification benefits the farmers market. It keeps us going. There's good there. Anything that helps the market, I support. That's the thing about it. I just know that's not our purpose, though. Our purpose is not to kick anybody out. We're here to support people, teach people how to eat healthy. We have no say in the other process. It just sucks how the process works. It does benefit some people, hurt others.

Terrance illuminates one of the primary contradictions that arise from food justice efforts in gentrifying neighborhoods. Gentrifiers can help to support food justice activities financially in ways that low-income, long-term residents cannot, as is the case with Phat Beets' CSA program. This helps maintain the functioning of food justice programs in the neighborhood and makes them available to those long-term residents who are aware of and feel comfortable making use of them.

Reflection and action

Phat Beets organizers also struggle with this contradiction, and reflect on the relationship between their food justice goals and the gentrification process. Karen, a white organizer who moved to Oakland from the East Coast to do urban gardening and food justice work, also struggles with this complexity:

> When things that are healthy and smart become really hip, it's really confusing to know what to do with it . . . We shouldn't be discouraging people from

doing healthy and smart things, but it certainly creates a different culture. When it's a "hip factor high," it's attracting a certain type of person.

Angelica takes Karen's comments even further, asserting that the association between health and hipness "serves to alienate and to welcome . . . [Phat Beets is] a bridge for something that alienates. We're not necessarily pushing people out. We're just welcoming people through a process of economic access, but that ends up pushing people out." These organizers realize that despite their intentions to the contrary, they create a space in which young, white newcomers feel comfortable with and enjoy access to affordable, fresh, organic produce, wholesome food, and political education. This helps to code the neighborhood as a space for these new residents, and a space ripe for investment by those who seek to profit from this demographic shift.

And yet they do not see this as a reason to cease their efforts. Ray, a young, white gender-neutral organizer going to school in LA and doing an allyship program with Phat Beets, explains that leaving behind programs that attract new residents does not address the structural causes of gentrification:

> Leave abandoned lots as abandoned lots? Or make a garden? I know gentrification will happen regardless . . . Everybody deserves a garden, [a] green space, [a] farmers markets around the corner. The fact that people are moving here in part because of that doesn't necessarily mean that we should abandon all efforts, because there are still historic residents living here.

As Ray, Karen and Angelica exemplify, Phat Beets organizers bring a healthy level of reflexivity to their role in the gentrification process. While they acknowledge the ways they are implicated in it, they also continue to support food justice work. Ray acknowledges that local food systems can be a draw for new residents, but can also serve the long-term residents who do not have other access to affordable, sustainably grown, healthy food. Moreover, organizers recognize that the absence of farmers markets and urban gardens will not slow gentrification in North Oakland. These reflections, however, make Phat Beets organizers more aware of gentrification—and more willing to explicitly resist it—than other local food and food justice activists. This was exemplified by their response to the NOBE realty campaign.

Saying "No" to NOBE

Scholars studying gentrification have often highlighted the role of real estate developers, who alter material conditions in order to make a neighborhood more attractive for new residents. Less attention has been paid to the ways that neighborhoods are rebranded—destigmatized of their associations with people of color, poverty, blight, and crime—in order to convince potential home buyers that the neighborhood is a place for them.

In North Oakland, the real estate company Better Homes and Gardens attempts to rebrand the neighborhood through its "NOBE" campaign. NOBE combines North Oakland, Berkeley and Emeryville into a kitsch, trendy-sounding acronym reminiscent of other gentrified areas including SOMA (South of Market Avenue) in San Francisco, NoHo (North Hollywood) in Los Angeles, and SoHo (South of Houston Street) and DUMBO (Down Under Manhattan Bridge Overpass) in Manhattan.

Phat Beets was particularly enraged that Better Homes and Gardens included the North Oakland Farmers Market and Healthy Hearts Garden (a local city park where Phat Beets and local residents created an edible landscape) on its website and asset map of the neighborhood. Better Homes and Gardens later released a video, painting the neighborhood as a "best-kept hidden secret" in order to sell "affordable" housing to first-time house buyers from San Francisco. Organizers felt that in doing so, Better Homes and Gardens had co-opted community assets and re-appropriated them as reasons for people to move to the area in ways that harmed long-term residents.

Recalling Norton's description of the increasingly dominant stories told by the automobile industry's public relations personnel from the 1920s onward (see Chapter 2 in this volume), Phat Beets responded by "culture jamming" the NOBE video with a response called "Neighbors Outing Blatant Exploitation." Culture jamming is a strategy adopted by many anti-consumerist social movements to disrupt or subvert dominant media culture (Lloyd 2003). Phat Beets released a counter-video mocking the real estate company's obvious attempt to remake the neighborhood.

The counter-video begins with white text on black screens, introducing the reason it was made. After offering statistics on foreclosure rates in Oakland (1 in 24 houses as of 2011) and defining gentrification, the text reads: "The video you are about to see was made by a local realtor. We merely added subtitles to ask some questions and to translate what is really being said."

The video goes on to do just that. For example, in the original, realtor Linnette Edwards defines NOBE through its geographic dimensions. The counter-video inserts text that redefines the acronym as "a term coined by realtors to destigmatize North Oakland in order to sell the foreclosed homes of long-term black and brown residents to affluent white people." In addition, Phat Beets asserts that NOBE's boundaries are nearly coterminous with a local gang injunction. Gang injunctions have long been criticized for criminalizing young people of color in low-income areas. In this case, Phat Beets asserts that it targets youth who may be seen as threats to investors that rely on environments that appear safe, secure, stable, healthy, clean, and preferably white for the profitability of their developments.

The heart of the video includes a series of assertions made by Edwards, followed by questions and responses from Phat Beets. When Edwards describes NOBE as "a great, up-and-coming community that is sort of this best-kept hidden secret that offers walkability, easy commute to San Francisco and all of these great restaurants and cafes," Phat Beets asks "best kept secret from who?" Edwards goes on to emphasize the neighborhood's affordability, with houses "selling in the $500,000 to $600,000 price range." In contrast, against a backdrop of typical North Oakland homes, Phat Beets provides statistics such as "during 2009, Blacks and Latinos were more than 70% more likely to lose their homes to foreclosure than white homeowners" and "Median household income of North Oakland is $33,556." These statistics prompt the textual narration to ask "Whose homes were these?"

Finally, Edwards explains that:

> [NOBE] is totally taking off as these hipsters and young professionals are coming in and really endorsing this community. Love it, live it! They can walk to so many different cafes and new, cool bars that I myself absolutely love. As an agent, it's so fun to sell the NOBE neighborhood because I can see this revitalization . . . [and] great buzz taking place.

The counter-video counters these class-coded statements with text asking: "Is this your neighborhood to sell?" and "Revitalization? Do you mean gentrification?" Clearly, Edwards and Better Homes and Gardens are trying to attract new, more affluent people to North Oakland by accommodating their lifestyles and sensibilities in the video, and Phat Beets resents the inclusion of its projects in this rebranding effort.

The use of Phat Beets' projects in the NOBE video also prompted the organization to release a formal statement on gentrification. The following is an excerpt from that statement:

> Because many forms of injustice intersect and reinforce one another, it is crucial that Phat Beets works across many different issues — including both food and housing justice — to not only support those most affected by these problems but also to eradicate the causes of them in the first place. This is why Phat Beets has chosen to address, challenge and resist gentrification in North Oakland.
>
> If working class people of color are displaced from North Oakland — which inevitably happens through gentrification – then Phat Beets farmers markets and CSAs become inaccessible to the community as a whole, which contradicts our mission and is therefore something we cannot support as an organization.

In this statement, Phat Beets frames gentrification as antithetical to its goal of food justice, as gentrification displaces the residents that food justice organizations seek to empower. Later in the statement, Phat Beets addresses its own positionality with regard to this process:

> Phat Beets sees gentrification as a structural process with many players and stakeholders, not an issue of individuals or families just trying to buy their first

home near good schools, parks and restaurants. Therefore, we do not blame individuals for their roles in gentrification. Many of the members, allies and supporters of Phat Beets are not historic residents of Oakland, and while we are aware and critical of our own role in gentrification through urban greening, we also understand the powerful possibilities that our programming can create when we unite in support of current residents and re-investment in the neighborhood.

In this way, Phat Beets acknowledges that, despite its desires to work to the contrary, it is nonetheless implicated in the gentrification process because its local food systems work is coded as affluent and white and is easily co-opted by those seeking to appeal to that demographic. Organizers maintain, however, that they remain distinct from Better Homes and Gardens because of their desire to empower local residents, rather than profit from their displacement.

Becoming the displaced

Ironically, as Phat Beets organizers reflected on their role as gentrifiers, they were forced out of the café space and eventually the market space as well. Investors in the café were not required to produce equal initial financial investments and were instead rewarded with differential positions in the business that matched their contributions. For example, cooks who invested more were rewarded with the more lucrative Saturday shifts, which built upon the farmers market's popularity, while those who invested less used the café on weekdays. One long-term local resident, who had been particularly involved in opening the café, became the leaseholder for the space, with Phat Beets holding a sublease for office space used to support both the Kitchen Incubator Program and the farmers market.

However, after only a few months, the leaseholder became dissatisfied with the café's rate of return on its investment. Phat Beets attempted to buy the lease, but instead, the original leaseholder sold it on Craigslist. The new owner was the Grease Box, a gluten-free soul food restaurant specializing in fried chicken. The owner of the Grease Box identifies as a mixed-race, queer woman originally from Louisiana, and had been running the Grease Box as a pop-up restaurant in San Francisco before finding more permanent space in Oakland. Like Phat Beets, most of her customers are new, white residents though unlike the collective, Grease Box's owner refuses to acknowledge her role in the gentrification process.

Crossroads and the Grease Box made some attempt to share the space, but were unable to come to an agreement as to who would use the kitchen when, and what ingredients were considered acceptable. For example, the Grease Box is entirely gluten-free and its management insisted that Crossroads vendors also not use gluten in the kitchen. This made it impossible for several vendors to cook their cultural foods, which was interpreted by Phat Beets as an assault on food sovereignty, that is, communities' rights to establish their own food and agriculture systems. As it became clear to Crossroads vendors that the Kitchen Incubator Program could not continue in that space, relationships with the Grease Box turned sour. Grease Box's owner called both the police and the Health Department, which Phat Beets organizers believe was done deliberately to intimidate and displace them. Indeed, the Health Department concluded that Phat Beets did have permission to use the kitchen with written permission from the Grease Box, which the latter declined to give. Not surprisingly, Phat Beets' sublease was not renewed for the following year.

In response, Phat Beets released a statement describing these events as an example of gentrification, and distinguishing its own role in the community from that of the Grease Box:

> Just to be clear, many members of the Phat Beets Produce collective are not long-term residents of North Oakland, but we do spend a great deal of time and energy in organizing with and supporting the interests and leadership of North Oakland residents in building the just food system we all need. In fact, Phat Beets has to fundraise and grant write in order to keep healthy, fresh and organic produce at our farmers market affordable to North Oakland residents, as well as fund the jobs of historic residents who staff the market itself. The food justice approach we take in working in North Oakland, and the approach of Grease Box, whose food costs don't take into consideration historic residents and their income level, is night and day. Unfortunately, Grease Box isn't the first such business that is symptomatic of a troubling gentrification pattern, which is why the North Oakland community can no longer afford to ignore it or merely refer to it as the 'G word'.

Despite this statement's labeling of Grease Box as a gentrifier and itself as community-based, organizers understood that they had helped to make Grease Box's entry into this space possible, and thus sown some of the seeds of their own displacement. Had Phat Beets not moved into a blighted building and helped make it a functional kitchen and farmers market with the support of long-term residents, it never would have been bought out by Grease Box because it would not have been economically viable for a new business to move into without an already established kitchen and customer base. It seems clear that the stream of young, artsy folks walking and biking from the surrounding neighborhood helped to convince the Grease Box that this could be a successful location. In essence, Phat Beets helped build a foundation for a future business to become successful, a business whose food and prices cater to new, white, hip, and affluent residents of North Oakland. This process has served both to displace Phat Beets and other Crossroads members from the kitchen they helped make viable, as well as to turn a community kitchen and non-profit kitchen incubator program into a for-profit business that does not address inadequate healthy food access in the community.

The beet goes on

Phat Beets is currently looking for a new space for its farmers market, offices and kitchen incubator program. Organizers have visited potential sites, but have yet to find the right match. Currently, organizers work from their homes, and hold meetings among themselves or with allies at local cafés. Many of the vendors displaced by Grease Box no longer come to the farmers market even to shop, given the loss of financial and emotional investment. Some vendors worked with Phat Beets to create videos describing how they were displaced just days after Grease Box came onto the picture. They are hoping to work with Phat Beets again once a new space is located.

In the interim, the organization is increasing its efforts to connect with long-term North Oakland residents. Organizers believe that deepening these ties will not only strengthen their programs, but help them to more fiercely resist gentrification. Organizers have developed a partnership with Bethany Baptist Church, a primarily African-American congregation of long-term and recently displaced North Oakland residents. Organizers initiated a series of meetings with church members to determine the social and political issues most relevant to them. Two themes that emerged were "economic development without displacement" and "community safety." Phat Beets is currently working to support long-term North Oakland residents in their desire to create a safe and economically thriving community, and to assist them in integrating urban agriculture and restorative justice into their programming. Organizers believe that working with long-term community members on the issues most important to them can support food justice work without the above described accompanying displacement.

With regard to economic development, Phat Beets and local community partners, stakeholders and organizations have initiated a working committee on "economic development without displacement." One of the goals of this committee is to engage long-term and recent North Oakland residents in preparing a comprehensive plan to present to the Oakland City Council to influence local revitalization projects that support economic opportunities for long-term residents.

On the theme of community safety, Phat Beets and Bethany Baptist have begun a series of 12-monthly restorative justice, community listening sessions. Facilitated by a formerly incarcerated North Oakland resident, these sessions are designed to bring together long-term and recent residents to build empathy and alliances around violence prevention campaigns. Second, Phat Beets is also working with the Bay Area Video Coalition to produce a documentary that captures stories from new and old residents about the history of North Oakland and how to make it safer without racial profiling, added policing and gang injunctions. The organization is also working to build a community safety text alert system that will alert local residents to incidents of violence in order to subsequently organize around it without calling the police. More directly, in order to heal around this violence, Phat Beets has begun working with families who have lost loved ones to violence to start memorial fruit tree plantings in their honor. These actions are not explicitly related to Phat Beets' food justice goals, but organizers believe they will help strengthen relationships with long-term community members so that future food justice work is more relevant to them.

Each of these initiatives serves to strengthen Phat Beets' connection to long-term residents and to more deeply integrate their work into community goals. Organizers believe that this will strengthen the ability of their food justice work to appeal to long-term residents, as the organization will be seen as a source of uplift in the community and therefore worthy of resident support. This way, when Phat Beets renews its farmers market, workshop series, and kitchen incubator program, they will do so in the context of strong community support, decreasing their projects' associations with new residents and gentrification.

Discussion and conclusion

Phat Beets has an ambiguous relationship with the gentrification process in North Oakland. Recognizing that displacement moves those they seek to empower further from resources such as fresh produce, organizers define it as inimical to their food justice goals. Thus, their official stance is to resist. This is clear from their published statements, and translates into actions such as hiring long-term residents, creating programming they believe will have broad appeal and co-creating economic ventures that help these residents to claim a stake in the local food system. However, the local food system that Phat Beets and their allies have created appeals mainly to young, middle-class, newcomers, providing them with access to low-cost healthy food and helping them to feel a greater sense of comfort in their new neighborhood. In this way, and despite their best intentions, the organization and its programs are implicated in gentrification.

These dynamics seem likely to be repeated among other food justice organizations in other gentrifying areas. Patrick Crouch, a white community activist who has been working for food justice in Detroit for over a decade, recently published a thought-provoking piece in *Grist* magazine, wondering if and how his work contributes to gentrification. He writes:

> Urban agriculture can be a force for good in under-resourced neighborhoods. It can provide job-training [and] access to healthy food . . . But many of the people of color I have known and worked with say it also inevitably attracts young white people, which—while not necessarily the cause of gentrification—is often a sure sign that it's on the way.

Crouch's intentions —using food justice activism to provide healthy food and jobs —resemble those of Phat Beets, as do the unintended consequences named by his allies. Crouch also points to other cities that have experienced similar dynamics, including the South Bronx, Harlem, the South Side of Chicago, and the Mission District in San Francisco, all of which, he writes, "have all been improved drastically by hard-working neighborhood activists only to see them increasingly vulnerable to gentrification as conditions improve."

Food activism, however, is only a small part of the neighborhood revitalization that has made these communities so vulnerable. A thriving arts and music scene, often building on those of historically marginalized and immigrant communities, also plays a role. In addition, walkability and ease of access to public transportation are other common attributes cited as appealing by first wave gentrifiers. This should raise concern among advocates of Complete Streets that their planning processes can contribute to displacement, ironically naming a neighborhood complete just as low-income people and people of color are pushed out.

In response to these concerns, planners advocating a Complete Streets approach in low-income, gentrifying neighborhoods should begin by listening to and working with long-term residents to ensure that their concerns are heard and represented. The lessons of participatory planning are commonly repeated, and yet their importance cannot be overstated. No street can be complete, and no development can be sustainable, if the communities surrounding them are left out of the planning process and if meeting their needs is not among planners' top priorities. Planners should learn from Phat Beets that developing relationships with long-term leaders is an essential part of the process of improving a neighborhood. This practice is particularly important when the improvements offered tend to appeal to newer residents with the economic ability to displace existing ones. Similar conclusions were reached by Miller and Lubitow in their analysis of bicycle planning in Portland in Chapter 14 of this volume.

Moreover, planners advocating Complete Streets may also want to think about other kinds of planning that can help to offset the pressure towards gentrification that their sustainable development goals may create. One obvious example is affordable housing, and planners may begin working with city officials to create affordable housing policies, rent control, and other tools that would help enable long-term residents to avoid displacement.

Lastly, planning scholars and fellow travelers can help activists and community members like those at Phat Beets and Bethany Baptist to flesh out the concept of economic development without displacement. What kinds of planning can improve low-income neighborhoods without making them vulnerable to gentrification? Are there particular best practices and lessons learned that community members may want to incorporate into their own development strategies?

At the heart of this question lie issues of social, spatial, and environmental justice. How can low-income people and people of color work with allies to improve the places they live, while maintaining their ability to live there? Developing tools to address this question will not only enrich scholarly understandings of gentrification, sustainable development and community activism, but will empower residents to create just and sustainable communities that can last for generations.

Notes

1   These are two common origin stories for the neighborhood's name, though there is no definitive answer.
2   In order to make the market more lucrative for farmers, farmers merely drop off their goods at the market, and they are then sold by Phat Beets' employees. Therefore, there is no labor cost for market participation.

References

Agyeman, J., 2003. *Just sustainabilities: Development in an unequal world*. Cambridge, MA: MIT Press.
Agyeman, J., 2013. *Introducing just sustainabilities: Policy, planning and practice*. London: Zed Books.
Alkon, A.H., 2011. Reflexivity and environmental justice scholarship: A role for feminist methodology. *Organization & Environment*, 24 (2), 130–149.
Alkon, A.H., 2012. *Black white and green: Race, farmers markets and the green economy*. Athens, GA: UGA Press.
Alkon, A.H., and Agyeman, J., 2011. *Cultivating food justice: Race, class and sustainability*. Cambridge, MA: MIT Press.
Bordo, S., 1990. Feminism, postmodernism, and gender-skepticism. In: L Nicholson, ed. *Feminism/Postmodernism*. New York, NY: Routledge, 133–156.
Brown-Saracino, J., 2004. Social preservationists and the quest for authentic community. *City & Community*, 3, 135–156.
Burawoy, M., 2009. *The extended case method: Four countries, four decades, four great transformations, and one theoretical tradition*. Berkele, CA: University of California Press.
Cameron, S., 2003. Gentrification, housing redifferentiation and urban regeneration: "Going for growth" in Newcastle upon Tyne. *Urban Studies*, 40 (12), 2367–2382.
Checker, M., 2011. Wiped out by the green wave: Environmental gentrification and the paradoxical politics of urban sustainability. *City & Community*, 23 (2), 201–229.
Cross, D., 2013. The 10 most exciting cities in America. Available from: www.movoto.com/blog/top-ten/10-most-exciting-cities/ [Accessed 28 December 2013].
Cutts, B.B., Darby, K.J., Boone, C.G., and Brewis, A., 2009. City structure, obesity, and environmental justice: An integrated analysis of physical and social barriers to walkable streets and park access. *Social Science & Medicine*, 69 (9):1314–1322.
Day, K., 2006. Active living and social justice: Planning for physical activity in low-income, black, and Hispanic communities. *Journal of the American Planning Association*, 72 (1), 88–99.
Dooling, S., 2008. Ecological gentrification: Re-negotiating justice in the city. *Critical Planning*, 15, 40–57.
Glantz, J., 2012. Report: Investors buy nearly half of Oakland's foreclosed homes. *The Bay Citizen*. Available from: www.baycitizen.org/news/housing/report-investors-buy-nearly-half-homes/ [Accessed 28 December 2013].
Guthman, J., 2008. Bringing good food to others: Investigating the subjects of alternative agrifood practices. *Cultural Geographies*, 15, 425–441.
Kennedy, M., and Leonard, P., 2001. *Dealing with neighborhood change: A primer on gentrification and policy choices*. Washington, DC: Brookings Institution.
Lees, L., 2000. A reappraisal of gentrification: Towards a "geography of gentrification". *Progress in Human Geography*, 24 (3), 389–408.
Lees, L., Slater, T., and Wiley, E., 2013. *Gentrification*. New York: Routledge.

Lloyd, J., 2003. *Culture Jamming: Semiotic Banditry in the Streets*. Available from: www.hums. canterbury.ac.nz/cult/research/lloyd.htm [Accessed 9 November 2013].

Ocejo, R., 2011. The early gentrifier: Weaving a nostalgia narrative on the Lower East Side. *City & Community*, 10 (3), 285–310.

Peck, J., 2005. Struggling with the creative class. *International Journal of Urban and Regional Research*, 29 (4), 740–770.

Pike, K.L., 1967, *Language in relation to a unified theory of the structure of human behavior*. The Hague: Mouton.

Project for Public Spaces, n.d. What is placemaking? Available from: www.pps.org/ reference/what_is_placemaking/ [Accessed 9 November 2013].

Quastel, N., 2009. Political ecologies of gentrification. *Urban Geography*, 30 (7), 694–725.

Self, R.O., 2003. *American Babylon: Race and the struggle for postwar Oakland*. Princeton, NJ: Princeton University Press.

Shaw, W.S., 2007. *Cities of whiteness*. Malden, MA: Blackwell Publishing.

Slater, T., 2006. The eviction of critical perspectives from gentrification research. *International Journal of Urban and Regional Research*, 30 (4), 737–757.

Slocum, R., 2007. Whiteness, space and alternative food practice. *Geoforum*, 38 (3), 520–533.

Smart Growth America, n.d. Benefits of Complete Streets. Available from: www.smartgrow thamerica.org/complete-streets/complete-streets-fundamentals/benefits-of-complete- streets/ [Accessed 9 November 2013].

Smith, N., 1987. Of yuppies and housing: gentrification, social restructuring, and the urban dream. *Environment and Planning D: Society and Space*, 5 (2), 151–172.

Smith, N., 1996, *The new urban frontier: Gentrification and the revanchist city*, London: Routledge.

The Onion, 2008. Nation's gentrified neighborhoods threatened by aristocratization. Available from: www.theonion.com/articles/report-nations-gentrified-neighborhoods-threatened, 2419/ [Accessed 9 November 2013].

Watson-Gegeo, K., 1988. Ethnography in ESL: Defining the essentials. *TESOL Quarterly*, 22 (4), 575–592.

Zukin, S., 2008. Consuming authenticity. *Cultural Studies*, 22 (5), 724–748.

Zukin, S., 1987. Gentrification: Culture and capital in the urban core. *Annual Review of Sociology*, 13 (1), 129–147.

10

REVERSING COMPLETE STREETS DISPARITIES

Portland's Community Watershed Stewardship Program

Erin Goodling and Cameron Herrington

Introduction

For a decade, Pacific Northwest rains regularly flooded St. Mary Ethiopian Orthodox Church in Portland, Oregon. Even after spending several thousand dollars in an attempt to repair the dry-well system in the parking lot, the small, immigrant-led congregation had to use sandbags and pumps to keep stormwater out of its converted warehouse church. Out of money, St. Mary decided to pursue a different approach. After months of planning and preparation, dozens of volunteers arrived on a sunny Saturday morning in summer 2013 with jackhammers, crowbars, shovels, and gloves. The volunteers worked with church members to remove 1,500 square feet of asphalt from the church's parking lot, "depaving" the way for a bioswale, a vegetated stormwater drain. After a contractor excavated the area and brought in new soil, volunteers returned to add hundreds of native plants that would soak up the parking lot's runoff and prevent future flooding. Time will tell, but church leaders report that the building has so far stayed dry after heavy fall rains.

St. Mary's congregation carried out this project with funding and technical assistance from the Community Watershed Stewardship Program (CWSP), a small program in the City of Portland's Bureau of Environmental Services (BES). Established in 1995, CWSP provides grants of up to $10,000 to community groups that take on projects that improve watershed health and manage stormwater. In this sense, CWSP sits at the nexus of two hallmarks of Portland's progressive ethos: environmental stewardship and civic engagement.

In this chapter, we draw on the example of CWSP to explain how the Complete Streets agenda in particular, and sustainability governance more broadly, may provide space for city planners and leaders to prioritize the needs of under-represented groups.[1] But in contrast to common sustainability claims (Wheeler and Beatley 2004), we assert that environmentally themed initiatives will not *inherently* result in equitable outcomes. Absent a focus on equity, sustainability and Complete Streets initiatives also produce *in*Complete Streets—those spaces both physical and socio-political in which "sustainability" and "Complete Streets" agendas fail to deliver on their social equity promises.

We highlight a handful of strategies that CWSP has employed to overtly prioritize social equity as part of its watershed health mission, and draw on the concept of equity planning to discuss ways that CWSP's experience might inform other environmental programs that aim to operationalize a social equity agenda through sustainability/Complete Streets programs. Our aim in this chapter is neither to thoroughly evaluate the specific approach that CWSP has taken, nor judge it against an alternative set of equity strategies. Instead, we discuss CWSP's equity focus as one example of how a municipal bureaucracy tasked with implementing a sustainability/Complete Streets agenda has intentionally sought to redress systemic disparities, rather than reproducing them.

Following this introduction, we describe the context in which CWSP operates, both locally in Portland and more generally in terms of "sustainable city" governance. Next, we summarize CWSP's *modus operandi* for its first 15 years, arguing that the program typified mainstream urban sustainability practice in that it assumed its community-led model would automatically result in "win–win–win" (Vos 2007) outcomes for economic development, environmental improvement, and social equity. We then problematize this mainstream understanding of sustainability, highlighting some of the shortcomings of an uncritical, ahistorical, de-politicized approach. Next, we turn to interviews with CWSP employees and others closely tied to the program to describe how it has recently come to more purposefully prioritize social equity. Finally, we outline some concrete strategies that CWSP has used to simultaneously improve watershed health and explicitly address the needs and desires of underrepresented groups.

Throughout our summary of CWSP's approach, we draw on Norman Krumholz's (1982) concept of equity planning to assert that bureaucrats and planners do in fact have agency to pursue equity agendas within urban sustainability and Complete Streets frameworks, at least in some circumstances. We caution, however, that isolated efforts have limited efficacy unless they are supported by— or inspire the development of—an institutional commitment to equity analysis and program reform. Indeed, overt equity objectives seeded in small programs such as CWSP can serve as catalysts, eventually trickling up to higher levels of governance and out to other programs and cities. We hope that, by shining a light on the evolution of CWSP's equity focus and describing some of its concrete tactics, we might provide planners and other leaders with inspiration and the foundations of a strategic approach to a more *just* sustainability (Agyeman 2005, 2013).

Portland, Oregon: model sustainable city?

Sustainability has been a dominant policy-making paradigm since the early 1990s, and municipal governments and city planning agencies often use the sustainability framework to articulate tripartite goals of economic growth, environmental quality, and social equity (Portney 2005; Gunder 2006; Krueger and Gibbs 2007). One iteration of this three-pronged sustainability approach is the "Complete Streets" ideal. Advocates of Complete Streets policies emphasize the need for roadways to cater to all users, not just drivers. They promote Complete Streets as smart investments that increase safety and make thoroughfares more "walkable" and welcoming, environmentally-friendly, and amenable to business (National Complete Streets Coalition 2013).

In Portland, Oregon, Complete Streets and watershed stewardship go hand-in-hand. Recognizing that streets serve as conduits not only for automobiles and bicycles, but also for polluted stormwater runoff, over the last decade BES has installed thousands of "green street" bioswales in the public right-of-way. Combined with other stormwater management facilities, this green system can reduce non-point source pollution. By allowing runoff from streets, parking lots, and other impervious surfaces to slowly infiltrate into soil onsite (see Figure 10.1), bioswales in some parts of the city help divert runoff from Portland's combined sewer pipes, which overflow into the city's waterways when the system exceeds capacity. In other areas, they act as a buffer to help prevent pollutants from going directly into creeks.

Portland's green street facilities have also made roadways more pedestrian- and bike-friendly by narrowing streets, slowing traffic, and creating buffers between cars

FIGURE 10.1 Portland bioswale

Source: Authors.

and people. Swales line many of Portland's designated "bicycle boulevards," which are a key ingredient of the city's implicit Complete Streets agenda. Though the specific phrase "Complete Streets" is not widely used by Portland's planners and municipal leaders, the city's push to create "20-minute neighborhoods" derives from the same sustainability/livability ethos that motivates the Complete Streets movement, and has contributed to Portland's reputation as one of the world's most progressive, livable cities (Seltzer 2004; SustainLane 2008) (Figure 10.2).

This green approach to planning and urban governance has translated into an economic growth strategy for Portland, attracting investors, businesses, tourists, and well-educated migrants (Jurjevich and Schrock 2012). Jonas and While (2007, p.129) suggest that the "new urban politics" is "as much about sustainability as it is about urban competition." Susan Anderson, City of Portland Planning Director, echoes this sentiment:

> We're not doing [sustainability] just to be altruistic. Part of the reason we're doing a lot of this: there's money to be made, to be crass . . . And most of these things are things we want to do to create better, healthier places anyway – but by doing that, you create a place where people want to live and have businesses.

> *(quoted in Minow-Smith 2012)*

Yet, while city officials, environmentalists, and eco-conscious consumers laud Portland's bike lanes and bioswales, eco-districts and electric cars, others perceive Complete Streets planning and its associated rhetoric of sustainability and livability as an evasion of messy political questions and direct engagement with social justice concerns. Cassie Cohen, executive director of Groundwork Portland, an

FIGURE 10.2 Mural depicting Portland's Complete Streets-oriented neighborhoods. Lead artist: Sara Stout

Source: Authors.

environmental justice non-profit organization that has received CWSP grants in recent years, explains:

> A lot of folks in positions of power in environmental groups pride themselves on having the city ranked highly — as a bikeable city, having lots of trees, certain parks, [and] MAX [light rail] lines. But it's been a convenient way for people to overlook the fact that they've kept out and isolated an entire group of Portlanders in the process of recognizing the city for these things. It leaves out communities that don't get to reap the benefits of the resources.
>
> *(Interview, 25 October 3013)*

Indeed, Complete Streets in some Portland neighborhoods are the correlates of *in*Complete Streets in others. Despite numerous accolades, not all of Portland's roughly 600,000 residents have regular access to neighborhood grocery stores, convenient public transit, parks, and streets made complete by sidewalks and crosswalks, bike lanes, and native plant bioswales (Curry-Stevens *et al.* 2010; Griffin-Valade *et al.* 2010; CLF 2013). And as in other U.S. cities (Hackworth 2007; McClintock 2011), Portland's disparities are both racial and spatial in nature. Over the last two decades, 82nd Avenue has been a fulcrum on which the demographics of poverty and race have shifted and rebalanced: to the west, the city has become more affluent and white; to the east, more diverse and poor. Rising property values and an incoming wave of wealthier, mainly white residents have displaced many lower-income households—especially African-Americans—from formerly redlined inner Portland neighborhoods (Gibson 2007; Bates 2013).[2] These same neighborhoods now constitute the epicenter of Complete Streets-oriented redevelopment, with walkable business districts, bike lanes, and a new light rail line. In contrast, many displaced African-Americans have joined refugee, immigrant, and working-class white populations in "the numbers" (east of 82nd Avenue), where there are substantially fewer Complete Streets amenities and a disproportionate number of high-crash traffic corridors (City of Portland 2013) (Figure 10.3).[3]

To borrow the title of China Miéville's (2011) novel, 82nd Avenue now serves as a visceral demarcation line between "the city and the city."[4] The media, local politicians, and scholars alike regularly refer to the existence of "two Portlands," a concept that rhetorically conjoins the city's spatial, racial, and cultural divides (Curry-Stevens *et al.* 2010; Mirk 2010; Pein 2011; City of Portland 2013). One Portland is the predominantly white, well-off, eco-conscious city depicted in the sketch comedy show *Portlandia* and celebrated by the *New York Times* (Scalza 2012). The "other Portland" (Pein 2011) includes the city's communities of color, lower-income residents, and immigrants. Gaps in income, home-ownership, education, and employment between whites and Portlanders of color are growing; by almost any measure, members of this other Portland are less likely than the city's more affluent, well-educated (generally white) residents to influence and benefit from muncipal sustainability initiatives (Figure 10.4) (Curry-Stevens *et al.* 2010; Griffin-Valade *et al.* 2010, CLF 2013).

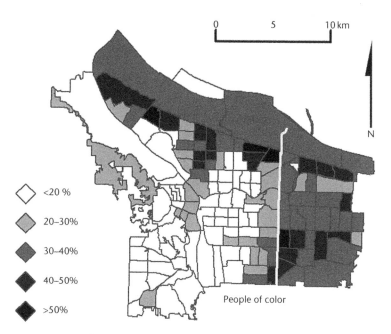

FIGURE 10.3 East Portland and other outer neighborhoods are home to far more people of color than Portland's inner-core neighborhoods, where Complete Streets amenities are concentrated

Source: Nathan McClintock; data from U.S. Census (2010).

FIGURE 10.4 An example of Portland's incomplete streets, heavily concentrated in neighborhoods inhabited by low-income residents, people of color, older adults, and children. Guy Dale makes his way up SE 162nd Avenue in East Portland, where it is not uncommon to see wheelchairs having to use roadways to get around

Source: Darryl James.

Local government has played a well-documented role in creating, exacerbating, and failing to address Portland's inequalities; acknowledging as much is now part-and-parcel of Portland's political rhetoric (Mirk 2010; City of Portland 2013; Law 2013). Organizations representing communities of color and low-income residents, however, have begun to advance their critique by explicitly drawing a connection between public investments in the sustainability branded revitalization of inner neighborhoods—streetcars, bike lanes, bioswales—and the dearth of investment, services, and even basic infrastructure in the numbers. "We have *Portlandia* and Poorlandia . . .We care more about bikes than people," states Kayse Jama (Panel discussion, 30 May 2013), executive director of Portland's Center for Intercultural Organizing.

It is in this context that CWSP has recently begun to push back against the inequities of Portland's sustainability politics and practices by explicitly prioritizing the needs of communities with histories of dispossession and displacement.

Community Watershed Stewardship Program: the early years

Throughout the 1970s and 1980s, Portland's heavy rains regularly overwhelmed the city's infrastructure and caused combined sewer overflows (CSOs) of raw sewage into the Willamette River and Columbia Slough. This contamination was the result of an antiquated system that channeled sanitary sewage and stormwater runoff into the same set of underground pipes. In 1991, the Environmental Protection Agency (EPA) and Oregon's Department of Environmental Quality (DEQ) mandated that the city clean up the mess.

BES responded with a three-pronged approach, resulting in a 99 percent reduction of CSOs into the Willamette and a 94 percent reduction into the Columbia. First, BES tunneled under the city to install the recently completed "big pipe," which has dramatically increased physical capacity for conveying sewage to a treatment facility. Second, it invested in a variety of green infrastructure measures, designed to soak rainwater into the ground and prevent it from entering the combined sewer system in the first place. This strategy has included construction of over a thousand bioswales, rain-gardens, and green streets facilities, and subsidies for eco-roof construction, pavement removal projects, and the disconnection of gutters and downspouts from the combined sewer system (BES 2011). Many of these features have benefits beyond stormwater management, such as traffic-calming and sidewalk beautification, making them congruent with Complete Streets style urban design.

Recognizing that the actions of negligent or uninformed residents could undermine the viability of these innovations, and hoping to create broad buy-in and political support for the Bureau's efforts, BES adopted community participation and watershed education as the third component of its holistic approach to stormwater management. "You can have great engineering, but if someone puts motor oil into a storm drain, that's a problem," explains Jennifer Devlin, CWSP's program manager (Interview, 25 October 2013). As a centerpiece of BES' community engagement strategy, CWSP was established as a grant program to fund watershed stewardship efforts such as the clean-up and restoration of streams and natural areas, "upland" projects such as rain-gardens that keep stormwater out of the combined sewer, and educational initiatives that spread the message of Portlanders' collective responsibility for watershed health (Figure 10.5).

From its inception, CWSP has been a partnership between Portland State University (PSU) and the City of Portland, and for the past decade has hired two graduate students each year to help Devlin coordinate the grant program. These students manage day-to-day operations, serve as liaisons to PSU classes that periodically work with grant recipients to implement projects, and bring innovative ideas (ibid.).

By cost-effectively wedding Portland's "urban imaginary of nature" (Huber and Currie 2007) with its tradition of neighborhood-based civic participation (Abbott 2001), CWSP embodies the triple bottom-line ideal of sustainability. In the first place, CWSP projects address environmental challenges related to stormwater management. Second, initiatives are fiscally efficient in that they leverage limited funds to attract many times the grants' value in in-kind donations and volunteer hours. And, third, CWSP projects are community-led. In other words, by setting aside a very small amount of money each year for community-based watershed projects—out of a total BES budget of $239.6 million in FY2013–14, CWSP

FIGURE 10.5 Typical CWSP stream restoration project

Source: Sarah Kidd.

awarded $95,000 in grants—BES efficiently invests not only in its core mission of stormwater management and watershed health, but also in developing communities. Environment, economy, and people: win–win–win.

Questioning the sustainability 'win–win–win'

Upon being established in 1995, "CWSP legitimized and validated community participation in what had been pretty much a top-down regulatory environment" within BES, recalls PSU professor and CWSP co-founder Barry Messer (Interview, 31 October 2013). Compared to more technical, expert-led approaches to environmental management, CWSP's community involvement strategy was relatively novel and progressive (Welsch and Heying 1999). But during its first decade, the majority of the program's grant applications came from environmentally focused, well-connected community groups—mainly representing white, middle-class, west-of-82nd Avenue Portland. Consequently, CWSP awarded almost all of its grants to a relatively narrow swath of neighborhoods and demographic sectors. In short, the program served as a resource for sustainability minded white Portland, and remained largely irrelevant for communities of color and other groups marginalized by the "sustainable city." This small watershed stewardship grant fund was unintentionally reproducing Portland's socio-economic—and increasingly spatialized—disparities.

It is well established that "sustainability," even when pursued with a community participation focus, is not a panacea for social injustice; an undercurrent of class, gender, and race/ethnicity-based conflict around socio-ecological relations persists even in sustainable cities, reflecting starkly disparate outcomes for different groups (Pulido 2000; Krueger and Gibbs 2007; Agyeman 2005, 2013). And in the absence of explicit measures to confront disparities, sustainability and Complete Streets initiatives often *reproduce* social inequalities, as many chapters in this book show. Jonas and While (2007, p.129) assert, "Even if in some cities attributes of the 'right' urban governance for *environmental* sustainability can be found, they often coexist with neoliberal urban forms that are *socially* regressive and with which they may be in conflict."

One key example is the link between green-themed livability and gentrification/ displacement, often obscured by sustainability and Complete Streets rhetoric (see Miller and Lubitow, Chapter 14 in this volume). When cities such as Portland invest public funds to "revitalize" neighborhoods with bike lanes, streetcars, and other Complete Streets elements, they seek to attract private development and affluent residents, often at the expense of lower-income households. Unless sustainability initiatives are controlled by vulnerable communities themselves, or are accompanied by anti-displacement strategies, low-income residents are frequently displaced, as property values rise (DeFilippis 2004; Bunce 2009; Quastel 2009).

As this potential for displacement suggests, there is rarely space for serious discussion of who benefits from and who pays for sustainability "improvements" (Agyeman 2005; Krueger and Gibbs 2007; Swyngedouw 2007). Alternative solutions to socio-environmental challenges are infrequently solicited from those most impacted (see Miller and Lubitow, Chapter 14 in this volume). Moreover, while there may be space to make small adjustments to specific policies or initiatives, there rarely exists space to question the overall sustainable development paradigm, which acquiesces to a political economic system predicated upon economic growth, a circumstance Swyngedouw (2007) refers to as "postpolitical." Sustainability research and policy instead focus on modifying economic valuation systems to better account for ecological variables, developing quantitative indicators and metrics, and designing technological solutions (e.g. green building practices) (Krueger and Gibbs 2007).

Messer describes the incredible complexity of managing urban stormwater: "[We're] dealing with an intractable urban environmental challenge like non-point source pollution—run-off—with ill-defined, multiple points of entry" (Interview, 31 October 2013). While technical fixes such as Portland's big pipe—and even its bioswales—may provide essential services in addressing such complex challenges, they also tend to supplant attention to the socio-ecological processes that come together to produce cities. Ecological variables, such as stormwater and sewage, do not exist in an apolitical world; rather, they become entangled with capital and deep-seated power dynamics, structuring outcomes according to political influence and access to resources (Harvey 1989, 2007; Heynen et al. 2006; Smith 2008).

In the case of Portland's stormwater and sewage challenge, engineers clearly had much to offer, but they could only address one aspect of the problem as it had been framed. Karyn Hansen, BES engineer and the Bureau's representative to the city-wide Equity Committee, explains how "objective" cost/benefit analyses can ignore layers of subjective and historically-contingent circumstances:

> Our engineers have used insurance claims as a proxy for the costs of basement flooding caused by insufficient capacity in our combined [sewer] system. It is a very objective assumption and fair in that it is applied without any discrimination. There is a difference between "fair" and "equitable," however. The very same real [flooding] event may be much more costly to a family that has little buffer in terms of specific resources to respond . . . like insurance, savings, alternate living quarters . . . And in terms of health resiliency, we know that people of color experience the cumulative impacts of stress on their health. It is worthwhile to "tunnel into" the decisions we make to see where having more information about the people impacted, including any history of disadvantage and subsequent disparities in health and economic outcomes, can be important.
>
> *(Email correspondence, 1 November 2013)*

Hansen describes how, in viewing challenges as purely environmental, as opposed to politically charged socio-environmental questions, experts and city leaders over-look complexities that determine access to the beneficial outcomes of environmental projects—including Complete Streets-oriented stormwater management projects. When decision-makers take pains to be "fair" and "nondiscriminatory," they may well reinforce existing racial and socio-economic disparities. Likewise, by not explicitly and proactively seeking to counteract disparities, CWSP's grant-making instead served to reify them. Seemingly neutral programs, operating in the context of the decidedly unequal, non-neutral city, merely perpetuate existing inequalities.

Worse yet, planning decisions and public investments can actually exacerbate inequalities. While the use of "objective" analytical tools such as maps and census data has led to the realization that incomplete streets are disproportionately located in low-income neighborhoods (Clifton et al. n.d.), planners are less likely to consider the possibility that the relationship between Complete Streets and housing affordability is more than coincidental. People of color and low-income residents do not merely happen to live in neighborhoods that lack sidewalks and bike lanes; it is precisely the absence of Complete Streets amenities that makes such neighborhoods unattractive to developers and households with higher purchasing power. Yet, when the "rent gap" between actual and potential ground rent becomes wide enough—for instance, when Complete Streets amenities are added to a previously low-rent neighborhood—"redevelopment and rehabilitation into new land uses becomes a profitable prospect, and capital begins to flow back" (Smith 1982, p.149). When planners target such areas for Complete Streets investments, the ostensible beneficiaries of those investments are frequently displaced.[5]

Likewise, by funding community gardens, bioswales, and other Complete Streets amenities that often accompany gentrification, municipal programs (like CWSP) can be implicated in the displacement of low-income residents.

CWSP's equity turn

By the mid-2000s, CWSP's staff was growing troubled by the program's tendency to reflect the city's racial and spatial disparities in its grant-making, and started thinking about how to make changes. Messer summarizes CWSP's thinking: "If you realize there's a hardship or inequitable way that things are working, it's the Bureau's responsibility to prioritize attention to those things" (Interview, 31 October 2013).

CWSP's first equity strategies were place-based. As early as 2003, the program adopted a policy of seeking to fund projects in each of the city's four watersheds.[6] In the years that followed, CWSP's graduate student employees conducted a GIS analysis to map past projects and target underserved neighborhoods for outreach. Beginning in 2006, CWSP held annual grant application workshops at libraries and community centers in targeted areas of the city. "We wanted to make sure grants did not just fund specific neighborhoods," Devlin explains (Presentation, 18 October 2013).

CWSP also began to offer assistance in completing the grant application and securing permits to carry out projects. Devlin describes some of the institutional barriers applicants faced: "[City permitting] is set up for developers; it's not set up for the church guy to build a garden" (ibid.). These initial steps laid the ground-work for more far-reaching reforms.

Though Devlin and her staff were beginning to analyze and address spatial disparities in the program's grant-making, they were limited in their capacity and resources, and felt constrained by BES' status as a ratepayer-funded bureau that needed to remain focused on its core mission of stormwater management. A mandate from City Commissioner Dan Saltzman's office in 2010, however, gave CWSP license to become more purposeful and explicit in taking an equity-oriented approach.[7] Devlin explains:

> The role [of Commissioner Saltzman] was really important . . . Since BES is funded by rate-payers, we can't just do whatever we think is "neat." We're very conscientious about using rates for our core mission . . . So to have the Commissioner direct us, "Do this [equity] work," that was huge. To hear they wanted it to be purposeful . . . "We want equity questions on the application"—they were very specific—that was very helpful in increasing our equity focus.
>
> *(Interview, 25 October 2013)*

Saltzman's directive did not come out of thin air. One of his advisors, Amy Trieu, had been on CWSP's application review committee for a few years. She recalls seeing Groundwork Portland's application seeking funds to pay young people to remove invasive plants as part of its environmental justice-focused summer employment program (Figure 10.6). "The application didn't score well. It wasn't very well-written, nor specific, and didn't offer many technical details [about how the project would help improve the watershed]," Trieu remembers (Interview, 30 October 2013). But the well-being of foster youth was already a high priority for Saltzman's office. "A youth program applying for an environmental grant was kind of unusual. But it connected with Saltzman's other stuff, including foster kids. The environmental impact seemed low, but it was high in community impact" (ibid.). Trieu sold Saltzman on the synergistic community and environmental outcomes that could come from funding projects such as stipends for youth employment, which led to the Commissioner's directive that CWSP take more purposeful, politically bold steps in implementing an equity agenda.

"There was a shift," Trieu says, "in CWSP selection committee members redefining community" (ibid.). Starting in 2010, the grant application asked applicants to explain the role that underrepresented communities played in their projects. Devlin and her staff adjusted the grant's budget restrictions so that groups could spend more money to pay young people for environmental work. "That changed the program in a huge way. It brought in different groups, and that was the intent," Devlin recounts (Interview, 25 October 2013). These few, basic changes to the program were successful in encouraging more applicants to partner with underrepresented community groups in order to carry out their projects.

FIGURE 10.6 CWSP grantee Groundwork Portland's Green Team at work

Source: Groundwork Portland.

Many of these partnerships, however, were superficial, and few applications came in for projects directly envisioned and led by communities of color and other historically marginalized groups. Projects located east of 82nd Avenue were also rare. Devlin felt that CWSP needed to do more. "I kept thinking in my head that Saltzman wants us to be more *purposeful* [about equity]," Devlin remembers (Interview, 25 October 2013). So in 2012, CWSP and PSU cobbled together funds to hire a third graduate employee, Cameron Herrington (co-author of this chapter), who was given the specific charge of analyzing CWSP's structure and practices, leading to changes that would deepen and institutionalize CWSP's commitment to equity.

A forward-looking view of equity planning: the nuts and bolts

With added analytical capacity and community outreach experience coming from Herrington's position, over the past two years, CWSP has implemented a handful of important reforms. While specific to the context of CWSP, these changes point to the more widely applicable strategies and principles heralded by equity planning practitioner and scholar, Norman Krumholz. Drawing on his experience as

Cleveland's planning director in the 1970s, Krumholz has spent much of his career thinking about how municipal employees can prioritize the needs of marginalized communities.[8] In his classic article, "A Retrospective View of Equity Planning," Krumholz (1982) describes the urgent challenges that existed in Cleveland in the 1970s, and summarizes his department's efforts to provide "a wider range of choices for those Cleveland residents who have few, if any, choices" (p. 163). Here we draw on Krumholz's reflections to help outline three areas in which CWSP has moved to become more responsive to underrepresented groups: (1) setting concrete goals; (2) infusing daily practices with an equity lens; and (3) spreading the word to other municipal programs.

Setting concrete goals

The most fundamental lesson that Krumholz learned in Cleveland is that there needs to be an explicit, overarching goal of social equity if results are to change. In order to move beyond the realm of equity rhetoric, and into the sphere of equity outcomes, goals must be *clearly defined* and *measurable*. In the case of CWSP, leaders decided that improving equity meant awarding more grants to projects that not only involved, but were *led by*, underrepresented groups. This entailed two steps: first, CWSP had to attract more applications for projects spearheaded by under-represented community groups. Second, from among submitted applications, CWSP's review committee had to prioritize those projects for funding.

In order to measure improvement, CWSP staff first needed to establish a baseline of equity performance, against which outcomes could be compared on a year-to-year basis. In 2012, CWSP staff analyzed all applications from the previous three grant cycles, and assigned each one a score based on the degree of underrepresented groups' participation and leadership.[9] This scoring system took an abstract equity goal and made it measurable, with higher scores going to projects that entailed higher levels of underrepresented group influence.

This initial baseline analysis confirmed assumptions that outreach efforts were not effectively reaching underrepresented groups: for the 2010–11 grant cycle (the first in which an equity question was asked in the application), 38 percent of applications had some involvement by underrepresented groups (usually a partnership with a dominant culture group that was the lead applicant), and only 9 percent were led by underrepresented groups (3 out of 34 total applications). Working from this starting point, CWSP could gauge improvements.

One key component of CWSP's goal-setting was an emphasis on acknowledging past injustices. For CWSP, examining Portland's history of uneven development (Smith 2008) associated with urban renewal policies, for example, helped underscore the idea that spatial equity approaches, while important, do not necessarily translate into socioeconomic equity outcomes. This is an especially prescient consideration in the context of rapidly gentrifying neighborhoods, where green development often involves the displacement of marginalized groups to underserved parts of the city. From 2012 forward, therefore, CWSP's concrete equity goals became focused on awarding grants to underrepresented *populations*, rather than just underserved *neighborhoods*.

Complete Streets planners, too, can become much more attuned to the complex relationship between spatial and socio-economic disparities. In order to ensure that underrepresented groups are the beneficiaries of Complete Streets enhancements (and other publicly funded projects that increase private property values), planners can advocate for explicit anti-displacement measures such as community benefits agreements, community controlled housing, and workforce development initiatives.

Infusing daily practices with an equity lens

For Krumholz (1982), clearly defined goals provide a framework for everyday decision-making. He asserts that planners and bureaucrats must ask "who benefits, and who pays" for every decision that crosses the desk; no decision is too small to be analyzed through an equity lens. There must be a "concentrated attack on these [day-to-day] problems" (ibid., p. 173). For CWSP, outreach and promotion, the application process, selection of grantees, and support for grantees constitute the everyday operations of the program. Such routine activities, on the surface, may appear as mere bureaucratic details. But in reality, these comprise the substantive elements that determine who benefits from CWSP's approximately $95,000 in annual grant funds. Staff asked how they could overcome obstacles to broader participation, while staying within the bounds of the core missions of CWSP and BES.

Communication and outreach

Shannon Jamison, one of CWSP's current graduate student coordinators, has helped implement the program's shift to a more purposeful equity agenda. She succinctly states:

> The onus is on us to make our program more relevant and accessible [to underrepresented communities]. We can't just change our grant selection priorities. We actually have to change our program so it's relevant to a broader swath of the city.
>
> *(Interview, 8 October 2013)*

CWSP reached out to underrepresented community groups to gain a better understanding of the barriers they faced in accessing the program, and to ask what would make it more relevant to their existing needs and priorities. Quite simply, "We asked people what was important to them," explains Jamison (ibid.).

Until 2012, CWSP's messaging and outreach had been focused on environmental projects that resonated with Portland's dominant—white, middle-class—sustainability culture. Its email announcements and flyers promoted the grant as a means of funding eco-roofs, stormwater management facilities, and nature-scaping projects, which reinforced the notion that CWSP was a program for environmentalists. Even CWSP's name, the Community Watershed Stewardship Program, poses an initial hurdle in reaching out to communities that are not familiar with the concept of watershed stewardship.

Whereas the watershed health message resonated with organizations that were already familiar with that language, and had time and resources to devote to explicitly environmental projects, it did not speak to communities that were contending with pressing priorities such as food insecurity or neighborhood safety. "I've seen your email announcements, but I delete them because we're not an environmental group," the director of one East Portland community-based organization told a CWSP staffer. The outreach and messaging challenge for CWSP was clear: it had to make the program relevant to groups that were motivated primarily by (seemingly) non-environmental concerns.

Through conversations with community leaders, and a review of past grant applications, CWSP staff compiled a list of community defined priorities and paired them with projects that are eligible for CWSP funding based on their watershed health benefits (see Table 10.1). "We can have different motivations—a community group is concerned with youth employment, BES wants to reduce stormwater runoff—but still work together on a project that meets both sets of goals," Jamison explains (ibid.). This analysis fed back into CWSP's messaging strategy, providing language to emphasize why non-environmentally oriented groups might want to apply.

Planning departments, for their part, can work to identify and prioritize under-represented community defined priorities, some of which might be addressed through Complete Streets initiatives. Moreover, rather than using common Complete Streets terminology such as sustainability, walkability, and livability, planning departments with equity objectives can more overtly state how Complete Streets initiatives are intended to address community defined concerns, such as pedestrian safety and public health.

Along these lines, CWSP staff began to send outreach emails and distribute posters with the headline, "Funding for YOUR community project!" This contrasted with previous years' materials, which said, "Fund your next watershed project" (see Figures 10.7a and 10.7b). For groups that weren't familiar with water-

TABLE 10.1 Index of CWSP projects that simultaneously respond to community and environmental concerns

Community priorities	Watershed projects
Food, nutrition, activities for elders and youth	Community gardens
Leadership and employment for youth	Youth summer programs with stipends
Crime and neighborhood livability	Re-greening properties, community spaces, art
Immigrant and refugee inclusion	Educational opportunities
Flooding, standing water	De-paving, bioswales

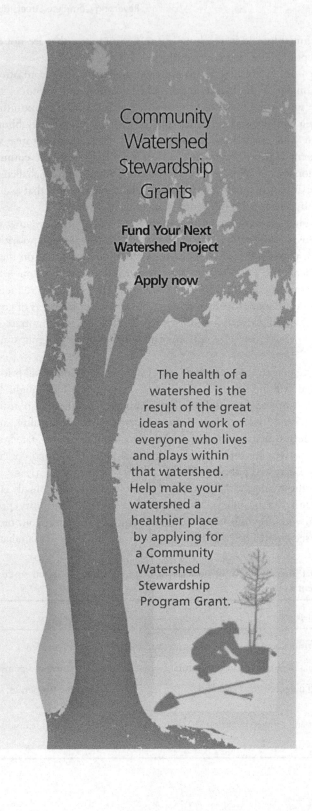

Community
Watershed
Stewardship
Grants

**Fund Your Next
Watershed Project**

Apply now

The health of a
watershed is the
result of the great
ideas and work of
everyone who lives
and plays within
that watershed.
Help make your
watershed a
healthier place
by applying for
a Community
Watershed
Stewardship
Program Grant.

Opposite and above: FIGUREs 10.7(a) and (b) Old and new CWSP brochures

Source: City of Portland, Bureau of Environmental Services. © City of Portland, courtesy Bureau of Environmental Services.

shed terminology, or that had never done a watershed project, the prospect of doing a "next" watershed project was presumably not very enticing (Herrington presentation, 18 October 2013). Messer sums up the messaging approach that CWSP has adopted over the last two grant cycles:

> There has to be something that provides a sense of efficacy. . . and relevance. You don't talk about an abstract thing called stormwater, you talk about food, a vacant lot that could be a garden, but it could also be a runoff area . . . You can't assume that all communities have that [mainstream environmental] knowledge. You have to make this work part of their world. And in so doing it furthers broader environmental objectives.
>
> *(Interview, 31 October 2013)*

Indeed, working with groups that did not have pre-existing environmental acumen and motivations has made CWSP a more effective program, in BES' own terms, by helping it to engage a more representative swath of Portlanders in watershed stewardship—a true win–win for the community and the city.

Armed with more effective messages and outreach materials, CWSP adopted a proactive plan in order to connect with groups that had not previously applied for grants. Staff now specifically reach out to organizations led by and representing people of color and other historically marginalized groups. Rather than expecting potential applicants to come downtown to BES' offices for meetings, staff members board buses and ride bikes across the city, meeting applicants at their churches, homes, and neighborhood coffee shops. Jamison says, "A huge part of the success is the people component. Having one-on-one meetings and talking about what they want and need, what communities are interested in, is really important" (Interview, 8 October 2013).

Furthermore, CWSP has relied upon a handful of city staffers who already have solid relationships with underrepresented groups to introduce and vouch for the grant program. Polo Catalani, director of the city's New Portlander Program, introduced CWSP staff to immigrant and refugee community leaders by hosting a dinner at an immigrant owned restaurant. Jamison reflects, "Figuring out who are the right messengers, and having those people make introductions, goes a long way" (ibid.).

As a result of its revamped messaging and outreach strategy, CWSP was able to meet its equity goal of attracting far more applications for projects envisioned and led by underrepresented community groups. For the 2013–14 grant cycle, 74 percent of the proposed projects had some degree of participation by under-represented groups, up from 38 percent in 2010–11. More importantly, one-third of the applications were for projects *led by* those groups, up from only 9 percent three years earlier.

The application process

Based on feedback from community organizations, CWSP streamlined the application process by eliminating unnecessary questions from the application form. Additionally, staff provided targeted support to assist new groups with the application process, and spent less time working closely with veteran applicants. "Our program asked people to talk very articulately about environmental issues. But several first-time applicants asked me, 'What is a watershed?' This puts people at a disadvantage," Jamison explains (ibid.). Staff now sit with applicants, helping them evaluate their project goals and adjust language in order to communicate both community and watershed health benefits and make applications more competitive. Cohen, Groundwork Portland Director, reflected, "CWSP can be a resource for smaller organizations [like us] to get introduced to watershed restoration work, even if they don't have the skill set ahead of time. They help get them going" (Interview, 25 October 2013).

Notably, many groups led by immigrants and communities of color told CWSP they'd like to use funds for community garden projects. They hoped to grow food, provide gardening education, and facilitate outdoor activities for youth and elders. But whereas CWSP had no explicit restrictions for other types of projects, a list of constraints that applied only to community gardens had been adopted in 2011. With the support of Devlin and BES managers, CWSP eliminated those garden restrictions prior to the 2013–14 grant cycle. The program's application guide instead now contains a table listing various components of a food garden project that can enhance watershed health, thereby making garden projects more likely to receive funding.

Selection criteria

While shifts in messaging, outreach strategy, and the application process were fundamental in helping CWSP attract applications from a more diverse range of groups, Devlin and her staff knew they also needed to address equity in the grant selection process. The selection committee had always made funding decisions based on the two aspects of CWSP's core mission: first, projects had to improve watershed health, and, second, they had to be community-based (that is, an individual or small group of people would be unlikely to receive funding). Over the past three years, however, CWSP has instituted a third evaluation variable, which assesses the role that underrepresented groups play in envisioning and implementing projects.

To ensure that the program has the capacity to accurately evaluate applications on the basis of the new equity criterion, CWSP recruits staff members from the city's Office of Equity and Human Rights and the citywide Equity Committee to serve on the selection committee. All selection committee members—including environmental scientists, stormwater experts, and environmental educators from BES—are now instructed to consider equity alongside the other two criteria, and the committee has taken that charge seriously. For the 2013–14 grant cycle, 100 percent of funded projects had some level of involvement by underrepresented community groups, compared to the 74 percent of the applications that met that standard. Projects *led by* underrepresented groups, meanwhile, made up two-thirds of the grant awards, after comprising one-third of the applications. Far from being accidental or coincidental, this "overfunding" of underrepresented communities' projects is by design, and is now institutionalized in the program's selection process.

Implementation support

The final component of CWSP's day-to-day operation entails supporting groups that receive funding as they implement their projects. CWSP staff remain limited in time and resources to invest in this area, and so call on past grantees to help support less-experienced groups. Such collaborations are imperative. Cohen says, "We met new partner organizations with the help of CWSP that have potential [work projects] for our young folks . . .This helps with job skills training and stewardship experience, and they get paid in the process . . . It's been critical" (ibid.). And two established environmental organizations that had received CWSP grants in past years, Depave and the Johnson Creek Watershed Council, were instrumental partners in remedying the parking lot flooding challenge at St. Mary Ethiopian Orthodox Church (described at the beginning of this chapter).

Jamison recounts some of the benefits of pairing mainstream environmental groups with community groups:

> [Mainstream environmental] groups are now partnering up with under-represented groups in order to get their watershed goals accomplished [due to the new funding criteria], and it's helping community groups get their goals

accomplished, too. There's genuine interest in how they can work with new groups to achieve goals. There doesn't seem to be any animosity [about the new funding criteria]. [Environmental groups] know they need to get savvy with our new equity focus—it's not going away. That's pretty powerful.

(Interview, 8 October 2013)

Spreading the word

Finally, Krumholz underscores the need to engage with the larger political arena beyond one's own bureau or program around equity issues, including talking with elected officials, other bureaucrats, and community leaders. For CWSP, in addition to engaging with energized PSU students that bring in new ideas, this has meant inviting policy analysts from elected officials' offices to help evaluate applications. As described above, such outreach played a decisive role in making CWSP's equity approach more explicit.

Krumholz (1982, p.174) stresses that activist-oriented city staff must remain politically engaged:

If [bureaucrats] consistently place before their political superiors analyses, policies, and recommendations which lead to greater equity, and if they are willing to publicly join in the fight for the adoption of these recommendations, some of them will be adopted when the time is ripe.

Portland's City Council became familiar with CWSP through yearly briefings, and when a budget crisis in 2013 caused the mayor to cut CWSP from his proposed budget, past grant recipients' testimony, along with pressure from the city's Office of Equity and Human Rights (OEHR), prompted the Council to reinstate funding for the program.

To share its equity approach more widely, CWSP has collaborated with OEHR to develop a 40-minute presentation documenting the program's "promising equity practices." Devlin describes the enthusiasm that has emerged in BES: "I have six groups in my own bureau that want the presentation. They want to know what the thinking looks like and how to get here . . .What are the nuts and bolts?" (Interview, 25 October 2013). OEHR, meanwhile, is working to schedule the presentation for other city bureaus. At one recent presentation, a Housing Bureau staff member reflected, "We are looking at the same thing [as CWSP] . . . I'm curious about looking at our language and seeing what kinds of embedded barriers there are [to our programs]" (Public comments, 18 October 2013).

Conclusion

The case of CWSP provides one example of how to operationalize equity aspirations in sustainability and Complete Streets-oriented programs. But feminist economic geographer J.K. Gibson-Graham (2006, p.105) reminds us that illuminating the practices of one city program, as we have done here, is not merely an exercise in exposing "what's out there." Rather, in researching and writing this chapter, we are making an active attempt to produce and transform discourses associated with Complete Streets. Along with sustainability and livability, emphases on Complete Streets in city planning and governance circles contain multiple and contradictory possibilities and outcomes. We hope that, in bringing attention to a handful of tangible ways that CWSP and its grantees have reimagined and reinterpreted the watershed health component of Complete Streets planning, we are helping to actualize more socially and environmentally just political projects and desires.

To be sure, CWSP and BES still have work to do to become even more responsive to the needs of all city residents. While CWSP's grant application has become more streamlined, for instance, a considerable amount of paperwork is still required for a relatively small amount of funding; this can quickly overwhelm small organizations, like St. Mary's congregation and Groundwork Portland.

But Hansen, BES engineer and Equity Committee representative, reiterates the importance of the steps CWSP has taken: "It's like planting seeds. It's easier to talk to other programs about how to translate this stuff into the concrete, day-to-day running of their programs with an example like CWSP." And Cohen, Groundwork Portland executive director, describes the substantial work her program's youth have done with the help of CWSP funding: "We've done brownfield tours and remediation projects.[10] These have helped young people from low-income households of color learn about environmental issues and learn valuable job skills for the green economy, while enhancing Portland's watersheds" (Interview, 25 October 3013).

Yet, we cannot rely solely on the work of grassroots community groups such as those funded by CWSP, nor individual municipal employees, to fight widespread socio-environmental injustices. The inclusive, hands-on approach we document here may well be effective in sharing a small pot of public resources with those who have historically been excluded. Fully addressing more profound injustices such as gentrification/displacement, however, will require commitments and effective policies at higher levels of sustainable city planning and governance. After all, the circumstances and histories that structure disparities operate at much greater scales than that of a church parking lot, a brownfield, a watershed, or even a city. Cohen describes the layers of history and institutional exploitation that merge to produce the poverty and inequities that many Groundwork youth and their families face:

> [Brownfield lots] have been vacant, sitting there for decades while the Black community was there, and now they're getting flipped and turned into beautiful coffee shops and bars. People can't afford to live here [in inner Northeast Portland] anymore and reap the benefits . . . There's systemic racism and oppression that affect folks here locally, and impact their lived experience . . . Youth tend to blame themselves. They think about change as "What can I as an individual do to pick up trash?," versus what are the systemic things that need to be fought and organized around?
>
> *(Interview, 25 October 2013)*

Confronting the historical and systemic injustices that Cohen references requires dedicated resources from public sector entities. Such resources have been vital for CWSP, which has hired graduate student employees specifically to perform equity analysis and push forward program reform. Messer emphasizes that student employees bring an invaluable "energy, vision, and persistence of attention to the sometimes neglected areas [such as equity] that frequently get lost in the day-to-day over-burdened world of city bureaus" (Email correspondence, 21 November 2013). Many municipal offices do not have such resources—nor the institutional backing to pursue such an agenda in the first place. "How do you do this without a dedicated person that can make you uncomfortable and call things out?" Devlin asks. "Change is an uphill battle. We are creatures of habit, and change is difficult" (Interview, 25 October 2013).

Nonetheless, Complete Streets-oriented programs that are purposeful in their equity work can have a broader impact. As the example of CWSP demonstrates, they can serve as a testing ground for new models and practices that translate equity rhetoric into tangible outcomes, thereby opening more space for social justice-oriented community groups to work, and providing immediate, compelling examples for like-minded planners, practitioners, and policy-makers.

Notes

1 Throughout this chapter, we follow CWSP's lead in defining underrepresented groups as communities of color, immigrants, refugees, elders, and others who have historically been discriminated against and excluded from access to economic and political power.
2 Redlining is the practice of drawing a red line around African-American neighborhoods on maps, and then deeming properties substantially lower in value than in other neighborhoods and/or charging more for banking, insurance, and other services within the boundaries; it was used as a discriminatory tool by real estate agents to segregate neighborhoods from the 1920s to 1968.
3 Some neighborhoods west of 82nd Avenue lack Complete Streets as well. Additionally, poverty is not confined to East Portland, and more affluent residents live in some East Portland census tracts. But disparities between East Portland and other areas are starker, steadily increasing, and reflect a history of locally uneven power relations (Schmidt 2013), making East Portland's lack of Complete Streets particularly notable.
4 Miéville's *The City and The City* is set in a quasi-fantastical, dual city-state, in which two separate cities occupy the same physical space. Residents of each city are trained from birth to ignore the people, streets and buildings of the other, despite their being constantly in plain sight. Transgressions across this cultural spatial divide are severely punished.
5 In this chapter we heavily emphasize the intersection of Complete Streets-oriented planning and gentrification/displacement, as this is a particularly pertinent theme in Portland. Moreover, as gentrification has become a globalized "consummate expression of neoliberal urbanism . . . mobilized [by] individual property claims via a market lubricated by state donation" (Smith 2002, p. 99), we contend that it is nearly impossible to discuss the production of urban space taking place through Complete Streets planning without putting gentrification/displacement issues at the center of analysis (though related themes, such as disparities in health outcomes, are certainly relevant as well).
6 There are four primary watersheds within Portland's city limits: Fanno/Tryon Creeks, Willamette River, Johnson Creek, and Columbia Slough.
7 In Portland's commission form of government, commissioners have both legislative and administrative authority. In addition to serving on the City Council, each commissioner

is assigned by the mayor to run specific bureaus. BES was in Commissioner Saltzman's portfolio at the time.

8 Planning theorist Firanak Miraftab (2009, p. 44) describes how virtually any actor (including activists, mothers, teachers, city workers) can be transformative ("insurgent") planners if they engage in "purposeful actions that aim to disrupt domineering relationships of oppressors to the oppressed, and to destabilize such a status quo through consciousness of the past and imagination of an alternative future." While CWSP staff and other bureaucrats implementing Complete Streets or sustainability initiatives may not have "city planner" as their job title, we contend that city employees seeking to implement an equity agenda in their programs and bureaus are dabbling in a political world more akin to that of city planners and community development practitioners than techno-rational experts, and therefore seek insights from the field of equity planning.

9 Scoring system: 0 for no participation by underrepresented groups; 1 for limited participation in a project led by a dominant culture organization; 2 for a fundamental partnership between a dominant culture group and an underrepresented community; and 3 for projects envisioned and led by underrepresented groups.

10 Brownfields are sites where future use is affected by past industrial or commercial contamination.

References

Abbott, C., 2001. *Greater Portland: Urban life and landscape in the Pacific Northwest.* Philadelphia, PA: University of Pennsylvania Press.

Agyeman, J., 2005. *Sustainable communities and the challenge of environmental justice.* New York, NY: NYU Press.

Agyeman, J., 2013. *Introducing just sustainabilities: Policy, planning and practice.* London: Zed Books.

Bates, L., 2013. *Gentrification and displacement study: Implementing an equitable inclusive development strategy in the context of gentrification.* Commissioned by the City of Portland's Bureau of Planning and Sustainability. Available from: www.portlandoregon.gov/bps/article/454027 [Accessed 20 August 2013].

Bunce, S., 2009. Developing sustainability: Sustainability policy and gentrification on Toronto's waterfront. *Local Environment*, 14 (7), 651–667.

Bureau of Environmental Services (BES), 2011. Combined sewer overflow program progress report, January 2011.

City of Portland, 2013. Top 10 high crash corridors. Available from: www.portlandoregon.gov/transportation/article/439832 [Accessed 16 December 2013].

Clifton, K., Bronstein, S., and Morrissey, S., n.d. The path to Complete Streets in underserved communities: Lessons from U.S. case studies. Available from: www.smartgrowthamerica.org/documents/cs/resources/complete-streets-in-underserved-communities.pdf [Accessed 20 December 2013].

Coalition for a Livable Future (CLF), 2013. *The regional equity atlas: Metropolitan Portland's geography of opportunity.* Available from: http://clfuture.org/programs/regional-equity-atlas/maps-and-analysis/ [Accessed 14 August 2013].

Curry-Stevens, A., Cross-Hemmer, A., and Coalition of Communities of Color, 2010. *Communities of color in Multnomah County: An unsettling profile.* Portland, OR: Portland State University. Available from: http://coalitioncommunitiescolor.org/docs/AN%20UNSETTLING%20PROFILE.pdf [Accessed 23 January 2012].

DeFilippis, J., 2004. *Unmaking Goliath: Community control in the face of global capital.* New York, NY: Routledge.

Gibson, K., 2007. Bleeding Albina. *Transforming Anthropology*, 15 (1), 3–25.

Gibson-Graham, J.K., 2006. *The end of capitalism (as we knew it): A feminist critique of political economy.* Minneapolis, MN: University of Minnesota Press.

Griffin-Valade, L., Kahn, D., and Adams-Wannberg, K., 2010. *City of Portland 20th Annual Community Survey Results.* Portland, Oregon: Office of the City Auditor.

Gunder, M., 2006. Sustainability: Planning's saving grace or road to perdition? *Journal of Planning Education and Research*, 26 (2), 208–221.

Hackworth, J., 2007. *The neoliberal city: Governance, ideology, and development in American urbanism.* Ithaca, NY: Cornell University Press.

Harvey, D., 1989. *The urban experience.* Baltimore, MD: The Johns Hopkins University Press.

Harvey, D., 2007. *Spaces of global capitalism: A theory of uneven geographical development.* London: Verso.

Heynen, N., Kaika, M., and Swyngedouw, E., 2006. Urban political ecology: Politicizing the production of urban natures. In: N. Heynen, M. Kaika, and E. Swyngedouw, eds. *In the nature of cities: Urban political ecology and the politics of urban Metabolism.* London: Routledge.

Huber, M., and Currie, T., 2007. The urbanization of an idea: Imagining nature through urban growth boundary policy in Portland, Oregon. *Urban Geography*, 28 (8), 705–731.

Jonas, A., and While, A., 2007. Greening the entrepreneurial city? In: R. Krueger and D. Gibbs, eds. *The sustainable development paradox: Urban political economy in the United States and Europe.* New York, NY: The Guilford Press.

Jurjevich, J., and Schrock, G., 2012. Is Portland really the place where young people go to retire? Working paper. Available from: http://mkn.research.pdx.edu/wp-content/uploads/2012/09/JurjevichSchrockMigrationReport1.pdf [Accessed 5 November 2013].

Krueger, R., and Gibbs, D., eds., 2007. *The sustainable development paradox: Urban political economy in the United States and Europe.* New York, NY: Guilford Press.

Krumholz, N., 1982. A retrospective view of equity planning: Cleveland 1969–1979. *APA Journal*, Spring, 163–174.

Law, S., 2013. East side squeaky wheel gets city's funding grease. *Portland Tribune*. Available from: http://portlandtribune.com/pt/9-news/135335-east-side-squeaky-wheel-gets-citys-funding-grease [Accessed 5 May 2013].

McClintock, N., 2011. From industrial garden to food desert: Demarcated devaluation in the flatlands of Oakland, California. In: A.H. Alkon and J. Agyeman, eds. *Cultivating food justice: Race, class, and sustainability.* Cambridge, MA: MIT Press.

Miéville, C., 2011. *The city and the city.* New York, NY: Ballantine Books.

Miller, T., and Lubitow, A., 2014. The politics of sustainability: Contested urban bikeway development in Portland, Oregon. In: S. Zavestoski and J. Agyeman, eds. *Incomplete streets: Processes, practices and possibilities.* New York, NY: Routledge.

Minow-Smith, D., 2012. Breaking: Portland sustainability chief admits 'Portlandia' isn't really a parody. *Grist*. Available from: from http://grist.org/cities/breaking-portalnd-sustainability-chief-admits-portlandia-isnt-really-a-parody/ [Accessed 18 November 2012].

Miraftab, F., 2009. Insurgent planning: situating radical planning in the Global South. *Planning Theory*, 8 (1), 32–50.

Mirk, S., 2010. East of Eden: East Portland is getting poorer—and angrier. *Portland Mercury*. Available from: www.portlandmercury.com/portland/east-of-eden/Content?oid=2462525 [Accessed 6 March 2012].

National Complete Streets Coalition, 2013. Available from: www.smartgrowthamerica.org/complete-streets [Accessed 20 October 2013].

Pein, C., 2011. The other Portland. *Willamette Week*. Available from: www.wweek.com/portland/article-18071-the_other_portland.html [Accessed 23 January 2012].

Portney, K., 2005. Civic engagement and sustainable cities in the United States. *Public Administration Review*, 65 (5), 579–591.

Pulido, L., 2000. Rethinking environmental racism: White privilege and urban development in Southern California. *Annals of the Association of American Geographers*, 90 (1), 12–40.

Quastel, N., 2009. Political ecologies of gentrification. *Urban Geography*, 30 (7), 694–725.

Scalza, R., 2012. A culture moves east in Portland, Ore. *The New York Times*. Available from: www.nytimes.com/slideshow/2012/10/21/travel/20121021-SURFACING.html?_r=2& [Accessed 31 October 2013].

Schmidt, B., 2013. East Portland's housing explosion tied to city plan without basic services. *The Oregonian*. Available from: www.oregonlive.com/portland/index.ssf/2013/12/east_portlands_housing_explosi.html [Accessed 21 December 2013].

Seltzer, E., 2004. It's not an experiment: Regional planning at Metro, 1990 to the present. In: C. Ozawa, ed. *The Portland Edge*. Washington, DC: Island Press.

Smith, N., 1982. Gentrification and uneven development. *Economic Geography*. 58 (2), 139–155.

Smith, N., 2002. New globalism, new urbanism: gentrification as global urban strategy. *Antipode*, 34 (3), 427–450.

Smith, N., 2008. *Uneven development: Nature, capital, and the production of space*. Athens, GA: University of Georgia Press.

SustainLane. 2008. SustainLane presents: the U.S. city rankings. Available from: www.sustainlane.com/us-city-rankings/ [Accessed 18 February 2012].

Swyngedouw, E., 2007. Impossible 'sustainability' and the postpolitical condition. In: R. Krueger and D. Gibbs, eds. *The sustainable development paradox: Urban political economy in the United States and Europe*. New York, NY: The Guilford Press.

Vos, R., 2007. Defining sustainability: A conceptual orientation. *Journal of Chemical Technology and Biotechnology*, 82 (4), 334–339.

Wheeler, S., and Beatley, T., 2004. *The sustainable urban development reader*. London: Routledge.

Welsch, A., and Heying, C.,1999. Watershed management and community building: A case study of CWSP. *Administrative Theory & Praxis*, 21 (1), 88–102.

PART III
Possibilities

11

COMPL(EAT)ING THE STREETS

Legalizing sidewalk food vending in Los Angeles

Mark Vallianatos[1]

Introduction

Take everything about LA and put it into one bite

Over the past several years, Los Angeles has been praised for its hybridizing and informal food scene. According to food writers and urbanists, the city and region seemed to be constantly spinning off not just innovative cuisines—but equally significantly, different ways and places to sell and enjoy food. In 2010, *Food & Wine* magazine named Roy Choi, chef of the Kogi BBQ Truck, a popular taco truck that sells Korean-Latin fusion food, as one of its ten best new chefs (Brion 2010). Choi and Kogi co-founders Alice Shin and Mark Manguera helped launch the national and now internatonal trend for gourmet food trucks that announce their stops on twitter (Arellano 2012, pp. 266–269). A week after the launch of the Kogi Truck in late 2008 (before its success made him famous), Choi defined its signature Korean BBQ taco as Los Angeles in a meal:

> Everything you get in that taco is what we live in LA. It's the 720 bus on Wilshire, it's the 3rd street Juanita's Tacos, the Korean supermarket and all those things that we live every day in one bite. That was our goal. To take everything about LA and put it into one bite.
>
> *(Behrens 2008)*

Gourmet food trucks, traditional taco trucks, and trailers serve the streets of Los Angeles (Figure 11.1). If you need groceries, look for produce trucks that take routes through immigrant neighborhoods. Street food is even more diverse on the sidewalks. Vendors push carts designed for mobile vending. Others sell food and drinks out of strollers or grocery carts jury-rigged for vending with an assortment

FIGURE 11.1 Vendor rides three-wheeled bike cart on sidewalk

Source: Photo by Rudy Espinoza.

of coolers, grilltops, propane tanks, tinfoil or sheetmetal walls/heatshields, utensils and condiments. Street food doesn't always move around and come to you. Sometimes it waits on metal grills, tables and tarps temporarily placed on the sidewalk. At its most basic, street food stands and walks in LA, held by vendors poised by the side of the road or in street medians waiting to sell bags of oranges or to carry ready-to-drink coconuts into traffic to hand through car windows.

This street food helps make streets and sidewalks in Los Angeles more "complete" places by expanding and blurring formal categories of route and place, cuisine and culture, sale and purchase, law and politics. From tacos or bacon-wrapped hotdogs after a night out to a stop at a cut fruit cart on a hot afternoon, carts and trucks extend the hours and places that people buy, sell and eat. These mobile meals create hotspots of social interactions in a city that too often lacks public life. The hybridizing of ingredients and recipes in what food critic Jonathan Gold calls "dripping plates of food drawn straight from the city's recombinant

DNA" (Gold 2012) lends an air of cultural solidarity, at least in the shallow form of epicurean appreciation, to a region where immigration has transformed demographics without always integrating society.

Street food is also a significant element of the informal economy and street life, with many vendors operating outside of the law. Despite its reputation as a hotbed of street food, Los Angeles, is, in fact, the only one of the ten most populous cities in the United States not to allow sidewalk vending of food (National Policy and Legal Analysis Network to Prevent Childhood Obesity and Public Health Law & Policy 2010).

As the City of Los Angeles attempts to reshape its roads and transportation system to incorporate more Complete Streets that are safe for pedestrians, bike riders, transit users, and drivers (City of Los Angeles 2010, 2012, 2013), it will need to reexamine whether there is a role for food vendors, with their distinct cultural signifiers and spatial practices, on city sidewalks. Can streets in a heavily immigrant metropolis, however multi-modal the distribution of lane space, be said to be "complete" if they fail to include the livelihoods and economic survival of vendors; the smells, sights and tastes of homelands; and places for people to pause, shop, and eat?

In this chapter, I will explore why sidewalk vending is illegal in Los Angeles, how unsanctioned vending impacts streets, and why and how it should be legalized. The chapter is organized into five parts. The first section provides a brief history of street food in Los Angeles. The second section describes the laws that regulate mobile food vending in the city. The third section analyzes how vendors use and transform sidewalks. The next section suggests why sidewalk vending of food in LA should be legalized and how a legal scheme for vending could be set up. The chapter concludes on a hopeful note with accounts of a campaign to legalize sidewalk vending.

History

Respect the architects

What seems new about tweeting food trucks does indeed represent innovation, but also draws upon the city's history as a magnet to immigrants and an epicenter of car culture and eating at the speed of driving. The Los Angeles region birthed the modern fast food industry (Schlosser 2001). Taco Bell, the first fast food chain serving Mexican food, modeled its tacos loosely on those its founder Glen Bell had eaten at Mexican restaurants in San Bernardino, a city east of Los Angeles (Arellano 2012, pp. 59–64).

As Ray Choi referenced with his shout-out to Juanita's Tacos, a traditional taco trailer that parks at 3rd and Western in Koreatown, there have been taco trucks in Los Angeles since at least the early 1970s. Originating mainly in East Los Angeles, these catering trucks are known as Loncheras. They traditionally parked during the day in industrial areas without many food options to sell to factory workers, and then at night sold on streets in neighborhoods with large Latino populations (Chee et al. 2009).

These trucks pioneered motorized street food in the Los Angeles region. Sociologist and music critic Oliver Wang, who mapped the stops of the first wave of twitter trucks, commented:

> I don't care if your truck is mashing up Vietnamese banh mi with Philly cheesesteak or serving Filipino chicken adobo wrapped in lavash bread; if you're a catering truck serving cheap food off the street, you're still following the lead of the old-fashioned taco trucks that have been a part of this city's food fare for 30+ years.
>
> Respect the architects.
>
> *(Wang 2010)*

Taco trucks are themselves heirs to earlier forms of street food that, like present day trucks and carts, sometimes drew the ire of competing merchants and the attention of regulators and inspectors. In the late nineteenth and early twentieth century, wandering "tamale men" in San Francisco, Chicago, New York, and other large cities sold tamales, often from buckets heated by steaming water. Gustavo Arellano relates in *Taco USA* that our local tamale vendors were vehicular from the start:

> Given Los Angeles' spread-out geography even in those embryonic days, wandering tamale men didn't take hold in L.A. as they did in the rest of the United States; a cart or wagon was necessary, not only to travel from home to downtown but also the better to procure a spot on the bustling streets . . . As dusk fell, a cavalry of two-by-four pushcarts and eight-foot-long wagons with walls that opened up to reveal cooks inside wheeled their way towards the Plaza [de Los Angeles] and its vicinity, setting up shop until last call and beyond.
>
> *(Arellano 2012, p. 55)*

By the turn of the twentieth century, downtown restaurants began urging the Los City Council to restrict tamale sellers. In 1910, to defend their livelihood, tamale wagon owners organized a counter-petition with the signatures of more than 500 customers. A century before the similar saveourtacotrucks.org petition (Winters Keegan 2008), it argued that "the lunch wagons are catering to an appreciative public and to deprive the people of these convenient eating places would prove to be a great loss to the many local merchants who sell the wagon proprietors various supplies" (Arellano 2012, p. 56). Vending on sidewalks was, however, banned in business districts by the 1930s and citywide in 1980.

Changing conceptions of what streets and sidewalks are for also contributed significantly to the banning of sidewalk vending. Early sidewalks, Anastasia

Loukaitou-Sideris and Renia Ehrenfeucht explain, were host to diverse activities: "Shopkeepers displayed fruit and vegetables . . . Street peddlers also made a living on the street. Public orators could highlight the ravages of capitalism or preach salvation. Children played around building stoops, and dandies strolled along the pavement" (Loukaitou-Sideris and Ehrenfeucht 2009, pp. 20–21).

City political and opinion leaders, supported by engineers who designed civic infrastructure, began to try to impose order on sidewalks, to remove obstructions like the display cases of adjacent businesses. Laws and street design pushed walkers off of streets and onto the sidewalks and redoubled efforts to keep sidewalks clear as unobstructed routes for pedestrians rather than as places to gather (ibid., pp. 20–26). Loukaitou-Sideris and Ehrenfeucht point out the irony of labeling food vendors and other sidewalk activities as obstructions. Without commerce, entertainment, and political attractions to draw and keep residents onto sidewalks, pedestrian activity in most parts of Los Angeles withered away, leaving streets with few people.

Sidewalk vending didn't reemerge as a significant activity in Los Angeles until the 1970s and 1980s, when immigration from Latin America and Asia coincided with a loss of industrial jobs from deindustrialization and the end of the Cold War. Many new arrivals turned to the informal economy, including vending, for work. As an example, LA's popular cut fruit carts trace their origins back to a single pioneering *frutero* who vended fruit in the Mexican state of Puebla before moving to the United States. He began selling cut fruit in Los Angeles sometime in the 1980s. His "fellow *paisanos* [hometown associates] emulated the business model," establishing fruit carts as a local institution (Rosales 2012, p. 9).

The association of vending with immigrant workers and immigrant communities helps explain the third reason why sidewalk vending is illegal in Los Angeles. From restrictions on Chinese laundries to racially restrictive property covenants, governmental and private land use controls in the city were long tinged by racist assumptions (Kolnick 2008). Although attitudes are changing, sidewalk vending has been viewed as a foreign, chaotic activity—a third world occupation— rather than as an opportunity to encourage business formation, make pedestrian-friendly streets and provide food in low-income areas.

Law

No person [...] shall

Street food vendors in the City of Los Angeles are subject to municipal, county, and state regulations that govern if, what, where, and how they may sell food on the public right of way: streets and sidewalks. The City of Los Angeles Municipal Code Section 42(b) prohibits sale of any products, including food, on sidewalks.

> No person, except as otherwise permitted by this section, shall on any sidewalk or street offer for sale, solicit the sale of, announce by any means the

availability of, or have in his or her possession, control or custody, whether upon his or her person or upon some other animate or inanimate object, any goods, wares or merchandise which the public may purchase at any time.

(Los Angeles Municipal Code 2013)

As a misdemeanor, violations of this ban face up to six months in jail and a $1,000 fine.

In 1994, this ban on sidewalk vending was amended to allow the establishment of up to eight "Special Sidewalk Vending Districts" (Los Angeles Municipal Code 1994). Vending Districts were meant to be pilot areas. Complicated regulations, including a requirement that 20 percent of surrounding landowners and residents sign the application in favor of a new district, and assignment of vendors to specified, fixed locations, made it difficult to establish vending districts. Only one vending zone, in McArthur Park, was ever created. According to those who participated in, regulated (Harris 2012), or observed this district, it failed due to the restrictions on participating vendors and from competition from illegal vendors operating nearby (Kettles 2004).

With no vending district currently existing, food vending is illegal on all sidewalks in the City of Los Angeles. Enforcement of this code falls to the city's Bureau of Street Services. The Bureau's 35 inspectors enforce over a hundred provisions of local and state law, including vending issues and illegal dumping. Gary Harris, of the Bureau's Investigation & Enforcement Division, explained that his staff tends to focus enforcement actions on vending violations that include additional offenses beyond simply selling on the sidewalks. For example, selling pirated DVDs can be a felony in California, so enforcement might target sidewalk vendors believed to have counterfeit or bootlegged items for sale. The Bureau does, however, make arrests for simply vending when they receive complaints and/or when they have already issued warning to illegal vendors (Harris 2012). In the almost eleven months between July 1, 2011 and May 23, 2012, they arrested 284 vendors for violating section 42(b) (City of Los Angeles Bureau of Street services 2012).

While the sidewalk portion of the streets is subject to municipal regulations, sale of food from vehicles in the road portion of streets in California is regulated by section 22455 of the California Vehicle Code. This state law states that a "commercial vehicle engaged in vending upon a street may vend products" upon "bringing the vehicle to a complete stop and lawfully parking adjacent to the curb." Local jurisdictions can "adopt additional requirements for the public safety regulating the type of vending and the time, place, and manner of vending from vehicles upon any street" (California Vehicle Code 2013).

The latter clause could seem to give localities the power to regulate food trucks. Courts have interpreted the law with a stress on "public safety." Ordinances banning catering trucks from doing business near restaurants or from parking in residential neighborhoods, and requiring trucks to move frequently have been struck down as conflicting with the state code, as restraints of trade, as vague or as not really enhancing safety (Eagly 2012).

All establishments that sell food to the public, including mobile vendors, are subject to the California Retail Food Code. The Los Angeles Department of Public Health enforces the code in LA County. Health requirements vary by the type of food to be sold, by whether any food is prepared on the vehicle, and by the type of vehicle (which health rules refer to as a "mobile food facility"). Some rules apply to all mobile vendors, such as the requirement to park vehicles within 200 feet of a bathroom that vendors are authorized to use, and to store vehicles at commissaries every day while not in use. Commissaries are places where trucks or carts can be cleaned and where waste products like dirty water and used cooking oil can be removed and replenished. It is never permissible for a vendor to keep a cart or truck at their home (California Retail Food Code 2013).

If vendors handle food, then their vehicle usually needs to have a hand-washing sink, with plumbing capable of heating water. If vendors cut or otherwise prepare food, they need an additional sink, ideally with three chambers, to clean utensils that have touched food (Powell 2012; California Retail Food Code 2013). Sidewalk vendors may apply for health permits from the county though this does not give them the right to sell on sidewalks in jurisdictions that outlaw such vending. Many sidewalk vendors utilize carts that cannot meet health codes but still take steps to handle food in ways that are safe, or at least, that project a sense of cleanliness:

> Vendors know that they must perform personal, professional, and symbolic hygiene if they hope to acquire and maintain customers. Personal inspection by discerning customers can lead to or destroy a regular customer base. Vendors often keep cleaning supplies [such as hand soap dispensers and spray cleaner bottles] in view to broadcast their hygiene; they also spend time between customers cleaning their cart.
>
> *(Rosales 2012, p. 26)*

County Department of Public Health enforcers are kept busy inspecting, citing, and seizing illegal vehicles. Every 45 days the department fills its 20,000 square foot warehouse with confiscated food carts and equipment. Most cited vendors do not appear in court to contest the seizure of their carts. Vehicles taken off the sidewalks are eventually sold for scrap metal (Powell 2012). With Bureau of Street Services inspectors and LAPD officers enforcing city restrictions and county health inspectors looking for code violations, a cat and mouse game can develop between vendors and law enforcement. According to inspectors (Powell 2012) and to scholars, vendors "use informal patrol and alert systems on the streets in order to relay information about ongoing crackdowns. This information is diffused through the use of cell phones or in drive-by warning shouts or whistles" (Rosales 2012, p. 21). When inspectors do catch vendors, they can issue citations, make arrests, seize carts and equipment, or, as in this eyewitness account, fight flavor with foulness and socialization with sterility:

> The corner was filled [with vendors and customers] one moment and then in another, it had changed. Vendors fled as police cars quickly arrived in order

to round up the vendors for questioning. Those that were caught looked disappointed, but not scared; they turned over their food for inspection. A health inspector put sour drops in their *champurrado* and liquid food . . . making it no longer salable. The vendors were told to go home and take their wares with them. Almost immediately, the fire department came and hosed down the street in an effort to clean the street from street vendors. In a matter of minutes, the street and its surroundings became isolated and empty, looking completely different than it had 15 minutes prior.

(Munoz 2008, p. 117)

Shaping sidewalks

Even with occasional crackdowns, sidewalk vending is a daily practice on many streets. According to a count of permits from the Bureau of Specialized Surveillance and Enforcement, Environmental Health Division, Los Angeles County Department of Public Health, in May 2012 there were 6,280 mobile vendors in the county with valid health permits to sell food. Of these more than 6,000 licensed mobile vendors, a little over 2,000 were carts, the rest were trucks. Terrance Powell from the Enforcement Bureau of the County's Department of Public Health, estimates that there are approximately 12,000 additional mobile and street vendors active in the county without health permits (Powell 2012). This makes for approximately 18,000 vendors operating in Los Angeles County. The large majority of unlicensed vendors are sidewalk vendors rather than truck operators, so it is safe to say that there are at least 10,000–12,000 sidewalk vendors in the county. These vendors have a transformative impact on streets designed for cars:

> Every Friday, Saturday, and Sunday evening, a one-block stretch just off the boulevard is transformed into a lively destination spot for Latino immigrant families. Customers stroll up and down the sidewalks, choosing from a smorgasbord of seafood cocktail, Salvadoran *pupusas*, Mexican tacos, *tamales*, and beverages like fruit-flavored water in the summer and thick, hot, corn-based *atole* and *champurrado* in the winter. The smell of beef and pork frying in vats wafts through the air. Vendors advertise their food by shouting "*tacos, tamales*," while other vendors selling Avon cosmetics, pirated CDs and DVDs, and inexpensive shoes are quieter. The food vendors sell from parked trucks and vans, and they also set up elaborate displays of brightly colored salsas on folding tables. It's hard to walk down the wide sidewalks because they are so packed with merchandise and customers chewing their food, most of them standing and holding paper plates, but a few sitting on stoops; one vendor has even set up a make-shift dining area with plastic crates as chairs.
>
> *(Estrada and Hondagneu-Sotelo 2011, p. 112)*

By returning commerce to (and placing culture on) the sidewalks, vendors have brought people back to streets as or more effectively than most intentional street-changing designs, programs, and policies. A number of observers have pointed out that the cultural practices and survival tactics of Latino immigrants in Los Angeles have transformed the built environment and experiences of daily life through what James Rojas has labeled "Latino urbanism." Residents of immigrant neighborhoods reshaped buildings and reclaimed streets by selling and buying products and labor in public places (Rojas 2003; Mendez 2005).

Immigrant practices of do-it-yourself space changing pre-date recent interest in "tactical urbanism" and "place making" that have emerged as popular strategies for urban improvement and economic development (Lydon 2012). Movements for Complete Streets often focus on infrastructure improvements. Advocates and agencies have developed recommended interventions and safer street standards for multi-modal mobility (Model design Manual 2011, NACTO 2013). Complete Street resources and best practices are certainly valuable tools but the practices of vendors show that low-income residents working from economic necessity can help infuse more organic, democratic, and site- and culture-specific tactics into the geometric recommendations of the Complete Streets movement.

Since some of the places that Latino urbanism is remaking are city sidewalks, it is worth considering in more detail how the simple act of selling, buying, and eating food on a sidewalk can change a street. Sidewalk vending acts on a street through at least five pathways: by attracting people; by engaging with and shaping the built environment; by changing local food environments; by creating a culture of place; and by inspiring political debates about the purpose and use of sidewalks and related public space. Each of these pathways creates (or evades) one or more "layers of microspatial organization" that govern public and private property through regulation, markets and cultural and social power (Soja 2010, pp. 32–33).

I have already referenced how the banning of sidewalk vending, along with other shifts towards car-based mobility and land use, served to reduce pedestrians' activity—and how the renaissance of vending in heavily immigrant areas attracts people back onto streets. The final two sections of this chapter address the policy and politics of vending. I'd like to briefly expand upon vending and the built environment, food environment, and culture of place.

To attract and serve customers and to avoid arrest, vendors interact with the built environment of the city in customary and creative ways. "Vending spaces are systematically organized at the street level in Los Angeles . . . with unofficial street rules regarding where [vendors] can sell, what they can sell, and how they sell it" (Munoz 2008, pp. 98–99). Among the first challenges of sidewalk vending is locating a spot, multiple spots, or a route to sell on. Some of the forces that influence vending location are social process and relationships. Sidewalk vendors informally or formally negotiate where they sell. Seniority is usually respected, so new vendors will not set up close to an existing vendor with the same products. Vendors believe that too many vending sites in close proximity will attract the attention of police or inspectors, so they often self-regulate to limit the number of vendors on a block or intersection. In some areas, vendors pay protection money to street gangs, which play a role in keeping vendors in their spots and in watching out for inspections. Families and hometown associations are more significant sources of labor, advice, moral support, and funding to start vending operations and to replace seized equipment (Munoz 2008; Rosales 2012).

Vendors in Los Angeles also adapt physical spaces and objects to create economic places on sidewalks. Some spots are considered good places to sell due to proximity to features of the sidewalks such as bus stops; or to features of adjacent buildings such as ATMS, which attract people and arm these potential customers with cash; or gates to schools, which disgorge hundreds of potential customers in the afternoon. Carts, tables on which condiments are placed, trash cans, and other tools of vending become temporary denizens of the sidewalks where vendors operate. Colorful umbrellas, for example, become "a functional signifier in the vending landscape," used for shade and as advertising (Munoz 2008, p. 93). Beyond the sidewalk, places like gas station bathrooms, produce markets and restaurant supply stores, apartment kitchens, and driveways or backyards become areas for preparing items, washing hands, and storing carts.

The vending spaces created by thousands of carts and stands alter the food environment of heavily vended communities. Although mobile food may sound like a transient phenomenon, the space-shaping strategies described above show how vendors embed themselves in public spaces. As a presence in neighborhoods, sidewalk vendors carry the potential to be hubs and spokes for local food transformation. Known by customers, linked into family and immigrant hometown networks, attracting knots of people on Los Angeles' often unfriendly streets, vendors are case studies of how "the process of crafting place-based identities determines the 'depth' of local food systems. The 'thicker' the sense of place, the deeper the food-related practices that a community sustains" (Mares and Peña, 2011, p. 205) (Figure 11.2).

In 2010 to 2011, to get a better idea of how vendors operate and whether mobile vending holds potential as a source of healthy food, our Urban & Environmental Policy institute partnered with the Community Redevelopment Agency of Los Angeles and Esperanza Community Housing Corporation to survey vendors operating in parts of South Los Angeles. This project grew out of a community food assessment that we had worked on in three neighborhoods in South and Central Los Angeles (Azuma et al. 2010). When we talked with residents about the challenges of accessing a healthy meal and ideas to improve the food environment in their neighborhoods, one of the themes that they came back to again and again was transportation. Mothers described the difficulty of taking transit to reach stores with better selection when they had to transfer lines and carry bags and manage children on crowded buses. The difficulties of getting around to shop for food meant that many people who don't own a car end up walking to the closest store, which probably doesn't have a great selection of fruits, vegetables, lean meats, etc.

Our analysis of food and transportation assets in Southeast Los Angeles revealed that mobile vendors were both a significant component of the food retail environment and a potentially important distribution channel for healthy food. Project

FIGURE 11.2 Cut fruit cart in Glassell Park

Source: Photo by Ana Vallianatos.

partners developed a survey tool to find out more about vendors' operations and attitudes. To overcome the concerns of vendors, some of whom were operating without permits and feared that inquiries were connected to law enforcement, surveys were conducted by Spanish-speaking health promoters from Esperanza, who, as neighborhood residents, found it easier to interact with vendors in a supportive, non-intimidating manner. Project staff interviewed 45 vendors operating in the project area, with questions about vehicles, foods for sale, economics and logistics, nutrition, experiences with law enforcement, and interest in legal vending (Vallianatos *et al.* 2011).

The largest portion of the mobile vendors surveyed (over 25 percent) were operating out of what we categorized as "push or pulled improvised vehicles" such as shopping carts. Most vendors (80 percent) owned their own vehicle. The most common items for sale were beverages and two food categories that would be considered to be of low nutritious value: fried foods and snack foods. But it is significant that a quarter of vendors surveyed sold either or both whole or cut fruit or vegetables, making them sources of healthy food. Sales ranged from $40–$500 per day with an average of $162.50. Of those interviewed, only 30.2 percent reported being aware of any laws governing street or mobile vending. 34.9 percent reported having had encounters with law enforcement in the past (Table 11.1). If a legal permit were available, 50 percent of vendors surveyed said they would pay

TABLE 11.1 Items sold by vendors surveyed in Occidental College, Esperanza, CRA-LA project

Type of food	Number (frequency, %)
Beverages, bottled	19 (44.2)
Fried foods	18 (41.9)
Snack foods (e.g. chips)	15 (34.9)
Cooked meals (e.g. tacos)	12 (27.9)
Fruit/vegetables, whole	11 (25.6)
Fruit/vegetables, cut	11 (25.6)
Beverages, poured (e.g. horchata)	7 (16.3)
Ice cream/frozen snacks	6 (14.0)
Hot dogs	4 (9.3)
Pre-packaged meal (e.g. sandwich)	2 (4.7)

Source: Vallianatos *et al.* (2011).

up to $100 for a permit. 16 percent of surveyed vendors said they would pay for a permit "no matter its cost". Only 4 percent said they would not pay for a permit.

Beyond the physical impacts of vending on sidewalks and on the mix of food available in local areas, vendors shape the culture of the places they operate in. From the recipes used to prepare meals for sale, to the clothes worn by vendors, to the sales slogans they call out, vendors create spaces that reflect their immigrant origins. This cultural place-making is contemporary in being set up day after day by thousands of vendors but is also linked to memories of ways of cooking, eating, and using public space in countries and neighborhoods of origins. As Lorena Munoz argues in her dissertation on Latino vending landscapes:

> These nostalgic memories are in part what is consumed and what creates a certain "sense of place" for the vendors as well as the consumers . . . when individual memories emerge in relation to other people's memories of street vending of traditional foods, there is a space of collective memory that is being created that in part creates "place" in the landscape.
>
> *(Munoz 2008, pp. 147–148)*

Policy recommendations

Legalize and incentivize

Given the diverse nature of vendors in the project area (as in Los Angeles as whole), the survey result on the desirability of a permit—a path to legalization—jumped out at us. Allowing vendors to transition to legal sales would help relieve them of the stress of facing inspectors, confiscation of their vehicles, and fines. Vending has economic benefits in that it can be an entry point into entrepreneurship in low-income communities where unemployment is high. Legal sidewalk vending could also potentially help improve access to healthy food in areas without enough full service grocery stores, farmers markets, or healthy sit-down restaurants. Produce trucks and carts can expand the number of places where fruits and vegetables are for sale, by locating at or moving through areas where fresh food is scarce. Much of the food currently sold by vendors is, like most food sold by stores and restaurants, high in fat, salt and/or sugar. But policy-makers have little influence over what food is sold as long as both fried snacks and fruit are both vended as black market items.

Legal sidewalk vending can improve the vitality and walkability of cities by giving people a reason to walk and be outside and recognizing that vendors are making meaningful spaces. Increasing the number of people out on city sidewalks can also make neighborhoods safer by ensuring more eyes on the street, and may have a positive spillover effect on local stores as more people are out strolling and shopping.

With these objectives in mind, the City of Los Angeles should allow permitted sale of food on city sidewalks. A legal permitting process would recognize the value of street and mobile vending, create opportunities for entrepreneurship in the legal economy, and allow the city to regulate and influence street food.

- How many? There should not be a cap on the number of permits available or the number of sidewalk vendors allowed to operate. In New York City, where the number of traditional food vending permits has been capped at 3,000 since 1979, there is a 20-year waiting period to get a permit. Vendors lucky enough to have a permit often illegally "rent" out their permit for $12,000–$20,000 per year (Wolan 2010).
- Where? Sidewalk vending should be allowed in all areas of the city where there is sufficient space on sidewalks and where vendors can abide by health requirements. Do not assign specific spaces to sidewalk vendors but do establish where on sidewalks vendors can station their carts so they do not block pedestrians, doorways, ramps, etc, as is done by regulation in cities such as Portland (City of Portland Office of Transportation 2009).
- What are the requirements to operate legally? Require vendors to have a vending permit from the city, a business license, and to carry liability insurance. Vendors will need to follow county health regulations and be responsible for the removal of their customers' trash.
- Who can vend? Many street vendors are undocumented workers. Set up the permitting process so that forms of identification and data available to undocumented residents are accepted.
- Who can veto? Do not require permission from adjacent/local restaurants or food stores. The city can encourage vendors to partner with small stores to avoid conflicts and allow small merchants to diversify their points of sale. In fact, stores or restaurants with appropriate facilities can become commissaries for vending carts (Los Angeles County Department of Public Health 2011, pp. 1–2).

- What must carts/vehicles look like? Do not mandate the aesthetics of carts. Work with the Los Angeles County Department of Public Health Department and manufacturers on standardized cart/vehicle designs that are easy to construct and operate, and that meet food handling/storage rules (Figure 11.3).
- How to help vendors? Create a "one-stop-shop" where vendors can apply for all necessary permits. Conduct outreach and training to encourage illegal vendors to apply for permits and to instruct vendors on their rights and responsibilities. For instance, workshops with information about New York City's

FIGURE 11.3 Cut fruit cart in West Los Angeles

Source: Photo by Mark Vallianatos.

Green Cart program are offered in multiple languages (New York City 2011). Link vendors with micro-finance programs as was done through Michigan's Neighborhood Food Movers program (State of Michigan 2010, p. 6).

In neighborhoods where there are not enough stores selling a wide selection of fruits and vegetables or restaurants with healthy meals, mobile and street food can be a source of affordable, healthy food. The city should use financial and locational incentives to encourage more vending of healthy items by food carts and other mobile vendors.

- Cheaper permits for healthy vendors. Offer a reduced price permit for vendors who sell all or a majority of healthy items. The city would need to define healthy by establishing nutrition criteria as Kansas City has done for vendors in parks (Kansas City Parks and Recreation 2006) or, what is probably easier to enforce, limiting a lower cost healthy vending permit to fruits/vegetables as New York City has done with its Green Cart program (New York City 2011).
- Access to more areas. The city should allow healthy vendors to sell in areas that are off limits to other mobile vendors. For example, only healthy vendors could sell near parks, schools or transit stations (Metro 2010).
- Priority access to public/private financing. The city should prioritize vendors of healthy items for public financing or private low cost loans.
- Links to sources of local, healthy food. The city should help vendors source local produce and local, healthy bread, dairy, meats and prepared food.
- Waiver of commissary requirement or support for community commissaries. The city could work with the county to explore whether vendors of fruits and vegetables can be exempted from having to store carts trucks in a commissary, as is done in San Antonio, Texas (National Policy and Legal Analysis Network to Prevent Childhood Obesity and Public Health Law & Policy 2010). They should also support vendors and community organizations who want to run vending commissaries for healthy vending. An Oakland zoning variance allowed a restaurant and commissary for fruit vendors active in a low-income neighborhood (Oakland City Planning Commission 2008).

In order to tap into the place-making, economic, and food access potential of sidewalk vending, rules governing sidewalks and streets should make physical and regulatory space for vending. States and municipalities are increasingly embracing the concept of Complete Streets, defined by the National Complete Streets Coalition (2010) as:

> Streets for everyone. They are designed and operated to enable safe access for all users, including pedestrians, bicyclists, motorists and transit riders of all ages and abilities. Complete Streets make it easy to cross the street, walk to shops, and bicycle to work. They allow buses to run on time and make it safe for people to walk to and from train stations.

Complete Streets legislation adopted in California requires the City of Los Angeles to "plan for a balanced, multimodal transportation network that meets the needs of all users of streets, roads, and highways, defined to include motorists, pedestrians, bicyclists, children, persons with disabilities, seniors, movers of commercial goods, and users of public transportation" (Assembly Bill 1358, 2008, p. 1). While updating the mobility element of its general plan to embrace the laudable complete street goals of streets for all users, Los Angeles should ensure that its streets meets the needs of sidewalk vendors as important users of streets.

- Streets as places as well as routes. While the Complete Streets concept of streets for all users is powerful, it is limited by assuming that people use streets solely for transportation (National Complete Streets Coalition, 2010). Streets are also important public places in and of themselves, not just links between places. Designing streets that work for sidewalk vendors reinforces that people like to stop and linger on sidewalks, that streets can be places where people make their livelihoods, and that people shape streets in subtle ways to create cultural experiences and individual identities.
- Space for vending. Sidewalks in heavily vended areas should be wide enough to allow carts, tables, trash cans, umbrellas to be set up and still allow space for pedestrians to move by safely.

Conclusion

You can still smell the food, but see nothing [...]

Former Los Angeles Mayor Antonio Villaraigosa created a Food Policy Council Task Force in 2009 to mark the 30th anniversary of farmers markets in LA. The task force produced a report on strategies to ensure good food for Los Angeles and recommended the establishment of a permanent Food Policy Council. In January 2011, the Council was launched (Los Angeles Food Policy Taskforce 2010). It established working groups, including a street food group. The working group brought together community-based organizations that work with sidewalk vendors; health and environmental advocates; gourmet and lunch truck operators; and staff from the City and County of Los Angeles.

Some participants were primarily interested in public health and in encouraging vending of produce in low-income neighborhoods. Others were concerned with vendor rights and legalization. The working group reached consensus that doing one required doing both. That is, healthy vending is a strong argument for legalizing sidewalk vending, and making vending legal increases the incentives and disincentives available to promote sale of healthy foods. By 2012, the working group had entered campaign mode to legalize sidewalk vending (Fine 2012). It developed a set of shared policy goals, dialogued with regulators to discover obstacles and see what type of permit system would be workable, and reached out to a broader set of allies interested in economic development, health, and a vibrant city (Los Angeles Street Vendor Campaign, 2013). Participants in the campaign, especially those representing or organizing vendors, can be seen as standing up for spatial justice in Los Angeles as have earlier efforts to improve the lots of janitors, bus riders, and other low-income workers (Soja 2010).

In November 2013, two Los Angeles City Council members representing heavily vended East and South Los Angeles districts, José Huizar and Curren Price, introduced a motion calling for "recommendations on possible regulation that could effectively permit and regulate *food street vending* on City sidewalks and parkways" (Los Angeles City Council, 2013). The motion also requested recommendations on legalizing the vending of non-food merchandise.

Hopefully this process will finally allow legal vending throughout the city. The current regime of unlicensed vending and intermittent crack-downs has allowed some vendors to scrape out a living on the streets, but at a cost of being confined to the shadows. County inspectors have told us how enforcement teams sometimes arrive on a street just in time to "still smell the food, but see nothing." Vendors have run off and hidden after being tipped off by lookouts (Powell 2012). Scattered enforcement of municipal and county regulations, low entry costs for sidewalk food vendors, and the demand for street food create an odd juxtaposition in which street food is forbidden but ubiquitous. Do we want these mainstays of Los Angeles' streets to continue to be marginalized, to fade away like ghosts—the scent of delicious food lingering on a street corner from which the vendors have vanished (Figure 11.4)?

Or may street vendors, through policy change and legalization, take on a more central and legitimized role in shaping truly Complete Streets, food and urban life?

FIGURE 11.4 Street food being grilled

Source: Photo by Rudy Espinoza.

222   Mark Vallianatos

Note

1   The author would like to acknowledge colleagues and partners working to research and legalize street vending in Los Angeles: Giulia Pasciuto, Melinda Swanson, Robert Gottlieb, Amanda Shaffer, Jesus Garcia, Jason Neville, Jessica Gudmundson, Heng Lam Foong, Jenny Scanlin, Matt Mason, Ana Nolan, Beth Weinstein, Michael Davies, Matthew Dodson, Yelena Zeltser, Antonia Ezparza, Gina Padilla; Jorge Barron, David Mendez, Jessica Mejia, Ana Vallianatos, Michael Sin, Anne Farrell-Sheffer, Gwendolyn Flynn, Gregg Kettles, Albert Lowe, Sandra McNeil, Faisal Roble, Rudy Espinoza, James Rojas, Nathan Baird, Julian Leon, Katherine Hulting, Kristin Jensvold-Rumage, Janet Favela, Erin Glenn, Carlos Ardon, Crystal Crawford, Lauren Dunning, Michele Grant, Mike Dennis, Jessica Durrum, Alexandra Agajanian, Claudia Martinez Mansell, Alexa Delwich, Paula Daniels, Xiomara Corpeño, Francesca de la Rosa, Isela Gracian, Paige Dow, Jared Weinman, Clare Fox, Alexa Delwich, Maria Cabildo, Gary Harris, Terence Powell and all the vendors seeking to make a living.

References

Arellano, Gustavo, 2012. *Taco USA: How Mexican food conquered America.* New York, NY: Scribner.
Assembly Bill No. 1358, 2008. An act to amend Sections 65040.2 and 65302 of the Government Code, relating to planning. September 30.
Azuma, Andrea Misako, Gilliland, Susan, Vallianatos, Mark, and Gottlieb, Robert, 2010. Food access, availability, and affordability in 3 Los Angeles communities, Project CAFE, 2004–2006. *Preventing Chronic Disease,* 7(2):A27. Available from: www.cdc.gov/pcd/issues/2010/mar/08_0232.htm?s_cid=pcd72a27_e [Accessed 9 May 2014].
Behrens, Zach, 2008. Eat this: Korean BBQ with the edge of a street taco. *LAist.* December 4, 2008. Available from: http://laist.com/2008/12/04/kogi_bbq.php#photo-1.
Brion, Raphael, 2010. *Food & Wine Magazine's best new chefs announced.* April 6, 2010. Available from: http://eater.com/archives/2010/04/06/food-wine-magazines-best-new-chefs-2010-announced.php [Accessed 9 May 2014].
California Retail Food Code, 2013. California Retail Food Code sections 114313, 114315, 114295. Available from: www.cdph.ca.gov/services/Documents/fdbRFC.pdf [Accessed 9 May 2014].
California Vehicle Code, 2013. California Vehicle Code 22455 (a) and (b). Available from: www.dmv.ca.gov/pubs/vctop/d11/vc22455.htm [Accessed 9 May 2014].
Chee, Morgan, Hermosillo, Jésus, and Joe, Lawrence, 2009. A sectoral analysis of the "Loncheras'" sub-sector in Los Angeles County. Los Angeles: UCLA Department of Public Affairs/School of Urban Planning, 19–20.
City of Los Angeles, 2010. *City of Los Angeles bicycle plan.* Available from: http://planning.lacity.org/cwd/gnlpln/transelt/NewBikePlan/Txt/LA%20CITY%20BICYCLE%20PLAN.pdf [Accessed 9 May 2014].
City of Los Angeles, 2012. LA/2B (Mobility Element Update). Available from: http://la2b.org/ [Accessed 9 May 2014].
City of Los Angeles, 2013. People St. Available from:http://peoplest.lacity.org [Accessed 9 May 2014].
City of Los Angeles Bureau of Street Services, 2012. Data from Investigation and Enforcement Division, City of Los Angeles Bureau of Street Services. June 20, 2012.
City of Portland Office of Transportation, 2009. *Sidewalk vending cart permit application packet.* Available from: http://www.portlandoregon.gov/transportation/article/275061 [Accessed 9 May 2014].

Eagly, Ingrid V., 2012. Criminal clinics in the pursuit of immigrant rights: lessons from the Loncheros. *UC Irvine Law Review*, 2. 2012.

Estrada, Emir and Hondagneu-Sotelo, Pierrette, 2011. Intersectional dignities: Latino immigrant street vendor youth in Los Angeles. *Journal of Contemporary Ethnography*, 40: 102.

Fine, Howard, 2012. Street vendors cook up challenge to sidewalk sales ban. *Los Angeles Business Journal*. October 8, pp. 1, 32–33.

Gold, Jonathan, 2012. How America became a food truck nation. *Smithsonian Magazine*. March, 2012. Available from: http://www.smithsonianmag.com/travel/How-America-Became-a-Food-Truck-Nation.html [Accessed 9 May 2014].

Harris, Gary, 2012. Interview with Garry Harris, Investigation and Enforcement Division, City of Los Angeles Bureau of Street Services. June 21, 2012.

Kansas City Parks and Recreation, 2006. *Vending policy*. December 12. Available from: http://www.kcmo.org/idc/groups/parksandrec/documents/parksrecreation/012710.pdf [Accessed 9 May 2014].

Kettles, Gregg W., 2004. Regulating vending in the sidewalk commons. *Temple Law Review*, 77(1). Available from: http://papers.ssrn.com/sol3/papers.cfm?abstract_id=897498. [Accessed 9 May 2014].

Kolnick, Kathy A., 2008. Order before zoning: Land use regulation in Los Angeles, 1880–1915. PhD dissertation, University of Southern California.

Los Angeles City Council, 2013. Council File 13-1493. November 6, 2013. Available from: http://cityclerk.lacity.org/lacityclerkconnect/index.cfm?fa=ccfi.viewrecord&cfnumber=13-1493. [Accessed 9 May 2014].

Los Angeles County Department of Public Health, 2011. Plan check facilities for mobile food facilities and mobile support unit. Los Angeles County Department of Public Health.

Los Angeles Food Policy Taskforce, 2010. The good food for all agenda: Creating a new regional food system for Los Angeles. July 2010. http://goodfoodla.org/wp-content/uploads/2013/02/good-food-full_report_single_072010.pdf [Accessed 9 May 2014].

Los Angeles Municipal Code, 2013. Los Angeles Municipal Code IV, 42 (b). Available from: http://www.amlegal.com/nxt/gateway.dll/California/lamc/municipalcode/chapterivp ublicwelfare?f=templates$fn=default.htm$3.0$vid=amlegal:lamc_ca$anc=JD_42.00. [Accessed 9 May 2014].

Los Angeles Municipal Code, 1994. Los Angeles Municipal Code IV, 42 (m). Added by Ord. No. 169,319, Eff. 2/18/94. Available from: http://www.amlegal.com/nxt/gateway. dll/California/lamc/municipalcode/chapterivpublicwelfare?f=templates$fn=default.htm$ 3.0$vid=amlegal:lamc_ca$anc=JD_42.00 [Accessed 9 May 2014].

Los Angeles Street Vendor Campaign, 2013. Available from: http://streetvendorcampaign. blogspot.com/ [Accessed 9 May 2014].

Loukaitou-Sideris, Anastasia and Ehrenfeucht, Renia, 2009. *Sidewalks: Conflict and negotiation over public space*. Cambridge, MA: MIT Press.

Lydon, Mike, 2012. *Tactical urbanism 2: Short-term action/long-term change*. Street Plans Collaborative. March 2012. Available from: http://www.cnu.org/cnu-news/2012/03/tactical-urbanism-20 [Accessed 9 May 2014].

Mares, Teresa M. and Peña, Devon G., 2011. Environmental and food justice: Towards local, slow and deep food systems. In: Alison Hope Alkon and Julian Agyeman, eds. *Cultivating food justice: Race, class and sustainability*. Cambridge, MA: MIT Press.

Mendez, Michael, 2005. Latino new urbanism: Building on cultural preferences. *Opolis: An International Journal of Suburban and Metropolitan Studies*, 1(1).

Metro, 2010. Status of food vendor programs. Los Angeles County Metropolitan Transportation Authority, Operations Committee. May 20, 2010.

Model Design Manual, 2011. Model design manual for living streets. Ed. Ryan Snyder *et al*. Available from: http://www.modelstreetdesignmanual.com/ [Accessed 9 May 2014].

Munoz, Lorena, 2008. Tamales. . . Elotes. . . Champurrado: The production of Latino vending landscapes in Los Angeles. PhD dissertation, University of Southern California.

NACTO, 2013. Urban street design guide. National Association of City Transportation Officials. Available from: http://nacto.org/usdg/ [Accessed 9 May 2014].

National Complete Streets Coalition, 2010. *What are Complete Streets?* Available from: http://www.smartgrowthamerica.org/complete-streets/complete-streets-fundamentals/complete-streets-faq [Accessed 9 May 2014].

National Policy and Legal Analysis Network to Prevent Childhood Obesity and Public Health Law & Policy, 2010. Mobile vending laws in the 10 most populous U.S. cities. Available from: http://changelabsolutions.org/sites/changelabsolutions.org/files/Mobile Vending_chart_FINAL_2010.02.17.pdf [Accessed 9 May 2014].

New York City, 2011. Green cart program. February 2011. Available from: www.nyc.gov/html/doh/downloads/pdf/cdp/green-cart-workshop.pdf [Accessed 9 May 2014].

Oakland City Planning Commission, 2008. "Agenda." July 16, 2008. Available from: www2.oaklandnet.com/oakca1/groups/ceda/documents/webcontent/oak035649.pd [Accessed 9 May 2014].

Powell, Terrance, 2012. Meeting with Terrance Powell, Bureau of Specialized Surveillance, Los Angeles County Department of Public Health, July 12, 2012.

Rojas, James, 2003. Latino urbanism: a new model for sustainable transportation. Paper presented at Latino New Urbanism conference, October 16–17, University of Southern California.

Rosales, Rocio, 2012. Survival, economic mobility, and community among Los Angeles fruit vendors. Program on International Migration, UCLA International Institute, UCLA. 2012. Available from: http://escholarship.org/uc/item/36q2c86b. [Accessed 9 May 2014].

Schlosser, Eric, 2001. *Fast food nation: The dark side of the American meal.* New York, NY: Houghton Mifflin.

Soja, Edward W., 2010. *Seeking spatial justice.* Minneapolis, MN: University of Minnesota.

State of Michigan, 2010. MI neighborhood food movers fresh food delivery program. Available from: http://web.archive.org/web/20100528054835/ http://michigan.gov/documents/foodmovers/MNFM_Manual_290427_7.pdf [Accessed 9 May 2014].

Vallianatos, Mark, Pasciuto, Giulia, Swanson, Melissa, and Shaffer, Amanda, 2011. *Bringing people to good food and good food to people: Enhancing food access through transportation and land use policies.* Los Angeles: Urban & Environmental Policy Institute. March 2011.

Wang, Oliver, 2010. Ode to the taco truck. *The Atlantic.* August 11, 2010. Available from: http://www.theatlantic.com/national/archive/2010/08/ode-to-the-taco-truck/61292/# [Accessed 9 May 2014].

Winters Keegan, Rebecca, 2008. *The great taco truck war. Time.* April 25, 2008. Available from: www.time.com/time/nation/article/0,8599,1735104,00.html; saveourtacotrucks.org petition. http://saveourtacotrucks.org/2008/05/13/sign-the-petition-page-5/#bottom. [Accessed 9 May 2014].

Wolan, Christian, 2010. Vendor rules promise less art, more cupcakes in city parks, *Gotham Gazette*, April 2010. Available from: www.gothamgazette.com/article/work/20100414/22/3244 [Accessed 9 May 2014].

12

FIXING THE CITY IN THE CONTEXT OF NEOLIBERALISM

Institutionalized DIY

Lusi Morhayim

Introduction

Today most American cities make automobile traffic the priority, and pedestrians seem like a disruption to efficient, fast moving traffic. There are cities that have even eliminated sidewalks, as if everyone can and has to drive, disregarding those with disabilities, youth, and the elderly. To what extent can one claim the existence of a public realm if streets are more or less devoid of people and social interactions? Examining car-free streets activism in San Francisco, California, alongside spatial changes in the last two decades, this chapter discusses both the possibilities offered by grassroots activism and its limitations in making cities socially, environmentally, and spatially just.

San Francisco is a city in which room for lower-income populations is shrinking rapidly. In most parts of the city, rents are only affordable by six-figure-income earners who work in the information technology sector at Silicon Valley companies. Hartman (2002) notes that "HUD's [US Department of Housing and Urban Development] 2000 Annual State of the Cities report concluded: 'A person earning the minimum wage in San Francisco would have to work the equivalent of 174 hours a week just to pay the median rent.'" Hartman adds that cases like "fifty-seven hundred applicants for fifty-five affordable housing units" for a new affordable housing development in the city become a cruel joke for many families. The shrinking space for lower-income populations is detrimental to social diversity and justice. While the quantity of spaces in which low-income and disadvantaged populations reside is already an issue, the quality of lower-income areas poses yet another spatial justice problem.

Urban form, health, and spatial justice

The quality of the built environment plays an important role in both determining public health and in environmental justice activism. The Centers for Disease Control and Prevention (CDC 1999) notes that physical activity reduces risks of coronary heart disease (the leading cause of death in the United States), hypertension, colon cancer, and diabetes, along with depression and anxiety. In the US, approximately 12.5 million children and adolescents are obese (CDC 1999). Pan *et al.* (2009) note that the rate of obesity is lower in non-Hispanic whites compared to other ethnic groups. A number of studies show that physical activity is linked to built environment variables, as well as income levels and ethnicities. Giles-Corti *et al.* (2005) suggest that "people who live within walking distance of urban parks are reported to be nearly three times more likely to get the recommended amount of daily physical activity" (cited in Cutts *et al.* 2009). Gordon-Larsen *et al.*'s (2006) study shows that lower socioeconomic status (SES) is linked to lower levels of physical activity due to lack of access to amenities. In a nationwide longitudinal study in which income levels, facilities for physical activity, and obesity rates are correlated, researchers conclude that "low-SES and high-minority block groups were less likely to have facilities" for physical activity and were "associated with decreased physical activity and increased [risk of being] overweight" (ibid.). The same researchers add: "Inequality in availability of physical activity facilities may contribute to ethnic and SES disparities in physical activity and overweight patterns." Such studies indicate the importance of creating urban forms that support physical activity as a way to make healthy lifestyles affordable for everyone but especially for those who are historically disadvantaged. More importantly, these studies underline that inequalities are built into the urban form, including inequalities in terms of access to health-promoting urban amenities.

Despite its fame for progressiveness, San Francisco for many years did not make it to the top of the list of the best bicycling cities in the United States. However, recent years have demonstrated a different trend. The city's bicycling infrastructure is now over 200 miles in total length, and new public plazas and parklets (sidewalk extensions for recreational use) are springing up fast. These cultural and spatial transformations can be attributed partially to grassroots activists and partially to an interesting dynamic between citizens who volunteer to transform the city and local governments that not only make citizen-initiated physical transformations in the city possible, but also encourage them.

San Francisco is a city that historically has accommodated multiple counter-culture movements, ranging from civil rights activism to alternative lifestyles. Car-free streets events (CFSEs) that have been flourishing in the city are one such movement. These events bring together those who are less interested in automobile-oriented urban form and lifestyles than the majority of urban residents. CFSEs such as Critical Mass and Park(ing) Day have been key elements in the continuous evolution of bicycling culture in San Francisco. In addition, these events are aligned with neighborhood-scale grassroots organizations, such as the Wigg Party and Fix Fell, which focus their efforts locally in their neighborhoods and streets. These events have not only been effective in promoting bicycle culture, but they have also resulted in a reimagining of the potential for public engagement in the quality of urban streets.

In multiple ways the CFSEs challenge automobile-oriented urban form and demonstrate alternatives. They stand out with their claims on the city and their drive to "fix" the city. Parallel to the cultural shift that these movements bring about in the city, there have been major changes in the form of the city and in the way in which spatial transformations take place.

This chapter focuses on an examination of CFSEs and protests, such as Park(ing) Day and Fix Fell, and the city's recent programs, such as the parklets, Pavements to Parks, and Better Streets programs. Using interview data gathered during the events, spatial analysis of physical urban transformations, and content analysis of the city's programs, this chapter discusses the extent to which the Complete Streets initiative has the potential to contribute to urban social and spatial justice, and under what circumstances it does not, and whether the ways in which governance and implementation of Complete Street principles take place may thwart the idea of just cities in the larger perspective, instead of enabling them.

Public space vs. parking automobiles

Today, relying on private transportation is the norm for many, and having parking space readily available is an absolute requirement for the urban driver. Public streets are utilized as parking spaces wherever possible, despite the fact that the city is also home to those who do not own an automobile. In fact, in San Francisco County there are 0.58 automobiles per capita; only 43.9 percent of workers commuted to work by driving (36.0 percent) and car-pooling (7.9 percent), and these numbers were lower by 4.5 and 2.9 percentage points respectively compared to 2000 data (SFMTA 2011).

This positions parking spaces at the heart of spatial politics of urban spaces. Parking spaces are leasable land and a valuable commodity in dense cities. Ferguson (2005) estimates that in commercial areas, parking lots comprise about 60 percent of the built cover. There are a total of 448,000 parking spaces in San Francisco, 281,700 of which are on-street parking places, and of those, 29,103 are metered parking spaces (SFMTA 2011). Parking meters generated $40,520,486 for the city of San Francisco in the 2010–2011 fiscal year (SFMTA 2011). Parking permits add $9,040,407, and parking tickets add $86,306,584 to the total revenue (ibid.). Individual residents, too, can capitalize on their parking spaces by renting them out.

Evidently, parking spaces have a direct influence on the socioeconomic diversity of cities. According to Jia and Wachs (1999), in San Francisco, minimum off-street parking space requirements for new housing developments increase housing costs by more than 10 percent. Thus, parking creates an obstacle in building more affordable housing (Henderson 2009). On the other hand, parking spaces are potential public spaces that can be utilized to enhance the quality of urban life.

As Putnam (2000) outlines, even though informal social connections do not necessarily lead to formal participation in civic life, they still play a significant role in sustaining social capital. Research shows that, independent of cultural differences, the more space devoted to motor vehicle traffic, the weaker the relations between neighbors (Appleyard *et al.* 1981; Hart n.d.; Transportation Alternatives 2006). Replication of the same research in other countries indicates that social relations are thwarted by automobile traffic despite geographical and cultural differences. On-street parking spots are potential extra public spaces for such casual interactions and extra green space in the city, at least in the view of the city's residents whose views are aligned with car-free streets and livable city ideas.

CFSEs and their role in urban production

A city like San Francisco, with an unmistakable heritage of activism, unsurprisingly gives birth to innovative urban grassroots movements and enables others to flourish. Scholars observe a wide variety in citizen-led production of urban space and more specifically, appropriations of urban space. Examples include community gardens; participatory projects led by community-based non-profit organizations (Hayashi 2010); individual appropriations in urban space, such as yarn bombing; community-driven appropriations of urban space mediated through a physical infrastructure provided by architects, such as the ECObox (Petcou and Petrescu 2011); and rather insurgent Chinese fan dancers' appropriation of public spaces (Chen 2010).

CFSEs are unique grassroots urban interventions. They present temporary opportunities in which marginalized groups of people, collectively and deliberately, in a certain time frame, and with a goal of long-term urban transformation, occupy a public space and appropriate it for their desired use. These events are directly about access to streets, and they depend on people to reclaim streets and occupy them for a variety of uses. The participants' marginalized quality warrants attention (Morhayim 2012). Bicyclists and pedestrians alike have not been the primary concern of automobile-centered planning until recently. Most cities do not provide easy and safe access to bicycling and other non-motorized means of transportation. Thus, on one hand, those who cannot drive, find not driving economically wiser, or simply prefer alternate modes of transportation are marginalized and limited in the context of access to streets. They are also limited in terms of freedom to choose their desired transportation mode and thus to maintain their lifestyle and identity. Similarly, in regards to pedestrians, streets are considered transportation corridors rather than social spaces.

However, on the other hand, advocates of livable cities and bicycling are not always from the marginalized sections of the society in terms of gender, socioeconomics, and race. For instance, in the case of bicyclists in the US, about 75 percent of bicyclists are male, and only 25 percent are female (Alliance for Biking and Walking 2012). While "bicycling levels are roughly evenly distributed among all income classes," higher-income people are more likely to bicycle for leisure and less likely to bicycle for utilitarian purposes (Alliance for Biking and Walking 2012).

Yet, the demographics of San Francisco bicyclists do not reflect the demographics of the city. Forty-nine percent of San Francisco's population is male, and 50 percent is female. While among bicyclists people from all ages, races, and genders are found, the majority of frequent bicyclists in San Francisco are men (72 percent), Caucasian (70 percent), and between the ages of 26 and 35; only 23 percent of frequent cyclists are women (SFMTA 2008). While Caucasians make up 53 percent of the city's population and Asians make up 32 percent, Caucasians make up 70 percent of frequent cyclists, whereas Asians only make up 12 percent. African-Americans (7 percent vs. 2 percent) and Hispanics (14 percent vs. 10 percent) are similarly underrepresented in the bicycling community in the city (SFMTA 2008).

Nevertheless, CFSEs as goal-oriented, focused, and locally organized urban appropriations by grassroots masses communicate a shared imagination from the bottom up due to cyclists' marginalized status in the context of access to safe streets and non-motorized transportation (Morhayim 2012). As Critical Mass bicyclists occupy streets and block automobile traffic, as participants of Park(ing) Day introduce a variety of social uses and additional green space into sidewalks and parking spaces, and as participants of Sunday Streets take up the whole street space for a variety of activities without any presence of automobiles on the streetscape, highly contrasting urban experiences replace the everyday use of streets.[1] These groups constitute counter-publics because of their marginalized position and because they introduce counter-discourses within the public sphere (ibid.). CFSE appropriations strike as overt dialogues between marginalized communities and the mainstream public over the uses of urban public spaces and access to the streets in the form of spatial performance. The events' participants communicate their desired uses of urban streets not in city hall meetings, but on the streets to those who reside there. Participants show what it would be like if streets accommodated a variety of social uses and non-motorized transportation modes. The communication takes place through appropriation of streets, rather than through the usual form of protest in the street such as demonstration rallies.

Park(ing) Day is one such CFSE. Rebar, a design studio based in San Francisco, created the first park(ing) spot in 2005. Rebar's designers/activists brought sod and chairs and paid a parking meter for two hours on a downtown street in San Francisco. Rebar's idea was quickly embraced locally and globally (Park(ing) Day 2013). The next year, residents of 13 other cities celebrated Park(ing) Day with 47 park(ing) spots. In 2011 there were 975 park(ing) spots in 162 cities in 35 countries. On-street park(ing) spots that people create during the annual Park(ing) Day feature all sorts of arrangements, such as mini-golf parks, grassy parks, sandy beaches, a setting for a grand piano recital, and yoga and meditation spaces, to name a few. Park(ing) spaces attract people in various ways, and the opportunities they create for social interactions are the highlight of the event for passers-by.

Besides play, leisure, social interaction, and greenery, the park(ing) spots also offer citizens the chance to be politically engaged with one another. Some of the park(ing) spots reflect general issues that are in debate, such as the legalization of marijuana, and others critique more land-related issues. For instance, a model of a state park with a dead fish in a pond surrounded with yellow crime scene tape in order to comment on the state's budget cuts that would result in the closing of 220 state parks in California. Many park(ing) spots make direct references to even more locally contingent issues, sometimes on the exact spot in the street or sidewalk where a group of people are demanding particular physical changes.

Various publics take advantage of Park(ing) Day in order to enact their ideal spaces in a street-theater manner. The events expose power struggles between counter and mainstream publics and values embedded in urban form. The tension over the right to urban streets is at times marked by devaluation and marginalization of fun and play in public spaces, and at times by prioritization of efficiency over green space and social interactions. Bicyclists, advocates of green space and spaces for sports and play, and citizens wanting more room for casual interactions present just a few examples of the many urban qualities that livable city proponents advocate.

Park(ing) Day provides an open canvas to the residents of the city to share their urban needs and temporarily recreate part of a public street to respond to their needs. Appropriation of space creates a public forum and fosters discussion in the public sphere. Park(ing) spots are free-speech platforms distributed in each neighborhood, rather than in one central town square, in exchange for on-street parking. The park(ing) spots foster spatial communication of right to the city claims and urban design ideas and enable residents to demonstrate their opinion. Some of the participants' reflections about Park(ing) Day can be outlined in the following categories.

Alleviating a sense of marginalization

Bicyclists comprise a significant public during the CFSEs. Riding a bicycle instead of driving an automobile is an overt choice, and the lack of bicycling facilities is an everyday obstacle for bicyclists. Participants of CFSEs often mention their feelings of marginalization in everyday life. Angela, who identified herself as a bicycle advocate, was interviewed at Rebar's park(ing) spot. In a setting decorated with inflatable cushions and a wall made of recycled milk crates containing potted plants that separated the park(ing) spot from the automobile traffic, she stated the following:

> We wanna go against how these spaces are taken for granted . . . it doesn't have to be car dominated. Cities don't have to be just designed around cars. It was a design choice, and we can make other choices . . . I really think the urban realm should be open to pedestrians, to people . . . we as taxpayers and citizens should be able to use the spaces that we pay for . . . Normally as a cyclist and as a pedestrian you are literally pushed off.

The feeling of being pushed off is a recurring theme in each CFSE. Interviews demonstrate that those who join the events identify themselves as part of a like-minded community (Morhayim 2012). The sense of being part of a like-minded community entails the belief that these individuals make the same rights demands regarding urban space and take a political stand about it by occupying streets. The opportunity to gather in public spaces of the city and collectively transform streets into their ideal spaces serves them as a way to gain a sense of community and empowerment.

Feeling connected

The CFSE participants' desires are not limited to the demand for adequate bike paths, lanes, and sharrows (shared lane markings). In a different park(ing) spot, three adjacent parking spaces were joined together by a team from a coffee shop who called their installation "Ritual State Park" (Figure 12.1). The ground was covered with sod, and the space exhibited a camping tent, a picnic table for four, and two people in bear costumes, a grizzly bear and a panda. Those who got their coffee from the shop were sitting outside, despite the overcast weather. A participant named Kevin said:

> There is grass instead of cars. It helps to connect a little bit more. Without grass I wouldn't stay more. It is life, it grows, it has color, adds a lot . . . Nothing disconnects you from air, grass, asphalt, rain drop, smell. Being connected is a pretty awesome thing . . . concrete is hard, nothing there . . . Here in park(ing) I am stationary. I am connected to the people, the elements of nature, to energies.

FIGURE 12.1 Ritual State Park park(ing) spot

Source: Aditi Rao.

As Kevin details, a green space on a street provides a spot to take a break. It transforms a street to a space where one can hang out, rather than just pass by. It allows one to have an attentive experience of the surroundings and the people who occupy the same space. Kevin, who says he is not an automobile hater but thinks there are too many cars, sees parallels with his park(ing) spot experience and bicycling. He says that driving can be a very negative experience, whereas on a bicycle, "I can really have a sense of openness . . . there is definitely a camaraderie amongst people on bikes . . . when inside the car you are separated from this."

Neil, another Park(ing) Day participant who seems to agree with this connecting experience, says, "It makes you stop and pause." The difference in the experience of the street during Park(ing) Day is a feeling of "openness, people are less closed off and just trusting." The sense of openness that both of these participants enjoy is about being connected to nature, people, and urban surroundings. As opposed to a desire to escape the chaos of the city, interviewees expressed a yearning to be more connected with one another in the urban setting and to enjoy what the city can offer.

Neil also notes the differences between park(ing) spots and city parks:

> This is definitely outside of the norm . . . public parks got a similar vibe . . . except obviously parks are sort of on their own, isolated . . . separate from the city . . . this is a lot more integrated into the fabric [of the city].

Public parks are isolated from the downtown area, while streets are integrated with urban life. Yet access to streets is limited in the sense that streets do not accommodate space for social life or green space, an amenity that would be useful for those who do not live close by city parks.

Collective imaginations

Urban streets are designed to accommodate automobile-oriented ways of life. The ease and accommodation provided by parking on the streets, entrances to garages, traffic lights, and all such design elements, which most people accept as necessities, are for other groups an obstacle to the multiple public uses that streets could offer as public spaces. Thus, the car-free streets grassroots communities, particularly bicyclists and pedestrians, take advantage of the events to enact spaces that match their values and present their counterdiscourses about urban form.

Bryan, a self-proclaimed bicycling advocate, thinks that "events like this, having a collective sense of streets being used differently . . . plays into these larger ideas of how we want to operate as a community, how we want our streets to look, and how we want to behave in these streets." Susan, a 34-year-old who does not drive a vehicle or have a driver's license, was interviewed at the California Institute of Integral Studies park(ing) spot and talked about her ideal urban space:

> I have a fantasy of living somewhere where vehicles are not allowed, especially the downtown core. Just it would be walking and a lot more lanes for bicycles

. . . we pay to have roads built but have we actually chosen to have roads built? Is that what we would choose to have where our tax money spent on? . . . To me it is more valuable to have space for bicycle parking and more emphasis on pedestrian traffic . . . being out and being able to have a place to sit down where you can comfortably . . . rest or eat lunch ... Reclaiming space is all about remembering that it is our city and our space.

Fixing the city

There are other parallels between the bicycling counterpublic and Park(ing) Day, and one particular similarity is the prevalence of "do-it-yourself" (DIY) culture. Bicyclists interviewed at CFSEs often stated that they enjoyed the sense of freedom, liberation, and empowerment one feels when bicycling. Taking their shared imaginations as a foundation, bicyclists project the everyday sense of freedom found on a bicycle onto urban space and claim their freedom to appropriate urban space according to their needs.

Regarding the DIY culture, Furness (2010, p. 142) refers both to "a process of fixing/building/altering bicycles and an expression of self-reliance." According to Furness, DIY culture is an extension of the punk culture, a culture also characterized as "cultural resistance rooted in the rejection of dominant norms and consumerist values . . . [and] a collective desire for more participatory technologies and more democratic modes of technological production." For example, customizing multiple-gear bicycles into single-gear ones is an expression of rejecting dependency on "expert" knowledge and technologies that bicycle companies impose on them to make consumers dependent on their services and bicycle parts (ibid.). The same idea of self-reliance and rejection of expert knowledge can be applied to rejecting urban forms generated based on knowledge and standards created by planners and engineers.

Bicyclists' rejection of expert knowledge and desire to be self-reliant are not limited to bicycle technologies and a desire to modify their bicycles. Evident in CFSEs, appropriations on urban streets are direct projections of the bicyclists' DIY ideology regarding bicycles onto the urban space; bicyclists actively try to fix the city the same way they fix their bicycles. With the ambition of making the city more "bikeable," these counter-publics have taken the matter into their own hands and occupy and fix their city while also manifesting their DIY/fixer culture.

The park(ing) spots on Fell Street (between Scott and Divisadero) were a telling example of bicyclists' desire to "fix" the urban form. Located on six adjacent on-street parking spots, the collective park(ing) space exhibited a banner that read "Fix Fell," taking its name from one of the organizing neighborhood communities that are comprised of bicyclists and residents. The park(ing) spots depicted a solution to bicyclists' safety concerns on the exact block where they feel most unsafe.

Fell Street is a major bike route for bicyclists. It is part of the least hilly route (the Wiggle) to travel from Market Street to the Panhandle and Golden Gate Park. Yet even though it is a residential street, it is like a one-way major highway with three car lanes. A dedicated bicycle path is located on the left side of the street, sandwiched between heavy vehicle traffic on the right and parking spaces on the left. Moreover, automobiles making left turns to enter a gas station—located on the corner of the block and at the end of the bike path, cut through the bicycle path, increasing the already existing safety concerns of bicyclists.

Given these conditions, residents have been demanding the city make Fell Street a better and safer place for pedestrians and bicyclists by separating the bike lane, adding physical barriers, and removing parking spots. Confrontations on this stretch of the street can be traced back to at least a few months before the Park(ing) Day in 2010 to the day in which a "bicycle spill" happened. Attempting to resemble the BP oil spill, bicyclists chained themselves to several junk bicycle pieces they laid down at the entrance of the gas station in order to block its entrance (Fix Fell 2010a). One of the city's supervisors attended the three-hour long protest and declared his support for the bicycle issues. Drake Logan, one of the activists, underlined the immediate connection between global environmental problems caused by oil dependency and everyday health and safety risks that people face on the streets because of planning that prioritizes oil-dependent lifestyles over creating safer and more livable streets: "Now it is the time to break the city laws when city laws aren't protecting us against injury or death on city sidewalks. And, when the government is not making BP or any other oil companies clean up what they have done in the Gulf of Mexico" (Fix Fell 2010b). The protest ended with arrests and fines, but the needs of bicyclists were presented in the public sphere in a noticeable way.

Park(ing) Day provided a different kind of opportunity for neighborhood organizations on Fell Street—Fix Fell and the Wigg Party—to demonstrate their vision for Fell Street: on-street parking removed and sidewalks extended and used as social spaces rather than travel-only spaces (Figures 12.2 and 12.3). The Wigg Party is a neighborhood bicyclist organization whose goal is the betterment of the overall Wiggle route. Its park(ing) spots echoed the ongoing discussion about the removal of parking spots on the street in order to make the bike lane safer. In addition, organizers aimed to introduce a more residential feel to the neighborhood by limiting the automobile presence and extending the sidewalk.

Park(ing) spaces on Fell Street transformed spaces normally occupied with cars into an outdoor living room, with couches, rugs, cushions, tea corners, and planters, all standing side-by-side with the heavy traffic, the only separation being the bicycle lane. Passers-by and residents alike sat in the park(ing) spots to read a book or chat with one another.

The park(ing) spots became an agora for residents with differing opinions, as activists reconfigured the street to accommodate their needs and lifestyles. Not all residents' ideals were in perfect alignment, however. While I was observing, a couple of confrontations happened between the neighbors and those who were setting up the park(ing) spots. One resident expressed her discontent regarding the bicyclist community being powerful and aggressive. She was worried that eventually bicyclists will take her parking space away, despite the fact that she has been

FIGURES 12.2 and 12.3
Fix Fell, Fell Street
Park(ing) Day spots
in 2010

Source: Author.

a home owner in the city for many years, whereas the bicyclists are primarily young people who are renters. Her point of view implied that owning land/property makes a person more eligible to decide for the city, but being a renter does not, despite the fact that both groups of people reside in the same city.

Another incident was a confrontation between a neighbor and those who were taking advantage of the park(ing) spots. The neighbor stopped to express her disapproval about the nature and ideology of the installations, adding that she finds the event ridiculous and not having enough parking spaces is unimaginable. Though she left dissatisfied after a few minutes of discussion, one of the Wigg Party organizers stated that in fact the park(ing) spot served its main purpose despite the bitter tone of the discussion. According to him, getting a chance to talk face-to-face about the conflicting demands of residents was the primary point of their installation, more so than a few hours of enjoying the extended social space. In that sense, the park(ing) spots they organized met both goals of creating a different space and fostering a debate about such physical transformation of the streets.

Events like Park(ing) Day are exactly about such contestation over urban space. CFSEs, by providing transitional experiences and creating a forum between mainstream groups and counter-publics, let the unspoken be spoken between opposing groups, in the heart of the city, in its public streets. They are an attempt at democratization of urban processes and claiming a share in decision-making. Rios (2010) argues that when identity groups claim public space, cultural imaginations of public space lead to "empowerment, and, ultimately, political efficacy." Park(ing) spots on Fell Street, in fact, were translated into a tangible urban transformation project.

Spatial changes: institutionalized DIY

Livable city advocates' visions of alternative streets become visible through CSFEs. Dissemination of their counter-discourses in spatial ways in the public sphere opens up possibilities for the creation of actual counter-spaces (Morhayim 2012). Thus, the events themselves may be temporary appropriations of urban space, but their impact on urban space is greater than that.

In the last two decades the city's physical form has changed to a great extent in order to accommodate bicyclists and pedestrians.[2] The city today accommodates over 129 bike lanes and shared roads and over 201 miles of total bicycle network (SFMTA 2008, 2012a). The San Francisco Bicycle Coalition's membership increased from the hundreds to over 11,000 between 1992 and 2011 (SFBC 2011). The coalition, through its members' support, has provided bicycle access to mass transit, helped extend the bicycle network, and organized communities to close Golden Gate Park to automobile traffic on Saturdays, in addition to car-free Sundays. Fell Street, which was a hotspot of confrontation during the Park(ing) Day in 2010, has been going through a series of transformations in order to make the street safer for bicyclists. The bike lane was already painted green and by the late 2012 the city approved proposals for adding poles to separate the bike path from the heavy traffic, the removal of on-street car parking and installation of concrete planters for further separation of the path from automobile traffic (SFMTA 2012b). Furthermore, the city organized temporary traffic closures under the Sunday Streets program together with a non-governmental organization and worked with Rebar to make parklets happen, in addition to a number of new plazas created in recent years.

CFSEs go beyond symbolically making a territorial claim on public space. Like any ritual or performance, these temporary events create collective meanings and contribute to shared imaginations. Some of the CFSEs, such as Critical Mass, also communicate that citizens are willing to cross legal boundaries in order to experience their city streets the way they want, even if it will be a temporary experience. Participants' willingness to reshape their city plays a major role in the process in which the city is being transformed.

The cultural and social capital of Rebar's partners is also worth noting in terms of their role in Park(ing) Day's success. "Trust for Public Land (2008), a nationwide non-profit that focuses on developing parks for public use, is another logistic and financial contributor that makes Park(ing) Day possible" (Morhayim 2012). Moreover, in an interview, Rebar stated that its first park(ing) spot installation received immediate support from the mayor of San Francisco's administration (Freedenberg and Jones 2009). A phone call from City Hall started the process of collaboration and led to the integration of the Park(ing) Day idea into the City's Pavement to Parks Program and the construction of parklets. As of January 2014, 42 fixed parklets and seven mobile parklets have been constructed (Pavement to Parks 2012a) (Figure 12.4). Thus, the bottom-up quality of these appropriations is strongly supported by the social and cultural capital of its players, and the events' success and ability to influence and bring about change are not disconnected from power dynamics.

The parklets are unique, given that a "community-partnership model" characterizes these projects. They are administered under the Pavement to Parks program. Those who would like to construct a parklet are required to go through a permit process. The Pavement to Parks program started in 2009 in order to increase the amount of public space in the city by rebuilding underutilized roadways. As part of this project, up through 2012, five new plazas have been constructed in San Francisco.

FIGURE 12.4 Valencia Street Parklet

Source: Author.

The implementation of these projects is made possible by a number of actors' contributions, such as local neighborhood/community/non-profit membership organizations' and nearby businesses' facilitation efforts, private donations, volunteer labor, and designer and construction companies' *pro bono* or reduced price services. Even the maintenance of the parks is supposed to be provided by one or more of these actors. For instance, the Divisadero Street parklet was made possible with the efforts and resources of several organizations, including the Great Streets Project, volunteers, and Mojo Bicycle Café (a café and bicycle shop located across from the parklet). Landscaping services and materials such as a decking system, cabling, wood, hardware, and planters were donated. Another portion of the funds came from an office that works under the direction of the mayor's office, the Office of Economic and Workforce Development's Neighborhood Marketplace Initiative, whose focus is to attract businesses to the city. Only "the first few parklets were sponsored by the City as demonstrations" (Pavement to Parks 2012b). The city's current website does not mention any government funds for the new parklets (Pavement to Parks 2013).

The *New York Times* reports that the new projects in San Francisco are part of a bigger traffic calming project that includes new traffic signals and planters, which has resulted in 53 percent collision rate reduction for the 11 blocks around Guerreo Park since 2004 (Arief 2009). These developments, paid for through community/ private partnerships, serve as both a traffic calming strategy and repurposed public spaces, a combination of services and urban amenities that would traditionally be provided by the city.

The first parklet on Divisadero Street that is still in existence today, was constructed initially as a six-month-long pilot project in 2010. It has been followed by 42 more parklets as of 2014. Parklets similarly benefit public health by increasing pedestrian activity, as evidenced by research on local case studies. According to the San Francisco Great Streets Project (a campaign initiated by San Francisco Bicycle Coalition, San Francisco Planning and Urban Research Association, and the Project for Public Spaces) survey on the Divisadero Parklet, the average number of weekday visitors doubled, and pedestrian activity (people per hour) increased by 37 percent on weekday evenings.

Parklets are supposed to be used as public spaces, yet unlike the rest of the streets, they are privately constructed and maintained. Although extra usable public space is added, the city does not always spend public money in order to bring the projects to life. The city's role in the construction of parklets is reduced to one of manager and permit provider, and in the case of objections during the 10-day public notice period, the city holds public hearings. The San Francisco Planning Department requires parklets to place signs that will make it obvious that they are open to the public and not only to customers of the businesses that established the parklets.

Shifting responsibility for public space from the city to individuals, businesses, and community organizations is a strategy that goes beyond the Pavement to Parks Program. Under the Better Streets project (www.sfbetterstreets.org), since 2012 the city has guided its citizens to "become active in creating Better Streets" in their neighborhoods by providing "a comprehensive 'how-to' guide on installing elements" that will make streets more livable/better (SFMTA 2012c). Under this program various actors in the city apply for permits to sponsor and improve the streets. Property owners, residents, or business owners can improve sidewalk landscaping, street trees, special sidewalk paving, outdoor café seating, sidewalk merchandise displays, bicycle racks, and parklets. Community organizations such as neighborhood groups, merchant associations, or community benefit districts can improve larger-scale projects. Any parties who apply to conduct changes on their streets are also expected to be responsible for the maintenance of the altered area.

Expecting various patrons in the city to take on a number of responsibilities—such as to determine the need for improvements in the public space, apply for a permit, generate and provide funds, carry out construction, and even later on provide maintenance—transcends boundaries between traditional public and private notions of space regarding use, maintenance, and responsibility of providing the public spaces.

Discussion

The relationship between activists' DIY sentiments found in CFSEs and the recent physical transformations taking place in the city is hard to dismiss. On one hand, these public spaces are much more *public* than many other public spaces in terms of the ways in which they come to life. First of all, grassroots movements disseminate ideas about alternative urban spaces in the public sphere. Regarding their actual construction, to some extent, they may be considered a step ahead in planning practices, given the variety of partners involved in the process, other than the city. The process of different actors collectively re-envisioning and constructing parts of the city's public spaces resonates with Lefebvre's (Lefebvre *et al.* 1996) idea of *œuvre*—collectively building the city as a work of art, and being an *inhabitant*. The projects come to life through processes in which experts, non-experts, and businesses act like *inhabitants*, rather than simply *habitants* of the city. Yet, many users and residents are still only involved to the extent that they are allowed to object to the new constructions during the 10-day public notice period and after the permits are granted.

The projects may also be seen to be more democratic because they respond to many San Franciscans' recent aspirations to make the city more environmentally friendly. When possible, reclaimed and recycled materials are used in the construction of the parks (such as with the fallen trees used in Guerrero Park), and green landscaping is added. Besides being "green," parklets also speak to both the social and healthy lifestyle aspirations of some San Francisco residents and to Complete Streets advocates, as these places may encourage casual interactions and discourage the use of motorized transportation. Thus, the projects make the public spaces of the city more inclusive of its many residents' urban needs, culture, and values.

While there are positive aspects of such community partnership processes, there are also negative ones. The appearance of new parklets depends on demands from nearby businesses or neighborhood groups' ability to organize and collect funds. Because the projects rely on resources provided by for-profit and non-profit organizations and strong social capital, they are more likely to take place in already economically vital neighborhoods. Thus, the future of extra public spaces holds the potential for unequal development throughout the city because the decision regarding where the parklet should be located is not made by a central organization or the city's planning department. This can create an even greater divide between upper- and lower-class neighborhoods in the city. Ocubillo (2012) argues that because the success of the parklets depends on pedestrian activity, and thus local merchants, and because of the parklets' local-scale focus, parklets may reinforce inequities. Lavine (2012) argues streets with parklets may become less accessible to low-income residents.

Joassart-Marcelli, Wolch, and Salim (2011: 707) note that if non-profits start to overtake the responsibility of providing resources for recreation from the governments, the absence of non-profits "from low-income and minority neighborhoods reinforces inequities in the distribution of park and recreation resources." The same is likely to be true for future development of parklets. The highest concentration of affordable housing units in San Francisco occurs in neighborhoods such as Western Addition, Downtown/Civic Center (Tenderloin), Bayview, Potrero Hill, Mission Bay, and South of Market (Figure 12.5). Yet those areas exhibit few to no parklets, despite the fact that already disadvantaged low-income communities would benefit most from health-promoting spaces.

Parklets' quasi-public/quasi-private character creates further confusion regarding their role in urban spatial justice. Despite the fact that parklets are public spaces, it is unknown whether they clearly communicate this to passers-by, since not everyone pays attention to the placards that are often placed below eye-level on the furniture. The parklets are often sponsored by coffee shops across the sidewalk, and they look like extensions of those coffee shops. Passers-by may not always know that they can use parklets without purchasing anything. Given that the projects are fairly new, however, over time more people may come to know about their open access.

The fact that sponsoring businesses are also responsible for the maintenance of the parklets may interfere with the ideal qualities associated with public spaces. The First Amendment gives every citizen the right to be in public spaces and the right to free speech, which includes the right to protest in public spaces. The initial private investment and continuing maintenance requirements by sponsors of the parklets and some parklets' outdoor coffee shop look raise questions regarding the public qualities of such places. After all, businesses make financial investments in these fixed structures with expectations of profit return. In this case, would the businesses let citizens hold protests and engage in free speech or let homeless people sit or sleep in parklets?

San Francisco residents' willingness to take action to make their streets more livable and bicyclists' DIY aspirations and the projection thereof onto urban space seem to have become a solution for a local government that lacks funding for public

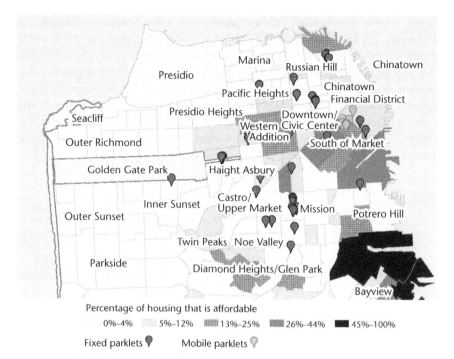

FIGURE 12.5 Map shows fixed and mobile parklets overlaid onto a map that shows affordable housing percentage in different parts of San Francisco. Darker colors indicate areas with higher percentage of affordable housing

Source: Reproduced based on information gathered from Pavement to Parks (2012a) and San Francisco Department of Public Health, Environmental Health Branch (2013).

projects in the aftermath of a crisis-hit economy. It appears that temporary CFSEs are less of a headache than previously thought and are even useful for local governments wanting to warm the mainstream, automobile-centered population up to the idea of creating a more livable city and limiting automobile access. Moreover, the city can tap into its residents' willingness and outsource the cost that it takes to provide more livable and healthier public space improvements. In the case of San Francisco, the DIY attitude seems to be institutionalized by the city.

These case studies highlight the complexity that characterizes urban processes, especially in terms of arguments about spatial justice. The projects such as those that happen under Pavement to Parks and Better Streets programs make the city more appealing and inclusive for populations such as non-motorists, who are marginalized by historically prevailing automobile-centric planning. However, at the same time, the social capital and private entrepreneurship required to make these projects happen, and lack of central land-use planning, hold the potential for unjust spatial development among different neighborhoods in the city, particularly for disadvantaged, low-income populations. Even though the civic sector's involvement in transforming the city appears to be a step towards sustainable and democratic production of urban space for certain populations, it may reproduce already existing social and spatial inequalities for low-income groups. Thus, the idea of Complete Streets should be evaluated not only by the end product in a vacuum, but also by the location, distribution of the redevelopment projects, partners involved in making the projects happen, and the social, cultural, and economic resources required to make the new livable streetscapes happen. Otherwise, the Complete Streets are bound to stay incomplete in terms of accessibility and ethnic and socioeconomic diversity.

Notes

1   Critical Mass and Sunday Streets are other examples of CFSEs taking place in San Francisco, CA. Critical Mass is a rather insurgent event in which bicyclists gather monthly and ride en masse in the city streets, blocking automobile traffic. Sunday Streets is a city-sanctioned event that closes select streets throughout the city to automobile traffic on designated Sundays to allow for casual car-free social gatherings and physical activity (for further discussion of these events, see Morhayim 2012).
2   Two decades ago corresponds with the start of Critical Mass, an iconic car-free streets event.

References

Alliance for Biking and Walking, 2012. *Bicycling and walking in the United States 2012. Benchmarking report* [online]. The Library of Congress, United States Copyright Office. Available from: www.peoplepoweredmovement.org/site/index.php/site/memberservices/2012_benchmarking_report/ [Accessed 30 December 2013].

Appleyard, D., Gerson, M.S., and Lintell, M., 1981. *Livable streets*. Berkeley, CA: University of California Press.

Arief, A., 2009. Pavement to parks: Opinionator. *The New York Times*, September 22, 2009. Available from: http://opinionator.blogs.nytimes.com/2009/09/22/pavement-to-parks [Accessed 11 June 2014].

Centers for Disease Control and Prevention (CDC), 1999. *Summary of physical activity and health: A report of the Surgeon General*. U.S. Department of Health and Human Services [online]. Available from: www.cdc.gov/nccdphp/sgr/summ.htm [Accessed 25 December 2013].

Chen, C., 2010. Dancing in the streets of Beijing: Improvised uses within the urban system. In: J. Hou, ed. *Insurgent public space: Guerrilla urbanism and the remaking of contemporary cities*. New York, NY: Routledge.

Cutts, B.B., Darby, K.J., Boone, C.G., and Brewis, A., 2009. City structure, obesity, and environmental justice: An integrated analysis of physical and social barriers to walkable streets and park access. *Social Science & Medicine*, 69 (9),1314–1322.

Ferguson, B.K., 2005. *Porous pavements*. Boca Raton, FL: Taylor & Francis.

Fix Fell, 2010a. Fix Fell protest update [online]. Last modified 4 November 2010. Available from: http://fixfell.wordpress.com/2010/11/04/fix-fell-protest-update/ [Accessed 21 June 2012].

Fix Fell, 2010b. A20 video coverage [online video]. Available from: http://fixfell.wordpress.com/2010/08/23/a20-video-coverage/ [Accessed 21 June 2012].

Freedenberg, M., and Jones, S.T., 2009. Seizing space: How Rebar and other artsy renegades reignited a movement to reclaim the urban environment. *San Francisco Bay Guardian*, November 18–24, 2009. Available from: http://rebargroup.org/wp-content/uploads/2009/11/sfbg2009-web.pdf. [Accessed 11 May 2012.]

Furness, Z.M., 2010. *One less car: Bicycling and the politics of automobility*. Philadelphia, PA: Temple University Press.

Giles-Corti, B., Broomhall, M.H., Knuiman, M., Collins, C., Douglas, K., Ng, K., et al., 2005. Increasing walking – how important is distance to, attractiveness, and size of public open space? *American Journal of Preventive Medicine*, 28 (2), 169–176.

Gordon-Larsen, P., Nelson, M.C., Page, P., and Popkin, B.M., 2006. Inequality in the built environment underlies key health disparities in physical activity and obesity. *Pediatrics*, 117 (2), 417–424.

Hart, J., n.d. *Driven to excess: Impacts of motor vehicle traffic on residential quality of life in Bristol, UK* [online]. Summary of research undertaken as part of a Master's dissertation in transport planning at the University of the West of England, UK, 2008. Available from: www.spur.org/misc_docs/LivableStreetsinBristol.pdf [Accessed 23 June 2012].

Hartman, C., 2002. *City for sale: The transformation of San Francisco*. Berkeley, CA: University of California Press.

Hayashi, Y., 2010. Machizukuri House and its expanding network: Making a new public realm in private homes. In: J. Hou, ed. *Insurgent public space: Guerrilla urbanism and the remaking of contemporary cities*. New York, NY: Routledge.

Henderson, J., 2009. The spaces of parking: Mapping the politics of mobility in San Francisco. *Antipode,* 41 (1): 70–91.

Jia, W., and Wachs, M., 1999. Parking requirements and housing affordability: Case study of San Francisco. *Transportation Research Record* 1685 (1): 156–160.

Joassart-Marcelli, P., Wolch, J., and Salim, Z., 2011. Building the healthy city: The role of nonprofits in creating active urban parks. *Urban Geography* 32 (5): 682–711.

Lavine, E., 2012. Spectacle in the new green city. *Berkeley Planning Journal* (25).

Lefebvre, Henri, Kofman, E. and Lebas, E., 1996. *Writings on cities*. Cambridge, MA: Blackwell Publishing.

Morhayim, L., 2012. From counterpublics to counterspaces: Livable city advocates' efforts to reshape cities through carfree-streets events. Dissertation (PhD), University of California, Berkeley.

Ocubillo, R.A., 2012. Experimenting with the margin: Parklets and plazas as catalysts in community and government. Master's thesis, University of Southern California. Available from: http://issuu.com/robin.abad/docs/experimentingwiththemargin_abadocubillo2012_ [Accessed 29 July 2014].

Pan, L., Galuska, D.A., Sherry, B., Hunter, A.S., Rutledge, G.E., and Dietz, W.H., 2009. Differences in prevalence of obesity among black, white, and Hispanic adults: United States, 2006–2008. *Morbidity and Mortality Weekly Report* 58 (27): 740–744. Atlanta, GA: National Center for Chronic Disease Prevention and Health Promotion, CDC.

Park(ing) Day, 2013. *Archive*. Available from: http://parkingday.org/archive/ [Accessed 23 December 2013].

Pavements to Parks, 2012a. *San Francisco map of parklets & projects* [online]. Available from: http://sfpavementtoparks.sfplanning.org/map.html [Accessed 10 October 2012].

Pavements to Parks, 2012b. *Pavement to Parks* [online]. Available from: http://dreamlets.sfplanning.org/parklets/built-projects-parklets/ [Accessed 10 November 2013].

Pavements to Parks, 2013. *Pavement to Parks* [online]. Available from: http://sfpavementtoparks.sfplanning.org/parklets.html [Accessed 23 November 2013].

Petcou, C., and Petrescu, D., 2011. At the ground level of the city. In: Z. Begg and L. Stickells eds. *The right to the city*. Tin Sheds Gallery, Faculty of Architecture, Design and Planning, the University of Sydney.

Putnam, R.D., 2000. *Bowling alone: The collapse and revival of American community*. New York, NY: Simon & Schuster.

Rebar, 2013. *Rebar workforce* [online]. Available from: http://rebargroup.org/studio/workforce/ [Accessed December 2013].

Rios, M., 2010. Claiming Latino space: Cultural insurgency in the public realm. In: J. Hou, ed. *Insurgent public space: Guerrilla urbanism and the remaking of contemporary cities*. New York, NY: Routledge.

San Francisco Department of Public Health, Environmental Health Branch, 2013. *Proportion of SF housing stock that is deed restricted, public, inclusionary or rent-controlled* [online]. Available from: www.sustainablecommunitiesindex.org/city_indicators/view/77 [Accessed December 2013].

SFBC (San Francisco Bicycle Coalition), 2011. *San Francisco Bicycle Coalition fact sheet* [online]. Available from: www.sfbike.org/download/press/SFBC_FactSheet.pdf and http://www.sfbike.org/download/press/SFBC_FactSheet_2011.pdf [Accessed 20 March 2011].

SFMTA (San Francisco Municipal Transportation Agency), 2008. *2008 San Francisco state of cycling report* [online]. Available from: www.altaplanning.com/App_Content/files/fp_docs/SF-State-of-Cycling.pdf [Accessed 4 April 2012].

SFMTA (San Francisco Municipal Transportation Agency), 2011. *San Francisco transportation fact sheet, November 2011* [online]. Available from: www.sfmta.com/cms/rfact/documents/SFFactSheet201111-29-2011.pdf [Accessed 8 June 2012].

SFMTA (San Francisco Municipal Transportation Agency), 2012a. *San Francisco state of cycling report* [online]. Available from: www.sfmta.com/cms/rbikes/documents/2012StateofCyclingReport8_9_12.pdf [Accessed 2012].

SFMTA (San Francisco Municipal Transportation Agency), 2012b. *Oak Street and Fell Street pedestrian and bike safety project* [online]. Last modified May 23, 2012. Available from: www.sfmta.com/cms/bproj/OakandFellBikeways.htm [Accessed 4 October 2012].

SFMTA (San Francisco Municipal Transportation Agency), 2012c. *Better streets plan* [online]. Last modified August 29, 2012. Available from: www.sfmta.com/cms/wproj/28717.html [Accessed 3 October 2012].

Transportation Alternatives, 2006. *Traffic's human toll: A study of the impacts of vehicular traffic on New York City residents* [online]. Available from: www.transalt.org/campaigns/reclaiming/trafficshumantoll.pdf [Accessed October 2006].

13

THE MOST COMPLETE STREET IN THE WORLD

A dream deferred and co-opted

Anna Livia Brand

Introduction

North Claiborne Avenue runs through the heart of New Orleans' historic black communities, Treme and the 7th Ward. A regional spine that connects Orleans with St. Bernard and Jefferson Parishes, Claiborne is also the site of a much contested expressway, whose 1960s construction decimated the black business corridor that once lined this wide, tree-lined boulevard and contributed to these neighborhoods' decline. Coupled with the construction of I-10 were other large-scale urban interventions, including the urban renewal-type development of Armstrong Park and the development of two public housing projects. Combined, these interventions mirrored national trends that supported white suburbanization (and in the case of New Orleans the suburbanization of the middle-class black community) and urban disinvestment. Across the country we saw the rise in concentrated poverty and high indices of social ills such as joblessness, crime, and poor public education within cities as federally subsidized highways supported the literal and figurative abandonment of the city center.

Now, the country is rethinking its urban commitments and planners are playing a role in encouraging whites, young entrepreneurs, and the "Creative Class"[1] to return to the city. In an effort to pave the way for this, planners and urban policy-makers have begun narrating and implementing new urban development visions and policies that seemingly promote a more equitable re-imagining of urban cores—a return to the center to foster growth and alleviate decline through mixed-use and mixed-income communities. Included in this thinking are new Complete Streets initiatives being written and implemented across the country and which propose to democratize streets by incorporating different modes of transportation into street redevelopment and thereby reduce the hierarchical accommodation of auto traffic. Complete Streets initiatives are a part of remaking cities in the name of economic growth and diversity in the twenty-first century. As such, they are a piece of how cities, previously disrupted and dismantled by urban policies such as suburbanization and federal highway construction, are being put back together and revitalized through new urban interventions.

In New Orleans, particularly in the wake of Hurricane Katrina, there has been both the explicit and implicit push to remake the downtown and its surrounding neighborhoods. Within this, there has been increased momentum on a past community-initiated goal to take down the urban portion of the I-10 expressway and restore the boulevard using a Complete Streets approach. This potential scenario, that planners say would develop "the most complete street in the world,"[2] has been advocated for within a local planning and citizen participation process, the Livable Claiborne Communities study,[3] focused on community revitalization and economic development along part of the Orleans Parish portion of the corridor. Yet much like national re-urbanization trends, the work to re-imagine Claiborne is a part of a larger whole of redevelopment in the city, particularly in and near the city's historic black core neighborhoods of Treme and the 7th Ward, which are located on higher ground and just north of the city's thriving tourist center, the French Quarter. The tremendous development pressures surrounding these two neighborhoods, including the Complete Streets redevelopment of their northern border, Rampart Street, and the redevelopment of all of the mid-twentieth-century projects that contributed to these neighborhoods' decline, signify a complete re-imagining of these urban spaces and their occupants. However, contrary to the notion of completeness, Claiborne's redevelopment is, to many long-term residents, a linchpin in the city's efforts to gentrify the downtown and displace the black community from their historical stronghold.

The rethinking of urban space in the early twenty-first century at the surface reflects a normative commitment to "ailing" urban cores, promoting diversity, and initiating urban revitalization. The economic, social, and racial segregation of the city that resulted from the combined forces of urban disinvestment, the con-centration of poverty in public housing, and the promotion of white flight to the suburbs, is seemingly transformed by new commitments to public and private urban investment strategies, new federal housing initiatives to de-concentrate urban poverty, and the promotion of vibrant, livable, shoppable, walkable, bikable, and transit-rich urban centers. However, as the Introduction and chapters in this book describe, the move back to the center and the remaking of cities into more vibrant and livable cores beg for more critical thinking about who will benefit from this new completeness and who will be pushed out by increased land values and gentrification. Are urban revitalization initiatives and new policies such as Complete Streets really complete for *all* citizens or will the repercussions be to displace urban poor and minority residents in order to build a wealthier, whiter, and more entrepreneurial city? In the words of poet Langston Hughes, what will happen to the deferred dreams of current residents who have inhabited the urban spaces once abandoned? The results so far are at best unclear and at worst, strikingly reminiscent of urban renewal—but in reverse.

This chapter considers the potential redevelopment of Claiborne Avenue in light of the larger redevelopment narratives and projects being undertaken in New Orleans' downtown neighborhoods.[4] This research takes a comparative approach and interrogates the racial and economic repercussions and undertones of the development schemes promoted by new residents and urban planners; questions the norms and policies promoted by these initiatives; and interrogates whose needs this redevelopment promotes and whose needs it undermines. Using discourse analysis and grounded theory to understand the narratives and visions of the new New Orleans, as well as interviews with residents and policy-makers and observations at public meetings, this chapter ultimately argues that this new vision of urban renewal, though premised on increasing equity and access, is ultimately incomplete for the least well-off and for the city's racial minorities who have occupied the downtown neighborhoods through its cycles of abandonment and revitalization. Further, I argue that the notion of completeness is itself constructed on narrow grounds and ignores alternative conceptualizations of the city's public spaces. I begin by briefly highlighting the history of the Treme and 7th Ward neighborhoods before turning to a discussion of the historical and contemporary accounts of redevelopment in this area of the city. I conclude with a discussion questioning the notion of completeness presented by the redevelopment of New Orleans' black core and argue that the city is being remade for a specific group of citizens while it is being dismantled for others.

Making and decimating New Orleans' historic black core: Treme and the 7th Ward

Like many US cities, New Orleans' history of racialized geographies has taken place at multiple geographic scales. From the regional scale to the city level to the neighborhood to the segregated public facilities, racial geographies in New Orleans have influenced and been influenced by daily life, planning, and public policies. New Orleans' population decline in the 1960s mirrored other US cities, with increasing suburbanization and white flight occurring at the same time that the post-Civil Rights city was supposedly integrating. Yet beyond national racial shifts, New Orleans' internal racial geographies have always been further complicated by the geographic implementation of urban slavery, racial differentiation, and urban segregation/integration, unique contextual realities that gave shape and meaning to the early formation of the Treme and 7th Ward neighborhoods.

In New Orleans, early racial segregation was shaped by topography, commerce-related development patterns, and racial difference/hierarchies (Campanella 2006; Lewis 2003; Sublette 2008). Blacks, people of color, and immigrants historically lived in lower-lying areas of the city (both north and east of the French Quarter), while the higher ground was reserved for whites (Campanella 2006; Lewis 2003). This complicated racial geography was made more so by the unique racial hierarchy that has further shaped development patterns and socio-economic relations in the city (Campanella 2006; Hirsch and Logsdon 1992). Because of New Orleans' history of French and Spanish occupation, slaves were able to buy their own freedom, producing a substantial population of Free People of Color. Further, with Spanish, Caribbean, and European ancestral lines, extensive racial intermixing led to the formation of a new social or racial caste, the Creole community, which largely settled in the Treme and 7th Ward neighborhoods just north of the French Quarter. Black Creoles in New Orleans historically separated themselves from African-Americans (both literally and physically), setting themselves apart (as an identity group) and above other blacks (Hirsch and Logsdon 1992). Prior to Jim Crow segregation, Black Creoles had more status than African-Americans in New Orleans and were able to own land and businesses, have bank accounts, lend money, marry freely, and even own slaves and this led to the formation of economically and culturally vibrant black geographies in the Treme and 7th Ward neighborhoods.

Treme is one of the oldest black neighborhoods in the United States and both Treme and the 7th Ward were the original home to Free People of Color and Black Creoles. The neighborhoods formed their social and physical fabrics out of their racial difference and the freedoms given to Black Creoles and Free People of Color to own land and businesses. Free People of Color and Black Creoles literally shaped the neighborhood with their extensive building trade businesses and high rates of property ownership. This local network of carpenters, plasterers, brick masons, and electricians built these neighborhoods and many homes throughout the city. Congo Square, located in what is now Armstrong Park and one of the only places in the city that blacks (both free and enslaved) were allowed to congregate dating back to the eighteenth century, was located in Treme and was the site where African-Americans (including a large population of blacks of Haitian descent) came together on Sundays to drum and dance, exchange news, and sell produce and other goods. The ability to congregate meant that African traditions such as dancing and drumming could be maintained and cultivated (eventually cultivating the foundation for jazz). By the late 1800s, Treme and the 7th Ward were prosperous and thriving communities, and by the 1950s, Claiborne Avenue was the vibrant economic and social corridor of black-owned businesses that traversed both neighborhoods. Claiborne's importance as a retail and social center for the black community was largely driven by their exclusion from patronizing the city's main retail center on Canal Street (Crutcher 2010). Thus, this tree-lined boulevard with its wide neutral ground became the economic center of black life—where blacks could both own and patronize businesses, and the social and recreational center of black life—where black families and children, segregated from many of the city's other recreational spaces, could play and relax.[5] The neutral ground space also played an important role in the African-American community's unique cultural traditions and it was where blacks congregated for African-American parades during Mardi Gras, which were segregated from the city's white Mardi Gras parades (ibid.).

Although the racial mixing and blacks' rights to purchase their own freedom produced two vibrant black neighborhoods within a wider citywide landscape of intense segregation, discrimination, and disinvestment, blacks still lived economically and socially inhibited lives. In response to basic inequalities, benevolent societies and social aid and pleasure clubs, and later black-owned insurance companies, emerged to assist the black community (ibid.). These social and insurance organizations, which emerged as early as the late eighteenth century, provided members with financial and burial assistance and continued to observe traditional ceremonial practices for burials. The social aid and pleasure clubs also contributed to the social dynamics of these neighborhoods, which became known for their second-line parades, jazz funerals, and local bars and music halls.[6]

Despite the economic and cultural vibrancy found in these two neighborhoods, these racialized landscapes continued to be shaped by inequitable policies and development patterns well into the early mid-twentieth century. New Orleans' patterns of segregation persisted and became more entrenched with the emergence of Jim Crow segregation and the move toward integration in the wake of Civil Rights gains (Campanella 2006). In the early twentieth century, new technologies and the invention of a new pump allowed the city to expand geographically and to drain the back swamps that had previously been uninhabitable. Development thus began to move toward the lakefront and away from the historic core. However, "the Wood pump, as it turned out, was a powerful agent to accelerate racial segregation in New Orleans" (Lewis 2003, p. 67) and the area toward the lake emerged as an affluent white area of the city, legally condoned through Jim Crow rules allowing real estate agents not to sell to blacks.[7] As the city expanded toward the lake from the 1920s onward, the city and the New Orleans levee district redesigned and redeveloped the lakefront, creating over 2,000 acres of new waterfront development that would eventually be used for both leisure and park space, a municipal yacht harbor and private suburban-style development (ibid.).

Alongside white flight toward the lake, increased suburbanization also occurred to outlying suburban parishes in the mid-twentieth century. The construction of the I-10 expressway was instrumental in this rapid depopulation of the urban core. In the 1960s, a well-organized white coalition, focused on the preservation of the French Quarter, successfully lobbied against the proposal to locate an expressway along the riverfront and as a result, the urban overpass portion of I-10 was constructed through the heart of the historic Treme and 7th Ward neighborhoods and above Claiborne Avenue (Baumbach and Borah 1981). Although "there is no record of anyone from Treme or other Downtown areas arguing against the destruction of their neighborhoods," local residents received little notice of the proposed location of the overpass (Crutcher 2010, p. 60). One local planner noted that many black residents in Treme and the 7th Ward felt that the decision had been made without their input and was a done deal.[8]

The construction of the I-10 overpass contributed to the decline of this vibrant economic and recreational corridor, where property values rapidly diminished and local businesses were closed or moved. Between 1960 and 2000, the number of businesses located on Claiborne in these communities declined from 132 to 35.[9] The large live oak trees that lined the boulevard were removed and the neutral ground became populated by a forest of large concrete columns supporting the expressway. As in many US cities, the expressway enabled the city's white and middle-class populations, as well as its retail center, to move out to the suburbs and more typical suburban-style developments. In New Orleans, this included the development of a predominantly middle-class black New Orleans East, which emerged in the 1960s and 1970s (Lewis 2003). With this increased suburbanization of middle-class blacks to New Orleans East, and whites to areas like Lakeview and the suburbs, Treme and the 7th Ward's populations declined significantly in the mid-twentieth century. New Orleans' exodus of whites in the 1960s represented a real population loss of nearly 65,000 whites and a real population gain of nearly 85,000 blacks between 1950 and 1970 in the city.[10]

The effects of suburbanization on blacks in the city meant economic shifts in terms of resources, and development shifts in terms of planning projects intended to protect and revitalize the historical core of the city. By the early 1970s, the black business core on Claiborne had been decimated and the recreational neutral ground space overtaken by the overpass. While the construction of the I-10 corridor through the heart of the city's black core was a critical part of this, the changes on Claiborne were not the only element leading to the decline of these neighborhoods. Additional development projects, including the construction of segregated public housing projects and the establishment of a new civic park, were made in the context of promoting tourism and racial segregation and contributed to the decline of these two neighborhoods. Both the Lafitte and Iberville public housing projects, located in Treme, pre-date the construction of the I-10 expressway, arguably contributing to white flight in the 1950s and 1960s. Built in the 1940s as part of the Housing Act of 1937 and as a part of slum clearance efforts in New Orleans, Lafitte and Iberville were predominantly lower-income black public housing developments similar to other segregated public housing across the country. Also pre-dating the construction of I-10 was the initial development of a new civic center located on a site adjacent to Rampart Street, the northern border of Treme and the border between Treme and the French Quarter. The city's new civic center and eventually the larger development of Armstrong Park in the 1970s, displaced more than 100 Treme families, the majority of which were nonwhite, and Globe Hall, one of the dance halls most frequented by the black community (Crutcher 2010). The location was chosen because the property values in Treme were low and because it was largely considered by planners and policy-makers to be a slum worthy of clearance (ibid.). As with the I-10 construction, there was little effort to include community partici-pation in the early planning of the civic center and little compensation for the loss of homes (ibid.). Although the black community in Treme raised more opposition by the time the larger park was constructed, the park's walls were literally and figuratively shut to the black community with the erection of tall fences along its Treme borders and its development plans, which emphasized high culture, rather than local culture or benefits to the black community (ibid.).

These types of projects that devastated two black neighborhoods are typical of the types of planning and development interventions made in the mid-twentieth century, many of which have served to further polarize the black and white communities in terms of urban resources and amenities. They often reflect urban investment, but in the name of tourist expansion or economic development, therefore contributing to unequal economies and disinvestment in the areas of the city that need it the most. Fast forwarding to 2000 and the years leading up to Katrina, New Orleans' racial differences, like many US cities, were marked by stark contrasts between blacks and whites in terms of employment and income, education, and other quality of life measures, including crime and poverty. In 2000, while blacks represented 67 percent of the population, they were far more likely to live in poverty, live in unaffordable housing situations, attend notoriously failing public schools, rely on public transportation, and work in accommodation and food service industries (Greater New Orleans Community Data Center 2014a). However, prior to Katrina, blacks in New Orleans were NOT less likely to own homes, were more likely to have lived in their neighborhoods for over 30 years and relied on social networks for childcare and transportation (ibid.).

Treme and the 7th Ward reflect this nuanced and racialized context. By 2000, though Treme was seeing the gradual gentrification of its boundaries near the French Quarter, these neighborhoods were still mired in the extreme racialized differences that characterize so many black urban areas in the US (Greater New Orleans Community Data Center 2014b). In 2000, Treme, which was 92 percent black, had an average household income of $25,600 and nearly 60 percent of its population was living in poverty (including a staggering 80+ percent of children under 5 living in poverty) (ibid.).[11] Similarly in the 7th Ward, a nearly 95 percent black community, 38 percent of residents were living in poverty and just over 50 percent of children under 5 were living in poverty in a neighborhood with an average household income of $34,702.[12] Both neighborhoods, known as the cultural heart of the city and the birthplace of jazz, second lines, and brass bands, were suffering from years of disinvestment, poor education, and poor employment prospects.

Although the decline of these neighborhoods can be measured in statistics and disinvestment, this is not the whole picture. As McKittrick and Woods argue, an over-emphasis on descriptive statistics, which is seen often in planning and used to fuel and rationalize redevelopment initiatives,

> importantly situate[s] the materiality of race and racism, [yet] it can also be read as naturalizing racial difference in place . . . identifying the "where" of blackness in positivist terms can reduce black lives to essential, measurable "facts" rather than presenting communities that have struggled, resisted, and significantly contributed to the production of space.
>
> *(2007, p. 6)*

Given this, the history of Treme and the 7th Ward can be read through these specific types of urban strategies that dismantled the black economic core and affected blacks' social, cultural, and economic lives. Understanding this history is important, given the revitalization narrative that has more recently been constructed about revitalizing these communities, as we will see in the next section. As James Jennings (2012) argues, an analysis of the spatialization of inequality is critical for planners' understanding of the systematic and historical spatial distribution of neighborhood distress. Yet at the same time, the history of these neighborhoods can also be read in their resistance, their continued cultural practices and weekly second-lines, their painting of the I-10 overpass columns with murals of the trees that once lined Claiborne, and their adaptive reuse of this space under the overpass for barbeques, second-lines, Mardi Gras Indian performances, and Mardi Gras gatherings. Despite the gradual decline of the Treme and 7th Ward neighborhoods, there still existed and exists a vibrant sense of social and cultural life that dominates these neighborhoods and marks residents' resiliency, adaptability, and political activism. Although as one Treme resident said, the community still "suffers from the loss of Claiborne Avenue," (Anonymous, personal communication, October 2010) this suffering is tempered by what Du Bois (1994) might call residents' double consciousness or ability to see themselves beyond the demonizing lens applied to them by white elites and with a view that encompasses their own resilience, dignity, and dreams for a different future. The duality of this view or way of understanding a community is critical to blacks' diagnosis of the newest redevelopment proposals affecting their communities.

Re-imagining and remaking New Orleans' historic black core: an old community dream resurfaces

It is in fact black residents' dream for a different future that has resurfaced in the wake of Hurricane Katrina, a storm that brought much devastation to the city and its residents, drastic populations shifts, and a new vision for development that emphasizes a remaking of urban space for those who once abandoned the city core. Of course, the question remains as to whether this dream will be realized or deferred further, or utilized as a tool of exclusion for those who first proposed a new vision for their own community. In this section, I discuss the myriad of development changes and new visions for the city's downtown neighborhoods before returning to a discussion of residents' deferred dream.

Katrina brought substantial demographic changes. Despite repopulation and rebuilding surges, the population loss from pre-Katrina levels persists, with a loss of over 140,000 residents (Greater New Orleans Community Data Center 2014a). Yet the population loss represents a demographic shift in the city and the most substantial changes have been in terms of the racial dynamics, including a substantial loss of black residents and an increase in Hispanic residents. This shift is represented by a loss of over 115,000 blacks and just over 24,000 whites, with a slight increase in the Hispanic population (just over 3,000 documented residents). The population decline between 2000 and 2010, mostly due to Katrina, is thus incredibly uneven and indicates the different economic realities of rebuilding for the black and white communities. Since 2000, both Treme and the 7th Ward have seen a loss in their black populations (-5,086 and -6,967 respectively), while Treme has seen a substantial increase in its white population (+66.9 percent) (Greater New Orleans

Community Data Center 2014a, 2014b). For the first time since the 1940s, the population of whites in Treme has increased to 17.4 percent of the neighborhood's population. Treme has lost about 50 percent of its population since 2000, which can be attributed to the combined changes in the neighborhood, including the closure and rebuilding of both the Lafitte and Iberville public housing developments, the effects of Hurricane Katrina, and gentrification. While Treme residents were able to resist earlier waves of gentrification due to their "active resistance and the neighborhood's proximity to public housing projects" (Crutcher 2010, p. 33), the 2010 population numbers indicate that this has begun to shift and that gentrification has been fueled by new redevelopment proposals and by the effects of Katrina making more valuable the higher ground that did not flood. Gentrification is perhaps less felt in the 7th Ward, where the population gain in the white community is very small. However, the 7th Ward will likely face increased gentrification in the future with the expansion of the streetcar system along Rampart Street/St. Claude Avenue and with new development along this corridor, Claiborne Avenue, and around these historic neighborhoods.

However, beyond the evidence of demographic shifts, the changing realities of federal support to cities, new economic realities, and new urban development visions are impacting lower-income and black communities in New Orleans. In the wake of Katrina, new visions for re-imagining the city's downtown are being implemented alongside continued commitments to an expanded tourist economy and the promotion of a new city for entrepreneurs and members of the creative class. Amidst the post-Katrina development climate, New Orleans' historic black core neighborhoods, located on high ground and adjacent to the city's French Quarter and Marigny neighborhoods, face tremendous development pressures. Post-Katrina redevelopment has included an entire rethinking, re-planning, and re-building of the mid-twentieth-century projects that contributed to both Treme and the 7th Ward's decline. The redevelopment of Armstrong Park and both the Lafitte and Iberville public housing projects are coupled with the potential removal of the I-10 overpass along Claiborne Avenue—re-signifying these former sites of neighborhood decline in a new narrative of regeneration and revitalization. Additionally, other urban development projects—including the Lafitte Greenway, the Bio-Medical District and related redevelopment along Tulane Avenue, the redevelopment of the neighborhoods' northern border—Rampart Street, using the Complete Streets redevelopment approach, and growing gentrification pressures all form a coherent, yet uncoordinated assault on the affordability and future of the Treme and 7th Ward neighborhoods for their current and long-time black residents. This section traces the nascent planning and development of each of these projects, including a discussion of the future of the I-10 corridor as an incompletely envisioned street, addressing them as a strategy to remake the city once again.

In the wake of Katrina, the city shut down nearly all of its public housing developments in the name of implementing new federal housing policies that reflected a commitment to de-concentrating poverty and building mixed-income communities. Both the Lafitte and Iberville housing projects are a part of this effort.

Lafitte, whose reconstruction began off-site in 2008 and on-site in 2009, is being redeveloped under the HOPE VI redevelopment policy. The redevelopment plan "reduces the total number of on-site units from 900 to 517 [141 home ownership and 376 rental], but calls for the development of an additional 983 in-fill units" (459 homeownership and 524 rental).[13] Former tenants of Lafitte have the opportunity to return, either on-site or in one of the off-site developments in the Treme and Tulane/Gravier neighborhoods.[14] Recently, with only just over half of units completed (including only 276 rental units), construction temporarily stalled due to funding hurdles, though it is expected to continue in 2014.[15]

In contrast, Iberville is being redeveloped under the more recent Neighborhood Choice program. The new Iberville, which broke ground in October 2013, will include the replacement of 821 of the former development's units both on-site and within the Neighborhood Choice boundary. The boundary encompasses the Treme neighborhood, as well as part of the 7th Ward, and stretches west to Tulane Avenue or Tulane/Gravier neighborhood (the site of the city's new Bio-Medical District). The first two phases of new development include 227 rental units, including 81 public housing units, 49 workforce units, and 97 market rate units, as well as 112 units for seniors.[16] The full project calls for a total of 880 units, including 304 public housing apartments, 315 market rate homes and 261 workforce units.[17] The redevelopment plan also calls for additional community investments in schools and grocery stores within the project area.

HOPE VI was a federal poverty de-concentration and housing program that focused on demolishing public housing in order to rebuild mixed-income communities in the late twentieth century. The program has yielded mixed-results for former tenants across the country, particularly given its reduction in the total number of locally sited affordable housing and public housing units and the subsequent dislocation of families from their communities (Goetz 2003). The Neighborhood Choice program counters the main criticisms of HOPE VI and focuses redevelopment within a specific geographic area. Still, given their initial development, both the Iberville and Lafitte projects fit with Vale's understanding of "twice-cleared" communities. Although Vale's focus was on HOPE VI sites, particularly in more notorious public housing projects in Chicago and Atlanta, he does note that the second clearing of these sites under HOPE VI, nearly half a century later, shares an impulse with the initial slum clearance and construction of these segregated facilities in that they "share a fundamental concern with improving the image of the city" (2013, p. 318) and mark the "demolition of discredited places" (ibid., p. 325). In this, Vale notes that the remaking of public housing in the late twentieth century entails "a strong social component, . . . economic imperatives and the dominant visual appeal of destructive creation, . . . it also entails a fundamental social reconfiguration of community identity" (ibid., p. 332). We see this in the rebuilding of both Lafitte and Iberville, whose common new aesthetic focuses on mirroring the historic fabric of the Treme and 7th Ward neighborhoods and re-knitting the neighborhoods, in contrast to the demonized view of these public housing projects prior to the storm.[18] Yet, Vale's understanding of "discredited places" is also a critical part of the new narrative dominating redevelopment in and around Treme and the 7th Ward which rests on a demonized or overly descriptive view of these communities in order to remake and revitalize them into more complete communities.

The re-imagining and rebuilding of Armstrong Park form another piece of the larger work to improve the image of the city and remake the downtown neighborhoods. Repairs and improvements to the park and to the civic center buildings made since Katrina were contested by Treme residents who felt excluded from the process and who noted that the continued lack of access to the park from the Treme community was unaddressed in the new development plans (Elie 2009). Although redevelopment has sparked new levels of engagement with the park, including the emergence of a local non-profit focused on the park and on promoting its use for community and cultural exchange, the exclusion of the community from formal planning process regarding the redevelopment of the park and the continued literal exclusion of the community from accessing the park, speak to the larger work of re-narrating the image of the city and these downtown neighborhoods and promoting a new vision for high culture and creativity, one that largely ignores the historical and local contexts.

Yet, beyond the re-imagining and rebuilding of these twentieth-century projects, there are new projects that potentially stand to affect the affordability of Treme and 7th Ward neighborhoods for long-time residents. The Lafitte Greenway and the new Bio-Medical District are two of these projects. The Lafitte Greenway is a new urban greenway project located on publicly owned land that once held a former shipping canal and railway. Starting at Armstrong Park and located along Treme's western edge, the Greenway stretches away from the downtown in a 3.1-mile long strip of future green, park, and recreational space. The amenities of the future park will include a bike and walking trail, formal and informal recreation spaces, community gardens, a dog park, and the integration of new regional water strategies.[19] The Lafitte Greenway is just east of the city's new Bio-Medical District, a state economic development district with taxing and bonding authority that was created in 2005. The Bio-Medical District is located in the Tulane/Gravier neighborhood—just west of Treme, and will house various elements of the city's biosciences industry, including two new hospitals, the Veterans Affairs Medical Center and the University Medical Center Hospital.[20] The clearing of this 1,500-acre site was controversial, given that the city had to demolish and move 81 historic homes in order to clear the way for this new development.[21]

Complete Streets: an old community dream resurfaces

The final element in the re-imagining and remaking of the city's downtown is the redevelopment of two critical thoroughfares: Rampart Street/St. Claude Avenue and Claiborne Avenue—both of which are being redeveloped under the city's new Complete Streets Ordinance, which was adopted in 2011. Similar to other Complete Streets policies across the country, the goal of this ordinance is to "accommodate and encourage travel for all users in a balanced, responsible, and equitable manner consistent with, and supportive of, the surrounding community."[22] Included in the city's street redevelopment plan is the northern border of the Treme and 7th Ward neighborhoods, Rampart Street/St. Claude Avenue. The proposed redevelopment of this corridor, set to open in 2015, includes a new streetcar line and bike lane, reducing traffic to one dedicated lane.[23] The inclusion of a streetcar, rather than improvements to the city's existing bus transit system or the adoption of a bus rapid transit system, is linked to federal emphasis on rail transit (Pickrell 1992), but also to nostalgic notions of the New Orleans streetcar, the promotion of upper middle-class redevelopment interests (Stone 1980; Boshken 1998), and the promotion of tourism and economic development (Guthrie and Fan 2013).[24] As Grengs (2004, p. 52) notes, "Mass transit is a new space of emerging social conflict over how the contradictions of neoliberalism will be resolved in cities."

He continues:

> This new space of conflict holds special relevance for planners, because the neoliberal agenda . . . contributes directly to changing urban spatial patterns, and the emerging spatial patterns raise new questions for planning theory about the role of social justice in cities where racial and economic segregation are worsening.
>
> *(ibid. p. 52)*

New Orleans' post-Katrina redevelopment fits squarely within a neoliberal redevelopment approach that emphasizes a new narrative of economic expansion through new spatial redevelopment policies such as those affecting its historic black core neighborhoods. While the prospects for the future of these two communities are unclear, the redevelopment of both Rampart Street/St. Claude Avenue and Claiborne Avenue is a critical part of this new spatial pattern.

The prospects for Claiborne's future redevelopment hinge on future environmental and transportation studies, yet the proposed redevelopment of Claiborne is in line with the city's Complete Streets approach. The potential removal of the I-10 overpass along Claiborne is actually a community-driven goal, born in the wake of its construction and the decimation of the vibrant business corridor along Claiborne. This community vision is documented in a 1976 study focused on the social, economic, cultural, and recreational potential of redesigning this corridor to meet community needs.[25] In the Preface to this study, one of the project leaders noted:

> The general situation among residents of the Claiborne Avenue corridor is one of noticeable frustration, permeated by a quiet evolving tension. The sordid conditions of the corridor must be acted upon with a sense of urgency and good faith. Local residents and visitors alike will suffer gravely if the CADT [Claiborne Avenue Design Team] area is allowed to continue the trend of deterioration which has adversely affected its character.[26]

The Preface went on to say that the vision represented in the plan was a community's dream for improving their urban environment and warned, in the words of poet Langston Hughes, that "some dreams deferred dry up, some fester like a sore, and others explode."[27] The origins of this study were rooted in the community work of the local black neighborhood and cultural organization, the Tambourine and Fan Club, who saw its work,

> oriented toward people generally bypassed or victimized for lack of participation in decisions or projects which seriously affect their lives. The organization sees itself as a reflection of the many unsung persons whose efforts have sustained the culturally unique traditions of the Claiborne Avenue corridor . . ..[28]

The 1976 proposed removal of the I-10 expressway along Claiborne Avenue is a tacit yet critical aspect of the newer effort to take down the expressway and create "the most complete street in the world."[29] Soon after Katrina, this proposal made its way into early planning processes and strategies, finally being reflected in the City's new Master Plan, which was adopted in 2010.[30] Also in 2010, the newly formed Claiborne Avenue Improvement Coalition, a coalition of developers, funders, neighborhood organizations, service providers, faith groups, schools, and government agencies and formed by NEWCITY neighborhood Partnerships, contracted the Congress for New Urbanism (CNU) to complete a study regarding the replacement of the I-10 Claiborne overpass with a newly restored boulevard.[31]

This 2010 study, focused largely on the traffic implications of taking down the overpass and the design implications of the new corridor, spurred the city into further action. The city received a HUD Challenge/DOT TIGER II planning grant to undertake a further study of this corridor. The study, the Livable Claiborne Communities Study (LCC), was launched in September 2012 and culminated in October 2013.[32] Over the course of this study the project team, led by the city and its consultant, Kittelson & Associates, held two sets of community meetings (December 2012 and March 2013), meetings with stakeholders and project advisors, and a culminating community meeting in October 2013 where they presented their proposed alternatives for the Claiborne corridor. The process will next move into yet unfunded environmental and funding assessment stages.

In the final community meeting, the project team presented three alternatives, two of which proposed minor changes to the infrastructure of the Claiborne overpass and the removal of a number of ramps that disrupt the fabric of the community and street network.[33] The final recommendation, broken into two alternatives, proposed the full removal of the urban portion of the I-10 overpass along Claiborne Avenue. Only the first of these three recommendations (Scenario 1) included the existing bus network as the major public transit mode along Claiborne. Scenarios 2 and 3 propose a new streetcar along North Claiborne and an enhanced bus system along the Broad Street, the northern border of the Treme and 7th Ward neighborhoods. Similar to the Rampart Street/St. Claude Avenue streetcar expansion, the inclusion here of a new streetcar line reflects both federal shifts toward rail projects and local nostalgia and tourism promotion, rather than local transit needs. As noted above, this illustrates new spatial and development conflicts about mass transit that reflect neoliberal redevelopment initiatives in urban centers (Grengs 2004).

The final LCC vision, which included these three scenarios, also reflected the community's push back toward earlier top-down visions that became evident early in this planning process. Residents in the Claiborne corridor area and along its regional spine were a part of this public participation process, yet residents most affected by the potential direct removal voiced their concerns over the repercussions of this redevelopment for the future of their neighborhood, particularly their ability to continue to afford to live in what they perceived would be an even more rapidly gentrified area in the wake of removing the I-10. One resident noted in an earlier interview that "the removal of I-10 will only further gentrification and development and price people who live here out."[34] The culminating recommendations therefore included such community-led ideas as workforce training and access to new jobs (particularly in the Bio-District), cultural preservation, and the inclusion of affordable housing.[35] Of course, at this point, it is entirely unclear which elements of these community goals will be honored and how the gap between these goals and the reality of a poorly educated and lower-income local workforce will be met.[36]

However, also presented at the October 8, 2013, LCC meeting were renderings of each of these three scenarios. The proposed vision for the third scenario reflected earlier renderings from the 2010 study of Claiborne Avenue and included a fully redesigned neutral ground on Claiborne that emphasized the city's new commitments to Complete Streets and water management.[37] This rendering included space for the streetcar expansion, a water retention canal, bike lanes, and a narrow strip for replanting trees. As discussed earlier, Claiborne was once the site of a much-used recreational space for residents excluded from racially segregated public parks. Once the I-10 overpass was constructed, the space under the overpass became in many ways a literal and perceived wall between the different sides of the communities. However, it was also the site of reclamation, and as noted earlier the community not only painted the new concrete columns with murals of the trees that once lined Claiborne, but used this space for community and cultural gatherings. In this sense, the space under the overpass marked both the decimation and the resilience of these communities, or as I argue earlier, what Du Bois (1994) would call a mark of black residents' double consciousness. The proposed new space of Claiborne, at least in one of the major visions proposed in the LCC study, completely eliminates any sense of community space along this wide neutral ground. In its vision for *completeness*, it is therefore an *incomplete* articulation and vision of the community's dream for reclaiming this space.

Together, the rebuilding of the twentieth-century projects that contributed to Treme and the 7th Ward's decline and newer redevelopment projects, signify a new vision for the city. By some measures, the projects discussed in this chapter and other projects either proposed or being implemented in and around the Treme and the 7th Ward neighborhood, signify billions of dollars of investment. The NEWCITY Partners estimate that these investments in the arts, housing, education, healthcare, greenspace, neighborhood amenities, and infrastructure, represent $3.7 billion in development investment in this area.[38] The question always remains as to who will benefit from this and whose dreams for a new city and new neighborhoods will be honored. Despite the fact that the dream of removing the I-10 overpass along Claiborne was a community dream, long deferred, it is unclear if the implementation of this dream will realize what residents then had in mind, a better place for residents who had long struggled and suffered from their community's decline.

The repercussions of all of this redevelopment for long-time Treme and 7th Ward residents remain unclear. Beyond the physical redevelopment or spatial reordering of the city and the effects of this on these neighborhoods, there are other forces that are shifting the social and cultural norms of place that also affect the community's cultural viability. Noted among these are new tensions between new residents (often gentrifying white residents) and long-time black residents about the noise levels during second lines or the perceived implications of neighborhood bars (Reckdahl 2007). Commenting that these new changes brought about by white gentrification and new noise ordinances have "shut down the bars", and are "restricting the flow of music on the street",[39] long-time residents point out that new residents are working to enforce new norms on their cultural expression, making culture into a nuisance. The nuisance laws go two ways, said one activist, showing how redevelopment is about "two different mindsets—one about culture and one about property values."[40] Another long-time resident reflected that the noise ordinances were like "people who buy beachfront homes and then decide they don't like the sand or the water . . . they call the police if the second line is too loud."[41] The fact that these new residents have been able to begin to re-shape these second lines by increased police presence, by requirements for permitting, and constraints on the food trucks that follow these second lines means that what once were community norms are being challenged by new bureaucratic norms and economic expectations, limiting the capacity of these second lines to roam freely through the streets of the neighborhood (Reckdahl 2007).

Yet while the black community feels the threats of displacement and gentrification, particularly in Treme, the narratives promoting redevelopment rely, contradictorily, on ideas of selling New Orleans' "authentic" black culture and planners have promoted an ideal of Claiborne as a "corridor of culture,"[42] an ideal that ignores the vivid culture already practiced in the streets of these communities—one that is also already threatened by new, gentrifying and neoliberal norms and one that is literally displaced from the spaces of Claiborne Avenue in these new visions. Robin Kelley importantly points out these contradictions in the gentrification and redevelopment of Harlem. In his Introduction to Alice Attie's book of photographs of a transitioning Harlem, Kelley argues:

Priced out, displaced, gentrified, the old Harlemites who have for so long lurked in the white imagination as a source of fear and fascination have begun to disappear. And yet, as this new army of developers, speculators, and investors march through Harlem behind the wrecking ball of global capital, they are banking on the neighborhood's rich history as the center of black culture and art.

(2003, p. 10)

We see something similar in Treme and the 7th Ward, where not only are developers and the army of urban policy-makers who support them (at the local, state, and federal level) leading the charge to redevelop this once and now twice-cleared community (Vale 2013), they are doing so with the contradictory narrative of *completeness*, *cultural restoration*, and *community dreams* that will likely create an unrecognizable Treme and 7th Ward, from its sounds to its people to its spaces.

Racial and spatial formation in the twenty-first century: Complete Streets and incomplete visions

The New Orleans historic black core is being re-imagined and remade. Whether Claiborne Avenue will become the "most complete street in the world" is yet to be seen.[43] However, this moment in the city's and these neighborhoods' history is an important point from which we might collectively check-in about what this re-imagining, re-investment, and rebuilding means for those whose ancestors built the landscape and culture, suffered from its demise, and adapted in the wake of changes that have long benefitted property value and economic expansion, but not their own immediate lives. The role and narrative about history are complicated, one that Doreen Massey argues is "constructed so as to confirm the views and convictions of the present. It is this which enables them to warrant the building of particular futures" (1995, p. 186). Places, Massey notes, "can be understood as articulations of social relationships," but she cautions that "the identity of places is very much bound up with the *histories* which are told of them, *how* those histories are told, and which history turns out to be dominant" (ibid., p. 186). Michelle Boyd (2008) similarly warns us that narratives about the past can be constructed to cleanse the most brutal aspects of racialized difference and segregation. In her research on the Bronzeville community in Chicago, Boyd found that the late twentieth-century work by black leaders to revitalize this community drew on narratives that emphasized the cultural vitality and economic independence of this predominantly black community during the Jim Crow era, an idealized narrative that erased the brutalities and violence of racial segregation and the vulnerability of blacks' economic and political lives.

Yet, as I noted earlier, the contrast between overly emphasizing descriptive inequalities (McKittrick and Woods 2007), a discrediting narrative that can, has been, and is being utilized to support redevelopment and revitalization and the "creative destruction" of these communities (Vale 2013), and understanding the brutal legacy of systemic and historic inequality (Jennings 2012) is a conflict for planners searching for ways to promote the often conflicting goals of economic expansion and social equity through new urban policies such as Complete Streets. However, together both Massey (1995) and Boyd (2008) caution our interpretations of the ways in which Treme and the 7th Ward's histories are being recalled to fit new development narratives. What Boyd (2008) calls the "collective invention of memory" is at work here, as New Orleans draws on a narrative emphasizing these neighborhoods as the cultural home of the city in an effort to attract and promote new development. Similarly, we see narratives identifying a new notion of *completeness* for the future of Claiborne Avenue, resting on ideas of culture and histories of economic vibrancy, but ignoring the central yet tacit fact that development goals of economic expansion are sometimes at odds with residents' connections to place. As Kelley (2003, p. 15) notes, "Harlem residents' sense of history . . . does not necessarily serve the interests of property." Together, Massey, Boyd, and Kelley warn us that not only are narratives of the past cleansed of the brutalities of racial discrimination and segregation, but that these cleansed histories are used to remake the present and future in the name of new development goals and new visions.

In this, I want to suggest, that missing from this discourse and narrative about the history of New Orleans' black core are not only the brutalities of segregation and racism and the effects of past redevelopment strategies in contributing to an unequal urban spatial pattern; the adaptability and resilience of these communities in the wake of these structural forces; and the community-led dream of a new, better, future,[44] but also the role of race and its implications in our geographical imaginations. Both Kelley's (2003) and Vale's (2013) arguments indicate that the notion of race is bound up in geography and redevelopment and in whites' perceptions and fears of urban space. Malcolm X once argued that, "'Negroes' do not exist outside of America's geographical imaginations, for they are a construct of American racial ideologies" (as quoted in Tyner 2006, p. 37). In their seminal work on racial theory, Omi and Winant (1994) argue that although "race" is a social construct, it has been and is used to define hierarchies between groups of people and to justify tangible outcomes in terms of economic, geographic, and political advantage. Their understanding of racial formation is critical here because it challenges us to re-engage a discussion of race—and its geographic implications—amidst a neoliberal development context that shuns all discussions of race while also contradictorily producing unequal and racialized outcomes. Neoliberalism, they argue, "seeks to downplay the continuing significance of race in society; indeed it promotes a false universalism which can only serve to mask underlying racial conflicts" (ibid., p. 152). I certainly see these contradictions at work in New Orleans and in the absence of any narrative that focuses specifically on the racial implications of development. The narratives of history, nostalgia, and culture bypass this critical lens and obfuscate the potential implications for what was once a black mecca. I see these trends at work in the new narratives, visions, and redevelopment projects of New Orleans—particularly those whose intention is to remake the downtown neighborhoods into more vibrant, walkable, complete neighborhoods.

This vision is incomplete and, in co-opting an old community vision, further defers and displaces the vision for racial and geographic equality. In 1976, the Claiborne Avenue Design Team asked, like Langston Hughes, what would happen if this dream were deferred. For now, the answer remains unclear. But given the contradictions and co-optation of this dream, it is unlikely that the current vision for the future of Claiborne will produce the "most complete street in the world".[45]

Notes

1 Richard Florida, *The Rise of the Creative Class*, 2002.
2 David Dixon, Principal for Planning and Urban Design, Goody Clancy, as quoted in Buchanan (2013).
3 Livable Claiborne Communities. Available from: www.livableclaiborne.com/ [Accessed July 29, 2014]
4 Although completed in October 2013, the future of the Livable Claiborne Communities study and recommendations are unclear, given that the study must now move through both environmental and transportation studies. The other projects discussed in this chapter, including the redevelopment of the Iberville and Lafitte housing projects, the Bio-Medical District, and the Rampart Street/St. Claude Avenue streetcar expansion are current projects and thus their ultimate repercussions cannot be measured at this point.
5 In New Orleans, the median or green space between lanes of traffic is known as the neutral ground.
6 Second-lines are a local tradition in which onlookers join in (the second line) behind brass bands (the first line) playing in the street. Jazz funerals are a local funeral tradition in which the brass band, playing a slow dirge, accompanies the mourners to the cemetery. Once the deceased is buried, the tempo of the band picks up in a celebration of the life of the deceased. See also Regis (1999, 2001).
7 Although predominantly black areas of the city, including the Lower Ninth Ward, eventually benefited from the new pump technology, these areas were the last to be drained (Campanella, 2006; Colten, 2005; Lewis, 2003).
8 Anonymous, personal communication, November 2013.
9 Restoring Claiborne Avenue: Alternatives for the Future of Claiborne Avenue, A Report to the Claiborne Avenue Improvement Coalition, Prepared by Smart Mobility Inc. and Waggonner & Ball Architects, 2010. Available from: www.cnu.org/cnu-news/2010/07/cnu-coalition-study-finds-restored-avenue-would-meet-traffic-needs-stimulate-rebirth [Accessed March 14, 2013].
10 Although the city population has continued to decline since the 1960s, the black population continued to gain population in real numbers and in relative percentages between 1970 and 2000 and prior to Katrina, blacks represented over 65 percent of the city's total population (Greater New Orleans Community Data Center 2014a).
11 The average household income in New Orleans in 2000 was $56,497. The average household income is shown in 2010 dollars. See Greater New Orleans Community Data Center (GNOCDC). Available from: www.datacenterresearch.org/data-resources/neighborhood-data/district-4/Treme-Lafitte/ [Accessed July 28, 2014].
12 The average household income is shown in 2010 dollars (Greater New Orleans Community Data Center 2014a).
13 The total number of rental housing units equals the original number of units in the Lafitte housing development as reported by Providence Community Housing in its "Lafitte Brochure".
14 There are two critical issues with repopulating the Lafitte housing development. One is the timing of construction and the schedule for when affordable and public housing units will come back online. The second issue is whether former tenants will undergo a more stringent screening process for returning to the new Lafitte. However, both of these analyses were outside the scope of this chapter.

15 Hernandez (2013).
16 Similarly to the redevelopment of Lafitte, there are critical issues of the timing/phasing of reconstruction and the screening of former residents in the redevelopment of Iberville. Again, both of these issues are outside the scope of this chapter. See White (2013).
17 According to these numbers, the total number of public housing units for the Iberville development does represent a loss of 436 public housing units. See White (2013).
18 Iberville Treme Transformation Plan. Available from: http://cnineworleans.org//wp-content/uploads/2012/01/ITTP_factsheet_011112.pdf [Accessed November 15, 2013].
19 Although outside the scope of this chapter, there has been increased momentum in the New Orleans region to rethink its relationship to water and to promote new design and development strategies that better deal with issues such as stormwater and street drainage. Lafitte Greenway Master Plan. Available from: http://lafittecorridorconnection.com/project-documents.html [Accessed November 15, 2013].
20 See http://biodistrictneworleans.org/wp-content/uploads/2013/02/130418_BROCHURE_LegalSize.pdf [Accessed November 15, 2013].
21 While the relocation of these homes was seen as a win by local preservationists, many of the homes remain vacant and in further disrepair on city-owned lots. See Webster (2012).
22 New Orleans' Complete Streets. Available from: www.nola.gov/dpw/complete-streets/ [Accessed October 22, 2013].
23 The first segment of this streetcar expansion will run from Canal Street to Elysian Fields, with six stops along this 1.4-mile stretch. At the present time, only this segment of the streetcar expansion is designed and funded, meaning that residents who live beyond the Marigny and 7th Ward neighborhoods (east of the French Quarter) will have to commute via both bus and streetcar. Available from: www.norta.com/norta/_meta/files/Streetcar_expansion/3-6-2013-Public-Meeting.pdf [Accessed November 15, 2013].
24 This recent study of the planned expansion of New Orleans' streetcar system along Rampart/St. Claude indicates that the expansion of this system could spur economic development in the form of neighborhood commercial/mixed-use revitalization (Guthrie and Fan 2013). However, this article also notes that this analysis does not account for the myriad of factors affecting redevelopment in this area of the city.
25 I-10 Multi-Use Study, Claiborne Avenue Design Team Report, 1976. Available from: www.livableclaiborne.com/what-is-the-lcc-study/planning-history.aspx [Accessed March 1, 2013].
26 Preface, Dr. Rudy Lombard, I-10 Multi-Use Study, Claiborne Avenue Design Team Report, 1976. Available from: www.livableclaiborne.com/what-is-the-lcc-study/planning-history.aspx [Accessed March 1, 2013].
27 Ibid.
28 Ibid., p. 14.
29 David Dixon, Principal for Planning and Urban Design, Goody Clancy, as quoted in Buchanan (2013).
30 City of New Orleans, Plan for the 21st Century. Available from: www.nola.gov/getattachment/962b415f-ce44-409b-8aaf-1252ab101c24/Vol-2-Ch-11-Transportation/ [Accessed October 3, 2013].
31 Restoring Claiborne Avenue: Alternatives for the Future of Claiborne Avenue, A Report to the Claiborne Avenue Improvement Coalition, Prepared by Smart Mobility Inc. and Waggonner & Ball Architects, 2010. Available from: www.cnu.org/cnu-news/2010/07/cnu-coalition-study-finds-restored-avenue-would-meet-traffic-needs-stimulate-rebirth [Accessed March 14, 2013].
32 Livable Claiborne Communities, Building on a Living Heritage of Culture and Innovation. Available from: www.livableclaiborne.com/download/project-info-sheet.pdf [Accessed October 8, 2013].
33 Livable Claiborne Communities, Building on a Living Heritage of Culture and Innovation, LCC project team, October 8, 2013. Available from: www.livableclaiborne.com/download/Presentation-10-08-13-Final.pdf. [Accessed October 10, 2010].
34 Anonymous, personal communication, October 2011.

35 Livable Claiborne Communities, Building on a Living Heritage of Culture and Innovation, LCC project team, October 8, 2013.
36 Although the LCC study notes that most of the job growth in the LCC project area will be in the health care industry, due to the development of the Bio-Medical District, 30 percent of residents living in this area do not have a high school diploma or its equivalent. Available from: www.livableclaiborne.com/download/Presentation-10-08-13-Final.pdf [Accessed October 10, 2010].
37 Please note this rendering was not included in the final presentation now accessible on the LCC website. However, a version of this rendering can be found in the 2010 study: Restoring Claiborne Avenue: Alternatives for the Future of Claiborne Avenue, A Report to the Claiborne Avenue Improvement Coalition, Prepared by Smart Mobility Inc. and Waggonner & Ball Architects, 2010, p. 26. Available from: www.cnu.org/cnu-news/2010/07/cnu-coalition-study-finds-restored-avenue-would-meet-traffic-needs-stimulate-rebirth [Accessed March 14, 2013].
38 Available from: http://cnineworleans.org//wp-content/uploads/2012/01/NEWCITY-mapHD.jpg [Accessed November 22, 2013].
39 Anonymous, personal communication, November 2010.
40 Anonymous, personal communication, October 2011.
41 Anonymous, personal communication, October 2010.
42 Buchanan (2013).
43 David Dixon, Principal for Planning and Urban Design, Goody Clancy, as quoted in Buchanan (2013).
44 I-10 Multi-Use Study, Claiborne Avenue Design Team Report, 1976.
45 David Dixon, Principal for Planning and Urban Design, Goody Clancy, as quoted in Buchanan (2013).

References

Baumbach, R.O., and Borah, W.E., 1981. *The second battle of New Orleans: A history of the Vieux Carre riverfront expressway controversy.* Tuscaloosa, AL: University of Alabama Press.
Boshken, H.L., 1998. Upper middle class influence on developmental policy outcomes: The case of transit infrastructure. *Urban Studies*, 35 (4), 627–648.
Boyd, M., 2008. *Jim Crow nostalgia.* Minneapolis, MN: University of Minnesota Press.
Buchanan, S., 2013. Residents consider options for the Claiborne expressway. *Louisiana Weekly*, 25 March.
Campanella, R., 2006. *Geographies of New Orleans: Urban fabrics before the storm.* Lafayette, LA: Center for Louisiana Studies.
Colten, C.E., 2005. *The unnatural metropolis: Wresting New Orleans from nature.* Baton Rouge, LA: Louisiana State University Press.
Crutcher, M., 2010. *Treme: Race and place in a New Orleans neighborhood.* Athens, GA: University of Georgia Press.
Du Bois, W.E.B., 1994. *The souls of black folk.* New York: Pocket Books.
Elie, L.E., 2009. Armstrong Park planning exclusionary, Treme residents complain. *Times-Picayune.* 8 August.
Florida, R., 2002. *The rise of the creative class: And how it's transforming work, leisure, community, and everyday life.* New York: Basic Books.
Goetz, E.G., 2003. *Clearing the way: Deconcentrating the poor in urban America.* Washington DC: Urban Institute Press.
Greater New Orleans Community Data Center, 2014a. Seventh Ward Statistical Area. Available from: www.datacenterresearch.org/data-resources/neighborhood-data/district-4/Seventh-Ward/ [Accessed 14 May 2014].

Greater New Orleans Community Data Center, 2014b. 'Treme'/Lafitte Statistical Area. Available from:www.datacenterresearch.org/data-resources/neighborhood-data/district-4/Treme-Lafitte/ [Accessed 14 May 2014].

Grengs, J., 2004. The abandoned social goals of public transit in the neoliberal city of the USA. *City*, 9 (1), 51–66.

Guthrie, A., and Fan, Y., 2013. Streetcars and recovery: An analysis of post-Katrina building permits around New Orleans streetcar lines. *Journal of Planning Education and Research*, 33 (4), 381–394.

Hernandez, M., 2013. Construction on major housing project stalled due to funding hurdles. WWLTV.com. Available from: www.wwltv.com/news/Construction-on-major-housing-project-stalled-due-to-funding-hurdles-228712501.html [Accessed 21 October 2013].

Hirsch, A.R., and Logsdon, J., eds., 1992. *Creole New Orleans: Race and Americanization.* Baton Rouge, LA: Louisiana State University Press.

Jennings, J., 2012. Measuring neighborhood distress: A tool for place-based urban revitalization strategies. *Community Development*, 43 (4), 464–475.

Kelley, R.D.G., 2003. Introduction. In: *Harlem on the Verge:* New York: Quantuck Lane Press. 9–17.

Lewis, P.F., 2003. *New Orleans: The making of an urban landscape.* Harrisonburg, VA: University of Virginia Press.

Massey, D., 1995. Places and their pasts. *History Workshop Journal*, 39, 182–192.

McKittrick, K., and Woods, C., eds., 2007. *Black geographies and the politics of place.* Cambridge, MA: South End Press.

Omi, M., and Winant, H., 1994. *Racial formation in the United States: From the 1960s to the 1990s.* 2nd edn. New York: Routledge.

Pickrell, D.H., 1992. A desire named streetcar. *Journal of the American Planning Association*, 58 (2), 158–177.

Reckdahl, K., 2007. Culture, change collide in Treme. *Times-Picayune*, 2 October.

Regis, H., 1999. Second lines, minstrelsy, and the contested landscape of New Orleans Afro-Creole festivals. *Cultural Anthropology*, 14 (4): 472–504.

Regis, H., 2001. Blackness and the politics of memory in the New Orleans second line. *American Ethnologist*, 28 (4), 752–777.

Stone, C.N., 1980. Systemic power and community decision-making. *American Political Sciences Review*, 74, 978–990.

Sublette, N., 2008. *The world that made New Orleans: From Spanish silver to Congo Square.* Chicago: Lawrence Hill Books.

Tyner, J., 2006. *The geography of Malcolm X: Black radicalism and the remaking of American space.* New York: Routledge.

Vale, L.J., 2013. *Purging the poorest: Public housing and the design politics of twice-cleared communities.* Chicago: University of Chicago Press.

Webster, R., 2012. Program to move homes from LSU-VA hospital site, rehab them, remains in disarray. *Times-Picayune*, 24 November. Available from: www.nola.com/politics/index.ssf/2012/11/program_to_move_homes_from_lsu.html. [Accessed 25 December, 2012].

White, J., 2013. Officials break ground on Iberville redevelopment. *New Orleans Advocate.* Available from: www.theneworleansadvocate.com/news/7375761-171/hud-secretary-mitch-landrieu-break [Accessed 25 October, 2013].

14

THE POLITICS OF SUSTAINABILITY

Contested urban bikeway development in Portland, Oregon

Thaddeus R. Miller and Amy Lubitow

Introduction

Portland, Oregon has built a reputation as "America's Bicycle Capital" (Figure 14.1) on a foundation of forward thinking planning laid by bicycle plans in 1973, 1996 and 2010. With 319 miles of bikeways and counting, the League of American Bicyclists awarded Portland platinum status as a *Bicycle Friendly Community* in 2008, and *Bicycling Magazine* has named Portland the most bike-friendly city in the US several times over (despite a brief fall to #2 behind Minneapolis in 2010). The City of Portland's ambitious *Portland Bicycle Plan 2030* seeks to increase ridership and expand the network of planned bikeways to 962 miles. This is supported through substantial community engagement and outreach activities and a network of cycling shops, community cycling centers, popular blog coverage, and bicycle advocacy groups. Many businesses now clamor for bike parking to replace car parking, brewpubs have stationary bikes that generate electricity, and new apartment developments tout bike-friendly accommodations. The bike and the cycling infrastructure that supports it serve as a prominent symbol of Portland as a green, livable city. This chapter tells the story of how a bikeway development and traffic operations project in North Portland became a topic of such intense conflict that, at its height in the fall of 2011, it was even covered in the *New York Times* and *Atlantic Cities*. How did a bikeway enhancement project become so contested in "America's Bicycle Capital"?

Lined with breweries, popular brunch spots, a local, organic market and shops that have been or are waiting to be featured in the next *New York Times* article on Portland, North Williams Avenue (N. Williams) is perhaps the living, breathing embodiment of the zeitgeist captured by *Portlandia*. Located in North Portland's Albina neighborhood, N. Williams has been the site of rapid gentrification over the last ten years and is a major south-to-north commute route (North Vancouver

FIGURE 14.1 Portland Bike City USA, downtown Portland

Source: Dillon Mahmoudi.

Avenue is parallel to N. Williams and runs north-to-south) for cyclists and a major thoroughfare for automobile and bus traffic. The N. Williams corridor sees an estimated 700–1,000 motor vehicles per hour, and certain segments of the street experience 3,000 bicycle trips each day, according to the City of Portland Bureau of Transportation (PBOT). Due to such heavy use and ongoing conflicts between different transit modes, PBOT identified N. Williams as a site for bikeway development in 2010.

Despite a relatively modest budget and limited goals around bikeway enhancement and pedestrian crossings, the North Williams Traffic Safety Operations Project would erupt into controversy. The ensuing public debate would bring to the surface legacies of racist policies and planning projects, frustrations over the city's priorities, concerns about continuing gentrification and equitable public participation in city decision-making. It would range from specific design elements related to the project, including the configuration of the bike lane and the addition of long sought-after streetlights, to more general, but certainly no less important, arguments for affordable housing and more equitable participation in city policy and planning. For a time, the debate seemingly pit cycling advocates against some community members, particularly African-Americans. Cycling advocates and others were focused on the all-too-real conflicts between the various modes of transportation on N. Williams. "It's a public safety issue," noted one interview subject involved in Portland's cycling community. Issues of gentrification and historical legacies of racism, while widely viewed as important, were also seen as a distraction from the pressing issues of bike safety and access. Community members, on the other hand, viewed the project as just the latest example of a city project that put the concerns of other groups above their own. As one long-time resident stated in an interview with one of the authors, "First, you [the City of Portland] took our businesses, then you took our homes, and now you want to take our street."

Bikes and bike lanes, those symbols of a livable Portland to some, have also come to serve as symbols of gentrification to others. As Zavestoski and Agyeman note in Chapter 1 of this volume, changes to the street are not simply physical, but are tied to social, discursive, and historical realities. The ongoing story of N. Williams illustrates this point. Alterations to N. Williams cannot be limited to lines painted on asphalt. They are inextricably tied to concerns about gentrification and the past, present, and future conditions and voice of the African-American community in the North Portland area.

This chapter explores how a traffic safety operations project with a relatively limited scope and budget brought to the surface long-simmering issues of racism, gentrification, and inclusion, highlighting the degree to which physical trans-formations of infrastructure are *political*. Following this, we examine how PBOT responded to this conflict by expanding the stakeholder advisory group to include more community members. We then discuss how this *process* opened up discursive space to engage in social, political, and historical issues *and* how the project out-comes and design were altered as a result. As such, the N. Williams case illustrates how inclusion and opening up affect the *possibilities* of creating both new infra-structural designs *and* new politics. Before describing the N. Williams case and its context in more detail, we first turn to a brief discussion of how infrastructure, including streets, and politics are intertwined.

The politics of infrastructure and the limits of Complete Streets

Contests over infrastructure design and the street, more specifically, are contests over social and political order and visions of our future. Our cities and the infrastructures that form, service, and maintain them are the embodiment of social, ethical, and political choices and contests that have played out over time and at multiple scales—from the community meeting to larger trends and city-building regimes (Hommels 2005). As urban historians Tarr and Dupuy (1988) put it, urban infrastructures are the technological sinews of the modern metropolitan area. They deliver essential services, such as drinking water and energy, and provide protection against climate and weather variability. Infrastructure—those background systems that make modern life possible and are often taken for granted (Edwards 2003; Hommels 2005)—and the technical, social, ethical, and political decisions that get built into it are "black-boxed" once constructed (Graham and Marvin 2001; Latour 1987). These social and political choices become settled in the engineered infrastructure and then hidden from view. We take for granted not only the physical systems and the services they invisibly deliver, but also the social and political values and contests that shape them.

We only notice infrastructure when it is in flux—in moments of creation, transformation, or destruction; when the services we rely on are severed or up for grabs. It is at these points that the politics in infrastructure and the implications for our communities and cities become clear to the broader public. The injustice of infrastructure, for instance, was laid bare in the levee failures during Hurricane Katrina. From national political debates over the Keystone XL pipeline to local debates over our streets, conflicts over infrastructure highlight the degree to which their design and purpose are not simply technical. They are deeply political in conception and construction, with implications for the distribution of services and risks among and between communities.

Yet, largely ignored is how a better understanding of the social and political dimensions of infrastructure can improve our understanding of cities, neighborhoods, and streets, social justice issues and efforts to address them. Examining how infrastructure can shape and motivate political debates and how, in turn, politics can shape infrastructure design, management, acceptability and accessibility is critical to understanding contests over Complete Streets. More broadly, uncovering the politics of infrastructure is crucial to comprehend, and affect, many debates about the current and future conditions of our cities (Graham and Marvin 2001).

In this context, the Complete Streets movement is a political one seeking to transform our streets so that transportation planners and engineers design with "all users in mind — including bicyclists, public transportation vehicles and riders, and pedestrians of all ages and abilities" (National Complete Streets Coalition). While certainly laudable, as Zavestoski and Agyeman in Chapter 1 and others in this volume note, the Complete Streets movement focuses narrowly on technical design choices and the discourse categorizes people according to their mode of transportation. This can depoliticize discussions about the street, its present conditions, proposed changes and future objectives, framing them as the purview of experts in transportation planning and engineering, and potentially masking political motivations and implications. Further, we suspect that despite best efforts to design for "all users," there will still be contests over the ideal mix of transportation modes.

While the Complete Streets discourse may open up space for a more diverse set of perspectives about the uses of the street and how it might fit into community wants and needs, it also marginalizes groups and individuals who do not view the street solely via their mode of transportation. The N. Williams case, detailed below, deals with a traffic safety operations project where cycling was the central component; it was not an explicit Complete Street project. The debate and issues that emerged, however, were broader and illustrate the tensions and limitations of the Complete Streets discourse. On N. Williams, technical issues such as mode conflict and pedestrian access were, for a time, overwhelmed by discussions about equitable access to public participation processes, legacies of planning policies and practices, and gentrification. To the frustration of some cycling advocates, issues could not be kept to strictly technical, apolitical questions of safety and access (Lubitow and Miller 2013). These issues are inherently political even if they are not acknowledged as such or even positioned as outside of or above political concerns. Claims to safety and access are claims to certain uses of the street by certain populations and driven by a set of values and views of what a good street, or city, ought to look like. One cycling advocate lamented in an interview that the N. Williams debate and other contests over cycling infrastructure set the city's efforts back:

> [W]e had an opportunity in Portland. We still do. We had an opportunity in this city to be the undisputed leader in building a city where it's easy to bike . . . it's important because it has the power to change every other city in America.
>
> *(personal interview with authors)*

Here proximate concerns over a safer, more accessible, bike route are linked to broader visions of a bike-friendly Portland and what it stands for (see also Hoffmann, Chapter 8 in this volume).

Does the Complete Streets movement have a place for such discussions? How are transportation planners and engineers expected to design for such concerns? The following case illustrates how decisions about streets are political and how an expanded process results in a different, physical design of the street. This is also a challenge to those who may feel marginalized by planning practices—how do those concerns and politics get built into the world? Importantly, the N. Williams story demonstrates the importance of considering the politics of infrastructure and how they get *built into* the world and into our streets. It also provides a window to the possibilities of politics when processes allow diverse groups and perspectives to meaningfully participate and shape our streets.

". . . now you want to take our street": understanding the historical context

The redlining and discriminatory lending practices that plagued many post-WWII American cities were visible and present in the North Portland neighborhood surrounding N. Williams. Political priorities and economic discrimination and marginalization resulted in the segregation of Portland's African-American community within the North Portland area during the 1950s and 1960s. As a result of these practices, the relatively small African-American population of Portland (which has historically made up less than 10 percent of the city's population) made up a large percentage of all residents in the North Portland area during this period. However, the subsequent consolidation of Africa-American businesses, homes, and churches in one area of the city made the community vulnerable to displacement as urban renewal and development contributed to major infrastructural changes to the neighborhood. As part of the broader dynamics of urban renewal that swept the nation in the mid-twentieth century, many areas of the North Portland neighborhood were cleared to make way for the construction of the Veteran's Memorial Coliseum in the early 1950s, Interstate 5 (which cut through the middle of North Portland) in the mid-1950s, and the erection of the Emanuel Hospital in the 1960s (Gibson 2007). These projects resulted in the destruction of large numbers of housing units, the displacement of many residents, and the closure of a number of local businesses, many of which were owned by African Americans (Abbott 1981; Teaford 2000; Roos 2008).

The impact of urban renewal has been long-lasting. Not only did these projects displace home and business owners, they have also contributed to a long-standing sense within this neighborhood that the city of Portland acted unjustly in selecting development locations and sites. As in other cities, the large-scale infrastructure projects separated major sections of the neighborhood and increased the amount of bridges, parking lots, and unused open spaces that eventually contributed to a decline in neighborhood vitality and livability (Teaford 2000). In the 1980s, this meant that property values in the neighborhood declined and the percentage of absentee landlords increased. This deterioration in the economic valuation of property in the neighborhood laid the foundation of the forces of gentrification that have swept through the neighborhood in recent years, a pattern observed in other cities around the world (Smith 2002).

Since the 1990s, Portland as a whole has experienced rapid population growth and seen the influx of many young, white, middle-class residents to the city core. The increased need for housing and amenities close to the city center has facilitated processes of gentrification in the North Portland area in which N. Williams runs. Developers swept through the North Portland neighborhood, buying up properties cheaply and transforming them into upscale housing and boutique businesses and restaurants. In recent years this has substantially shifted the demographic characteristics of North Portland such that certain swaths of the neighborhood that were once majority black are now majority white. This change in the demographics of the neighborhood has not only reduced the affordability of housing, but also resulted in a significant change in the makeup of retail stores in the area with many of the historically African-American shops closing. Sociological research in this part of the city demonstrates that there are competing and contrasting viewpoints on the costs and benefits of gentrification in the neighborhood. For example, though new demographic developments may have led to the decline of segregation in the area, there remains a deep divide between white residents and residents of color which is, in part, influenced by historical legacies of displacement and power.

Given these dramatic changes, in 2010, PBOT prioritized the North Williams Avenue corridor (Figure 14.2) as a site for bikeway development due to ongoing safety issues related to traffic conflicts among motor vehicles, bicycles, buses, and pedestrians. With an estimated 700–1,000 motor vehicles/hour throughout the corridor and certain segments of the street experiencing 3,000 bicycle trips each day, the city was interested in reducing this congestion and enhancing accessibility for all modes of transit. A report prepared by Kittleson and Associates, Inc. for

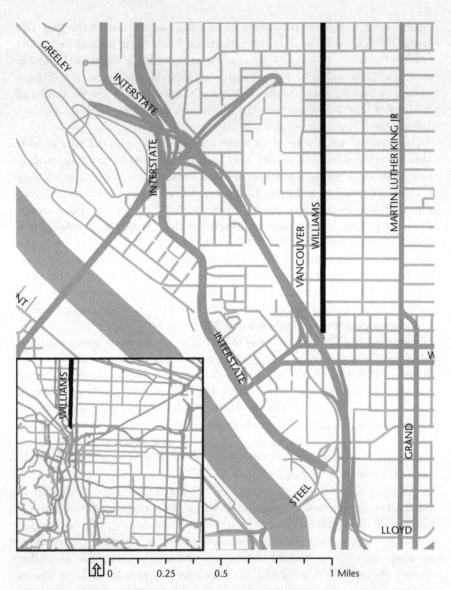

FIGURE 14.2 Map of North Williams Avenue Corridor

Source: Authors.

PBOT on the existing conditions of N. Williams noted that conflict between modes of transit on the street—motor vehicles, buses, bicycles, and pedestrians—was a significant safety issue needing attention, particularly at the Fremont and Cook Street intersections.

Today, N. Williams is home to one of the few north–south bike lanes in the North Portland area and serves as a major bike commute route for many residents.

Historically, the bikeway had been rated as one of the best bike lanes in the city (Bower *et al.* 2007). However, beginning in 2006, bike traffic increased dramatically on the street as the relatively affordable Northeast neighborhoods experienced an influx of young white residents, many of whom were regular cyclists, ultimately stifling the flow of bike traffic. These demographic shifts led to increased ridership on many of the streets in the northeast part of the city and contributed to on-street conflicts between different modes of transportation (Figure 14.3). Along with this, the *Portland Bicycle Plan 2030* categorized the N. Williams–Vancouver corridor as a major city bikeway, setting a precedent for this street as a critical source of the bike infrastructure in the area.

The North Williams Traffic and Safety Operations Project

As noted above, the N. Williams corridor, located on the northeastern side of the Willamette River, was identified in 2010 by PBOT as a site for bikeway development due to ongoing conflicts between different transit modes. The prioritization of safety enhancement project on this street typically involved a public engagement process that solicited neighborhood perspectives on the planning and design of changes to the street. This public process model seeks to enhance public dialogue on city planning efforts as political representation at the neighborhood level is loosely managed by volunteer-run and led neighborhood associations. While these neighborhood associations present a unique and fertile ground for public participation, they are not necessarily designed to provide direct input into city decision-making processes.

Therefore, public input in relation to transportation projects of this nature has typically been managed by the creation of a stakeholder advisory committee (SAC) of interested business owners, residents, and key stakeholders living or working in the affected area. Rather than having city officials or politicians seek public comment, the city's practice of including residents and business owners in a planning advisory capacity has typically worked to ensure community support and engagement in project design and implementation. In the case of the N. Williams corridor, PBOT made efforts to set up a similar stakeholder advisory committee

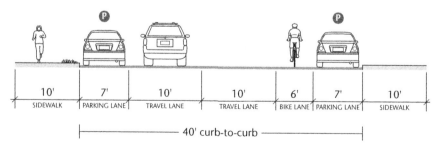

FIGURE 14.3 Existing street cross-section along high traffic sections of N. Williams
Source: PBOT Final Report, 2012.

who would be tasked with advising the city on how to best alter the street. Typically SAC meetings are convened for four to six months and the committee concludes by presenting their recommendations for how the city should proceed. In late 2010, efforts to start soliciting participants for the N. Williams SAC began and city staff engaged a variety of outreach methods intended to target a diverse group of stakeholders. A consultant hired by the city to help with recruitment sought community participants by canvassing door-to-door, by sending postcards to all residents and businesses along the street, and by sending emails to local neighborhood associations and community organizations. Open meetings were also held to secure participation, while the African-American churches on or adjacent to the street were contacted.

These forms of outreach were utilized to form the initial SAC in early 2011; 18 members of the committee were white and four members were people of color. This lack of diverse representation, when coupled with historical legacies of racism and inequality that characterized the African American experience in the North Williams area, served as a catalyst for community grievances around the type of streetscape development to emerge.

Methods and data

This chapter is based upon a case study of a bikeway development project in Portland, Oregon, called the North Williams Traffic and Safety Operations Project. We build our discussion from a review of relevant public documents, including Portland Bureau of Transportation websites and meeting minutes, newspaper and blog coverage, as well as observation at public meetings from August 2011 through June 2012, and interviews with 19 individuals, including citizens and governmental employees involved in the decision-making process. As researchers interested in the public process around this issue, we attended official public meetings related to the project as well as community-based forums or discussions devoted to the topic of N. Williams. We continually made the public and the stakeholders engaged in the planning process aware of our research interests and found that PBOT staff and community stakeholders were often eager to participate in formal interviews to discuss the implications of the project and their experiences as participants.

The 19 semi-structured interviews we draw from in this chapter lasted between 30 minutes and one hour. Each interview was digitally recorded, transcribed, and imported into the qualitative data analysis program Dedoose. A structured coding scheme was developed collaboratively by the authors and a research assistant after each interview had been reviewed for content and thematic trends. Subsequently, each interview was analyzed and coded by one author according to this scheme and reviewed by the other author and the research assistant to ensure the reliability of the application of codes. Field notes and public documents were used to help verify the accuracy of statements made by interview participants and coded data was used to help build the arguments presented here.

"This is much deeper than I had understood before . . .": access, history, and inclusion

To begin to understand the dynamics that shaped some initial opposition to the North Williams project, the process surrounding public engagement must be clarified. Our data suggest that the African-American community's lack of access and inclusion in both previous city decision-making processes and in the present case was a key factor in opposition to the proposed street redesign. Not only did historical marginalization impact contemporary responses to the project, but current city practices surrounding cycling infrastructure contributed to a sense among some interviewees that the project was limited in scope from the beginning, tending to favor certain perspectives on street design over others.

Historical and contemporary marginalization in planning and decision-making

Although the demographics of the North Portland area have shifted dramatically in recent years, many long-term residents of color remain in the neighborhood and continue to keep the history of a close-knit black Portland alive. With some African-American homeowners still residing in the area and a number of black churches situated in the neighborhood, some of the cultural and social capital of the neighborhood prior to gentrification remains despite the fact that this community may no longer be as geographically connected as it once was. For example, one of the prominent black churches in North Portland provides transportation to and from church for residents who have been displaced by rising real estate prices in the neighborhood (Scott 2012). Given the historical importance of the North Portland area as a critical focal point of the black community, previous marginalization from city planning and decision-making in this neighborhood was a collectively recalled concern for many people of color. The dynamics of urban renewal that had displaced many residents in the 1950s and 1960s (one interviewee reported that her family was displaced three different times during her childhood due to eminent domain; another reported that her family was forced to move twice) contributed to a sense among those interviewed that the city had a past of imposing decisions on the black community without adequate community engagement or participation. One African-American woman noted her experiences growing up in the area and the lack of engagement she observed in past decision-making:

> We have these huge ginormous monstrosities that are being built . . . [land use laws were changed] during the time when nobody wanted to live in the neighborhood. My family lived there, but nobody else really wanted to live in that neighborhood. What I'm learning now is that a lot of these laws were passed through in a time when people weren't paying attention.

This same resident continued later on to lament the history of exclusionary decision-making in relation to planning in the neighborhood, and connected that exclusion to current practices:

> A lot of decisions were made about a community, and people that lived in
> the community, their needs . . .were not taken into account. [The city was]
> like, 'We're just going to do this over here . . .' It even goes back to where
> freeways were built. There are only two houses left on the street right in Eliot
> where my family grew up because they built the high school, the freeway,
> and the Coliseum. The homes were just wiped out, and nobody had a say
> . . . So it doesn't surprise me, but it's still very disturbing and angering to see
> that happen in 2013.

Another long-time African-American resident echoed the notion that the city's
historical exclusion of African-Americans in planning processes was visible in the
present scenario:

> [This project] was the city doing its normal thing of not being inclusive;
> disrespecting, not acknowledging the fact that the community had already
> been gentrified. Not even taking into consideration what impact this is going
> to have on the African-American community that's left— there's not much
> left—so what impact is that going to have?

One prominent member of one of the black churches similarly noted how his
concern emerged at a public meeting convened by the Portland Bureau of
Transportation after the stakeholder advisory committee process was already
underway with only four people of color on the 22-person committee:

> I started recognizing that at that point they were literally drawing conclusions,
> and making decisions and . . . how can you draw conclusions and make
> decisions when it is pretty clear we have not been involved? We, the [black]
> community, have not been involved, and this feels like another city grab like
> what has been done in the past.

The above perspectives demonstrate some of the African-American community's
concern surrounding the decision-making process for this project. The relatively
recent history of exclusion in relation to urban renewal projects was brought to the
forefront as black residents, business owners, and local church officials realized that
the PBOT stakeholder advisory committee process was already underway and a
truly diverse group of stakeholders was not participating. The historical exclusion
and marginalization experienced by minorities in this neighborhood, when coupled
with a lack of representation in the current context, contributed to the emergence
of negative community responses to the North Williams project. Community
apprehension around the project even caught the attention of national media, being
highlighted in *The New York Times* and *The Atlantic Cities* whose coverage
highlighted the seeming surprise around "bike lane backlash, even in Portland"
(Goodyear 2011).

The sense of present-day exclusion that was felt by many black residents is best
clarified by examining the trajectory of public process and community outreach on

the part of the city that, while well-intentioned, had failed to bring a diversity of voices to the original advisory committee process. Interviews and participant observation reveal that the outreach process to secure participants for the SAC was inadequate. Of particular importance were issues related to the methods of outreach and the language and framing used to describe the project and solicit participation.

As noted earlier, when beginning the process of convening a stakeholder advisory committee in late 2010, PBOT hired a consultant to aid the city in conducting outreach for the North Williams project. Project manager, Ellen Vanderslice of PBOT, noted that she recognized that the city needed to make every effort to bring together a SAC that was broadly inclusive. In reflecting upon early efforts to organize a stakeholder advisory committee, she noted that she was aware of the history of the neighborhood and the need for inclusiveness:

> [B]ecause this was a sensitive area . . . we really wanted to begin, we really wanted to be more intentional about [this] before we convened our stake-holder advisor committee—to begin by trying to get out into the community, put out feelers in all sorts of different ways, and build relationships in the community.

Starting with the recognition that additional effort needed to be made in a neighborhood with such a complex history with the city of Portland, a consultant was hired to help conduct outreach in and around the street. However, Vanderslice noted that there may have been a mismatch early on, as the consultant's efforts to connect to the minority residents "didn't always meet with success, because a young, hip, white, bike-riding woman comes to the door of a church, she doesn't necessarily get the best reception." Interviewees further illustrated that, though the city had been well-intentioned in hiring a consultant to guide the outreach process, the methods of outreach that were utilized were inadequate to engage the black community. When interviewed for this study, the consultant noted that she employed a range of strategies to get people engaged, including sending emails and postcards, canvassing local homes, businesses and churches, and making phone calls. Despite the range of tactics used, her initial efforts did not succeed in getting a group of actively engaged participants to commit to participating in the stakeholder committee. One interviewee who had been a part of the committee from the beginning of the project noted the tendency for the city to "use the same tools over and over and that gets the same people." He went on to say:

> It's the email resources lists from the Office of Neighborhood Involvement and . . . there are certain email distribution lists from the Portland Development Commission that they use, the Bureau of Transportation had its own that it uses. All of those tend to be squeaky wheels.

Other interviewees echoed the point that the methods of outreach did not appropriately target minorities and the consultant herself noted that, though she felt she had engaged a range of strategies to solicit participation, she wished she had had more time and resources with which to spend engaging with the local churches. Ultimately both Vanderslice (the project manager) and the hired consultant recognized that the SAC that had been convened and was beginning to hold meetings in early 2011 was not diverse enough. To some extent PBOT staff believed that this was due, in part, to a lack of participation from those who had originally committed to participate:

> Although, the list of people who agreed to be on the stakeholder advisory committee was representative enough . . . a lot of the people who agreed to be on the stakeholder advisory committee at the beginning did not come. And they tended to be people of color. And so we very quickly ended up with a committee that was almost entirely white. So now I did not think it was representative.

PBOT staff reported that these individuals were largely cyclists, property owners, and those already actively involved in their neighborhood associations. As the consultant noted, 'The most available and responsive people I encountered when going door-to-door were those who were already involved in their neighborhood association, owned property, or were developers and architects working on the corridor' (email communication to Amy Lubitow, 28 August 2012). Another PBOT staff member reported his recognition that initial outreach efforts did not go far enough:

> We went out and our consultant started talking to people on the street, and we knew that it was a diverse community and we knew that history there. We did really make an effort to try to get some involvement from the African-American community, but we weren't very successful, and we didn't push all that hard. It was sort of like, 'Would you like to be involved?' 'Not really.' We didn't really look at the churches enough.

One African-American woman who had been part of the committee from the beginning noted that:

> I actually sent the city an email [to say], 'This makes me uncomfortable. This is an area that's been disregarded over time. There aren't enough people of color on this committee. I can't believe the city didn't go out and do a better job to see if they could find people of color who've lived in this community; who don't ride bikes and have been here for many, many years.'

Portland has consistently been lauded as one of the most bike-friendly cities in the US and perhaps deservedly so with a large infrastructure devoted to making cycling safe and accessible, and an active population of devoted cyclists. The dominance of this vision of Portland has meant that both resources and city priorities have been shaped by ideas and expectations around continued support and expansion of cycling amenities and infrastructure. The N. Williams project, though deemed a "Traffic Safety and Operations Project" illustrates this notion as it was initially conceived as a bikeway enhancement project, not simply a safety improvement project. PBOT's Vanderslice, in reflecting upon the beginnings of this project noted that there was always an emphasis on bikes:

> There was a pot of money associated with a number of projects that we called the Bikeway Development Projects. And these were streets that had bikeways on, already had . . . some bike facility, but there was . . . some deficiency . . . The idea was to take these places where people were already biking, and make it better . . . This is also coming out of the implementation of the Bicycle Plan for 2030 that really tells us to try . . . to appeal to a broader range of potential bicyclists . . . These projects were looked at as a way to try to find lower stress facilities on these busier streets. So that's where, when it started, so it truly started as a bike project.

This original understanding of the project as a bike lane enhancement project was somewhat obscured when the project did not have the word "bike" or "cycling" attached to it. The language used to frame this particular project can therefore been seen to have contributed to a lack of diversity in the public process along with the outreach efforts described above. In particular, the naming of the project and the ways in which the city elected to message and publicize the project did not succeed in signifying to many minority residents that this was, in fact, a project about redesigning bike lanes on N. Williams. The lack of clear and direct language about the project's intended goals of altering the bike lanes on the street (and potentially reducing the existing two-car lane to one lane to make room for additional bike lanes) did not motivate a lot of minority residents to become participants in the public process during initial meetings. It was only later on, as black residents began to recognize the significant impacts the project could have, that the project became more visibly associated with bike lane alterations.

Two African-American interviewees who became SAC members once the committee was expanded noted the history of bike lane projects being prioritized over other safety enhancements and reported that black residents were accustomed to the city neglecting basic safety mechanisms in favor of bike lanes. At one public meeting about the project in July 2011, a local resident (who was not a part of the SAC) highlighted the tensions of many residents who felt that the city routinely overlooked safety enhancements in the area:

> You say you want it 'safe' for everybody, how come it wasn't safe 10 years ago? That's part of the whole racism thing . . . we wanted safe streets back then; but now that the bicyclists want to have safe streets then it's all about the bicyclists getting safe streets.
>
> *(Schmitt 2011)*

PBOT's outreach consultant also noted that she was aware of this dynamic:

> Politically and socially you really should not put the bike lane in before you put in the signals and the pedestrian improvements because we were told very clearly by the African American neighbors . . . that [the city] comes in, the [African American community] tells their opinion, it becomes phase two, it never happens.

Another member of the SAC who joined after its expansion offered:

> That could have been the assumption before, that people in the Black community weren't interested in the project. I don't know why we were left out, but we were. I just think that this is a good example of bringing everybody to the table, especially in a very torn community at this time.

Perceptions that minority residents were not interested or motivated to participate appear to be unfounded, as public meetings and interviews conveyed the import with which black residents viewed these matters on the street. Rather than a lack of motivation, the utilization of language that spoke more directly to the dominant cycling culture than to minority residents should be recognized as a critical barrier to inclusive public processes and engagement.

Importantly, the language used *did* appear to resonate with avid cyclists in the neighborhood and succeeded in conveying to those parties the nature of the project; ultimately securing a great deal of engagement from local bikers. The "squeaky wheels" of the city outreach process, and the usage of language related to safety and traffic succeeded in tapping directly into the more active and engaged cyclists. Given the range of city projects related to bicycling, many white cyclists were familiar with the framing of bike infrastructure projects and were already clued into the various networks through which information about public process traveled. As such, initial SAC meetings and larger public meetings were dominated by cyclists who were heavily invested in supporting proposals to significantly expand the bike lanes on North Williams Avenue.

Building trust and honoring history

In April of 2011, PBOT held a public meeting to share some of the project details. This meeting was held at a local church and was well attended by community members. At this meeting, it became clear to many residents that some of the proposed street alterations were extensive, and that those making decisions about the street were a mostly white group of residents and business owners.

Following this meeting, the SAC reconvened in early May 2011 to discuss public comments from the open house and one of the proposed ideas for street redesign. At the close of that meeting, an informal vote occurred regarding whether or not PBOT should commit to exploring the proposed redesign. In recounting this event, interviewees who were part of the initial SAC noted that all of the

African-American SAC members rejected the idea. Vanderslice, PBOT Project Manager, stated that this was when she fully realized the social and historical dynamics that were bearing on the project: "This is much deeper than I really had understood before . . . we're going to need to do some kind of digging in here." The April public meeting demonstrated that much of the initial concern was related to a lack of diversity on the SAC, but also hinged on historical marginalization of the black community in Portland.

At the SAC meeting the following month, on June 6, 2011, Vanderslice requested support from the SAC to extend the public process for this project and abandon the July deadline for beginning construction. In her letter to SAC members to explain this process, she noted "We are broadening our outreach and doing more listening to ensure that we achieve the first objective for the project: to conduct an open planning process through which all voices can be heard by the City" (E. Vanderslice, 9 June 2011, letter to the SAC).

Thus, although the city made a range of attempts to attract and retain a more representative group of SAC participants, community responses during the public meeting in Spring 2011 demonstrated that they had not gone far enough. In an attempt to meet community requests for a more representative SAC, during the summer of 2011 PBOT made additional efforts to expand the original SAC. New outreach efforts targeted black churches specifically, and also centered around a process of targeting prominent members of the black community in helping to spread the word about the opportunity to join the SAC. One resident who joined the expanded SAC noted that the outreach process the second time around was much more visible and targeted—the use of key point persons was seen as a key piece of this approach:

> There were flyers were posted at places like the Elks and elementary schools in the neighborhood. Churches knew about this. In the African-American community, a lot of things are word of mouth. We do have our community newspapers, and people read those community newspapers and look to them for information, but you've got to go to the people. If you're really looking for their input, you have to go to them.

Following this new outreach process, by late summer 2011, the SAC had been expanded to include a more diverse group with 27 members, 12 of whom were people of color (PBOT 2011). PBOT's efforts to acknowledge historical grievances and build new relationships was a first step in generating trust between community members and the city, as well as among residents themselves. Expanding the SAC and seeking additional community input at public meetings demonstrated to many that the city was serious about taking all opinions into account. As one SAC member offers:

> I think what's happened over the years is that there has been this culture of distrust that has been built up, and to break down those barriers is difficult.

I'm hoping this project goes most of the way towards finishing that so that when the next project comes, it won't be as contentious as this.

Overwhelmingly, the members of the SAC who were interviewed agreed that PBOT, despite initial missteps during outreach efforts, had made a range of successful decisions. Most importantly, the efforts made to slow down the decision-making process and to expand the SAC were seen as critically important actions. As one SAC member noted, "I felt the city did well to recognize that they may have been on a time track, and revised that time track, and revised it again, and again." Similarly, another African-American SAC member reported that:

> The city's approach was . . . excellent in one way—because they were driving home to a conclusion, and they backed off. I give them a great deal of high marks for that . . . for saying, 'It's pretty obvious that we are not representative enough, and therefore we need to add other people to the board.'

This expanded SAC included both the original members as well as the new participants; the next phase of the project therefore required a process of engaging old and new committee members and providing a space for dialogue about the contentious aspects of the project itself. Notably, the early meetings of the new iteration of the SAC centered around dialogue about the history of the neighborhood rather than about the technical aspects of the street design. The expanded SAC agreed that discussing historical grievances in the committee itself was vital to the project's evolution. The use of some meeting time at both SAC meetings and at open houses and public meetings to describe and discuss the North Portland neighborhood's evolution and the repeated marginalization of black residents was critical to building trust and overcoming PBOT's initial missteps in relation to outreach.

Making space for discussion of the social context of the neighborhood was particularly important in building rapport among members of the SAC, but also served to clarify to the community more broadly that the PBOT was committed to an inclusive decision-making process. As an SAC member noted in an interview:

> As we started through the process, honoring the history of North Williams Avenue became a real important issue to the African Americans on the committee. And what we were able to do was demonstrate to the rest of the stakeholder advisory committee members the importance of that. And I know for a fact many of them embraced that. They understood it. Their heart really understood that. And so just through the education of having different people come in and talk about what was there and making references to the different books for people to read and all the different resources that were made available. I think the committee, the staff got it.

Another SAC member spoke of the efforts of PBOT staff, after expanding the SAC, to facilitate discussions about the history of the community into the project discussions:

The very first SAC meeting we had opened with a PBOT staff member . . .
I want to say at least half of that meeting . . . [was about] the history of the
neighborhood, talking about [the urban renewal projects] . . . red-lining and
various other aspects of the pain and suffering that this neighborhood has
occurred. That was part of the conversation, and part of the awareness of the
SAC at that time.

In providing this space to discuss the social history of the neighborhood and some
of the specific experiences of members of the SAC, the PBOT allowed members
to better understand one another and move forward with a clearer sense of
collective purpose:

I feel like a lot of the key leaders on that committee were really good about
talking about any of the tension and the history of the community and the racial
dynamics and all sorts of stuff . . . I mean that community has an identity the
way it is because of a history of racist Portland. So it's not possible to have a
conversation about [North Williams] without bringing race into it or the history
into it. And, if you think that there is, then you have no cultural context.

Restarting the SAC process and beginning from an acknowledgement of the
historical marginalization of the black community in the area served to build a more
cohesive and connected group of committee participants. These initial discussions
ultimately led the SAC to collectively develop a "Guiding Statement" for their
committee that acknowledged past grievances while developing a set of criteria for
moving forward. As one SAC member noted:

The purpose of the guiding principles were to say, 'Let's figure out a way to,
one, embrace and help people understand that we respect the past, we don't
like it but we respect it, and we don't want to do work like that again.' I give
the city high marks for saying not only do we want to do that here, but it's
possible, I will say even probable that the city has done that in other
neighborhoods as well, so that these guiding principles could potentially be
used elsewhere.

As another member noted, "We developed the guiding principles that you have
seen. In my view what was important about that is the first three or four meetings
. . . we spent the majority of the meeting listening to people." Although other SAC
members reported feeling that the Guiding Principles took too long to devise, most
agreed that they served the goal of bringing the committee together and devising
a way to move forward, given earlier tensions. Excerpts from this two-page
document illustrate the concerted effort the SAC made to bring the historical
context of the neighborhood into the present-day discussion:

We honor the descendants and the collective memory of the community and
all those who have suffered or watched their families or businesses suffer due

to systemic processes of racial residential segregation, and housing condemnation to make way for urban renewal, and institutional disinvestment, when governmental or institutional goals collided with neighborhood dreams, goals, and hopes . . . We vow to do everything in our power to reverse that legacy and intentionally use this project to begin the healing process . . . We understand that the members of the community are the experts in their neighborhoods, and that the City has expertise in traffic planning and engineering.[1]

The statement provided a clear set of agreed-upon ideas that brought the committee together, while also clarifying how the historical dynamics of the neighborhood continued to impact the SAC process. This document not only acknowledged that past injustices continued to impact contemporary processes and served to bring the diverse SAC together, but also stood as a reminder that the legacies of racism, displacement, and marginalization were still felt in the neighborhood. The second page of the document also made a series of "future requests" to the city of Portland that would serve to remedy some of the problematic aspect of the N. Williams outreach process, including reassessing their approach to outreach and prioritizing community engagement in more cognizant ways. The process of building this statement also generated a SAC sub-committee dedicated to "Honoring History" that met outside of SAC meetings to generate plans to rename certain streets in the neighborhood to commemorate local black history. The revised SAC process demonstrates the necessity of integrating social context into planning processes. Redesigning a street is not simply a technical project, but is also a social and political project. The final project proposal, for which additional funding was requested from the Oregon Department of Transportation's Bicycle and Pedestrian Program, contained explicit plans to incorporate an "honoring history" component to the project through public art installations (Oregon Department of Transportation, *Notice of Intent*, 2012).

The public process surrounding the N. Williams street design demonstrates how dominant ideologies regarding planning and the presumed universal desirability of certain infrastructural elements (here, bicycles and bikeway development) can result in less inclusive planning processes. In this case, original outreach mechanisms and language used spoke directly to those most invested in bike lane expansion while failing to engage minority residents. This reality, when coupled with the historical legacies of racism in relation to planning, created tensions and conflict. This process illustrates Zavestoski and Agyeman's claim in Chapter 1 of this volume that, "If any of the historical narratives are absent from the dominant picture of who the community is, that picture will therefore be distorted." In Portland, such narratives were indeed missing in early planning processes. The framing of the N. Williams project as a simple safety and transportation project overlooked the reality that streets are living spaces with their own unique social history and that planning is not merely a series of technical decisions, but is informed by a host of social and political realities, both past and present.

Conflicting visions and future possibilities

Despite substantive efforts by PBOT in outreach, the community, particularly the long-term African-American community in North Portland, did not see much reason to get involved initially and when they did, they fundamentally disagreed with key aspects of the project. This was due to the ways in which different groups framed or assigned meaning to the project and the infrastructural changes to the street (Bijker 1995).[2] Different groups interpreted the bike and cycling infrastructure differently and, at least initially, incompatibly.

PBOT, cyclists, cycling advocates and others who supported the project from the start saw the changes to the street as providing critically important enhancements for bike and pedestrian safety, by mitigating conflicts between different modes of transportation (which included eliminating one lane of automobile traffic), and improved access for cyclists, further cementing N. Williams place as a major bikeway. These changes were widely viewed as urgent due to current high traffic levels and expected increases from continued rapid development on N. Williams. These groups were *highly included* in the safety and access frame. That is, there was broad agreement on the need for the project and its goals and meaning. Further, there was a shared understanding of how such changes on N. Williams fit into broader visions and goals for the street and for the city of Portland, like the *Portland Bicycle Plan 2030*.

This also helps to explain how some advocates of the project could not see or understand the relevance of emerging concerns around racism and gentrification. "I came here for a discussion of the safety issues," said one resident at a public meeting on the project, "but I honestly don't understand how a safety campaign on Williams is an issue of gentrification or racism." Later, the same resident would add, "If we delay this safety campaign and project for a year, and in that time another first grader is hit and killed, I'd feel that it was a huge failure on our part as a community" (BikePortland.org). When you are so highly included in a frame, it's difficult to see outside of it. Issues outside of that frame, such as institutional racism, do not have meaning to those highly included and therefore do not help to shape concerns, meanings or designs. The Complete Streets movement would do well to consider what issues and groups are included or excluded from the ways they frame their projects and concerns.

While PBOT, cycling advocates, and other concerned citizens were highly included in the safety and access frame, for others it did not resonate or register. As one African-American resident noted in an interview:

> I was going in there [to the community meeting] thinking, 'we're going to be talking about lighting on the street, you know, talking about pedestrians having access to get across' . . . I had no idea [what] the whole thing was . . . and I didn't know that a bicycle plan exists for the city of Portland, I didn't know that the city was looking to [be]come, a cutting-edge cycling city in America. I mean, I didn't know that.

When groups or actors do not share in the dominant frames and meanings of a particular issue, they have a *low inclusion*. According to Hommels (2005, p. 332), "For them, the technology presents a 'take-it-or-leave-it' choice. They see no possibilities for variation within a given . . . frame, so they are left with the choice of either accepting it or abandoning it." They are "closed-out" of the popular frame—the discourse and designs are not theirs nor do the issues, as framed, resonate.

Precisely because, to PBOT's credit, there was room for public discussion and some concerned residents spoke up, the dominant frame of safety and access was dislodged and the issue attained a new interpretive flexibility. There was space to debate and provide new meaning to the project and to the changes to the street. What we saw is that current conditions and proposed technical changes were inextricably tied to race and the historical social and physical development, not just of N. Williams but also of north and northeast Portland. More than any other group, the African-American community problematized popular, taken-for-granted framing of cycling infrastructure. This is summarized succinctly and emphatically by the African-American resident quoted above who asked, "You say you want it "safe" for everybody, how come it wasn't safe 10 years ago?" The limits of the safety and access framing, and of the Complete Streets discourse, are illustrated here. Safety for whom? Why are some perspectives heard by the city, and others seemingly ignored?

The debates that emerged here then led to an expanded SAC and more open discussion as detailed above. The open and honest discussions of history, racism, gentrification, and also of specific proposed changes to the street highlight the importance of listening, discussion, and building trust. That is, they highlight the importance of *process*. This process then opened up and led to new *possibilities*. The cycling community and PBOT realized the limitations of their framings and the importance of issues that had previously been closed out. The African-American community fought for a pathway to meaningfully participate and have their voices and concerns heard. Critically, this process not only changed the discourse but altered the very designs considered for the street (Figure 14.4). By opening up and changing the politics, the SAC and PBOT also changed the design.

Completing the street?

PBOT delivered its final report on the North Williams Traffic Operations Safety Project in August 2012. PBOT adopted the proposed outcomes from the SAC, including more pedestrian crossings and enhanced visibility, the reduction of motor vehicle speeds, and the management of conflicts between bikes and buses. The final recommended design concept was "informed by twenty-three public meetings, four community workshops, two open houses and a number of one-on-one conversations with community leaders and business owners" (PBOT 2012, p. 11). At its center, it proposes a left-side buffered bikeway in some segments and a shared left-side bikeway and turning lane in others. This would

Buffered Bike Lane Cross Section

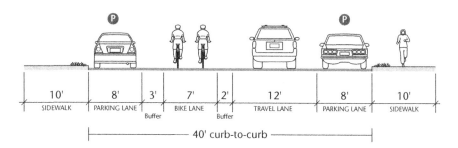

Shared Left-Side Bikeway and Left-Turn Lane Cross Section

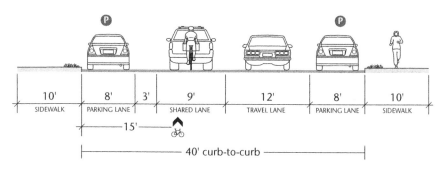

FIGURE 14.4 Final design proposal for major segments of N. Williams from PBOT final report

Source: PBOT Final Report, 2012.

maintain two lanes for motor vehicles in certain high traffic areas. The design also includes curb extensions and a new traffic signal. The left-side bikeway configuration is a unique design element that would be a first in the city. In addition, cyclists remain skeptical that it provides adequate safety. Unfortunately, the original funds for the project were no longer available by the time the final recommendations were delivered. PBOT was forced to search for external funding. PBOT applied for and was awarded $1.48 million from the Oregon Department of Transportation's Transportation Alternatives and Oregon Pedestrian & Bicycle Program. This award, however, would not fund the Honoring History public art installation. Given its importance to the community, PBOT agreed to fund the installation with $100,000 of bureau funds. The project is expected to break ground in summer 2014.

The N. Williams case demonstrates, as Zavestoski and Agyeman urge us to consider at the outset, that streets are physical spaces that shape and are, in turn, shaped by more symbolic, social, cultural, and political dimensions. N. Williams is certainly now considered as a street that is more than a mix of transportation modes and choices. It's a vibrant, diverse, gentrifying, congested (by Portland standards), walkable street with a deep history of immigrant groups and connection to Portland's African-American community.

When described in this sense, our streets will never be complete—they are always being materially and discursively made, always and necessarily *incomplete*. This is why, if we are concerned with "Complete Streets" and issues of justice and equity, we need to be sure that the *processes* are in place to foster constructive debate and ensure that a diverse set of politics and values have the opportunity to shape our infrastructure. Otherwise, not only will marginalized communities and perspectives continue to be closed-out, but marginalization then is reflected in our built environment. N. Williams shows that debates about the street and its design as a physical place are inseparable from politics, community, and visions of its past and future. Finally, N. Williams, we believe, points a pathway beyond the limits of the Complete Streets movement—*possibilities* emerge from processes that include diverse values and perspectives that will change the vision of the street and its physical design.

Acknowledgments

This study would not have been possible without the cooperation and enthusiasm of the Stakeholder Advisory Committee and the Portland Bureau of Transportation project management team. The authors thank all the interviewees for their time and effort. The authors also thank the graduate research assistants who provided critical support at various points during the research project: Dillon Mahmoudi, Jeff Shelton, and Elisabeth Wilder. This research was funded by an award from the American Sociological Association Fund for the Advancement of the Discipline.

Notes

1   The full document is available online: http://www.portlandoregon.gov/transportation/article/381521.
2   Work on technological frames and interpretive flexibility emerges from the literature on the social construction of technology (SCOT). Unfortunately, this is not the space to provide an overview of that literature and its usefulness in considering infrastructure, cycling and Complete Streets. For an overview of SCOT, see Bijker (1995).

References

Abbott, C., 1981. *The new urban America: Growth and politics in sunbelt cities*. Chapel Hill, NC: University of North Carolina Press.
Bijker, W.E., 1995. *Of bicycles, Bakelites, and bulbs: Toward a theory of socio-technical change*. Cambridge, MA: MIT Press.
Bower, D., Geller, R., Ginenthal, L., Igarta, D., Lear, M., and Waltz, J., 2007. *Portland's platinum bicycle master plan: Existing conditions report*. Portland, OR: City of Portland.
City of Portland Bureau of Transportation (PBOT), 2011. Stakeholder Advisory Committee Meeting Minutes: North Williams Traffic Safety and Operations Project.

City of Portland Bureau of Transportation (PBOT). 2012. *North Williams Traffic Operations Safety Project: Final Report.* Available from: https://www.portlandoregon.gov/transportation/article/417219 [Accessed 4 May 2014].

Edwards, P.N., 2003. Infrastructure and modernity: Force, time, and social organization in the history of sociotechnical systems. *Modernity and Technology*, 134, 185–225.

Gibson, K.J., 2007. Bleeding Albina: A history of community disinvestment, 1940–2000. *Transforming Anthropology*, 15 (1), 3–25.

Goodyear, S., 2011. Bike lane backlash, even in Portland [online]. *The Atlantic Cities.* Available from: http://www.theatlanticcities.com/neighborhoods/2011/09/portland-bike-lanes-open-racial-wounds/138/ [Accessed 5 November 2013].

Graham, S., and Marvin, S., 2001. *Splintering urbanism, networked infrastructures, technological mobilities and the urban condition.* New York: Taylor & Francis.

Hommels, A., 2005. Studying obduracy in the city: Toward a productive fusion between technology studies and urban studies. *Science, Technology & Human Values*, 30 (3), 323–351.

Latour, B., 1987. *Science in action: How to follow scientists and engineers through society.* Cambridge, MA: Harvard University Press.

Lubitow, A., and Miller, T.R., 2013. Contesting sustainability: Bikes, race, and politics in Portlandia. *Environmental Justice*, 6 (4), 121–126.

Oregon Department of Transportation, 2012. *Notice of Intent*: North Williams Traffic Safety and Operations Project, City of Portland.

Roos, R.E., 2008. *The history of Albina.* Roy E. Roos.

Schmitt, A., 2011. On gentrification and cycling [online]. *Streetsblog.* Available from: http://streetsblog.net/2011/07/22/on-gentrification-and-cycling/ [Accessed 5 November 2013].

Scott, A., 2012. By the grace of God [online]. *Portland Monthly.* Available from: http://www.portlandmonthlymag.com/news-and-profiles/culture/articles/african-american-churches-north-portland-march-2012 [Accessed 5 November 2013].

Smith, N., 2002. New globalism, new urbanism: Gentrification as global urban strategy. *Antipode*, 34 (3), 427–450.

Tarr, J.A., and G. Dupuy, eds., 1988. *Technology and the rise of the networked city in Europe and America.* Philadelphia, PA: Temple University Press

Teaford, J.C., 2000. Urban renewal and its aftermath. *Housing Policy Debate*, 11 (2), 443–465.

15

INCOMPLETE STREETS, COMPLETE REGIONS

In search of an equitable scale

Karen Chapple

Complete Streets are designed to accommodate safe travel for all modes and all users. In essence, the idea is that this public space should embrace diversity. Yet, decades of policy experimentation in fostering and maintaining diversity—for instance, in public schools or mixed-income housing—have shown that it is always more challenging than anticipated. What is diversity? A population that perfectly represents the universe or an equal mix of different groups defined by ethnicity or class? And in the specific case of urban design, given the impossibility of envisioning all potential users, how can designers keep diversity in mind when planning a public space?

This chapter examines the needs for street space in the travel patterns of low-income families, and in particular, low-wage workers. Both the work and non-work travel needs of low-income groups differ from those of upper-income metropolitan residents. The industries that employ most low-wage workers have distinct location patterns, typically with poor transit accessibility. Most low-income families thus rely on cars: in US metropolitan areas, 88 percent of low-income workers commute by car (versus 91 percent of other workers), and 86 percent of low-income households own at least one car (versus 95 percent of other households) (Blumenberg and Waller 2003). Several factors are increasing auto dependence among the low income, including the suburbanization of poverty and the space-time constraints of life, particularly for the working poor.

Given these special activity patterns, "completing" streets by accommodating bicycles, pedestrians, and other alternative modes may mean taking away capacity—and reducing mobility—for low-income residents and their jobs. This chapter argues that the movement to Complete Streets through diversifying modes and land uses may paradoxically increase segregation and poverty in the region. In other words, making some neighborhoods less welcoming to cars and trucks may displace economic activity to different parts of the region. These costs are disproportionately borne by the low-income residents—and may actually increase the region's ecological footprint. A more equitable approach would take regional economic patterns into account when replanning urban street space.

I begin with a brief description of the geography of employment and poverty, focusing on the region of San Francisco. San Francisco provides an interesting, albeit extreme, case study because of its high level of income inequality, as well as its embrace of the Complete Streets concept and supporting movement. At the same time as San Francisco, Oakland, Berkeley, and other cities are increasingly dedicating street space to alternative modes of transportation, their economies are increasingly dominated by low-wage service jobs.

The San Francisco region provides two illustrations of the challenges Complete Streets present for the lives of low-income residents. One of the most important sources of low-skill jobs is the industrial sector, or more broadly, the production, distribution, and repair (PDR) sector. Yet these districts and the trucks that they bring are often the first target of twenty-first-century place-making. With Complete Streets projects, this truck traffic does not just vaporize, but is displaced to other neighborhoods, often those with low-income residents. Another potential unanticipated impact is on activity patterns for low-income households. Low-wage work tends to be dispersed throughout the region, making accessibility a major issue. Low-income households depend on cars even more for non-work travel patterns, since goods and services may not be located within the neighborhood. In reducing vehicular traffic within certain parts of the region, Complete Streets projects may place inequitable restrictions on the movements of low-income residents and workers disproportionately who are dependent on autos.

The metropolitan geography of employment and poverty

Location theory tells us that firms tend to concentrate in more central areas due to the benefits of agglomeration: knowledge spillovers, the availability of both skilled and immigrant labor pools, and proximity to suppliers and markets (Gottlieb 1995). In the service sector, as well as in crafts manufacturing, the more specialized the firm, the more it gravitates towards central locations (Fujita *et al.* 1999). Consumer services tend to disperse more, locating near decentralized residential areas; large-scale or heavy manufacturing and logistics increasingly decentralize as well in search of low land costs (Daniels 1985).

Overall, low-wage work, which is typically low-skill as well, accounts for about half of all employment. In the San Francisco region, the economy is particularly bifurcated between high-wage and low-wage sectors: 58 percent of the jobs pay low wages (supporting households at 80 percent of the regional median income or less). Almost one-fourth of these jobs are related to tourism and entertainment, and an additional 16 percent are in retail. Other major sectors are business services, manufacturing, health care, education, and government. In contrast, sectors like finance, information, construction, and professional services primarily employ high-wage workers.

As predicted by location theory, low-wage work tends to disperse. A look at Bay Area job densities for sample sectors illustrates these differences (Figures 15.1–15.4). Overall, jobs are concentrated in the downtown centers of San Francisco, San Jose, Oakland, Berkeley, and the suburban communities along the I-680 corridor. But health care and social assistance establishments, as well as retail businesses, tend to co-locate with residences. Manufacturing jobs concentrate outside but nearby downtowns.

At the same time, poverty is growing throughout the region, just as it is throughout the US. From a peak of 15.1 percent in 1993, the poverty rate decreased to 11.3 percent in 2000, only to rise again to 15 percent in 2011, due to a sharp increase after the Great Recession (Center on Budget and Policy Priorities 2013). As poverty has grown nationally in the 2000s, it has also increased in both cities and suburbs, and in concentrated poverty neighborhoods—but not evenly across and between metropolitan areas. In general, poverty is growing fastest in the suburbs; however, their poverty rate remains just over half of the urban poverty rate. When poverty rates change, it is not because of the poor being pushed from one place to another; instead, poverty in both city and suburb follows metropolitan and national fortunes (Cooke 2010; Pendall et al. 2011). Although historically housing moved to the suburbs followed by jobs, the situation is now more complex: jobs are sprawling to more affluent suburbs but avoiding those with growing poverty (Raphael and Stoll 2010).

The conflicts between Complete Streets and industrial districts

PDR uses—including a variety of industries from auto repair, to crafts manufacturing, to food preparation, to bus parking, to warehousing and logistics—bring noise, pollution, and most visibly, trucks. In most cities, they have long located in older industrial or mixed-use neighborhoods near the downtown—the areas that, due to their proximity and architectural quality, are often the first to transform when city fortunes reverse. PDR firms then find themselves in conflict with new residential and commercial users who demand quiet in their buildings and more room to maneuver and park outside. In this context, where trucks dominate street life, a "Complete Streets" policy means making space for bikes, pedestrians, and alternative transit. This, in turn, makes it challenging for PDR businesses to function. PDR businesses have an active relationship to streets: they need sidewalk space for staging and driveways and streets for loading goods.

This battle over industrial land is playing out in New York City, Boston, San Francisco, Chicago, Los Angeles, Denver, Baltimore, Minneapolis, Charlotte, Portland, Seattle, much of the DC metropolitan area, and many other smaller cities (UC-Berkeley Center for Community Innovation 2009). But why should we care about protecting the existing industrial businesses? The line of argument typically put forward by the local chamber of commerce is that these businesses are mostly heavy manufacturers who have been leaving the city for decades anyway, or distributors who are using the land inefficiently, mostly for parking. Often an odd

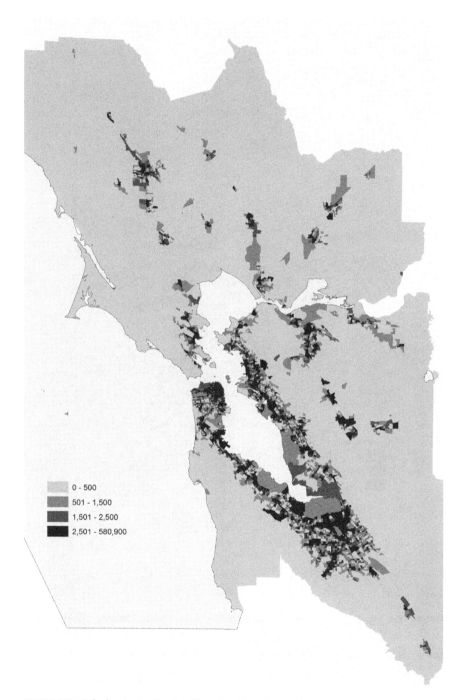

FIGURE 15.1 Job density in the San Francisco Bay Area, 2010

Source: Author's calculations from Longitudinal Employer-Household Dynamics dataset.

Legend:
- 0 - 500
- 501 - 1,500
- 1,501 - 2,500
- 2,501 - 580,900

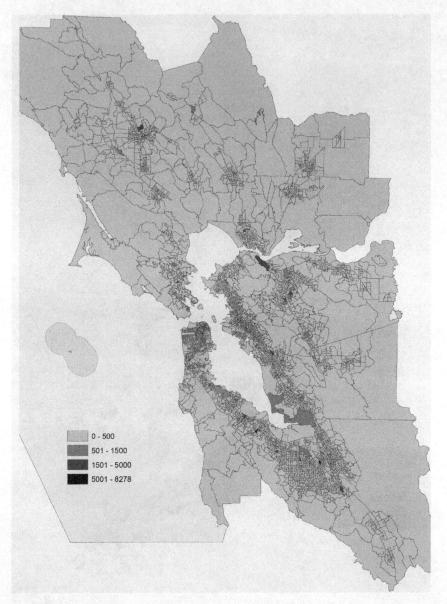

FIGURE 15.2 Job density in the San Francisco Bay Area, Health Care/Social Assistance, 2010

Source: Author's calculations from Longitudinal Employer-Household Dynamics dataset.

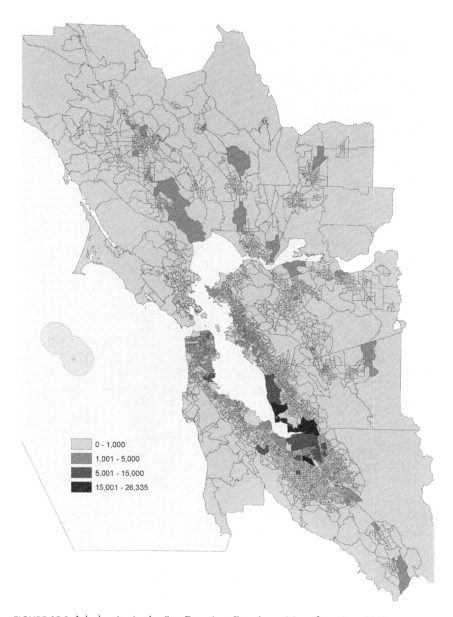

FIGURE 15.3 Job density in the San Francisco Bay Area, Manufacturing, 2010

Source: Author's calculations from Longitudinal Employer-Household Dynamics dataset.

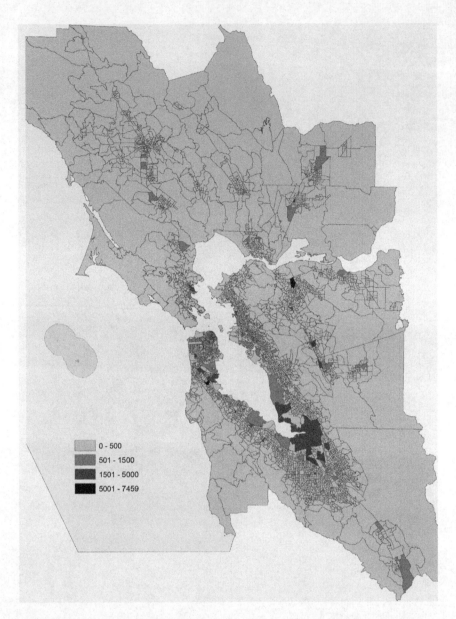

FIGURE 15.4 Job density in the San Francisco Bay Area, Retail and Entertainment, 2010

Source: Author's calculations from Longitudinal Employer-Household Dynamics dataset.

growth machine coalition in support of converting industrial land emerges. This might include not just the chamber and developers, but non-profit housing developers concerned about the need for affordable or workforce housing downtown, planners interested in more housing to achieve jobs/housing balance, politicians seeking retail and the sales tax revenue it brings, and environmental justice advocates concerned about pollution from productive businesses in high-density areas.

Yet, studies show that industrial areas contribute to the regional economy in multiple ways: as job and tax revenue generators; providers of supplies and services, such as back-office functions or automobile repair, to businesses and households; and reservoirs of low-cost space that can incubate startup businesses (Howland 2010). To function efficiently, they need to be located close to their customers downtown (Dempwolf 2010). Land that generates employment, whether in industrial or commercial uses, tends to have net positive fiscal benefits (Strategic Economics 2004). Most importantly, businesses in industrial zones are much more likely to expand than those in other zones, adding employees at four times the rate of commercial zones and nine times the rate in residential zones (Chapple 2014). Location on industrially zoned land in relatively large buildings gives firms the flexibility to spill into available space. Finally, this land is most likely to accommodate the middle-skill jobs that support a middle class. PDR businesses typically provide jobs in industries that pay well over a living wage, such as auto repair, construction, landscaping, and utilities (San Francisco Planning Department 2002).

The location of PDR businesses within the region also has important implications for regional sustainability. Locating logistics businesses in particular—e.g., wholesale distributors—in the urban core, near major trading ports, helps ensure the efficient movement of goods. Displacing these firms from the core into peripheral areas—a trend that is already occurring—would mean a significant increase in vehicle miles travelled (VMT) from trucks (Hausrath Economics Group and Cambridge Systematics 2004). But though demand from these businesses is steady or growing, the amount of warehouse and manufacturing space in the central areas of strong markets like San Francisco is declining. This is causing many PDR businesses to shift location to the region's periphery, or even adjacent lower-cost regions, with increasing VMT and its implications for greenhouse gas emissions.

The primary threat to industrial businesses, and impetus for the new demand for Complete Streets, is the mixing of uses. Although the single use district dominated metropolitan structure for almost a century, planners reacting to urban renewal (and taking their cues from Jane Jacobs) have gradually modified zoning regulations since the 1980s. Mixed-use districts permit and intensify the mixture of uses—residential, commercial, open space, institutional, and less frequently, industrial (Grant 2002). New Urbanists, particularly the transit-oriented development (TOD) advocates, are strong proponents of mixed-use, touting its ability to maximize efficient use of infrastructure and reduce VMT through co-location of diverse uses (Grant 2002). Proponents of traditional neighborhood design focus more on the quality of life, with the mixing of home and work in the dense and diverse European city as their model (Foord 2010). But even planners who have embraced mixed-use see challenges in including industrial businesses in the mix (Grant 2002).

When cities open up their industrial land to a variety of uses, including commercial and residential, they risk unsustainable rent increases that will gradually displace PDR businesses. In the face of competition for land from higher rent-paying office uses, rents will escalate beyond the means of some of the firms that are contributing more (and higher quality) jobs to the economy. Some argue that only the inefficient firms, that should be located on cheaper land anyway, are displaced. But from a social equity perspective, either the loss or the decentralization of jobs hurts life chances for low-income workers. What can we do?

Policies to protect industrial land

Policy recommendations for the preservation of industrially zoned land generally follow three tactics: regulation, penalties, and incentives. Regulatory tools are the most powerful; they include restricting the types of uses that can locate within a zone, instituting criteria for land conversion, and rezoning land.

Policies that preserve industrial zoning are essentially "exclusionary zoning"; they prohibit higher uses despite market interest (Heikkila and Hutton 1986). This policy has costs in that it may mean inefficient use of resources, slowdown of the transition away from industrial uses, and impacts on the local tax base in ways that are rarely made explicit. However, it may be appropriate to pursue exclusionary zoning under certain conditions, in particular: (1) when the industrial district is economically viable, functioning as a business incubator or housing businesses linked to other local clusters; (2) when there is a high level of structural unemployment; or (3) negative externalities are an issue (ibid.). Exclusionary zoning cannot only keep rents low for businesses but also provides certainty to developers about city intentions.

In practice, exclusionary zoning for industrial use has existed in a few cities since the 1980s, due to fears that demand from commercial and residential uses was displacing viable industrial businesses (Fitzgerald and Leigh 2002). Some of these districts—called Planned Manufacturing Districts in Chicago, Industrial Protection Zones in San Francisco, and Industrial Business Zones in New York—permit the mixture of uses in the districts, but limit land availability for non-industrial users.

The case of San Francisco is notable not only for protecting much of its industrial land but also planning strategically for its location. In the late 1990s, almost 2,800 acres or 12.6 percent of land in the city was available for industrial use—though in reality, this includes the port and buffer zones where most businesses cannot locate, so the total was closer to 5 percent. In any case, zoning in most of these areas allowed various types of office and, with a conditional use permit, housing as well as, of course, heavy and light industrial and commercial. Housing moved into industrial areas, the so-called Eastern Neighborhoods, because it was cheaper to build, there was less neighborhood opposition, and the zoning permitted it. As developers built live-work lofts in the area, mostly for a market interested more in living in a chic industrial area than actually producing anything, businesses were displaced and jobs lost. Meanwhile, the new residents complained about the lack of neighborhood services and the nuisances and noise from the PDR firms. Interestingly, this area has seen significant investment in new bike infrastructure as part of San Francisco's Complete Streets plan—as well as numerous bicyclist accidents.[1]

But in the 2000s, after a public planning process, the city acted to preserve its industrial land. To accommodate housing, it ceded over half of its industrial land near downtown to mixed-use zoning, with housing, and preserved the rest in industrial protection zones. The most transit accessible areas were opened up, but a short distance away, still within a mile of the downtown, the city protects its PDR uses. To maintain the dynamism of industrial districts, which often provide valuable low-cost incubator space, these zones also permit startup firms, but only in a few industry sectors such as cleantech and digital media.

The conflict between Complete Streets and travel for low-income families

Another way in which claiming street space for alternative modes may hurt diversity goals is through failing to support the complicated travel needs of low-income families. Historically, transportation engineers have focused on improving mobility for the journey to work, mostly through increasing capacity for cars on major arterials and highways. Given this unilateral focus, it is perhaps not surprising that a movement has arisen to make space for other modes. Who might this displace?

Overall, only 20 percent of all travel is for work; most trips are made for shopping, family or personal needs, or recreation (National Surface Transportation Policy and Revenue Commission 2007). Non-work travel patterns may be particularly complex for low-income families, who may suffer from time poverty, or the inability to meet complex multiple responsibilities within a set schedule. For instance, family sizes are larger, necessitating more trips to more places for education, health, and recreation. A family orientation leads to higher levels of auto dependency (Fan and Khattak 2012). Dependency on an array of public, private, and non-profit providers for services may mean traveling longer distances (Allard 2008). Relying on family and friends for assistance (e.g., for child care or errands) may complicate daily travel further, if they are not local. Lower-income households, particularly with working mothers, tend to make more trips (Blumenberg 2004). This occurs in part because they experience challenges in developing efficient trip chaining strategies, due to their reliance on multiple modes, as well as their fixed work schedules that don't allow for stops to and from work (Bhat 1997; Clifton 2003).

Ideally, families would be able to meet these needs within their own neighborhoods—a vision of the "complete communities" movement. As described by Reconnecting America, complete communities include:

a quality education, access to good jobs, an affordable roof over our heads, access to affordable healthy food and health services, the ability to enjoy artistic, spiritual and cultural amenities, access to recreation and parks, meaningful civic engagement, and affordable transportation choices that get us where we need to go . . . Complete communities are inclusive, measured by how residents and workers benefit and not necessarily the shape or form they take, and may likely require other supportive assets.

(Reconnecting America 2012)

Likewise, the Ahwahnee Principles of the New Urbanist movement state: (1) "all planning should be in the form of complete and integrated communities including housing, shops, workplaces, schools, parks and civic facilities essential to the daily life of the residents" and (2) "community size should be designed so that housing, jobs, daily needs, and other activities are within easy walking distance of each another" (Pivo 2005, p. 1).

Despite this push, the number of retail and service options in low-income neighborhoods is actually declining. As store sizes are growing, so are market areas, forcing low-income consumers to travel further (or pay more at smaller local shops) (Clifton 2003). This also increases auto dependence, as walking or biking is not an option. Ironically, where upper-income households can readily benefit from the alternative mode choices supported by Complete Streets, low-income shoppers may find their challenges exacerbated (to the extent that projects remove street capacity for vehicular traffic without creating alternatives for movement). The impact may be disproportionate on low-income groups because of their higher degree of auto dependence.

Despite comprising only a small share of overall travel, the challenges of the commute to work for low-income workers have garnered much more policy attention. Beginning shortly after the urban riots that occurred in a number of American cities in the 1960s, awareness arose of a potential "spatial mismatch" between poor inner city residents and suburban job opportunities (Kain 1968). Poor access to jobs explains much of why some groups experience disproportionately high rates of unemployment. With greater proximity to jobs, unemployment and welfare usage decrease slightly, and earnings increase slightly (Blumenberg and Ong 1998; Carlson and Theodore 1997; Immergluck 1998).

Still, there are reasons to rethink the notion that the problem is a simple mismatch of space. Evidence is accumulating that poor employment outcomes may be due to "automobile mismatch." With a car, workers can access many more job opportunities than by relying on transit (Taylor and Ong 1995; Shen 1998; Blumenberg and Hess 2003; Kawabata 2003; Blumenberg and Manville 2004; Grengs 2010; Fan 2012). This is obviously true for the sprawling cities of the American West; more surprising are findings that even in a city like Detroit, center city workers with a car have greater accessibility than suburban workers without (Grengs 2010). Owning a car typically improves job accessibility and increases employment rates and wages, regardless of whether jobs are nearby or not (Ong

1996, 2002; Shen 1998; Raphael and Stoll 2001; Cervero *et al.* 2002; Blumenberg 2004; Ong and Miller 2005; Fan 2012).

Transit is often not a viable alternative, even though the poor are relatively more dependent on transit than upper-income workers. It is not well designed to meet their travel needs because of the dramatic shifts in metropolitan spatial structure, particularly the rise of suburban job centers (Lang and Simmons 2003). Many of these jobs will be high-wage and high-skill; most of the low-skill jobs in construction, retail, and services tend to locate near residential neighborhoods or in individual homes, i.e., more auto-oriented locations, often with alternative work shifts (Fan 2012). For instance, in San Diego, rail transit lines and stations provide accessibility to only 20 percent of the city's low-wage jobs (Cervero 2010). The share of transit commuters increases dramatically near office buildings, but only those in high job density areas that house government or knowledge-based industries such as professional services, information, and financial services—all with a disproportionate share of high-wage workers (Belzer, Srivastava and Austin 2011). Thus, public transit may improve employment outcomes, but not as effectively as autos (Sanchez 1999; Cervero *et al.* 2002; Fan 2012).

Given these constraints, it makes sense that most low-income families rely on cars for travel. But even without owning a car, low-income families often have access to an automobile. Coping strategies to improve mobility include getting rides from others, borrowing cars, or relying on others, often through barter, to run errands or deliver goods (Clifton 2004).

Policies to support mobility for low-income families

Given the constraints of transit to reach jobs throughout the region, most initiatives to link low-income urban residents to suburban jobs (for instance, the Jobs Access and Reverse Commute program, which has provided almost $900 million in funding from 1999 to 2009) have had little success (Rosenbloom 1992; O'Regan and Quigley 1999). One evaluation of a van-pooling experiment called Bridges to Work, which provided job placement and transportation services to help urban low-skilled workers access suburban jobs in five regions (Baltimore, Chicago, Denver, Milwaukee, and St. Louis), concluded that it was not an effective solution in terms of increasing employment or earnings (compared to a control group) (Roder and Scrivner 2005). The findings indicated that workers will not take on long reverse commutes if they cannot realize substantially higher wages in return.

Given the accessibility challenges of a region's low-income residents, as well as the overwhelmingly positive impact of auto ownership on employment outcomes, the most equitable approach might be to improve access to automobiles among the poor. Low-income households are still likely to drive fewer miles than higher income; if the goal is reducing vehicle miles traveled, the primary target should be higher-income drivers. In any case, a vehicle miles traveled tax will be less regressive than other taxes like the sales tax (Schweitzer and Taylor 2008).

Thus, many states and cities have implemented programs that improve mobility through automobile access, whether via auto-ownership, car-sharing, or taxi voucher programs (Clifton, 2004). Car ownership programs offer great promise in terms of overcoming the barriers to work in both city and suburb, as well as supporting the non-work travel that constitutes the bulk of daily activity. Over 150 non-profit car ownership or loan programs for low-income groups have also emerged around the country, with one early evaluation showing significant and positive effects on wages and probability of employment for a very small sample of participants (Lucas and Nicholson 2003).

Complete Streets by completing the region

The challenge of creating places that are truly diverse, accommodating all users, is that we may not be able to anticipate who all the users are. In an architect's rendering of a lively street, or a livable place, we rarely see the trucks that are transporting goods made by locals, or the family struggling to get the kids to school on time. Yet, behind every iconic great place—the walkable neighborhoods of San Francisco, the boulevards of Paris—is an urban economy that supports and is supported by low-income workers and their families operating under severe mobility constraints.

As the Complete Streets movement removes capacity for cars and trucks from the region's most prominent streets, it will shift them elsewhere. Although this chapter does not analyze this displacement, it will likely follow a pattern that is typical when major arterials are removed: some vehicles shift to more minor streets nearby, some move to other parts of the region, and some disappear altogether. Each pattern has implications for social equity. As activity is displaced to more minor streets, it increases noise and pollution, often in residential areas. If it moves to other parts of the region, it increases vehicle miles traveled both for trucks delivering goods and workers commuting. If it disappears altogether, it may take with it the livelihood of low-wage workers. Ironically, the overall effect may be to increase segregation—and vehicle miles traveled—in the region.

Policies are in place to protect industrial districts and promote auto ownership. Complete Streets approaches may be able to work around those policies, for instance, avoiding encroachment on industrial areas and impact on travel patterns for low-income groups. As yet, however, the strategies have not even acknowledged that these users, too, need their Complete Streets. A more equitable approach would analyze these needs and impacts. Ultimately, this will mean developing an understanding of each street's role in facilitating the movement of people and goods throughout the complete region.

Note

1   See the bike accident map at https://www.baycitizen.org/data/bikes/bike-accident-tracker/.

References

Allard, S.W., 2008. *Out of reach: Place, poverty, and the new American welfare state.* New Haven, CT: Yale University Press.

Belzer, D., Srivastava, S., and Austin, M., 2011. *Transit and regional economic development.* Oakland, CA: Center for Transit-Oriented Development.

Bhat, C., 1997. Work travel mode choice and the number of non-work commute stops. *Transportation Research-B*, 31, 41–54.

Blumenberg, E., 2004. En-gendering effective planning: Spatial mismatch, low-income women, and transportation policy. *Journal of the American Planning Association*, 70 (3), 269–281.

Blumenberg, E., and Hess, D.B., 2003. Measuring the role of transportation in facilitating welfare-to-work transition: Evidence from three California counties. *Transportation Research Record*, 1859, 93–101.

Blumenberg, E., and Manville, M., 2004. Beyond the spatial mismatch: Welfare recipients and transportation policy. *Journal of Planning Literature*, 19 (2), 182–205.

Blumenberg, E., and Ong, P., 1998. Job access, commute and travel burden among welfare recipients. *Urban Studies*, 35 (1), 77–93.

Blumenberg, E., and Waller, M., 2003. *The long journey to work: A federal transportation policy for working families.* Washington, DC: Brookings Institution.

Carlson, V., and Theodore, N., 1997. Employment availability for entry-level workers: An examination of the spatial-mismatch hypothesis in Chicago. *Urban Geography*, 18 (3), 228–242.

Center on Budget and Policy Priorities, 2013. *By the numbers.* Washington, DC: Center on Budget and Policy Priorities. Available from: www.cbpp.org/research/index.cfm?fa= topicandid=36 [Accessed June 4, 2013].

Cervero, R., 2010. Destinations matter. Presentation at TOD and Social Equity Conference. Available from: http://communityinnovation.berkeley.edu/presentations/ Cervero_Destinations_Matter.pdf [Accessed July 29, 2014].

Cervero, R., Sandoval, O., and Landis, J., 2002. Transportation as a stimulus of welfare-to-work: Private versus public mobility. *Journal of Planning Education and Research*, 22 (1), 50–63.

Chapple, K., 2014, forthcoming. The highest and best use? Urban industrial land and job creation. *Economic Development Quarterly.*

Clifton, K.J., 2003. Examining travel choices of low-income populations: Issues, methods, and new approaches. Paper presented at 10th International Conference on Travel Behaviour Research.

Clifton, K.J., 2004. Mobility strategies and food shopping for low-income families: A case study. *Journal of Planning Education and Research*, 23 (4), 402–413.

Cooke, T.J., 2010. Residential mobility of the poor and the growth of poverty in inner-ring suburbs. *Urban Geography*, 31 (2), 179–193.

Daniels, P.W., 1985. *Service industries: A geographical appraisal.* London: Methuen.

Dempwolf, S., 2010. An evaluation of recent industrial land use studies: Do theory and history make better practice? Unpublished paper.

Fan, Y., 2012. The planners' war against spatial mismatch: Lessons learned and ways forward. *Journal of Planning Literature*, 27 (2), 153–169.

Fan, Y., and Khattak, A., 2012. Time use patterns, lifestyles, and sustainability of nonwork travel behavior. *International Journal of Sustainable Transportation*, 6 (1), 26–47.

Fitzgerald, J., and Leigh, N.G., 2002. *Economic revitalization: Cases and strategies for city and suburbs.* Thousand Oaks, CA: Sage Publications.

Foord, J., 2010. Mixed-use trade-offs: How to live and work in a compact city neighbourhood. *Built Environment*, 36 (1), 47–62.

Fujita, M., Krugman, P.R., and Venables, A.J. 1999. *The spatial economy: Cities, regions and international trade.* Cambridge, MA: The MIT Press.

Gottlieb, P.D., 1995. Residential amenities, firm locations, and economic development. *Urban Studies*, 32 (9), 1413–1436.

Grant, J., 2002. Mixed use in theory and practice: Canadian experience with implementing a planning principle. *Journal of the American Planning Association*, 68 (1), 71–84.

Grengs, J., 2010. Job accessibility and the modal mismatch in Detroit. *Journal of Transport Geography*, 18, 42–54.

Hausrath Economics Group and Cambridge Systematics, Inc., 2004. MTC Goods Movement Study Phase 2, Task 11 Working Paper: A land use strategy to support regional goods movement in the Bay Area. Oakland, CA: Hausrath Economics Group.

Heikkila, E., and Hutton, T.A., 1986. Toward an evaluative framework for land use policy in industrial districts of the urban core: A qualitative analysis of the exclusionary zoning approach. *Urban Studies*, 23, 47–60.

Howland, M., (2010). Planning for industry in a post-industrial world. *Journal of the American Planning Association*, 77(1): 39–53.

Immergluck, D., 1998. *Neighborhood jobs, race, and skills: Urban unemployment and commuting.* New York: Garland Publishers.

Kain, J.F., 1968. Housing segregation, negro employment, and metropolitan decentralization. *The Quarterly Journal of Economics*, 82 (2), 175–197.

Kawabata, M., 2003. Job access and employment among low-skilled autoless workers in US metropolitan areas. *Environment and Planning A*, 35 (9), 1651–1668.

Lang, R.E., and Simmons, P.A., 2003. Boomburbs: The emergence of large, fast-growing cities in the United States. *In*: B. Katz and R.E. Lang, eds. *Redefining cities and suburbs: Evidence from Census 2000.* Washington, DC: Brookings Institution Press, 51–62.

Lucas, M., and Nicholson, C.F., 2003. Subsidized vehicle acquisition and earned income in the transition from welfare to work. *Transportation*, 30, 483–501.

National Surface Transportation Policy and Revenue Commission, 2007. Implications of work and non-work travel patterns on passenger travel demand. Commission Briefing Paper 4A-07. Washington, DC: National Surface Transportation Policy and Revenue Commission.

Ong, P., 1996. Work and car ownership among welfare recipients. *Social Work Research*, 20 (4), 255–262.

Ong, P., 2002. Car ownership and welfare-to-work. *Journal of Policy Analysis and Management*, 21, 255–268.

Ong, P.M., and Miller, D., 2005. Spatial and transportation mismatch in Los Angeles. *Journal of Planning Education and Research*, 25 (1), 43–56.

O'Regan, K.M., and Quigley, J.M., 1999. Spatial isolation and welfare recipients: What do we know? Working Paper W99-003. Berkeley, CA: Institute of Business and Economic Research.

Pendall, R., Davies, E., Freiman, L., and Pitingolo, R., 2011. *A lost decade: Neighborhood poverty and the urban crisis of the 2000s.* Washington, DC: Joint Center for Political and Economic Studies.

Pivo, G., 2005. *Creating compact and complete communities: Seven propositions for success.* Practicing Planner Case Study. Chicago, IL: American Institute of Certified Planners.

Raphael, S., and Stoll, M., 2001. Can boosting minority car-ownership rates narrow inter-racial employment gaps? *Brookings-Wharton Papers on Urban Affairs*, 2, 99–137.

Reconnecting America, 2012. *Are we there yet? Creating complete communities for 21st century America*. Oakland, CA: Reconnecting America.

Roder, A., and Scrivner, S., 2005. *Seeking a sustainable journey to work: Findings from the National Bridges to Work Demonstration*. Philadelphia, PA: Public/Private Ventures.

Rosenbloom, S., 1992. *Reverse commute transportation: Emerging provider roles*. Washington, DC: Urban Mass Transportation Administration, U.S. Department of Transportation.

Sanchez, T., 1999. The connection between public transit and employment: The cases of Portland and Atlanta. *Journal of the American Planning Association*, 65 (3), 284–96.

San Francisco Planning Department, 2002. *Industrial land in San Francisco: Understanding production, distribution and repair*. San Francisco, CA: San Francisco Planning Department.

Schweitzer, L., and Taylor, B., 2008. Just pricing: The distributional effects of congestion pricing and sales taxes. *Transportation*, 35, 797–812.

Shen, Q., 1998. Location characteristics of inner-city neighborhoods and employment accessibility of low-wage workers. *Environment and Planning B*, 25, 345–365.

Strategic Economics, 2004. *Building San Jose's future: Jobs, land use, and fiscal issues in key employment areas, 2000–2020*. Report prepared for the City of San Jose. Berkeley, CA: Strategic Economics.

Taylor, B.D., and Ong, P.M., 1995. Spatial mismatch or automobile mismatch: An examination of race, residence, and commuting in U.S. metropolitan areas. *Urban Studies*, 32 (9), 1453–1473.

UC-Berkeley Center for Community Innovation, 2009. *Industrial land reports from cities and regions throughout the US and Canada: A repository*. Available from: http://community innovation.berkeley.edu/industrial-land-report.html [Accessed July 28, 2014].

16

TOWARDS AN UNDERSTANDING OF COMPLETE STREETS

Equity, justice, and sustainability

Stephen Zavestoski and Julian Agyeman

Problematizing Complete Streets

We began our book by asking whether Complete Streets narratives, policies, plans, and efforts as envisioned and implemented might be systematically reproducing and even amplifying many of the urban spatial and social inequalities and injustices that have characterized cities for the last century or more. We also argued that there are important missing people—namely people of color, immigrants, the poor, and other historically disenfranchised individuals—in popular narratives of Complete Streets. The overwhelming majority of our authors have laid out evidence that there are "silent" or "silenced" voices and there is indeed reproduction, and in some cases an amplification or deepening, of inequalities/injustices. In supporting our introductory ideas they have helped problematize the Complete Streets concept in one or more of three ways, each of which raises concerns about the prospects for equity, justice and sustainability in the evolving urban landscapes of the twenty-first century.

First, they argue that streets are complex spaces and places with many functions. To assume that a street can ever be complete, in the sense of being fixed and unchanging, is folly. Even if physical streetscapes remain relatively unchanged, the human stories we tell about our streets are constantly evolving. Second, the movement towards Complete Streets appears, in many instances, to be part of the neoliberal project in which urban planning itself becomes co-opted and shaped by the goals of economic growth and connectivity with the global economy. In this sense, Complete Streets become synonymous with the highly regulated walkable, livable cities that are assumed to be vibrant and successful only to the extent that they attract and retain the "Creative Class" (Florida 2002). Third, using Complete Streets as a neoliberal tool to attract the Creative Class is perceived by many to be a harbinger of gentrification, which in turn raises concerns for the diversity and equitability of cities. Related to this, inasmuch as Complete Streets increase cycling and walkability, making urban dwellers less dependent on carbon-burning private automobiles, concomitant increases in sustainability may result in what Dooling (2008) has called "environmental gentrification."

Can streets ever be "complete"?

That streets are never fixed in space nor time is abundantly clear in Norton's account of the stories about streets told by competing interests at the dawn of the automobile age. In the early years of the car, there was anger and a public backlash at pedestrian road deaths, with Cincinnati petitioning for 25mph speed governors on cars. Soon, however, Motordom's public relations massaged stories of automobiles as being emblematic of progress, freedom, individuality, and American values won the day and today few would contest the historical assertion that "streets are for cars." The Complete Streets movement aims to challenge the assertion, yet Norton shows us that the struggle is not a new one. Complete Streets advocates have simply "entered a stage as players in a new act of an old drama." Streets and their stories are the arenas in which everyday life is played out. For the past century, the dominance of the automobile has meant that everyday life must find cracks and crevices within the autocentric spaces of streets. On the timescale of a day, streets may appear to be fixed. But over a lifetime or generations, the drama of everyday life in street space shifts, as do the stories we tell about what streets are for.

Langegger's account of the regulation of street space in North Denver to curb the largely Latino cultural/spatial practices of lowriding and cruising illustrates this fact well. Langegger quotes an anti-cruising advocate who argues that "[r]esidents of the affected neighborhoods often hear the assertion that they must show respect for culture. Respect is a two-way street. The desire to spend a quiet weekend at home is no less respectable than the desire to show off cars, flirt, see friends, have fun, etc." So, whose culture gets to dominate how streets are designed and used? Brand more or less asks the same question in pointing out that "changes brought about by white gentrification and new noise ordinances have," according to her interviewees, "'shut down the bars,' and are 'restricting the flow of music on the street.'" Some of the long-time residents Brand interviewed expressed the feeling that the new white residents want to enforce new norms that essentially make culture, at least the African-American culture of the long-time residents, into a nuisance.

Cultural expression, conflict, and negotiation play out in streets, but top-down decision-making with respect to street design and transportation planning can also generate new cultural norms told through new stories. Lee demonstrates this through the concept of "cumulative irresponsibility." Streets are for cars, the story goes, and as such the mass harm produced by cars becomes "a naturalized burden of everyday life." But Lee also points to the Dutch *woonerf* principles that aim to "break down the socially constructed segregation of the interiority of private cars and the exteriority of public spaces" as an example of how redesigning streets can create new stories that question or even rupture cumulative irresponsibility. Morhayim also shows how activists in San Francisco have aimed to alter the physical streetscape and in so doing tell new stories about streets as spaces for human social interaction. Observing that "[t]he tension over the right to urban streets is at times marked by devaluation and marginalization of fun and play in public spaces, and at times by prioritization of efficiency over green space and social interactions," Morhayim asks, "To what extent can one claim the existence of a public realm if streets are more or less devoid of people and social interactions?"

Like Langegger and Brand, Vallianatos vividly illustrates how people practicing culture through social interactions make streets public. For Vallianatos, everyday life plays out in the diminishing spaces in which Latino street food vendors can legally sell their food. In the contestation over street space, the story of the importance of Latino street food vendors to the history of Los Angeles is lost. Yet, as Vallianatos suggests, street vendors' "mobile meals create hotspots of social interactions in a city that too often lacks public life." In fact, Vallianatos contends that "street food helps make streets and sidewalks in Los Angeles more 'complete' places by expanding and blurring formal categories of route and place, cuisine and culture, sale and purchase, law and politics. [C]arts and trucks extend the hours and places that people buy, sell and eat." Indeed, in an amusing play on words he talks of compl(eat)ing the streets. Here Vallianatos hints at another theme we will return to shortly: a vision of streets where mobility is not the sole or primary function.

Other examples of individuals and groups striving to create new stories in and about streets include the efforts of Phat Beets, the food justice organization described by Cadji and Alkon. Yet Phat Beets' story—one that respects the neighborhood's historical roots in African-American culture and the socioeconomic status of most of its long-term residents—is undermined by a local real estate company that "co-opted community assets and re-appropriated them as reasons for people to move to the area in ways that harmed long-term residents." Whereas developers in New Orleans, as Brand describes, aim to co-opt the history of a culturally rich neighborhood in ways that ultimately exclude its long-time residents, the Oakland real estate company described by Cadji and Alkon dismisses the neighborhood's past while aiming to capitalize on Phat Beets' efforts to revitalize the neighborhood in a way that benefits long-time residents. In each case, we see how the streets that are talked about as rich stories, as Norton reminds us in Chapter 2, are often completely removed from the physical, technical, and ultimately cookie-cutter urban design guidelines that city officials use in creating their versions of Complete Streets.

Neoliberalism, regulation, racism, and the mobility bias

At their core, our stories about streets communicate the functions people value for their streets. Whether conscious and concerted or spontaneous and organic, the functions of streets are always contested, as chapters by Golub, Chronopoulos, Hoffmann and Brand show us. For Golub and Chronopoulos, neoliberalization of cities leads to urban planning rooted in the objective of attracting economic activity and the use of economic rationalizations to justify everything from expensive light rail projects to congestion pricing schemes. For Golub, "the key questions for Complete Streets and their impacts on social equity must surround their planning process, and not technical issues," as the neoliberal approach to cities insists. Golub concludes by asking if "Complete Streets [are] being implemented because it is something a planning or streets department prioritizes," or if they are being "used to attract investments." Chronopoulos further assails neoliberal notions of streets, especially their privileging of projects on sustainability grounds:

> [U]rban spatial mobility with an automobile is rendered as environmentally and socially unsustainable, transformed into a transaction, and marketed as a product that in theory is governed by the forces of the free market. In practice, this type of spatial mobility becomes a privilege for affluent individuals who can afford to pay the fee and drive without experiencing interference from lower income drivers.

Chronopoulos nevertheless believes that socially just sustainabilities are possible, "but not when they are based on the requirements of a neoliberal political-economic system and its urban growth narratives."

Brand sees neoliberal policies in New Orleans neatly sidestepping the city's complex racial and cultural politics. She notes:

> We see narratives identifying a new notion of completeness for the future of Claiborne Avenue, resting on ideas of culture and histories of economic vibrancy, yet ignoring the central yet tacit fact that [neoliberal] development goals of economic expansion are sometimes at odds with residents' connections to place.

She suggests that:

> [M]issing from this discourse and narrative about the history of New Orleans' black core are not only the brutalities of segregation and racism and the effects of past redevelopment strategies in contributing to an unequal urban spatial pattern; the adaptability and resilience of these communities in the wake of these structural forces; and the community-led dream of a new, better, future—but also the role of race and its implications in our geographical imaginations.

Invoking Omi and Winant, Brand argues that an "understanding of racial formation is critical . . . because it challenges us to reengage a discussion of race—and its geographic implications—amidst a neoliberal development context that shuns all discussions of race while also contradictorily producing unequal and racialized outcomes."

Neoliberal justifications for Minneapolis' investment in infrastructure to support bicycle transportation, as demonstrated by Hoffmann, are employed unabashedly by the city's mayor who explicitly seeks to attract the Creative Class with his investments in bicycling infrastructure. She quotes Mayor Rybak as saying: "The key to economic growth is attracting talent. Especially in the creative field, talent is very mobile. [Our bicycle infrastructure] has attracted this wide swath of people to get something they can't find in a freeway-oriented place like Houston." In New Orleans, rather than economically mobile bicycle-riding urban dwellers, the attraction of tourists is the aim of city planners and developers. According to Brand, they intend to succeed through implementation of a Complete Streets project that foregrounds and ultimately exploits a community's racial heritage and historical significance.

A final common theme in our authors' critiques of the neoliberal underpinnings of Complete Streets is that Complete Streets policies and approaches largely retain the "mobility bias" of the automotive century. If streets are never fixed or static, it is because they serve many functions, including non-mobility functions. The mobility bias of Complete Streets, albeit giving increased rights to environmentally friendly pedestrians, cyclists, and public transit, is part and parcel of the neoliberal approach to the city inasmuch as one's ability to move freely about a city is seen as linked to one's ability to consume and one's economic productivity. Yet, as Golub observes, "even the very idea of mobility and the historical struggle for the right to mobility may differ among communities." Similarly, Lee contends:

> While Complete Streets represents a shift toward a model that seemingly does not privilege the car over other modes of transportation (Smart Growth America, 2013), the emphasis remains centered upon mobility, which may subtly strengthen the conceit that the right to the street belongs to those who contribute to economic productivity through their movement.

Gentrification and environmental gentrification

Other chapters in this volume demonstrate how Complete Streets projects, perhaps especially those driven by the neoliberal approach to urban management and planning, result in actual or perceived gentrification of neighborhoods. Invoking Harvey's (2008, p. 23) admonition that "The freedom to make and remake our cities and ourselves is . . . one of the most precious yet most neglected of our human rights," Langegger argues that regulation of Latino lowriding and cruising on North Denver's streets created what he calls "a *rights-rift*: a disconnect between rights attached to [Latino] people and the regulation of [Latino] people's behavior." This was part of a long-term transition of the neighborhood into a whiter, more middle-class, hip part of the city with more expensive real estate and "highly regulated spaces that facilitated predictable mobilities and a middle-class notion of livability." In a volte-face, Cadji and Alkon describe what may come to be an increasingly common conundrum for just sustainability-based organizations: how Phat Beets became a victim of gentrification that was, in part, a function of its own efforts to promote a successful neighborhood farmers market. Miller and Lubitow best illustrate how Complete Streets efforts such as bicycle transportation projects can be seen as part of a white, middle-class agenda. Goodling and Herrington, on the other hand, provide the lone case study suggesting that Complete Streets-related projects, namely the City of Portland's Bureau of Environmental Services' Community Watershed Stewardship Program, can benefit low-income and communities of color but only through operationalizing an explicitly social equity-focused approach to sustainability. This case provides a glimmer of hope that purposeful programs can be designed to mitigate the worst effects of gentrification.

Indeed, Goodling and Herrington's chapter points to an important question: Is it possible to introduce environmental amenities into a neighborhood without causing environmental gentrification? As suggested in a number of chapters, cities are increasingly playing the environmental and sustainability cards as a way to justify urban planning and other policies without critically considering whether these policies might increase income gaps and the problems of inequality. Complete Streets projects, when hailed for their potential to shrink a city's ecological footprint by reducing per capita vehicle miles traveled, are often not examined for their potential to create the type of "environmental gentrification" described by several authors in this volume.

Invoking the originator of the term, Dooling (2008), Cadji and Alkon note that environmental gentrification is the "displacement of vulnerable human inhabitants resulting in the implementation of an environmental agenda driven by an environ-mental ethic" (Dooling, 2008, p. 41). As Hoffmann points out, a form of environ-mental gentrification occurs when new residents move into a neighborhood to avail themselves of sustainability-related amenities like bicycle infrastructure. Yet the very improvements attracting the new eco-conscious class are perceived by planners and city officials to be politically neutral, thus obscuring the fact that the end result is greater, and ultimately unsustainable, urban inequality and injustice.

Although she does not describe it as such, Chapple also points to the potential downsides of ostensibly pro-sustainability transportation planning and policies like Complete Streets. At the regional scale, Chapple's focus, the poor and people of color are the most dependent on the automobile for transportation given the often great distances between housing they can afford and the location of jobs. Chapple wonders whether Complete Streets projects might make driving more expensive or more time-consuming. If they do, the impacts will be spread unevenly. Chronopoulos demonstrates exactly this potential in his analysis of congestion pricing, a policy approach that, in theory, makes streets more complete by reducing automobile dominance. In actuality, argues Chronopoulos, "[s]chemes like con-gestion pricing seek to restore class privilege to the elites in a realm that their affluence has been unable to penetrate." In other words, we need to ask about Complete Streets not just "Complete for whom?" but also "Sustainable for whom?"

In sum, we've distilled from the preceding chapters three primary critiques of Complete Streets—that streets can never be "complete" because they are not fixed, that the concept seems to be rooted in a neoliberal conception of the city that sees streets in terms of their potential to attract economic activity either through provision of amenities and services appealing to the Creative Class or by enhancing mobility, and that as currently conceived many Complete Streets projects seem to carry the potential for inequality exacerbating environmental gentrification. These critiques are intended to help us work through the ultimate question: "How can we achieve simultaneously the goals of ecologically sustainable cities, economically viable cities, and socially equitable and just cities?"

Our authors have a number of recommendations for how Complete Streets might move us towards this goal. Cadji and Alkon advise planners advocating a Complete Streets approach in low-income, gentrifying neighborhoods to "begin by working with long-term residents to ensure that their concerns are heard and represented" and "to think about other kinds of planning that can help to offset the pressure towards gentrification that their sustainable development goals may create." Cadji and Alkon go on to point to affordable housing, rent control, and other mechanisms "that would help enable long-term residents to avoid displacement," especially driven by Complete Streets initiatives.

Other authors' conclusions were less prescriptive and more cautionary. Chronopoulos warns that unless organizations that advocate Complete Streets "take into consideration the needs of ordinary people and understand that not everyone benefits from the neoliberal vision of sustainability, initiatives like Complete Streets will remain incomplete." Lee warns that "without examining and addressing fundamental issues of how responsibility for car damage is constructed, erased, and misdirected, Complete Streets may instead perpetuate unjust inequalities that privilege some and exclude others in the streetscape." Hoffmann's warning is aimed specifically at bicycle advocates: "[I]f bicycle planning continues to be used as a tool to recruit young 'creative talent,' then we do a huge disservice to the rest of the community. Those not hailed by Complete Streets visions are not ignorant of their unacknowledged presence." Based on her analysis of bicycle planning in North Minneapolis, Hoffmann concludes that:

> Residents may expect to be left out of future visions of bicycle infrastructure. And when these residents are used to and expect to be left out of these conversations, they may automatically reject the idea of the infrastructure on the grounds of their exclusion.

Furthermore, they may come to see bicycle infrastructure as a springboard to gentrification.

Goodling and Herrington also caution against the potential for Complete Streets projects to result in gentrification. Relying on grassroots community groups or individual municipal employees "to fight widespread socio-environmental injustices," they contend, is inadequate. "Fully addressing more profound injustices such as gentrification/displacement . . . will require commitments and effective policies at higher levels of sustainable city planning and governance." Morhayim, critiquing once again the Complete Streets perspective's mobility bias, suggests the need for a far broader metric of Complete Streets than mere mobility: "[T]he idea of Complete Streets should be evaluated . . . by the location, distribution of the redevelopment projects, partners involved in making the projects happen, and the social, cultural, and economic resources required to make the new livable streetscapes happen." Finally, Miller and Lubitow advocate that "the processes [be put] in place to foster constructive debate and ensure that a diverse set of politics and values have the opportunity to shape our infrastructure." They maintain that their case study "shows that debates about the street and its design as a physical place are inseparable from politics, community, and visions of its past and future." But their analysis also points to where "possibilities emerge from processes that include diverse values and perspectives that will change the vision of the street and its physical design."

An ecology of streets

Perhaps the most fundamental challenge to the Complete Streets concept as currently understood and practiced is Mehta's "ecology of streets" concept. He argues that we should not complete our streets and that the contemporary Complete Streets concept is "inadequate and even deceptive as it flattens this rich ecology to a set of limited mobility-related 'quality of life' goals." In this he is employing a different critique but is taking aim at the same neoliberal environmental gentrification processes that offer up measurable, quantifiable, community attributes such as increases in "walkability" and "livability" that often portend gentrification, as several of our authors argue.

Mehta's "ecology of streets" idea, in contrast, picks up many of our points about streets as dynamic, fluid social places, not physically fixed in space and time:

> Appreciating the street as ecology means understanding it as a space of dynamic relationships that result from complex webs of interconnected activities and phenomena. This translates into accepting the street as a place that thrives on the coexistence of diverse people, activities, forms, and objects, and modes of control and negotiation, as it operates as a social, cultural, economic, and political space. As a corollary, this also means not to think of the street as complete and in a stable state of equilibrium, but to recognize the street as a place in flux with some level of conflict.

Such dynamic, open streets are also adaptable in ways that highly planned streets with extensive and expensive infrastructure are not. Yet it is the latter type of street whose story is currently winning out in the drama over the function of streets.

Understanding Complete Streets: equity, justice, and sustainability

Our aim in this volume has been to problematize the Complete Streets concept in ways that might provoke its more critical use and application by urban planners, policy-makers, and academics. We have done this by focusing on some of the very real challenges to equity and justice introduced by the Complete Streets concept and the processes and practices resulting from the concept's application. We undertook this project not because we believe the concept is somehow wrong, or that it cannot be reconceived in ways that could make it more equitable and just, but because we feel the time is right to join in the growing contestation and debate over our most used public space: the street.

In the neoliberal city there has been a "trenchant reregulation and redaction of public space" (Low and Smith 2006, p. 1). This volume adds to the growing evidence that neoliberalism imposes a particular order on streets—an order that ultimately serves the purpose of sustaining and expanding the economic engine linking a city to the global economy. The chapters in this volume make the case that in many ways the Complete Streets movement is a new language for describing and justifying this order. More importantly, they caution that the order of Complete Streets may erase the "everyday" spaces where a diversity of cultures and people engage and interact while silencing dissident voices. These erasures and silencings are part and parcel of the environmental gentrification that is being catalyzed and given a livability and "green" sustainability veneer by cities implementing Complete Streets projects without regard to how, or whether, "just sustainabilities" (Agyeman 2013) can be achieved. In this way, social inequality not only persists but is deepened. More bluntly, the order imposed by neoliberalism erases the realities of race and difference. As Brand points out, it is profoundly important to remember that space matters when it comes to race since the "neoliberal development context . . . shuns all discussions of race while also contradictorily producing unequal and racialized outcomes." Neoliberalism is also a key factor behind the mobility bias that assumes streets can be "completed" through simple physical (re)design.

We close by returning to Massey's (1995) argument that streets, as places, are "constantly shifting articulations of social relations through time" and are not simply some physical infrastructure that is amenable to arm's-length planning by city hall bureaucrats under pressure from eager developers. We urge our readers to conceive streets as ecologies with rich and layered meanings, to be sensitive to this broader context and to consider issues such as income inequality, affordable housing, and economic opportunity at all levels of the socioeconomic ladder when (re)considering their Complete Streets programs.

References

Agyeman, J., 2013. *Introducing just sustainabilities: Policy, planning and practice*. London: Zed Books.

Dooling, S., 2008, Ecological gentrification: Re-negotiating justice in the city. *Critical Planning*, 15, 40–57.

Florida, R., 2002. *The rise of the creative class: And how it's transforming work, leisure, community and everyday life*. New York, NY: Basic Books.

Harvey, D., 2008. The right to the city. *New Left Review*, 53 (Sept–Oct), 23–40.

Low, S., and Smith, N., eds., 2006. *The politics of the public sphere*. London: Routledge.

Massey, D., 1995. Places and their pasts. *History Workshop Journal* 39 (1), 182–192.

Smart Growth America, 2013. *National Complete Streets Coalition*. Available from: http://www.smartgrowthamerica.org/complete-streets/complete-streets-fundamentals/complete-streets-faq [Accessed 16 May 2013].

INDEX

Note: Page numbers followed by 'f' refer to figures, and followed by 't' refer to tables, and followed by 'n' refer to notes.

reliance on 290, 291, 299, 300, 301; "Merrily We Roll Along" 17–18, 20, 30, 31; numbers of households without 41f; ownership improving job prospects 300; ownership programs 302; ownership, rising costs of 43–4, 57; policies to improve access among poor 301–2; public relations, industry 22, 23, 24, 29, 30, 31; as spaces of sensory privacy 83, 84; thwarting of social connection 228; use of alternatives by race 44–5, 45f; when streets were not for 21–3 *see also* automobility

casualties of road traffic accidents 22, 23, 25, 26, 41, 77–8, 80, 81

Centers for Disease Control and Prevention 2, 226

Checker, M. 68, 147, 158

Chicago, Bronzeville community 260

childhood obesity 2

children: apportioning of blame in traffic accidents 25, 26; casualties of road traffic accidents 22, 81; invading of play areas for 81; rights on the street 21; safety education in schools 25; withdrawal from street life 84

Cincinnati campaign for speed governors 23, 24, 27

Citi Bike Share program 87

Claiborne Avenue redevelopment, New Orleans 10, 246, 255–60; 1976 study of community vision for 256–7; Claiborne Avenue Improvement Coalition 257; Livable Claiborne Communities study 246, 257–8

Cohen, C. 179–80, 194, 195, 197–8

Cohen, S. 120, 121, 123

collective responsibility 78; fragmenting of 79, 85

Community Watershed Stewardship Program (CWSP), Portland 176–98, 311, 312; acknowledgement of past injustices 189–90; adjusting budget to pay young people for environmental work 187, 188f, 197; application assistance 186–7; application process 194, 197; background to 182–3; bioswales 176, 178, 178f, 179, 180, 182, 185, 186; cautioning against potential gentrification 197, 312; City Commissioner's backing for equity-oriented approach 187; communication and outreach 190–4, 191t, 193f, 196; community garden projects, releasing funds for 194; creation of 183; engaging

with larger political arena 196; equity strategies 186–8; equity strategies, extending 188–96; graduate student employees 183, 186, 188, 190, 198; inequalities in benefits of environmental projects 184–6; inequities in Portland's politics of sustainability 177–82, 181f; Krumholz's version of equity planning influencing 188–9; meeting equity goals 189, 194, 195; "overfunding" of underrepresented communities 195; partnerships 187–8, 195–6; place-based equity strategy 186; presentation on equity program 196; selection criteria 195; setting concrete goals 189–90; St. Mary Ethiopian Orthodox Church project 176; three-pronged approach to sustainability 178, 183–4

competition: between cities to recruit creative talent 140–1; in streets, neoliberal 87–8

complete communities movement 299–300

Complete Streets 3–5, 245–6; affordable housing and relationship with 186; completed for middle-class consumption 134, 135; conflict between industrial districts and 292, 297–8; congestion charging supported by 61, 70, 73; definitions 3, 219; "ecology of streets" a challenge for 94, 96–7, 219–20, 313; food vending to make streets "complete" 206, 207, 219–20; gentrification/displacement potential 120, 177, 179–80, 184, 186, 190, 310–13, 314; gentrification, ways of avoiding 173, 311, 312–13; health benefits of 1–2; inadvertently contributing to racial segregation and poverty 290; legislation adopted in California 220; missing narratives 7–8, 306; mobility bias 89, 97, 219–20, 310, 313; narrow focus on technical design choices 269; neoliberal underpinnings 308–10, 314; never "complete" 288, 307–8; as a new act in an old drama 20; New Orleans Ordinance for 255–6; New York policies 54, 55; power dynamics between bicycling and rhetoric of 139–40; problematizing 4–7, 306–7; public space, disregarding streets as 120, 130, 135, 220; race, sidestepping issues of 260–2, 309, 314; revolution 1–3; social context of 36–7, 46–7; social equity issues 5, 6–7, 47–8, 198, 288, 302, 309, 314; Transportation

Made in United States
Orlando, FL
23 December 2024

56477979R00189